TCP/IP and
Related Protocols

Uyless Black Series on Computer Communications

BLACK • *The V Series Recommendations: Protocols for Data Communications Over the Telephone Network*

BLACK • *The X Series Recommendations: Protocols for Data Communications Networks*

BLACK • *Network Management Standards: The OSI, SNMP and CMOL Protocols*

HUGHES • *Data Communications*

KIMBERLY • *Electronic Data Interchange*

RADICATI • *Electronic Mail: An Introduction to the X.400 Message Handling Standards*

WHITE • *Internetworking and Addressing*

TCP/IP and
Related Protocols

Uyless Black

McGraw-Hill, Inc.
New York St. Louis San Francisco Auckland Bogotá
Caracas Lisbon London Madrid Mexico Milan
Montreal New Delhi Paris San Juan São Paulo
Singapore Sydney Tokyo Toronto

Library of Congress Cataloging-in-Publication Data

Black, Uyless D.
    TCP/IP and related protocols / Uyless Black.
        p.   cm. — (Uyless Black series on computer communications)
    Includes index.
    ISBN 0-07-005553-X
    1. Computer networks.   2. Computer network protocols.   I. Title.
    II. Series.
    TK5105.5.B5663   1992
    004.6'2—dc20   91-37187
                                                                        CIP

*McGraw-Hill Series on Computer Communications, Uyless Black,
Series Advisor*

1 2 3 4 5 6 7 8 9 0   DOC/DOC   9 8 7 6 5 4 3 2

ISBN   0-07-005553-X

*The sponsoring editor for this book was Neil Levine, the editing
supervisor was Fred Dahl, and the production supervisor was
Pamela A. Pelton. It was set in Century Schoolbook by McGraw-Hill's
Professional Book Group composition unit.*

Printed and bound by R. R. Donnelley & Sons Company.

To my wife Holly, for all her efforts in the building of our new home (and just about everything else). She kept the contractors going while I finished this book and completed a long lecture tour. I could not possibly do all that I do without her.

Contents

Preface   xv
Acknowledgments   xvii

Chapter 1. TCP/IP and the Internet   1

Introduction   1
  Organization of Internet   3
  Request for Comments (RFCs)   4
TCP/IP and the OSI   4
Internetworking Architecture   5
  Terms and Concepts   5
  Connectionless and Connection-Oriented Protocols   6
The Internet Layers   9
Example of the Layer Operations   10
The TCP/IP Model: A Closer Look   12
Ports and Sockets: An Introduction   12
Challenges of Internetworking   13
Typical Internet Topologies   15
Summary   18

Chapter 2. Introduction to Networks, Bridges, Gateways, and Routers 19

Introduction   19
A General Taxonomy   19
Wide Area Networks (WANs)   22
  Circuit Switching   22
  Message Switching   22
  Packet Switching   23
Local Area Networks (LANs)   27
  LAN Components   27
Types of LANs   28
  Carrier Sense, Collision Detection   28
  CSMA/CD and IEEE 802.3   29
  Token Ring   31
  Token Bus   33
The LLC Sublayer   33
  Classes of Service   34
Repeaters, Bridges, Routers, Brouters, and Gateways   34

Source Routing and Spanning Tree Bridges   36
Summary   36

Chapter 3. Naming, Addressing, and Routing in an Internet   39

Introduction   39
Upper Layer, Network, Data Link, and Physical Names and Addresses   40
  Physical Addresses   40
  Universal Physical Addresses and Protocol Identifiers   41
  The CSMA/CD Frame and MAC Physical Addresses   44
  Link Layer Addresses (LSAPs)   45
  Extension to the LSAP Header (SNAP)   46
  Network Addresses   47
  Physical and Network Address Resolution   48
  Are All These Addresses Necessary?   49
  Upper Layer Addresses and Names   50
Example of a Complete Naming and Addressing Operation   50
The IP Address Structure   54
Destination Addresses and Routing   57
  Direct and Indirect Destinations   57
  IP Routing Logic   57
  Multihomed Hosts   60
Address Resolution Issues   60
The Address Resolution Protocol (ARP)   61
  ARP Address Translation Table   65
Proxy ARP   66
Reverse Address Resolution Protocol (RARP)   67
  Primary and Secondary RARPs   68
IP and X.121 Address Mapping   69
  International Numbering Plan for Data Networks (X.121)   69
  DDN IP Addresses   69
  Mapping X.121 and IP Addresses   70
Subnets, Subnet Addressing, and Address Masking   70
  Subnet Masks   73
Summary   75

Chapter 4. The Domain Name System (DNS)   77

Introduction   77
The Domain Name System (DNS) Architecture   78
Domain Name Space   79
Top-Level Domains   80
Domain Name Resolution and Mapping Names to Addresses   80
Name Server Operations   82
Resource Records (RR)   83
  RDATA Field   85
Explanation of DNS Types   86
  IN-ADDR-ARPA   88
  Example of a Resource Record   90
DNS Messages   93
RR Compression   96
Summary   96

Chapter 5. The Internet Protocol (IP)   87

Introduction   97
Major Features of IP   97
IP and Subnetworks   98
The IP Datagram   99
Major IP Services   106
   Internet Header Check Routine   106
   IP Source Routing   107
   Route Recording Option   109
   The Timestamp Option   109
   Fragmentation and Reassembly   111
IP Address and Routing Tables   116
   Address Table   116
   Routing Table   117
IP Service Definitions and Primitives   119
   IP/ULP Primitives   119
   IP/SNP Primitives   122
   Network Layer/LLC Primitives   122
Multicasting   124
Internet Group Management Protocol (IGMP)   126
Other Thoughts on IP   127
Connectionless-Mode Network Service (ISO 8473)   127
   The ISO 8473 PDU   128
   Quality of Service (QOS) Functions   128
   Protocol Functions   129
   Traffic Management between Subnetworks   129
   CLNP and IP   133
Summary   134

Chapter 6. Internet Control Messsage Protocol (ICMP)   135

Introduction   135
ICMP Message Format   137
ICMP Error- and Status-Reporting Procedures   137
   Time Exceeded   138
   Parameter Unintelligible   139
   Destination Unreachable   139
   Source Quench   140
   Echo Request and Reply   140
   Redirect   141
   Timestamp and Timestamp Reply   142
   Information Request and Information Reply   143
   Address Mask Request and Address Mask Reply   143
Other Thoughts on ICMP   144
Summary   144

Chapter 7. Transmission Control Protocol (TCP) and User Datagram Protocol (UDP)   145

Introduction   145
Value of the Trasnport Layer   145

TCP Overview   146
Major Features of TCP   147
Another Look at Ports and Sockets   180
  Examples of Port Assignments and Port Bindings   150
Passive and Active Opens   153
The Transmission Control Block (TCB)   154
TCP Window and Flow-Control Mechanisms   154
Retransmission Operations   156
Estimating Timers for Time-Outs and Retransmissions   160
TCP and User Interfaces   162
The Segment (TCP PDU)   162
The TCP Connection Management Operations   167
  Examples of the TCP Open, Data Transfer, and Close Operations   167
  TCP Connection Table   174
Other Considerations in Using TCP   176
User Datagram Protocol (UDP)   177
  Format of the UDP Message   177
Summary   179

Chapter 8. Route Discovery Protocols   181

Introduction   181
Terms and Concepts   181
  Routing Based on Fewest Hops   182
  Routing Based on Type of Service Factors   184
  Core and Noncore Gateways   186
  Exterior and Interior Gateways   186
  Border Routers and Boundary Routers   187
  How Autonomous Systems or Areas Exchange Information   188
  Who Participates in Exchanging Routing Information and in Executing
  Routing Logic?   190
  Clarifying Terms   191
The Gateway-to-Gateway Protocol (GGP)   192
  Introduction   192
  Neighbor Connectivity Analysis   193
  Exchanging Routing Information   193
  Computing Routes   194
  GGP Message Formats   196
  Example of a GGP Update Message   199
External Gateway Protocol (EGP)   199
  Introduction   199
  Major Operations of EGP   201
  The EGP States   201
  Types of Messages   202
  EGP Message Types   203
  Example of an EGP Update Message   208
  EGP Events   210
  EGP Operations During the Up State   210
  Other Features of EGP   213
Interior Gateway Protocols (IGPs)   214
Routed (Routing) Information Protocol (RIP)   214
  RIP Timers   215
  Example of RIP Operations   216

RIP Problems   216
The RIP Message Format   218
The RIP Request and Response   218
RIP versus OSPF   219
The Hello Protocol   219
The Hello Message Format   220
Gated   221
Summary of Vector-Distance Protocols   221
Choosing the Optimum Path with a Shortest Path Algorithm   221
Open Shortest Path First (OSPF) Routing Protocol   226
Introduction   226
OSPF Operations   227
Classification of Routers   229
Types of Advertisements   230
Example of the OSPF Shortest Path Tree   230
OSPF Data Structures   233
The OSPF Packets   237
Summary   249

Chapter 9. The Major Application Layer Protocols   251

Introduction   251
The TELNET Protocol   251
Network Virtual Terminal   252
TELNET RFCs   253
TELNET Commands   256
Example of TELNET Commands   257
Trivial File Transfer Protocol (TFTP)   258
TFTP and Other Protocols   258
TFTP Packets   259
File Transfer Protocol (FTP)   261
Data Types   263
FTP Commands and Replies   263
Sequence of Operations in an FTP Session   265
Examples of FTP Operations   267
Example of a File Retrieval   269
Minimum Implementation of FTP   269
Simple Mail Transfer Protocol (SMTP)   271
SMTP Model   271
Address Field Format   272
Examples of SMTP Operations   273
SMTP and the Domain Name System (DNS)   274
Summary   275

Chapter 10. Other Protocols   277

Introduction   277
X Windows   277
The X Window System Protocol   279
A Display Connection   280
Remote Procedure Call (RPC)   281
Network File System (NFS)   282
The NFS Server Procedures   282

Remote Exec Daemon (REXECD)   283
PING   283
HOSTNAME   284
Host Monitoring Protocol (HMP)   284
Discard Protocol   285
Finger   286
The Bootstrap Protocol (BOOTP)   286
Network Time Protocol (NTP)   288
Daytime   290
Summary   290

Chapter 11. Internet Network Management Systems   293

Introduction   293
Summary of the Internet Network Management Standards   293
Layer Architecture for Internet Network Management   294
The Internet Naming Hierarchy   295
Structure of Management Information (SMI)   297
    SMI Syntax and Types   297
The Management Information Base (IMIB)   298
    Overview of the Object Groups   299
    Templates to Describe Objects   302
    Definition of High-Level MIB   303
The SNMP   304
    SNMP Administrative Relationships   304
    Example of an SNMP Operation   306
    SNMP PDUs   306
    The SNMP MIB Managed Objects   308
CMOT   308
    The CMOT Layers   310
    The Lightweight Presentation Protocol (LPP)   311
Summary   311

**Chapter 12. Operating TCP/IP with Other Protocols
(and Other Protocols without TCP/IP)   313**

Introduction   313
A Minimum TCP/IP and LAN Stack   314
A Word about Operating System Dependency   314
TCP/IP over LLC   315
Replacing TCP with UDP   316
NetBIOS over TCP or UDP   317
IP over NetBIOS   318
XNS over IP   319
IP Router Stacks   320
Relationship of IP and LAN Bridges   321
IP and X.25   321
    IP, X.25, and LANs   321
    IP, X.25, and Public Data Networks (PDNs)   322
    IP, X.25, and Amateur Packet Radio   323
Using IPX with UDP/IP Networks   323

Transmitting 802 LLC Traffic over IPX Networks   324
Transmitting IP Datagrams over ARCNET Networks   325
Transmitting IP Datagrams over FDDI Networks   326
IP over Switched Megabit Data Service (SMDS)   327
OSI's Transport Protocol Class 0 over TCP   328
OSI Connectionless Transport Layer over UDP   329
TCP/IP over ISDN   330
Stacks for the 1990s   331
Summary   332

Chapter 13. TCP/IP and Operating Systems   333

Introduction   333
UNIX and TCP/IP   333
  Connection-Oriented Services   334
  Other Input/Output Calls   337
  Datagram Services   338
  Closing a Connection   338
  Other System Calls   339
  Example of Programs to Invoke UNIX-based TCP/IP Services   339
PC Interface Program   339
  Sending Mail Through SMTP   341
  Sending a File Through TFTP   344
  Sending a File Through FTP   345
  Using tn to Invoke TELNET Login Services   346
  Retrieving Network Statistics   347
  Using PING to Obtain Echo Services   347
  Using Route to Manipulate the IP Routing Table   348
Summary   349

Chapter 14. Management Considerations   351

The Vendor Strategies with the Internet-Based Products   351
  The Vendors React to the Marketplace   352
A Comparison of the TCP/IP and OSI Stacks   353
  IP and CLNP   356
  TP4 and TCP   356
Migration Issues   358
  Gateway Migration Issues   359
  Network Migration Issues   359
  Host Migration Issues   361
Migration of Internet to OSI Network Architectures   361
  Internetworking DOD and Non-DOD Architectures   361
  Dual DOD/OSI Protocol Hosts   362
  Application Layer Gateways   362
Activities of the Vendors   362
  Limited OSI Capability   363
  Equivalent OSI Capability   363
  Advanced OSI Capability   363
Summary   364

Index   365

Preface

I became involved with TCP/IP a few years ago when a client asked me to examine the feasibility of operating X.25 with the TCP/IP protocols. At about the same time, another client had received an IP-like protocol in a LAN package and asked me to evaluate its performance capabilities.

At that time, I had experience in several aspects of data communications networks. My background was principally in SNA, X.25, X.75, SDLC, LAPB, the V Series specifications, and the design of packet switching topologies to support connection-oriented network interfaces.

As I began to unravel the TCP/IP operations, I was struck by (1) how fast TCP/IP operated (in comparison to X.25) and (2) how little it did. Yet, it served the basic needs of my clients.

As I learned more about the operations of TCP/IP, I was also struck by the wealth of related standards that I could not find in the Open Systems Interconnection (OSI) suite. As examples, address mapping and route discovery were well established in TCP/IP but simply were not available in the CCITT and ISO standards. I was very pleasantly surprised to find many of these related protocols readily available in the marketplace.

I also found the documentation on the TCP/IP protocols easy to read and assimilate, but in some instances, incomplete and incorrect. This gap in the TCP/IP specifications made my introduction to TCP/IP an interesting one, to say the least.

In one respect, I have found the use of the TCP/IP protocols (and their rapid growth) has made my life easier, because of the ability of my clients to work with common communications protocols. Ironically, in another respect, the success of TCP/IP has made my life (and the lives of many of my clients) more difficult, because of the problems TCP/IP presents to the migration to the OSI Model. I have more to say about this issue in the book.

In the past few years, my clients have asked me to evaluate the TCP/IP suite for use on numerous other systems: the OSI suite, ISDN, frame relay, SMDS, etc. I provide the reader with my TCP/IP background, because you should know that I consider myself a user of TCP/

IP and not a developer. This book reflects this user-oriented view. It also reflects the fact that most of my experience with TCP/IP is with its use on private networks.

Intended Audience

This book is written for the reader who is a newcomer to the TCP/IP suite of protocols, or a person who is interested in filling some gaps about these protocols. For the more advanced reader, I highly recommend Volume II of *Internetworking with TCP/IP* by Douglas E. Comer (Prentice Hall, Inc.).

Some of the protocols associated with TCP/IP are not communications protocols and reside in a conventional applications layer of a layered protocol model. The emphasis of this book is on the lower communications layers of the TCP/IP standards with an overview of the applications layer.

Insofar as possible, the book is designed to be modular in that the reader can skip around the chapters without loss of continuity. It should also be emphasized that this book assumes the reader has a basic understanding of data communications systems and computer networks. Therefore, the book does not spend time discussing aspects of modems, why communications systems are used or needed, the rationale for layered protocols, etc.

Uyless Black
The Shenandoah Valley area, Virginia

Acknowledgments

The many individuals who participated in the development and nurturing of the TCP/IP suite of protocols deserve a medal. The pioneering efforts of the Internet Activities Board (IAB) have paved the way for the acceptance of standardized communications protocols and the sharing of valuable information about internetworking. Their efforts have solved many problems that heretofore were not being addressed in the data communications network industry. Their efforts have also paved the way for numerous international standards.

On a personal note, I owe thanks to many programmers, designers, and engineers who have listened to my ideas about how network and transport protocols should operate. I also owe them thanks for their input that led to the creation of this book.

I would also like to acknowledge several individuals at Bell Atlantic Education Services (BAES) with whom I have worked this year. Charlie Wortmann, John Hartin, Mary Jean Woland, and Peter Grubb have provided great support for many of my efforts.

I welcome comments from the reader about this book. They must be forwarded through my publisher.... I have moved to the country and have rid myself of electronic mailboxes.

TCP/IP and
Related Protocols

TCP/IP and the Internet

Introduction

Data communications networks were developed to allow users to share computer and information resources as well as a common communications system. As organizations have brought the computer into almost every facet of business, it has become obvious that a single network, while very useful, is inadequate to meet the information needs of businesses and individuals. For example, a user of one network often needs to access and share the resources of computers and databases that "belong" to another network. It is prohibitively complex and expensive to merge all resources into one network.

In the late 1960s and early 1970s, networks were not designed to allow resource sharing between users residing in different networks. Network administrators also were reluctant to allow users to tap into their resources due to concerns about security as well as excessive utilization of their network resources. As a result, it was difficult for a user to extend the use of an information system to another user across different networks, because the networks were either incompatible with each other or were not allowed to communicate with each other due to administrative problems.

During this time, it became increasingly acknowledged that it made good sense to share resources among user applications. But in order to do so, it was recognized that network administrators would have to agree upon a set of common technologies and standards to allow the networks to communicate with each other. It also followed that applications, such as electronic mail and file transfer, should be standardized to permit interconnections of end user applications (not just networks).

In the early 1970s, several groups around the world began to address the problem of network and application compatibility. At that time the term "internetworking," which means the interconnecting of computers and/or networks, was coined. The concepts of internetworking were pioneered by the CCITT, the ISO, and especially the original designers of the ARPANET. (The term *ARPA* refers to the Advanced Research Projects Agency, which is a U.S. Department of Defense [DOD] organization.) In fairness to the pioneers of internetworking concepts (and layered protocols, discussed shortly), the ARPA protocols were well in existence before the ISO and the CCITT took an interest in this important subject.

The procurement for ARPANET took place in 1968. The machines selected for this procurement were Honeywell 316 interface message processors (IMPs). The initial effort was contracted through Bolt Bernak & Newman (BBN) and the ARPANET nodes were initially installed at UCLA, University of California at San Bernardino, the Stanford Research Institute (SRI), and the University of Utah. The well-known "Request for Comments" (RFCs) came about from this early work.

These initial efforts were organized through the ARPANET Network Working Group. It was disbanded in 1971, and the Defense Advanced Project Research Agency (DARPA) assumed the work of the earlier organization. DARPA's work in the early 1970s led to the development of an earlier protocol, the network control program, and later the Transmission Control Protocol and the Internet Protocol (TCP/IP).

Two years later, the first significant parts of the Internet were placed into operation. At about this time, DARPA started converting some of its computers to the TCP/IP suite of protocols. By 1983 DARPA stated that all computers connected to ARPANET were required to use TCP/IP.

Perhaps one of the most significant developments in TCP/IP was DARPA's decision to implement TCP/IP around the UNIX operating system. Of equal importance, the University of California at Berkeley was selected to distribute the TCP/IP code. Some implementors have said that releasing such complex and functionally rich code was a "license to steal." Whatever one's view on the matter, it was a very significant and positive move in the industry. Because the TCP/IP code was nonproprietary, it spread rapidly among universities, private companies, and research centers. Indeed, it has become the standard suite of data communications protocols for UNIX-based computers.

At that time, other networks were coming into existence based on funding from the government and other research agencies and using TCP/IP protocols. The NSFnet was established as a high-capacity network by the National Science Foundation. Its goal is to provide a communications backbone for scientific and research centers, initially in the United States and now in other parts of the world. Its high-capacity lines are designed to support supercomputer transmissions. The supercomputer centers perform backbones from which lower-speed networks are attached. Today, NSFnet has evolved from the 56 Kbit/s carrier lines to T1 speeds of 1.544 Mbit/s and MCI has installed optical fiber connections over the NSF backbone network.

Organization of Internet

The organization of Internet is now administered by the Internet Advisory Board (IAB)(see Fig. 1.1). The IAB consists of a number of subsidiary organizations, but their main function is to coordinate the Internet Task Forces, which are responsible for developing the protocols for Internet. The two major groups within the IAB are the Internet Research Task Force (IRTF) and the Internet Engineering Task Force (IETF). The IRTF is responsible for ongoing research activities. The IETF concerns itself with tactical issues (implementation and engineering problems).

This organization reflects the change made to the IAB in 1989. The original IAB was formed in 1983 by DARPA. Its original charter was relatively simple: Coordinate research information exchange between researchers and encourage intercommunications through the Internet. The 1989 alignment reflects the growing complexity of the Internet system and the need for better coordination of its many activities.

The Federal Networking Council (FNC) serves as an advisory body for Internet. In addition, it coordinates activities of the U.S. government federal agencies on the use of Internet and other networks. The federal government agencies provide the funding for the research and development of the Internet system and protocols, and the FNC pro-

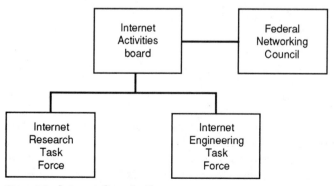

Figure 1.1   Internet Organization.

vides the important coordination function between the IAB and government agencies. The FNC board is actually chartered under the Federal Coordinating Committee for Science, Engineering, and Technology (FCCSET).

Until recently, membership in the FNC consisted of government agencies or members that were sponsored by government agencies. Today, any organization can be granted Internet identifiers. In addition, the FNC has developed a method that will allow a network to determine if it wishes to accept traffic from other networks. This technique, called the *usage database,* describes the volume and traffic type each member anticipates. It allows a network manager to examine the database when building routing tables. In its simplest form, it will provide information to guide network managers in their decisions to accept or not accept traffic from other networks.

Request for comments (RFCs)

A brief reference was made earlier to RFCs. The RFCs are technical notes dealing with an Internet protocol. They represent the documentation of the Internet. An RFC is submitted to the RFC Editor in Chief. Indeed, anyone can submit an RFC, if they wish, by using the instructions for authors of RFC in RFC: AUTHOR-INSTRUCT.TXT.

Some RFCs are de facto standards for the Transmission Control Protocol/Internet Protocol (TCP/IP); others are published for informational purposes; and still others are a result of research and may eventually become standards. Presently, there are over 1000 RFCs in existence, although quite a number of these specifications have been superseded.

As stated earlier in the Preface, the intent in this book is to gain a general understanding of TCP/IP. However, there is no substitute for the actual source documents (the RFCs). They can be obtained from

SRI International, Room EJ291
333 Ravenswood Avenue
Menlo Park, CA 94025
(800) 235-3151

TCP/IP and the OSI

Before we move into some tutorial discussions of networking architectures, it should be stated that the use of TCP/IP and related protocols continues to grow in the industry. This situation has raised some interesting points vis-à-vis the Open Systems Interconnection (OSI) Model. A substantial number of people believe that TCP/IP is a more viable approach for a number of reasons. First, TCP/IP is here; it works. Second, a wealth of products are available that use the TCP/IP protocol suites. Third, it has a well-founded, functioning administrative structure through the IAB. Fourth, it provides easy access to documentation. Fifth, it is used in many UNIX products.

Notwithstanding the preceding comments, it is the intent of the original Internet sponsor, the Department of Defense, to move away from the TCP/IP protocol suites. (We will discuss these issues in Chap. 14.) However, it should also be stated that the Internet approach is to stay with the existing standards and protocols and to write new specifications, if necessary. The stated approach is also to include the international standards if they are available. Lastly, the Internet approach is to remain vendor independent as far as possible. Again, we will have more to say about the OSI, TCP/IP issue in Chap. 14.

Internetworking Architecture

Terms and concepts

In order to grasp the operations of TCP/IP, several terms and concepts must first be understood. To begin this discussion, please examine Fig. 1.2. The Internet uses the term *gateway* or *router* to describe a machine that performs relaying functions between networks. Figure 1.2 shows a gateway placed between networks A, B, and C. (Terms *router* and *gateway* are defined further in Chap. 2.)

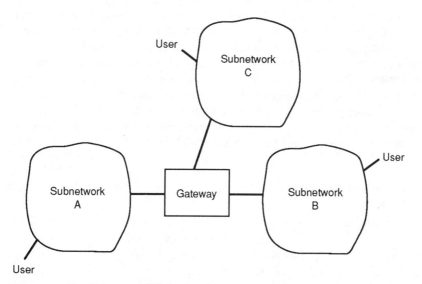

Figure 1.2 The Gateway and Subnetworks.

Networks A, B, and C are often called subnetworks. The term does not mean that they provide fewer functions than a conventional network. Rather, it means that the three networks consist of a full logical network with the subnetworks contributing to the overall operations for internetworking. Stated another way, the subnetworks comprise an internetwork or an internet.

An internetworking gateway is designed to remain transparent to the end user application. Indeed, the end user application resides in the host machines connected to the networks; rarely are user applications placed in the gateway. This approach is attractive from several standpoints. First, the gateway need not burden itself with application layer protocols. Since they are not invoked at the gateway, the gateway can dedicate itself to fewer tasks, such as managing the traffic between networks. It is not concerned with application level functions such as database access, electronic mail, and file management.

Second, this approach allows the gateway to support any type of application because the gateway considers the application message as nothing more than a transparent protocol data unit (PDU).

In addition to application layer transparency, most designers attempt to keep the gateway transparent to the subnetworks and vice versa. That is, the gateway does not care what type of network is attached to it. The principal purpose of the gateway is to receive a PDU that contains adequate addressing information to enable the gateway to route the PDU to its final destination or to the next gateway. This feature is also attractive because it makes the gateway somewhat modular; it can be used on different types of networks.

However, it should be emphasized that this transparency is not achieved by magic. Software must be written to enable communications to take place between the subnetwork protocol and the gateway. These procedures are usually proprietary in nature, and standards do not describe this interface between the gateway and the subnetwork. The exception to this statement is the publication of IEEE, OSI, and Internet service definitions that describe procedures (in an abstract way) between the host and gateway protocols (layers). These service definitions are examined later in this book.

Connectionless and connection-oriented protocols

The concept of connectionless and connection-oriented operations is fundamental to any communications protocol, and the Internet standards use both. It is essential that the reader have a clear understanding of their features. Their principal characteristics are as follows:

- *Connection-oriented operations:*   A user and a network set up a logical connection before the transfer of data occurs. Usually, some type of relationship is maintained between the data units being transferred through the user/network connection.

- *Connectionless-mode operations:*   No logical connection between the user and the network is established prior to the data transmission. The data units are transmitted as independent units.

The connection-oriented service requires a three-way agreement between the two end users and the service provider (for instance, the network). It also allows the communicating parties to negotiate certain options and quality of service (QOS) functions. During the connection establishment, all three parties store information about each other, such as addresses and QOS features. Once data transfer begins, the protocol data units (PDUs) need not carry much overhead protocol control information (PCI). All that is needed is an abbreviated identifier to allow the parties to access the tables and look up the full addresses and QOS features. Since the session can be negotiated, the communicating parties need not have prior knowledge of all the characteristics of each other. If a requested service cannot be provided, any of the parties can negotiate the service to a lower level or reject the connection request.

The connection-oriented service also provides (with a few exceptions) for the acknowledgment of all data units. Additionally, if problems occur during the transmission, a connection-oriented protocol provides mechanisms for the retransmission of the errored units. In addition to these services, most connection-oriented protocols ensure that the data arrives in the proper order at the final destination. Figure 1.3 summarizes the characteristics of connection-oriented networks.

The connectionless type of service manages user PDUs as independent and separate entities. No relationship is maintained between successive data transfers, and few records are kept of the ongoing

---

- Connection mapped through network

- Abbreviated addressing

- Usually fixed routing between networks

- Accountability provided

Figure 1.3   Connection-Oriented Networks.

user-to-user communications process through the network(s). Options are not negotiated, nor are tables created and maintained about the data transfer.

Generally, the communicating entities must have a prior agreement on how to communicate, and the QOS features must be prearranged. Alternately, QOS can be provided for each PDU that is transmitted. If so, each PDU must contain fields that identify the types and levels of service.

In contrast to the connection-oriented service, the connectionless service provides neither positive acknowledgments (ACKs) nor negative acknowledgments (NAKs). Additionally, connectionless networks are not concerned with flow control or any type of resequencing operations at the final destination.

By its very nature, connectionless service can achieve (a) a high degree of independence from specific protocols within a subnetwork, (b) considerable independence of the subnetworks from each other, and (c) a high degree of independence of the subnetwork(s) from the user-specific protocols.

A connectionless network is likely more robust than its connection-oriented counterpart, because each PDU is handled as an independent entity. Therefore, data units can take different routes to avoid failed nodes or congestion at a point in the network(s). However, connectionless protocols do consume more overhead (in relation to the length of the headers and in proportion to the amount of user data in the PDU) than their connection-oriented counterparts. The characteristics of connectionless networks are summarized in Fig. 1.4.

Before leaving the subject of connectionless and connection-oriented protocols, it should be stated that the practical network manager recognizes that it is efficacious to implement both connection-oriented and connectionless layers within a system. The choice depends on the type of service needed by the end user vis-à-vis the cost and overhead to obtain it. Since most vendors provide for a variety of connection-oriented and connectionless products, it becomes a matter of deciding in which layer one wishes to obtain the options of the various services.

- Limited end-to-end mapping
- Full addressing with data unit
- Can use alternate routing
- Limited accountability

Figure 1.4   Connectionless Service.

But let there be no mistake, if one cares for one's data, it must be accepted that there will be a connection-oriented protocol residing somewhere in the system.

The Internet Layers

The software and hardware operating on TCP/IP networks typically consist of a wide range of functions to support the communications activities. The network designer is faced with an enormous task in dealing with the number and complexity of these functions. To address these problems, an internet is structured by "layering" the functions.

Even though modern networks are now described by dividing them into seven conceptual layers, the Internet architecture is based on four layers. Figure 1.5 depicts the Internet layer architecture. The bottom layer of Internet contains the subnetworks and the subnetwork interfaces. They provide the capability of delivering data within each network. Examples of subnetworks are Tymnet, Transpac, ARPANET, and an Ethernet local area network (LAN). Even though this layer includes a "subnetwork," in actual implementations the data link and physical layers are required in all machines that are communicating with a subnet or a gateway. Therefore, be aware that Fig. 1.5 is quite abstract, because this layer must also include the data link and physical layers. Later figures will show this lower layer in more detail.

The next layer is the internetwork. This layer provides the functions necessary for connecting networks and gateways into a coherent system. This layer is responsible for delivering data from the source to the final destination. This layer contains the Internet Protocol (IP) and the Internet Control Message Protocol (ICMP). As discussed later, other supporting protocols for route discovery and addressing mapping also reside with IP at this layer.

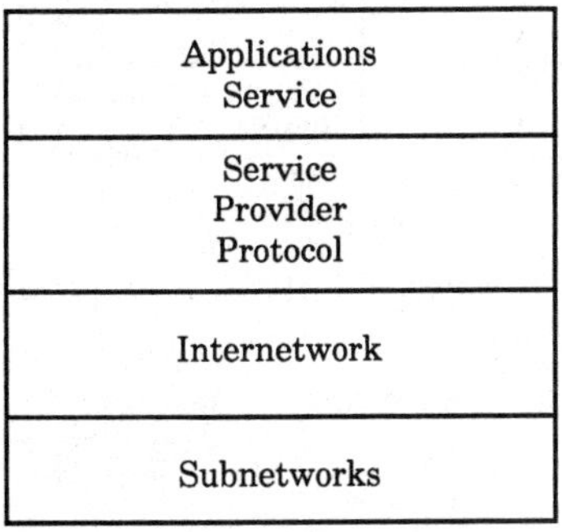

Applications Service
Service Provider Protocol
Internetwork
Subnetworks

Figure 1.5   The Internet Layers.

The third layer is known as the service provider protocol layer. This layer is responsible for end-to-end communications. If connection-oriented, it provides reliability measures and has mechanisms that account for all traffic flowing through an internet. This layer contains the TCP and the User Datagram Protocol (UDP).

Finally, the upper layer is called the applications service layer. This layer supports the direct interfaces to an end user application. The Internet applications are responsible for functions such as file transfer, remote terminal access, remote job execution, electronic mail, etc. This layer contains several widely used protocols, such as the File Transfer Protocol (FTP).

Example of the Layer Operations

Figure 1.6 shows the relationship of subnetworks and gateways to layered protocols. The layers depicted earlier in Fig. 1.5 have been changed to show the lower data link and physical layers, and the upper layers have been renamed with terms that are now more widely used in the industry.

In this figure it is assumed that the user application in host A sends an application PDU to an application layer protocol in host B, such as a file transfer system. The file transfer software performs a variety of functions and sends file records to the user data. In many systems, the operations at host B are known as *server* operations and the operations at host A are known as *client* operations.

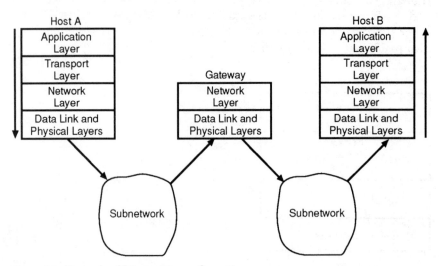

Figure 1.6 Example of Internet Layer Operations.

As indicated by the downward arrows in the protocol stack at host A, this unit is passed to the transport layer protocol. This layer performs a variety of operations (discussed in later chapters) and adds a header to the PDU passed to it. The unit of data is now called a *segment*. The PDU from the upper layers is considered to be data to the transport layer.

Next, the transport layer passes the segment to the network layer, also called the IP layer, which again performs specific services and appends a header. This unit (now called a datagram in Internet terms) is passed down to the lower layers. Here, the data link layer adds its header as well as a trailer, and the data unit (now called a *frame*) is launched into the network by the physical layer. Of course, if host B sends data to host A, the process is reversed and the direction of the arrows is changed.

The Internet protocols are unaware of what goes on inside the network. The network manager is free to manipulate and manage the PDU in any manner necessary. However, in some instances the Internet PDU (data and headers) remain unchanged as it is transmitted through the subnet. In Fig. 1.6, we see its emergence at the gateway where it is processed through the lower layers and passed to the IP (network) layer. Here, routing decisions are made based on the addresses provided by the host computer.

After these routing decisions have been made, the PDU is passed to the communications link that is connected to the appropriate subnetwork (consisting of the lower layers). The PDU is reencapsulated into the data link layer PDU (usually called a frame) and passed to the next subnetwork. As before, this unit is passed through the subnetwork transparently (usually), where it finally arrives at the destination host.

The destination (host B) receives the traffic through its lower layers and reverses the process that transpired at host A. That is, it decapsulates the headers by stripping them off in the appropriate layer. The header is used by the layer to determine the actions it is to take; the header governs the layer's operations.

The PDU created by the file transfer application is passed to the file transfer application residing at host B. If host A and B are large mainframe computers, this application is likely an exact duplicate of the software at the transmitting host. However, the application may perform a variety of functions, depending on the header it receives. It is conceivable that the data could be passed to another end user application at host B, but in many instances, the user at host A merely wants to obtain the services of a server protocol, such as a file transfer or electronic mail server. If this is the case, it is not necessary for an end user application process to be invoked at host B.

In order to return the retrieved data from the server at host B to the client at host A, the process is reversed by the data being transferred down through the layers in the host B machine, through the network, through the gateway, to the next network, and up the layers of host A to the end user.

The TCP/IP Model: A Closer Look

Figure 1.7 depicts an architectural model of TCP/IP and several of the major related protocols. The choices in the stacking of the layers of this model vary, depending on the needs of network users and the decisions made by network designers. For the present, we see some of the protocols that were explained in the previous material, specifically, IP and TCP. The protocols that rest over TCP (and UDP) are examples of the application layer protocols, also labeled applications service in Fig. 1.5. The lower two layers represent the data link and physical layers and, as the figure depicts, are implemented with a wide choice of standards and protocols. This figure will be used later in the book to explain the layers' operations in more detail.

Ports and Sockets: An Introduction

Each application layer process using the TCP/IP protocols must identify itself by a *port* number. This number is used between the two host computers to identify which application program is to receive the incoming traffic.

The use of port numbers also provides a multiplexing capability by allowing multiple user programs to communicate concurrently with

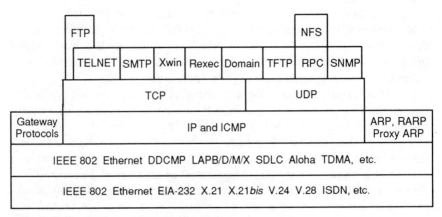

Figure 1.7   The IP Suite. (*IBM GG24-3376-00*)

one application program, such as TCP. The port numbers are used to identify these application entries. The concept is quite similar to a service application point (SAP) in the OSI Model.

In addition to the use of ports, TCP/IP-based protocols use an abstract identifier called a *socket*. The socket was derived from the network input/output operations of the 4.3 BSD UNIX system. It is quite similar to UNIX file access procedures in that it identifies an endpoint communications process.

In the Internet, some port numbers are preassigned. These are called *well-known ports* and are used to identify widely used applications, called *well-known services*. The well-known port numbers occupy values ranging from 0 to 255. An individual organization should not use the numbers within these ranges because they are reserved. An organization that wishes to assign a port number to any specific application should use a number above 255. Later discussions will examine ports and sockets in more detail.

Challenges of Internetworking

With this background information behind us, it should prove useful to examine several difficult issues and problems a network administrator encounters in providing internetworking services. They are discussed throughout the book in regard to TCP/IP. For the present, we will keep the discussion on a general level.

Different networks may use different length sizes for PDUs. If different length sizes are used, the networks or a gateway must provide for the fragmentation of the data units. In so doing, the identity of the data units must not be lost. The varying length sizes of the data units does not eliminate the requirement to maintain a sequence number relationship on an end-to-end basis. In Chap. 5, we learn that an IP gateway has the ability to fragment data units and that the receiving host computer will reassemble the fragments into the full PDU.

The timers, time-outs, and retry values often differ between subnetworks. For example, assume network A sets a wait-for-acknowledgment timer when a data unit is forwarded. The timer is used to ensure that an end-to-end acknowledgment occurs within a specified period. The data unit is passed to network B, but this network does not have an end-to-end timer. Thus, we have a dilemma. Should network A return an acknowledgment to the transmitting user upon passing the data unit to network B and assume the second network will indeed deliver the data unit? A false sense of security would result from the user in network A since the data unit may not arrive at the end destination. TCP/IP provides for end-to-end timing support, but the function is not invoked during the data unit's traversal through the subnetworks, only at the host computers. Therefore, a network is free to devise any type of timer it needs.

Subnetworks may use different addressing conventions. For example, one may use logical names and another may use physical names. In such a case, address resolution and mapping could differ between the two subnetworks. Indeed, most networks use network-specific addresses. For example, an SNA address simply does not equate to a DECnet address. Fortunately, the Internet provides standards to support several types of addresses. In addition, Internet systems are available to support address mapping from network-layer-to-physical-layer addresses. Other systems can be invoked that derive network addresses from user friendly names.

Subnetworks may exhibit different levels of performance. For example, one subnetwork may be slower and experience more delay and less throughput than another network. The Internet protocols do not concern themselves to any significant extent about these issues. As we learned earlier in this chapter, the protocols are designed to operate transparently on different types of networks. Of course, the network manager must be concerned with these problems and can use some of the Internet software as tools to help solve these problems (as discussed later, TCP is a valuable tool in this regard).

Subnetworks may employ different routing methods. For example, one may use a fixed routing directory and another may use an adaptive routing directory. In the former case, the network logic for resequencing is sparse. In the latter case, resequencing logic is extensive. The TCP/IP suite contains many protocols to support gateway routing but does not become involved in intranetworking routing, although many organizations use these protocols within their networks.

Subnetworks may require different types of user interfaces. For example, a subnetwork may employ a connection-oriented, user-to-subnetwork interface and another may use a connectionless, datagram protocol. The interface type influences error recovery and flow control. As we shall see in several of the chapters of this book, the internetworking of connectionless and connection-oriented protocols poses several very challenging problems (and opportunities) for the network manager.

Subnetworks may require different levels of security. For example, one network may require encryption and another may only support clear-text transmissions. TCP/IP does not concern itself with security, other than allowing a user to specify a level of security desired for the transmission of the data. The security designation is then used by the network to implement in any fashion it chooses.

Troubleshooting, diagnostics, and network maintenance may differ between the subnetworks or they may not be used across more than one network. A problem created in one subnetwork may affect another subnetwork, yet the affected subnetwork may have no control in the error analysis and correction. Any exchange of network management information between networks is carried transparently by the Internet protocols. However, the emerging Internet network management standards, discussed later, are intended to provide considerable support for network management.

Clearly, the internetworking task is not simple, and it requires considerable analysis and forethought before it is implemented. Yet the task is not insurmountable. As we shall see in this book, the TCP/IP product vendors and standards organizations have developed and implemented many effective internetworking techniques.

Typical Internet Topologies

During the discussions of TCP/IP and related protocols, we will be using several figures to illustrate some points. Figure 1.8a shows two networks connected by a gateway (labeled G). The networks are identified with network addresses (network id). The network on the left of the figure is identified as network 11.4 and the other network is network 128.1. (The scheme for creating these numbers is described in Chap. 3.) The term *network cloud* is used in this figure because the topology and operations of the networks are not shown. The topologies of the networks are depicted in the subsequent figures.

In some instances, the network cloud figure will be used as depicted in Fig. 1.8a when the explanations do not require a discussion of the operations within the network. Other instances require the examination of the operations within the network, in which case other examples in Fig. 1.8 will be used. For example, Fig. 1.8b shows the topologies of a conventional packet-switched network (network 11.4) and an Ethernet-type LAN (network 128.1). The boxes labeled A, B, C, and D inside network 11.4 symbolize packet switches, which are connected with communications links. They may also be computers which serve the dual function of hosts and packet switches. The boxes inside network 128.1 symbolize host computers, workstations, or file/print servers. Figure 1.8b shows that the two networks are connected with a gateway.

Figure 1.8c shows that host B in network 128.1 is acting as a gateway to packet switch D in network 11.4. In the case of the packet switch serving as a gateway, this arrangement is quite common. In the case of the host serving as a gateway, the arrangement is less common, because the host may not have the resources to run user applications and the gateway functions.

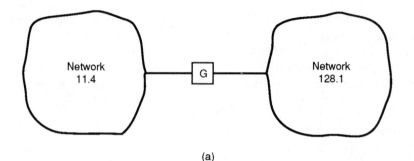

(a)

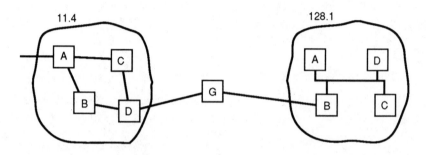

(b)

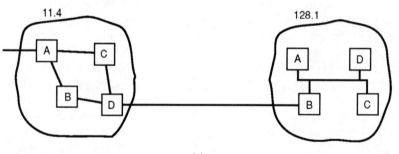

(c)

Figure 1.8   Typical Internet Network Topologies: (a) Network Clouds and Gateway; (b) Gateway Connecting Networks; (c) Packet Switches or Hosts Acting as Gateways.

Figures 1.8d and 1.8e are drawn without the network cloud. In several instances in this book, this is the approach taken.

Figure 1.8d will also be used in explaining LAN configurations. The reader will notice that two interconnected gateways are attached to an Ethernet-type topology (network 128.1) and a token ring topology (network 128.2). This configuration is common within office buildings that have a number of interconnected LANs.

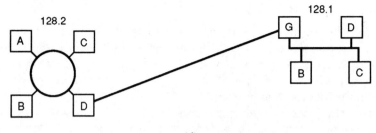

(d)

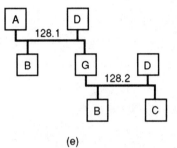

(e)

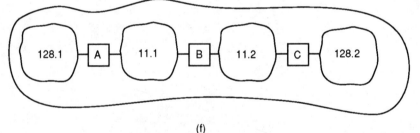

(f)

Figure 1.8 (*Continued*): (*d*) LAN Gateways; (*e*) Common Gateway between LANS; (*f*) Multiple Gateways in the Internet.

Figure 1.8*e* shows one gateway (G) connecting two Ethernet-type networks together. This approach is also quite common.

Finally, Fig. 1.8*f* shows several network clouds. From the perspective of an Internet user, the outer cloud represents the user's virtual network. The user is not concerned with the fact that user data may traverse four networks (128.1, 11.1, 11.2, and 128.2) and three gateways (A, B, and C) to reach its final destination.

Finally, this discussion has used the term *gateway* to describe the internetworking function. Chapter 3 expands this description to examine and contrast gateways, bridges, and routers.

Summary

The Internet protocols are designed to permit and facilitate the sharing of computer resources across different networks. Due to their sponsorship by the U.S. government and their simple yet effective operations, they have become one of the most widely used set of data networking protocols in existence.

Although the Internet protocols are called "TCP/IP," these two standards represent only a small part of a wealth of standardized data network standards.

Chapter 2

Introduction to Networks, Bridges, Gateways, and Routers

Introduction

TCP/IP has been implemented on both wide area and local area networks (WANs/LANs). The purpose of this chapter is to describe several prominent types of WANs/LANs and to explain their primary operating characteristics. We also examine routing schemes used to relay traffic between networks (internetworking) and examine bridges, routers, and gateways. We finish the chapter with an introduction to source routing and spanning tree protocols and their relationship to TCP/IP. This chapter serves as an introduction to the Internet routing and gateway discovery protocols, which are discussed in Chap. 8, and the IP routing algorithm, discussed in Chaps. 3 and 5.

A General Taxonomy

Communications systems on many WANs employ switches to route traffic from multiple users on a limited number of links. The stations attached to the network use the switch to share the links. Without the switch, each station would need multiple lines to communicate with the other stations. Indeed, a fully meshed network requires many lines—clearly an impossible task if many stations are involved.

An alternative to a switched network for sharing links is the broadcast network. Only one link is used. The multiple stations "copy" all the data units and discard those that are not addressed to a particular station. Most LANs use some type of broadcast protocol.

Figure 2.1 depicts the layers of WANs and LANs from the context of the seven-layer OSI Model. As the figure reveals, WANs reside in the lower three layers or LANs in the lower two layers of the OSI Model. Does this mean that we need not be concerned with the upper layers of the model when dealing with TCP/IP? Indeed not; the TCP/IP model also encompasses the transport layer and the application layer. These layers are highlighted during this discussion as well.

The left side of Fig. 2.1 shows the layers for a WAN. These layers encompass the physical, data link, and network layers of the OSI Model. The physical layer typically consists of modems for analog lines and digital service units (DSUs) for digital lines. As the figure shows, the modem or DSUs are connected to a telephone company (telco) medium such as a twisted wire pair. The connection between the user device and the modem or DSU is usually effected through an EIA 232-D connector and one of the appropriate CCITT V-Series modem standards.

Resting above the physical layer is the data link layer. Its principal function is to provide for error detection and retransmission of damaged data; that is, data that have encountered problems on the communications link (media). Today, most vendors support the data link layer with HDLC-type protocols such as LAPB, SDLC, etc.

The network layer is concerned with switching and routing traffic through the network. In addition, standards such as X.25 define the interface procedures for the user device and the network.

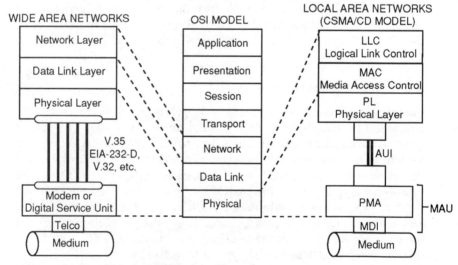

Figure 2.1 Layers of Local and Wide Area Networks.

The right side of Fig. 2.1 shows the layers for a LAN. The physical layer performs the same functions as a WAN. The parts of the physical layer (PL) are labeled in this figure as *attachment unit interface* (AUI), *medium attachment unit* (MAU), *physical medium attachment* (PMA), and *medium dependent interface* (MDI).

The AUI provides the attachment between the physical layer of the unit device and the LAN medium. It contains connectors quite similar to EIA 232-D or connectors similar to telephone jacks such as RJ 45. The MAU actually consists of both the PMA and MDI. Its principal function is to manage the connection of the DTE to the cable (LAN media) and provide services for transmitting and receiving data, detecting problems, testing operations, and checking for the quality of the signal.

The PMA contains the circuitry to support the functions of the MAU (discussed in the previous paragraph). The MDI provides the mechanical and electrical interfaces between the medium and the PMA.

The *media access control (MAC)* layer is responsible for managing the traffic on the LAN. It performs functions such as determining when the LAN media is free to transmit data, detects collisions of data on certain types of LANs, and determines when retransmissions should occur. It is media independent but specific to a particular protocol, such as token bus or token ring.

The *logical link control (LLC)* layer provides the interface between the LAN and the user layers. LLC can be configured to provide a very basic service (connectionless) or a very elaborate service dealing with connection-oriented operations. It is based on the widely used data link standard called *high-level data link control (HDLC)*; thus it can be configured to provide data link service with the unnumbered information (UI) frame or connection-oriented service with the asynchronous balanced mode (ABM) frame. The choice of how to configure LLC for operations with TCP/IP is an important one and will be discussed in several parts of this book.

The reader may wonder why a LAN does not contain the network layer. Indeed, the very idea seems anomalous since a LAN is a network. The reason is simple. The network layer (as originally conceived through the OSI Model) serves to support (a) routing and (b) interface operations. The routing aspect of the network layer is not found in the vast majority of LANs because they are broadcast networks and do not utilize switching techniques. Second, network interfaces were conceived to define the interface between the user and the network and to negotiate quality of service (QOS) features for the user/network connection. These needs do not exist in most LANs, because the interfaces are quite simple and QOS options are usually not available. Consequently, the network layer in a LAN is either nonexistent or very "lean." If it exists, it is usually implemented with a simple protocol, such as IP.

Now that we have an understanding of the layers of WANs and LANs, we turn our attention to more detailed aspects. For WANs, three switching techniques are explained: (1) circuit switching, (2) message switching, and (3) packet switching. The emphasis is on packet switching since it has become the prevalent approach for switched data networks and for control networks in telephone systems. For LANs, the emphasis is on broadcast technology implemented in Ethernet and token networks.

Wide Area Networks (WANs)

Circuit switching

Circuit switching provides a direct connection between two components. The direct connection of a circuit switch serves as an open "pipeline," permitting the two end users to utilize the facility as they see fit—within bandwidth and tariff limitations. Many telephone networks use circuit switching systems.

Circuit switching is arranged in one or a combination of three architectures: (1) concentration (more input lines than output lines), (2) expansion (more output lines than input lines), and (3) connection (an equal number of input and output lines). In its simplest form, a circuit switch is an $N*M$ array of lines that connect to each other at crosspoints. In a large switching office, the N lines are input from the subscriber (terminals, computers, etc.) and the M lines are output to other switching offices.

Circuit switching provides only a path for the sessions between data communications components. Error checking, session establishment, frame flow control, frame formatting, and selection of codes and protocols are the responsibility of the users. Little or no care of the data traffic is provided in a pure circuit switching arrangement. Consequently, the telephone network is often used as the basic foundation for a data communications network, and additional facilities are added by the value-added carrier, network vendor, or user organization. Other switching technologies (e.g., message and packet) often use circuit switching as the basic transmission media and then provide additional value-added functions and facilities such as store-and-forward services and protocol conversion.

Message switching

In the 1960s and 1970s, the pervasive method for switching data communications traffic was message switching. The technology is still widely used in certain applications, such as electronic mail. The message switch is typically a specialized computer. It is responsible for accepting traffic from attached terminals and computers (through dial-up or leased lines). It examines the address in the header of the message and switches (routes) the traffic to the receiving station or the next switch in the route. Unlike circuit switching in telephone networks, message switching is a store-and-forward technology; the messages are stored temporarily on disk units at the switches.

Since the data are usually stored, the traffic is not considered to be interactive or real-time. Of course, selected traffic can be sent through a message switch at very high speeds by establishing levels of priority for different types of traffic. High-priority traffic is queued for a shorter period than low-priority traffic. This approach could support interactive applications.

Storing the messages temporarily on disk storage also provides a method to smooth traffic by the practice of queuing the lower priority traffic during peak periods. The queuing also decreases the chances of blocking traffic due to network congestion. For example, the traffic can be stored temporarily and later routed to stations when they are available to accept it.

The message-switching technology usually operates in a master/slave relationship. Typically, the switch performs polling and selection functions to manage the incoming and outgoing traffic. For example, assume user A has data for user D. The switch performs a polling cycle of the attached computers on which the users are operating. Upon polling A, the data (message) are transmitted to the switch. Based on the message's priority, it is stored in one of several disk queues. Depending on overall traffic conditions and the message priority, the switch de-queues the message and sends a select command to D. At site D, an ACK to the select may be sent to the switch, after which the message is transmitted to D.

Message switching has served the industry well, but it suffers from three deficiencies. First, since it is inherently a master/slave structure, the entire network can be lost if the switch fails, because all traffic must go through the message switch. Consequently, many organizations install a duplicate (duplexed) switch, which assumes the role of the primary switch in the event of failure. The second major deficiency stems from the hub arrangement of a message switch. Since all traffic must go through one switch, the switch itself is a potential bottleneck. Degraded response time and decreased throughput can result from such an arrangement. Third, message switching does not utilize the communications lines as efficiently as other techniques discussed in the next section.

Packet switching

Because of the problems with message switching, the industry began to move toward a different WAN switching technique in the 1970s:

packet switching. Packet switching distributes the risk to more than one switch, reduces vulnerability to network failure, and provides better utilization of the lines than does message switching.

Packet switching is so named because user data (for example, messages) are divided into smaller pieces. These pieces, or packets, have protocol control information (PCI) headers placed around them and are routed through the network as independent entities.

A packet-switching network contains multiple switches which allow the network load to be distributed to multiple switching sites (see Fig. 2.2). Also, additional communications lines are attached to the switches. The arrangement provides the opportunity to perform alternate routing to avoid failed or busy nodes and channels. For example, in Fig. 2.2, a packet switch has the option of routing the packets to more than one packet switch.

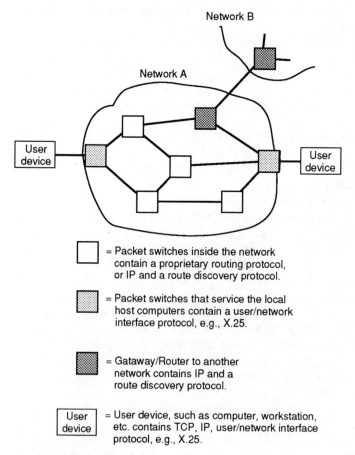

□ = Packet switches inside the network contain a proprietary routing protocol, or IP and a route discovery protocol.

▨ = Packet switches that service the local host computers contain a user/network interface protocol, e.g., X.25.

■ = Gataway/Router to another network contains IP and a route discovery protocol.

User device = User device, such as computer, workstation, etc. contains TCP, IP, user/network interface protocol, e.g., X.25.

Figure 2.2 Packet Switching.

Packet switching works well with data communications traffic, because many devices, such as keyboard terminals, transmit traffic in bursts. The data is sent on the channel, which is then idle while a terminal user inputs more data into the terminal or pauses to think about a problem. The idle channel time could translate into wasted line capacity, but a packet switch interleaves multiple transmissions from several terminals onto one channel. In effect, packet switching achieves statistical time division multiplexing (STDM) across the communications line. This approach provides better use of the expensive communications channel.

Packet switching goes one step further than the simple multiplexing of the communications lines. Packet logic can also multiplex multiple user sessions onto a single communications port on the computer. Instead of dedicating a port to one user, the system interleaves the bursts of traffic from multiple users across one port.

Packet switching also provides an attractive feature for connecting the terminals and computers together for a session. In a circuit-switched telephone structure, connect time is often slow. A switched telephone call requires that a number be dialed and that all resources be set up before the call can be routed to the destination. However, with a packet-switching system, dedicated leased lines are available for multiple users to transmit and receive their data traffic. The lines do not require any circuit setups, since they are permanently connected through the system. This technique can improve the slow connect time associated with multiple telephone circuit switches.

Figure 2.2 also shows the relationship of some of the TCP/IP protocols to the packet-switching components. This illustration shows one of several configurations that exist in the industry; it is not meant to be all inclusive. Typically the user device (a host) interfaces into a packet-switch network with a user/network interface protocol. The most widely used network interface protocol in the industry today is CCITT's X.25 standard. It provides several interface options for connecting the user to the network, such as reverse charge, call forwarding, and QOS features (such as throughput and delay negotiations). The Internet Protocol (IP) is also stored at the host machine because the gateways rely on the IP header to be created by the host computer. Additionally, TCP resides at the host machine to provide end-to-end integrity for the transmission between the two end user devices. Inside the network the packet switches may contain a vendor's proprietary routing protocol, or in some instances, IP is employed with a companion route discovery protocol. Remember that IP is a routing protocol but not a route discovery protocol.

The gateways in this figure could be configured with IP as in the case with an Internet. In a large number of public packet networks, such as Tymnet, Telenet, and in Europe the PTTs (Postal Telegraph and Telephone Administration), the gateway protocol is often X.75. The X.75 protocol, although a gateway protocol, is quite different from IP because it is a connection-oriented gateway protocol.

Choosing the packet route. Packet-switched networks are designed to route user traffic based on a variety of criteria, generally referred to as a least-cost routing (also called the cost metric), which is examined in Chap. 8. The name does not mean that routing is based solely on obtaining the least-cost route in the literal sense. Other factors are often part of the routing algorithm:

- Capacity of the link
- Number of packets waiting for transmission onto the link
- Load leveling through the network
- Security requirements for the link
- Type of traffic vis-à-vis the type of link
- Number of intermediate links between the transmitting and receiving stations
- Ability to reach (connect to) intermediate nodes and, of course, the final receiving station

Whatever the least-cost criteria may be, the network designer's goal is to determine the best least-cost, end-to-end path between any two communicating stations.

Even though networks vary in least-cost criteria, three constraints must be considered: (a) delay, (b) throughput, and (c) connectivity. If delay is excessive or if throughput is too little, the network does not meet the needs of the user community. The third constraint is obvious: The communications devices must be able to reach each other. Otherwise, all other least-cost criteria are irrelevant.

The algorithms used to route the packets through the network vary. Some algorithms are set up at a central site or executed at each individual packet switch. They may provide a static, end-to-end path between the two users of the network, or they may route the traffic through different packet switches. They vary in how they adapt to changing network conditions. Some algorithms adapt only to failures, and some adapt as traffic conditions change.

In many WANs, the TCP/IP protocols are not invoked. Typically, a vendor uses a proprietary product to manage packets within the network and then uses a gateway protocol like IP or X.75 to manage the data between networks. However, this approach is changing. Since the TCP/IP suite has several protocols to support very powerful packet routing arrangements, some networks have adopted the philosophy of "Why re-invent the wheel?" and have adapted the TCP/IP standards.

Before leaving the subject of routing, it should be emphasized that IP routes datagrams by using a routing table (directory). However, it does not create this table. The table is created by what this writer calls a *route discovery protocol,* which is examined in Chap. 8. Therefore, IP is of little use unless a route discovery protocol has created the IP routing table.

Local Area Networks (LANs)

TCP/IP is now found in many LANs. Indeed, many LAN vendors offer TCP/IP as part of their overall LAN package. These vendors use TCP/IP as an integral part of their product. Therefore, a brief description of this technology is in order.

Definitions of LANs are plentiful. While one definition has not gained prominence, most definitions include the following:

- The connections between the user devices are usually within a few hundred to several thousand meters.

- The LAN transmits data (and sometimes voice and video) between user stations and computers.

- The LAN transmission capacity is usually greater than that of a WAN. Typical bit rates range from 1 to 20 Mbit/s, with the emerging optical LANs operating in the 100 Mbit/s range.

- The LAN channel is typically owned by the organization using the facility. The telephone company is usually not involved in channel ownership or management.

- The error rate on a LAN is considerably better than a WAN-oriented telephone channel—for instance, error rates in $1:10^9$ bits transmitted are not uncommon.

LAN components

A LAN contains four major components to support the transmission of data between end users: (1) the channel, (2) the physical interface, (3) a protocol, and (4) the user station.

1. LAN channels (media) consist of coaxial TV cable, coaxial baseband twisted pair cable, or optical fiber. Coaxial cable TV (CATV) is used on many networks because it has a large transmission capacity, a good signal-to-noise ratio, low signal radiation, and low

error rates. Twisted pair cable and microwave are also found in many LANs. Coaxial baseband is perhaps the most widely used transmission path, giving high capacity as well as low error rates and low noise distortion.

Thus far, optical fiber paths have seen limited application, but their positive attributes ensure their use. The immediate use of lightwave transmission on LANs is for point-to-point, high-speed connections of up to 10 mi (16 Km). A transfer rate of over 100 Mbit/s can be achieved on this type of path.

2. The interface between the path and the user station can take several forms. It may be a single cable television (CATV) tap, infrared diodes, microwave antennas, or laser-emitting semiconductors for optical fibers. Some LANs provide regenerative repeaters at the interface; others use the interface as buffers for data flow.

3. The protocol control logic component controls the LAN and provides for the end user's access onto the network. The LAN protocols employ methods and techniques discussed later in this chapter.

4. The last major component is the user workstation. It can be anything from a word processor to a mainframe computer. Several LAN vendors provide support for other vendors' products, and several layers of the OSI Model are also supported by some LANs.

Types of LANs

Carrier sense, collision detection

Carrier sense, collision detection is widely used in LANs. Many vendors use this technique with Ethernet and the IEEE 802.3 specification.

A carrier sense LAN considers all stations as peers; the stations contend for the use of the channel on an equal basis. Before transmitting, the stations are required to monitor the channel to determine if the channel is active (that is, if another station is sending data on the channel). If the channel is idle, any station with data to transmit can send its traffic onto the channel. If the channel is occupied, the stations must defer to the station using the channel.

Figure 2.3 depicts a carrier sense, collision detection LAN. Stations A, B, C, and D are attached to a channel (such as coaxial cable) by bus interface units (BIU). Let us assume stations A and B wish to transmit some traffic. However, station D is currently using the channel, so the BIUs at stations A and B "listen" and defer to the signal from station D that is occupying the channel. When the line goes idle, A and B attempt to acquire the channel.

Since the A station's transmission requires time to propagate to other

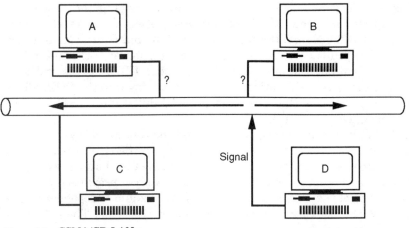

Figure 2.3   CSMA/CD LANs.

stations, they may be unaware that A's signal is on the channel. In this situation, A station could transmit its traffic even though another station has supposedly seized the channel. This problem is called the *collision window*. The collision window is a factor of the propagation delay of the signal and the distance between the two competing stations.

Carrier sense networks are usually implemented on short-distance LANs because the collision window lengthens with a longer channel. The long channel provides opportunity for more collisions and can reduce throughput in the network. Generally, a long propagation delay (a long delay before the stations know each other is transmitting) coupled with short frames and high data transfer rates gives rise to a greater incidence of collisions. Longer frames can mitigate the effect of long delay, but they reduce the opportunity for competing stations to acquire the channel.

Each station is capable of transmitting and listening to the channel simultaneously. As the two signals collide, they create voltage irregularities on the channel, which are sensed by the colliding stations. The stations must turn off their transmission and, through a randomized wait period, attempt to seize the channel again. The randomized wait decreases the chances of the collision recurring since it is unlikely that the competing stations will generate the same randomized wait time.

CSMA/CD and IEEE 802.3

The best-known scheme for controlling a LAN on a bus structure is carrier sense multiple access with collision detection (CSMA/CD). The most widely used implementation of CSMA/CD is found in the Ethernet specification. Xerox Corporation was instrumental in providing the research for CSMA/CD and in developing the first base-band commercial products. The broadband network was developed by MITRE. In 1980, Xerox, the Intel Corporation, and Digital Equipment Corporation jointly published a specification for an Ethernet LAN. This specification was later introduced to the IEEE 802 committees and, with several modifications, has found its way into the IEEE 802.3 standard. (Be aware that the Ethernet and 802.3 interfaces differ in some formatting conventions.)

CSMA/CD Ethernet is organized around the concept of layered protocols (see Fig. 2.1). The user layer is serviced by the two CSMA/CD layers, the data link layer, and the physical layer. Each of the bottom two layers consists of two separate entities. The data link layer provides the actual logic to control the CSMA/CD network. It is medium independent; consequently, the network may be broadband or baseband. The 802 standard includes both broadband and baseband options.

The MAC sublayer consists of the following sublayers:

Transmit data encapsulation

- Accepts data from LLC.
- Calculates the CRC value and places it in the FCS field.

Transmit media access management

- Presents a serial bit stream to the physical layer.
- Defers transmission when a medium is busy.
- Halts transmission when a collision is detected.
- Reschedules a retransmission after a collision is detected.
- Inserts the PAD field for frames with a LLC length less than a minimum value.
- Enforces a collision by sending a jam message.

Receive data decapsulation

- Performs a CRC check.
- Recognizes and accepts any frame whose destination address (D/A) field is an address of a station.
- Presents data to LLC.

Receive media access management

- Receives a serial bit stream from the physical layer.
- Discards frames that are less than the minimum length.

The physical layer is medium dependent. It is responsible for such services as introducing the electrical signals onto the channel, providing the timing on the channel, and data encoding and decoding. Like the data link layer, the physical layer is composed of two major entities: the data encoding/decoding entity and the transmit/receive channel access (although the IEEE 802.3 standard combines these entities in its documents). The major functions of these entities are as follows:

Data encoding/decoding

- Provides the signals to synchronize the stations on the channel (this sync signal is called the preamble).
- Encodes the binary data stream to a self-clocking code at the transmitting site and decodes the Manchester code back to binary code at the receiver.

Channel access

- Introduces the physical signal onto the channel on the transmit side and receives the signal on the receive side of the interface.
- Senses a carrier on the channel on both the transmit and the receive side (which indicates the channel is occupied).
- Detects a collision on the channel on the transmit side (indicating two signals have interfered with each other).

In a CSMA/CD network, each station has both a transmit and receive side to provide the incoming/outgoing flow of data. The transmit side is invoked when a user wishes to transmit data to another DTE on the network; conversely, the receive side is invoked when data is transmitted to the stations on the network.

Token ring

The token ring topology is another powerful LAN protocol offered by a number of vendors, and it is published as a standard as IEEE 802.5. IBM has based many of its LAN products around the token ring. It is illustrated in Fig. 2.4. The stations are connected to a concentric ring through a ring interface unit (RIU). Each RIU is responsible for monitoring the data passing through it, as well as regenerating the signal and passing it to the next station. If the address in the header of the transmission indicates the data are destined for a station, the RIU copies the data and passes the information to the user device.

If the ring is idle (that is, no user data occupies the ring), a "free" token is passed around the ring from node to node. This token indi-

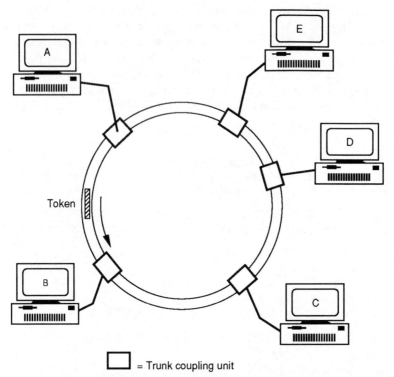

= Trunk coupling unit

Figure 2.4   Token Ring LANs.

cates that the ring is available and any station with data to transmit can use the token to transmit traffic. The control of the ring is passed sequentially from node to node around the ring.

During the period when the station has the token, it controls the ring. Upon acquiring the token (i.e., marking the token busy), the transmitting station inserts data behind the token and passes the data through the ring. As each RIU monitors the data, it regenerates the transmission, checks the address in the header of the data, and passes the data to the next station. Upon the data arriving at the transmitting station, this station makes the token free and passes it to the next station on the ring. This requirement prevents one station from monopolizing the ring. If the token passes around the ring without being used, the station can once again use the token and transmit data.

Some systems remove the token from the ring, place the data on the channel, and then insert the token behind the data. Other user frames can be placed behind the first data element to allow a "piggybacking" effect on the LAN with multiple user frames circling the ring. This approach requires that the token be placed behind the last data transmission. Piggybacking is useful for large rings that experience a long delay in the transmission around the ring, but the short propagation delay on a LAN is not worth the added complexity of a piggybacking LAN.

Many token ring networks use priority schemes. The object of the priority is to give each station an opportunity to reserve the use of the ring for the next transmission around the ring. As the token and data circle the ring, each node examines the token, which contains a reservation field. If a node's priority is higher than the priority number in the reservation field, it raises the reservation field number to its level, thus reserving the token on the next round. If another node does not make the reservation field higher, the station is allowed to use the token and channel on the next pass around the ring.

The station with the token is required to store the previous reservation value in a temporary storage area. Upon releasing the token, the station restores the network to its previous lowest priority request. In this manner, once the token is made free for the next round, the station with the highest reservation is allowed to seize the token.

Token bus

Token bus LANs (IEEE 802.4) use a bus topology, yet provide access to the channel as if it were a ring. The protocol eliminates the collisions found in the carrier sense collision detection systems but allows the use of a bus-type channel. The token bus requires no physical ordering of the stations on the channel. The stations can be logically configured to pass the token in any order.

The protocol uses a control frame called an access token or access right. This token gives a station the exclusive use of the bus. The token-holding station uses the bus for a period of time to send and/or receive data. It then passes the token to a designated station called the *successor station*. In the bus topology, all stations listen to the channel and receive the access token, but the only station allowed to use the channel is the successor station. All other stations must await their turn to receive the token. The stations receive the token through a cyclic sequence, which forms a logical ring on the physical bus.

The LLC Sublayer

Figure 2.1 served to introduce the LLC protocol. This section examines it in more detail, since many LANs use it to interface with the network layer (for example, IP). The IEEE 802 standards split the data link layer into two sublayers: MAC and LLC. As discussed earlier in this chapter and illustrated in Fig. 2.1, MAC encompasses

802.3, 802.4, and 802.5. The LLC includes 802.2. This sublayer was implemented to make the LLC sublayer independent of a specific LAN access method. The LLC sublayer is also used to provide an interface into or out of the specific MAC protocol.

The MAC/LLC split provides several attractive features. First, it controls access to the shared channel among the autonomous user devices. Second, it provides for a decentralized (peer-to-peer) scheme that reduces the LAN's susceptibility to errors. Third, it provides a more compatible interface with WANs, since LLC is a subset of the HDLC superset. Fourth, LLC is independent of a specific access method while MAC is protocol specific. This approach gives an 802 network a flexible interface with upper layer protocols (ULPs), such as IP or the OSI's connectionless network protocol (CLNP) (discussed in Chap. 5).

Classes of service

The 802 LAN standards include four types of service for LLC users:

Type 1:   Unacknowledged connectionless service

Type 2:   Connection-oriented service

Type 3:   Acknowledged connectionless service

Type 4:   All of the above services

All 802 networks must provide unacknowledged connectionless service (Type 1). Optionally, connection-oriented service can be provided (Type 2). Type 1 networks provide no ACKs, flow control, or error recovery. Type 2 networks provide connection management, ACKs, flow control, and error recovery. Type 3 networks provide no connection setup or disconnect, but they do provide for the acknowledgement of data units.

Most Type 1 networks use a higher-level protocol (i.e., TCP in the transport layer) to provide connection management functions. IP can rest over LLC as well. Therefore, a LAN layered model could be as follows: Physical, MAC, LLC, IP, TCP, and an application layer.

Chapter 5 discusses the relationship of TCP/IP and LLC in more detail.

Repeaters, Bridges, Routers, Brouters, and Gateways

Networks were originally conceived to be fairly small systems consisting of relatively few machines. As the need for data communication services has grown, it has become necessary to connect networks to-gether for the sharing of resources and distribution of functions and administrative control. In addition, some LANs, by virtue of their re-stricted distance, often need to be connected together through other devices. These devices are called a number of names in the industry; in this section we will explain and define each of these machines.

Figure 2.5 shows the relationships of these devices vis-à-vis a lay-ered model. A *repeater* is used to connect the media on a LAN, typi-cally called media segments. The repeater has no upper layer func-tions; its principal job is to terminate the signal on one LAN segment and regenerate it on another LAN segment.

The term *bridge* is usually associated with an internetworking unit (IWU). It operates at the data link layer (always at the MAC sublayer and sometimes at the LLC sublayer). Typically, it uses MAC physical addresses to perform its relaying functions. As a general rule, it is a fairly low-function device and connects networks that are homoge-neous (for example, IEEE-based networks).

A *router* operates at the network layer because it uses network layer addresses (for example, IP, X.121, E.164 addresses). It usually contains more capabilities than a bridge and may offer flow control mechanisms as well as source routing or nonsource routing features (discussed in the next section).

The term *gateway* is used to describe an entity (a machine or soft-ware module) which not only performs routing capabilities but may act as a protocol conversion or mapping facility (also called a conver-gence function). For example, such a gateway could relay traffic and also provide conversion between two different types of mail transfer applications.

Yet another term that has entered the market is *brouter*. (As if there were not enough terms.) The term *brouter* is used to describe a machine that combines the features of a router and a bridge. At first

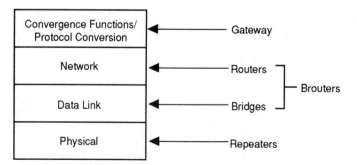

Figure 2.5 Placement of Internetworking Operations.

glance this seems redundant, but we shall see that the brouter is a powerful and flexible addition to internetworking products.

To avoid any confusion about these terms, some people use the term *internetworking unit* (IWU). An IWU is a generic term to describe a router, a gateway, a bridge, or anything else that performs relaying functions between networks.

Source routing and spanning tree bridges

The method in which internetworking protocol data units (PDUs) (datagrams or packets) are routed between networks is sometimes a source of confusion. The two major methods to perform routing are *source routing* and *nonsource routing*. Source routing derives its name from the fact that the transmitting device (the source) dictates the route of the PDU through an internet. The source (host) machine places the addresses of the "hops" (the intermediate networks or IWUs) in the PDU. Such an approach means that the internetworking units need not perform address maintenance, but they simply use an address in the routing field to determine where to route the frame.

In contrast, nonsource routing (using spanning tree techniques) makes decisions about the route and does not rely on the PDU to contain information about the route. Spanning tree routing is usually associated with nonsource routing and bridges and is quite prevalent in LANs.

The TCP/IP protocol suite utilizes source or nonsource routing but does not use spanning tree logic. These operations are found in the IP module and are introduced here and discussed in more detail in Chaps. 5 and 8.

An example of source routing on a LAN is illustrated in Fig. 2.6. The routing information field contains the LAN and bridge identifiers for each intermediate hop through the LAN network. Routing is accomplished by each bridge examining successive LAN numbers and bridge numbers in the routing information field and making a routing decision accordingly. As an example in Fig. 2.6, bridge 5 may receive a frame from LAN 3. Based on the routing information in the routing field, it might be required to route the frame out of its port to LAN 6 or out of another port to LAN 2. Again, under these conditions, the bridge has no control over how to route the frame.

Figure 2.7 depicts the operations of a spanning tree bridge. The bridge processor in the spanning tree bridge forwards frames based on an examination of the destination address. It compares this address to its bridge and routing information database. If the destination address is found in the forwarding table in this database, it determines the direction of the frame. If the frame is not intended for the port from which it came, it is forwarded on the correct port to the address indi-

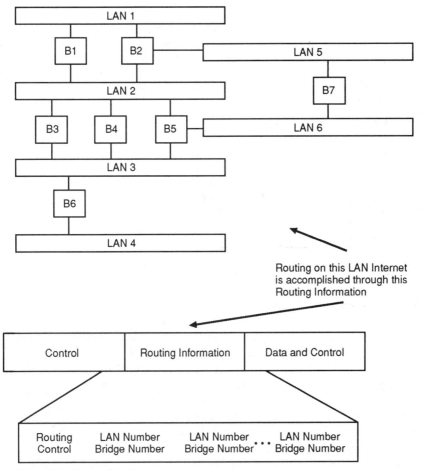

Figure 2.6   Source Routing.

cated in the database. Otherwise, it is discarded. If the source address in the frame is not contained in the database, this address is then added with the appropriate port on which it was received and a timer is started. The purpose of the timer is to keep the forwarding database updated in as timely a manner as possible.

As an example, assume that a frame is received at port A on the LAN in Fig. 2.7. The source MAC address in this frame is 1234. The bridge inspects this address to see if it is in the forwarding database. If not, it stores address 1234 with a notation that it can be found at port A.

Later, assume that a frame arrives at port B at destination address 1234 in the frame. The bridge processor examines its forwarding table and determines that station 1234 can be found at port A; consequently, it forwards this frame to the network attached to port A.

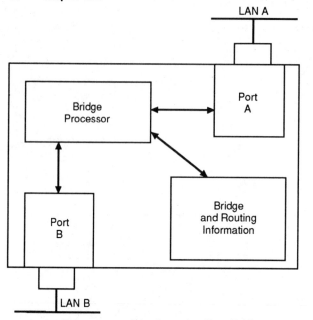

Figure 2.7   Components of the Spanning Tree Bridge.

The IP is not aware of the spanning tree operations on the LAN because the IP PDU resides in the I field of the LAN frame. The bridge does not process the I field, but treats it transparently. Consequently, the bridge is only concerned with MAC source and destination addresses. Any higher-level addresses (for example, a network address) that reside in the IP PDU are not acted upon by the spanning tree bridge. However, as we shall see in later chapters, these network addresses become vital for processing PDUs across WANs because the MAC addresses are stripped away before the frame is sent through a wide area internet.

Summary

TCP/IP runs on both LANs and WANs. Indeed, the TCP/IP logic is unaware of the type of network, since it is isolated from the LAN physical and data link layers and the wide area subnetwork logic, such as packet routing.

The IP module of TCP/IP can support both source routing and nonsource routing. Any type of spanning tree bridging on a LAN remains transparent to IP. The addresses used in IP remain transparent to the LAN bridges.

Chapter

3

Naming, Addressing, and Routing in an Internet

Introduction

A newcomer to data networks is often perplexed when the subject of naming and addressing arises. Addresses in data networks are similar to postal addresses and telephone numbering schemes. Indeed, many of the networks that exist today have derived some of their addressing structures from the concepts of the telephone numbering plan.

It should prove useful to clarify the meaning of names, addresses, and routes. A *name* is an identification of an entity (independent of its physical location), such as a person, an applications program, or even a computer. An *address* is also an identification but it reveals additional information about the entity, principally information about its physical or logical placement in a network. A *route* is information on how to relay traffic to a physical location (address).

A network usually provides a service which allows a network user to furnish the network with a name of something (another user, an application, etc.) that is to receive traffic. A network *name server* then uses this name to determine the address of the receiving entity. This address is then used by a routing protocol to determine the physical route to the receiver.

With this approach, a network user does not become involved and is not aware of physical address and the physical location of other users and network resources. This practice allows the network administrator to relocate and reconfigure network resources without affecting end users. Likewise, users can move to other physical locations but their names remain the same; the network changes its naming/routing tables to reflect the relocation.

This chapter introduces the issues surrounding naming and addressing and the concepts of physical and network address resolution (mapping). Chapter 4 continues with an examination of naming and the Domain Name System (DNS). Due to the relationship of addresses and routing, we also introduce the Internet Protocol (IP) routing in this chapter, which is explained further in Chap. 8.

Upper Layer, Network, Data Link, and Physical Names and Addresses

Communication between users through a data network requires several forms of addressing. Typically, three addresses are required: (a) a physical address, (b) a data link address, and (c) a network address. Practically speaking, other addresses are needed for unambiguous end-to-end communications between two users, such as upper layer names and/or port addresses.

Physical addresses

Each device (such as a computer or workstation) on a communications link or network is identified with a physical address. This address is often called the hardware address. Many manufacturers place the physical address on a logic board within the device or in an interface unit connected directly to the device. Two physical addresses are employed in a communications dialogue; one address identifies the sender (source) and the other address identifies the receiver (destination). The length of the physical address varies. Many implementations use two 48-bit addresses; however, other address sizes are also used. Indeed, the 48-bit address structure is considered too long by some designers, but the Ethernet and IEEE protocols use it, so it is widespread.

From the context of a layered data communications model, the physical address is used at the physical layer. The physical layer logic of a device examines the destination address of an incoming protocol data unit (PDU). If the address matches the physical address of the device, it is passed to the next upper layer. If the address does not match the device's address, it is ignored. In this manner, a physical address detection prevents the data from being passed needlessly to upper layers.

The physical address detection operation on a LAN is illustrated in Fig. 3.1. Device A transmits a frame onto the channel. It is broadcast to all other stations attached to the channel, namely stations B, C, and D. We assume that the destination physical address (DPA) contains the value C. Consequently, stations B and D ignore the frame. Station C accepts it, performs several tasks associated with the physical layer, strips away the physical layer headers and trailers, and passes the remainder of the PDU (it is no longer called a frame) to the next upper layer.

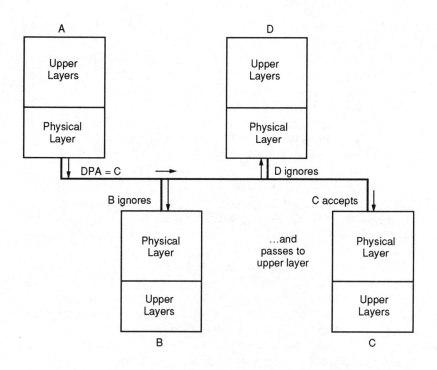

DPA = C means Destination Physical Address is C.

Figure 3.1   Physical Address Detection.

Universal physical addresses and protocol identifiers

The IEEE has assumed the task of assigning universal LAN physical addresses and universal protocol identifiers. Previously this work was performed by the Xerox Corporation by administering what were known as block identifiers (Block IDs) for Ethernet addresses. The Xerox Ethernet Administration Office assigned these values, which were three octets (24 bits) in length. The organization that received this address was free to use the remaining 24 bits of the Ethernet address in any way it chose.

Due to the progress made in the IEEE 802 project, it was decided that the IEEE would assume the task of assigning these universal identifiers for all LANs, not just CSMA/CD types of networks. However, the IEEE continues to honor the assignments made by the Ethernet administration office, although it now calls the block ID an *organization unique identifier (OUI)*.

Each OUI gives an organization the 24-bit address space (which is quite large), although the true address space is 22 bits because the first two bits are used for control purposes (described shortly). This means that the address space is 2^{22}.

The format for the OUI is shown in Fig. 3.2. The least significant bit of the address space corresponds to the individual/group (I/G) address bit. The I/G address bit, if set to a zero, means that the address field identifies an individual address. If the value is set to a one, the address field identifies a group address which is used to identify more than one station connected to the LAN. If the entire OUI is set to all ones, it signifies a broadcast address which identifies all stations on the network.

The second bit of the address space is known as the local or universal bit (U/L). When this bit is set to a zero, it has universal assignment significance—for example, from the IEEE. If it is set to a one, it is an address that is locally assigned. Bit position number two must always be set to a zero if it is administered by the IEEE.

The OUI is extended to include a 48-bit universal LAN address (which is designated as the *media access control [MAC]* address). This address is also shown in Fig. 3.2. The 24 bits of the address space is the same as the OUI assigned by the IEEE. The one exception is that the I/G bit may be set to a one or a zero to identify group or individual addresses. The second part of the address space consisting of the remaining 24 bits is locally administered and can be set to any values an organization chooses.

The locally administered 24 bits allows an organization to develop approximately 16 million unique and unambiguous addresses. In the event that this address space is exhausted, the IEEE will assign an additional OUI, but it will not assign an additional OUI until an organization uses all the values in the 24-bit address space.

Is the 48-bit address space sufficient for the future? Forty-eight bits provide for a 2^{48} value, which can identify about 281.475 trillion unique addresses, so it should be sufficient for a while.

The IEEE 802 project also administers a protocol identifier. This value is not a physical address but is discussed here due to its relationship with the other IEEE addressing schemes. The format for the identifier is shown in Fig. 3.2c. The first 24 bits are for the OUI discussed earlier. The remaining 16 bits are locally administered by an organization. However, in some instances these values are reserved for well-known protocols.

The idea of the protocol ID is to allow a link service access point (LSAP) to be used by the subnetwork access protocol (SNAP). The protocol identifier that is assigned by the IEEE requires that the bit position 2 (formerly known as U/L bit in other formats) be set to zero. If this bit is set to one, the locally administered protocol ID has no rela-

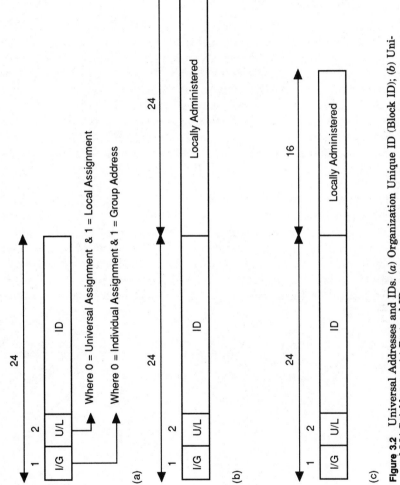

Figure 3.2 Universal Addresses and IDs. (*a*) Organization Unique ID (Block ID); (*b*) Universal MAC Addresses; (*c*) Protocol ID.

43

tionship to the IEEE assigned values. The LSAP and SNAP are discussed in the next sections of this chapter.

The reader interested in obtaining more information about these three formats may contact the IEEE standards office at 445 Hoes Lane, Piscataway, NJ 08855-1331.

The CSMA/CD frame and MAC physical addresses

The MAC level CSMA/CD frame for 802.3 is shown in Fig. 3.3. The *preamble* is transmitted first to achieve medium stabilization and synchronization. The *start frame delimiter (SFD)* follows the preamble and indicates the start of the frame. The 16- or 48-bit physical address fields contain the MAC addresses of the *destination* and *source stations*. The destination address can identify an individual workstation on the network or a group of stations. The *data length* field indicates the length of the LLC and data fields. If the *data* field is less than a maximum length, the PAD field is added to make up the difference. The *cyclic redundancy check (CRC)* value is contained in the FCS field.

The MAC level CSMA/CD for Ethernet is shown in Fig. 3.4. The formats of the Ethernet frame and the format of the 802.3 frame differ. First, the 802.3 frame contains an SFD which in actual practice becomes part of the 64-bit preamble. The 802.3 standard allows the use of 16- or 48-bit length addresses. The next 16 bits also are used differently by the two protocols. The *type* field in Ethernet is used to identify different protocols that are running on the network. The same set

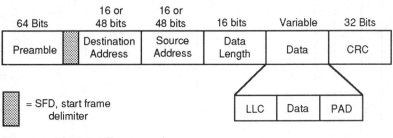

Figure 3.3   The 802.3 Frame.

Figure 3.4   The Ethernet Frame.

of bits is used in the 802.3 frame to determine the length of the data field.

The issue of compatibility naturally arises when one looks at the formats. The older versions of Ethernet (Version 1.0) are not compatible with the 802 standard. Newer releases of Ethernet have made these two standards compatible at the physical layer. However, they remain incompatible at the data link (LLC) layer.

Link layer addresses (LSAPs)

The IEEE 802 standards make use of yet another address called the LSAP. Its purpose is to identify the type of link protocol that is being used above the MAC layer. Table 3.1 lists the IEEE LSAP assignments and provides a description of the protocol. An 802 protocol must carry both a source and destination LSAP.

It is possible to use only one address at the physical and data link layers. If so, the address identifies the station (computer, workstation, etc.) on the link (channel) but usually nothing else. This practice is found on some wide area networks (WANs) but is less common on LANs. As an example, the LAPB link layer protocol uses the value of A to identify a user device and B to identify the network switch on a point-to-point X.25 link.

The IEEE also specifies a code to identify the EtherType assignments. These codes are contained in Table 3.2. Their purpose is to identify the upper layer protocol (ULP) that is running on the LAN. The LAN vendor should be questioned to determine how the vendor's LAN products support the IEEE 802.3 and the Ethernet frame formats. No technical reason exists why these frames cannot coexist at

TABLE 3.1   The LSAP

Link service access point		
IEEE binary	Internet Decimal	Description
00000000	0	Null LSAP
01000000	2	Individual LLC Sublayer Management
11000000	3	Group LLC Sublayer Management
00100000	4	SNA Path Control
01100000	6	DOD Internet Protocol
01110000	14	Proway-LAN
01110010	78	EIA-RS511
01110001	142	Proway-LAN
01010101	170	Subnetwork Access Protocol (SNAP)
01111111	254	ISO DIS 8473
11111111	255	Global DSAP

TABLE 3.2 EtherType Assignments

Ethernet decimal	Hex	Description
512	0200	XEROX PUP
513	0201	PUP Address Translation
1536	0600	XEROX NS IDP
2048	0800	DOD Internet Protocol (IP)
2049	0801	X.75 Internet
2050	0802	NBS Internet
2051	0803	ECMA Internet
2052	0804	Chaosnet
2053	0805	X.25 level 3
2054	0806	Address Resolution Protocol (ARP)
2055	0807	XNS Compatibility
4096	1000	Berkeley Trailer
21000	5208	BBN Simnet
24577	6001	DEC MOP Dump/Load
24578	6002	DEC MOP Remote Console
24579	6003	DEC DECnet Phase IV
24580	6004	DEC LAT
24582	6005	DEC
24583	6006	DEC
32773	8005	HP Probe
32784	8010	Excelan
32821	8035	Reverse ARP
32824	8038	DEC LANBridge
32823	8098	Appletalk

the physical level on the LAN network. Ideally, the vendor provides the capability to discern which frame format is being used.

Extension to the LSAP header (SNAP)

Due to the separate evolution of the Ethernet, TCP/IP, and IEEE LAN standards, it has been necessary to define some additional RFCs to provide guidance on the use of IP datagrams over Ethernet and IEEE networks. Figure 3.5 shows the approach recommended by the Internet with RFC 1042 (a standard for the transmission of IP datagrams over IEEE 802 networks). The LLC destination and source service access points (DSAP and SSAP, respectively) are each set to a decimal value of 170. The LLC control field is not affected by this standard. The SNAP control field can identify a specific protocol ID, but it is normally set to an organization code equal to 0. Thereafter, the EtherType field is used to describe the type of protocol running on the LAN. The EtherType field is coded in accordance with the conventions shown in Table 3.2. The reader should note that Table 3.1 shows the convention for coding the SAP values (i.e., 170) for the SNAP convention.

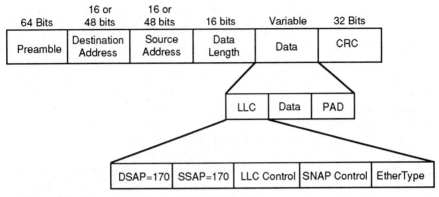

Figure 3.5   The Subnetwork Access Protocol Format.

Network addresses

The easiest way to think of a network address is that it identifies a network. Part of the network address may also designate a computer, a terminal, or anything that a private network administrator wishes to identify within a network (or attached to a network), although the Internet standards place very strict rules on what an IP address identifies.

A network address is a higher-level address than the physical or data link addresses. Higher-level addresses are not concerned with lower-level addresses. *Therefore, the components in a network or an Internet that deal with network addresses need not be concerned with physical addresses until the data has arrived at the network link to which the physical device is attached.*

This important concept is illustrated in Fig. 3.6. Assume that a user (host computer) in Los Angeles transmits packets to a packet network, such as Tymnet, ARPANET, etc., for relaying to a workstation on a LAN in London. The network in London has a network address of 128.1 (this address scheme is explained shortly).

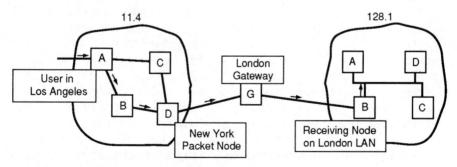

Figure 3.6   Network Level Addressing.

The packets are passed through the packet network (using the network's internal routing mechanisms, discussed in Chap. 2) to the packet switch in New York. The packet switch in New York routes the packet to the gateway located in London. This gateway examines the destination network address in the packet and determines that the packet is to be routed to network 128.1. It then transmits the packet onto the appropriate communications channel (link) to the node on the LAN that is responsible for communicating with the London gateway. In this example, the node is labeled B in network 128.1.

Notice that this operation did not use any physical addresses in these routing operations. The packet switches and gateway were only concerned with the destination network address. Data link addresses may have been used—depending on the vendor's preference.

Physical and network address resolution

The reader might question how the London LAN is able to pass the packet to the correct device (host). As we learned earlier, a physical address is needed to prevent every packet from being processed by the upper layer network level protocols residing in every host attached to the network. Therefore, the answer is that the target network (or gateway) must be able to translate a higher-level network destination address to a lower-level physical destination address.

In explaining how this task is accomplished, please examine Fig. 3.7. Node B on the LAN is a server that is tasked with address resolution. We assume that the destination address contains a network address, such as 128.1, *and* a host address, say 3.2. Therefore, the two addresses could be joined (concatenated) to create a full internet network address, which would appear as 128.1.3.2 in the destination address field of the IP PDU (datagram). (A later section in this chapter explains the structure of an internet address.)

Once the LAN node receives the datagram from the gateway, it must examine the host address and either (a) perform a look-up into a table that contains the local physical address for the network address, or (b) query the station for its physical address. Then it encapsulates the user data into the physical layer frame, places the appropriate physical layer address in the destination address of the frame, and transmits the frame onto the LAN channel. All devices on the network examine the physical address. If this address matches the device's address, the PDU is passed to the next upper layer; otherwise, it is ignored.

It is conceivable that the host address 3.2 also could be the actual physical address, but it is more common to assign different address values to a host address and its hardware physical address. For example, the value of 3.2 could be mapped into an IEEE MAC 48-bit physical address.

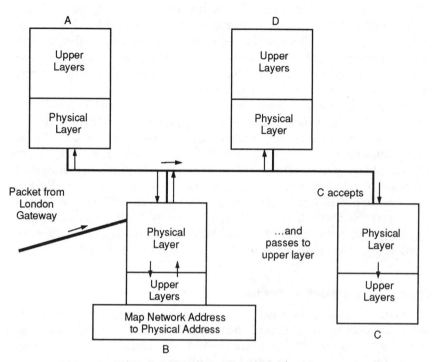

Figure 3.7   Mapping Network Addresses to Physical Addresses.

Are all these addresses necessary?

A number of this writer's clients have complained about the need to use physical as well as network level addresses. After all, an address space for a MAC address of 2^{48} provides over 281 trillion unique identifiers. From these people's perspective, it seems reasonable that this address space should be sufficient to provide unique addressing without the use of additional address fields. Several reasons exist for the use of different levels of addressing schemes in any network (although I must say I am intrigued by my clients' arguments).

Historically, the address spaces for LANs and Internet networks were developed by separate groups. Each group recognized the need for unique identifiers and devised them. The evolution of LANs and the Internet was such that the identifiers remained separate. Second, link capacity is still important in networks and will be for many years (notwithstanding optical fiber capacity). The use of a large address identifier, such as a 48-bit versus a slightly smaller 32-bit network address, is a savings of 50% of addressing bits transmitted. Third, under the present scheme, if the hardware interface (the board) of a computer station on a LAN becomes faulty, the board is replaced. If these addresses were used for network routing, each replacement of a board would require the changing of the network routing tables. Fourth, designers believe it efficacious to hide lower layer physical addresses from upper layer software. It provides for cleaner interfaces and gives network administrators more flexibility in configuration of network resources in various parts of the network.

All these arguments have merit. On a more general level, this writer wishes for a little common sense application of the multiplication principle. For example, a nine-digit number such as a social security number is more than adequate to distinguish any entity in the United States (for example, 10^9 = 1 billion). As another example, if we wish to identify something with, say, a more user friendly six-letter sequence in the English alphabet, we could still obtain unique identifiers of more than 300 million things with a 26^6 notation. Frankly, it is easy to lose patience with different companies, department stores, etc., that construct long and complex identifiers.

Upper layer addresses and names

Physical, data link, and network level addresses are insufficient to move the packet to its final "destination" on the host machine, and other higher-layer addresses are needed. For example, a packet may be destined for a specific software application, such as an electronic mail or a file transfer system. Since both these applications reside in the same upper layer (the application layer), some means must be devised to identify the application that is to process the packet. A ULP name or address is used by the host machine to determine which application receives the data.

The upper layer names or addresses are identified by a variety of terms. The Internet convention is to use the terms *protocol id, port,* and *socket.* The OSI convention is to use the term *service access point (SAP).* The Internet terms are explained in the next section.

Example of a complete naming and addressing operation

Figure 3.8 shows an example of the names and addresses used in the Internet layers, both at a sending and receiving computer.

The left part of the figure shows that a sending computer creates various names and addresses at different layers, which is used by the peer layer of the receiving computer (the right part of the figure) to identify the destination, protocols to invoke, and functions to perform.

The user application at the sending computer (such as a COBOL, C,

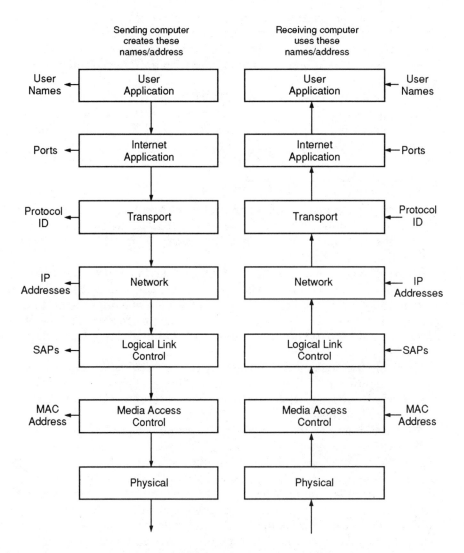

Figure 3.8 Relationships of Names and Addresses to the Internet Layers.

or Fortran application) is responsible for creating its own user name. Typically, this is done in accordance with an organization's specific protocols, or in some instances standards may define what a user name is. This user name is passed along with data to the internet application layer.

The specific internet application (such as file transfer or electronic mail) is identified with a port number. Frequently used applications have reserved port numbers and are called *well-known ports.* Consequently, if the sending computer wishes to invoke the internet application dealing with, say, file transfer, it would code a port number of 20 in the destination port field.

The user name created by the user application may actually be identified with the port number. A source port number may be used in lieu of a user name to identify the end user application. The reader should check with the specific installation to see how this upper layer convention is handled.

The traffic is passed next to the transport layer entity, which is either TCP or UDP. Whatever the case may be, this transport entity is identified by a *protocol number.* At the receiving machine the protocol number identifies the transport entity that is to receive the traffic. Consequently, the transport protocol ID would identify UDP, TCP, OSI's TP4, etc.

Next, the traffic is passed to the network layer which deals with the network addresses, called *IP addresses.* These addresses are used in the network layer to determine where the traffic is to be routed through an internet.

After processing at the IP module, the traffic is passed to logical link control (LLC). As discussed earlier, LLC works with destination and source SAPs. The concept of the SAP is quite similar to the concept of the port at the upper layer. The source SAP identifies the entity operating above LLC that is sending the traffic, and the destination SAP identifies the entity operating above LLC that is to receive the traffic. Ordinarily this would be the IP residing at the network layer, but as we have learned from Table 3.1, it could identify other entities such as SNA's path control or the ISO's IP equivalent (DIS 8473).

The last set of addresses to be used is the IEEE 48-bit MAC addresses. MAC receives the traffic from LLC and creates the destination and source MAC addresses. As shown at the bottom of Fig. 3.8, these names and addresses are sent to the receiving computer if it is on the same LAN or LAN segment as the sending machine. If the PDU is sent across a WAN, the addresses are stripped off before the unit is transmitted.

At the receiving end, the destination MAC address is used by MAC to determine if the traffic is be received at this station. If so, MAC accepts the traffic and passes the traffic (after stripping off the MAC fields) to LLC. LLC, in turn, uses the destination SAP to determine the proper protocol at the network layer.

Once the traffic is passed to the network layer, the IP address is used by gateways/routers to determine a route through the network. If the traffic has finally arrived at the receiving host computer, the IP address is used in conjunction with the port number to provide a unique and unambiguous connection between the two machines, known as the *socket*. We shall examine the socket in more detail in the chapter on TCP.

Next, the protocol identifier is used to determine which transport layer protocol is to receive the traffic. The traffic is then passed up to an internet application, where the destination port number is examined to determine which internet application entity (such as file transfer) is to receive the traffic.

Finally, the traffic may be passed to an end user application at the receiving machine, although it should be emphasized that in many scenarios today the end user application resides only at the originating computer. This approach means that the internet application (such as the file transfer example) would receive the data, service it, and perhaps return a reply. This approach is quite common in a client-server relationship where the sending computer contains the client and the receiving computer contains the server but not (in this example) an end user application.

Of course, the process can be reversed. In Fig. 3.8, the direction of the arrows can be changed and data can be sent from the computer on the right side of the figure to the computer on the left side of the figure.

The actual PDU transmitted on the channel contains considerable overhead just in names and addresses. But the situation suggested at the bottom part of the figure is not quite as onerous as it might appear, because the destination and source MAC addresses are not transported across a WAN. As we have learned earlier, these are inserted at the receiving network or computer through a process called *address mapping*. This topic will be discussed shortly.

In summary, the Internet standards (used in conjunction with IEEE LANs) use the following names and addresses at these layers:

Layer	Name/address used at this layer
User application	End user IDs
Internet application	Port numbers
Transport	Protocol names
Network	IP addresses
Logical link control (LLC)	LSAP numbers
Media access control (MAC)	MAC addresses
Physical	None

The IP Address Structure

TCP/IP networks use a 32-bit address to identify a host computer and the network to which the host is attached. The structure of the IP address is depicted in Fig. 3.9. Its format is **IP ADDRESS = NETWORK ADDRESS + HOST ADDRESS.**

It is important to note that the IP address does not identify a host per se, but a host's connection to its network. Consequently, if a host machine is moved to another network, its address space must be changed.

IP addresses are classified by their formats. Four formats are permitted: class A, class B, class C, and class D. As illustrated in Fig. 3.9, the first bits of the address specify the format of the remainder of the address field in relation to the network and host subfields. The host address is also called the local address (also called the REST field).

The *class A* addresses provide for networks that have a large number of hosts. The host ID field is 24 bits. Therefore, 2^{24} hosts can be identified. Seven bits are devoted to the network ID, which supports an identification scheme for as many as 127 networks (bit values of 1 to 127).

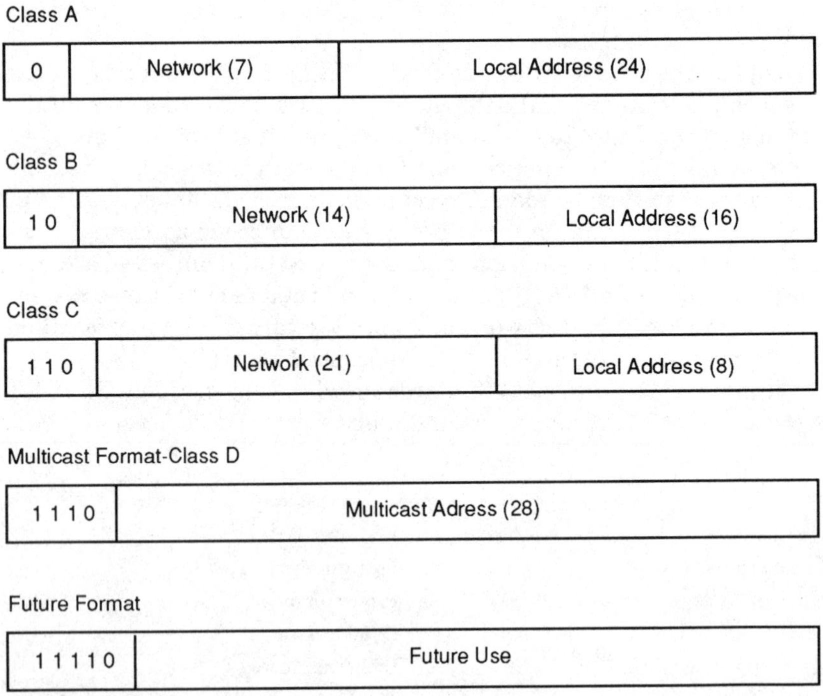

Class A

0	Network (7)	Local Address (24)

Class B

1 0	Network (14)	Local Address (16)

Class C

1 1 0	Network (21)	Local Address (8)

Multicast Format-Class D

1 1 1 0	Multicast Adress (28)

Future Format

1 1 1 1 0	Future Use

Figure 3.9 IP Address Formats.

Class B addresses are used for networks of intermediate size. Fourteen bits are assigned for the network ID, and 16 bits are assigned for the host ID. *Class C* networks contain fewer than 256 hosts (2^8). Twenty-one bits are assigned to the network ID. Finally, *class D* addresses are reserved for multicasting, which is a form of broadcasting but within a limited area. Multicasting is described in later chapters.

In summary, the IP address space can take the following forms:

	Network address space values
A	0–127*
B	128–191
C	192–223
D	224–254

*Numbers 0 and 127 are reserved.

The maximum network and host addresses that are available for the class A, B, and C addresses are as follows:

	Maximum network numbers	Maximum host numbers
A	126*	16,777,124
B	16,384	65,534
C	2,097,152	254

*Numbers 0 and 127 are reserved.

For convenience, the Internet addresses are depicted with decimal notations. As an example, a Class B internet address of binary 1000000 00000011 00001001 00000001 is written as 128.3.9.1. This address translates to network ID = 128.3 and host ID = 9.1. These notations may seem somewhat strange to humans, but the scheme works quite well with computers. Chapter 4 examines how user friendly names can be used and translated into the IP format.

In summary, the decimal notations for the IP address space can take the following forms:

A	network.host.host.host
B	network.network.host.host
C	network.network.network.host
D	(not applicable)

Some gateways and hosts can have multiple connections to other networks throughout an internet. These machines have two or more physical connections and are called *multihomed* hosts. Multihomed hosts must have a unique IP address for each of their physical connections. We shall see that the multihomed hosts, while providing flexible routing, can create some problems in managing traffic.

The IP address structure depicted in Fig. 3.9 can be coded with all 1s in the network or host ID fields. This coding identifies the datagram as a broadcast signal and can be used for sending the datagram to all networks and/or all hosts on a network. For example, the address of 128.2.255.255 means all hosts on network 128.2. Be aware that some TCP/IP software implementations do not support the broadcast option.

The IP address can also be coded with all 0s in the host ID. This means that the address is identified as "this host." Also, the network ID can be coded with all 0s, and that refers to "this network." For example, the 128.2.0.0 means this network; that is, network 128.2. The use of a network ID of 0 is helpful if a host does not know its IP address. It sends a datagram with 0s in the network ID field. Other hosts interpret this address as this network.

The capability to code either all 1s or all 0s in the internet address space can provide some useful capabilities. However, the use of these features requires some thought. For example, sending all 0s in the address space means this host on this network. This coding should be used only when a host is trying to learn its own IP address. The same holds true for coding all 0s in the network address space with the host number in the host address space. As another example, consider the coding of all 1s in the entire IP address space. This simply means that the destination address will be interpreted and received by every host on the connected network; however, it will not be forwarded outside that one network. Other combinations can be developed with these capabilities. It is prudent for the reader to check with a software vendor to see how these capabilities are implemented as well as their implication on performance and operations.

Formal Internet addresses are issued only to those users that are communicating through the DARPA internet network. These addresses are administered by the Network Information Center (NIC), which is part of SRI International. Many users do not communicate through ARPANET or the Internet. Therefore, they are free to choose their own internet addressing structure. While users are free to choose their own private internet addresses, considerable thought should be given to which class of address to use. Obviously, the ratio of networks to host machines is the principal consideration in choosing the address format. Additionally, the address format should be chosen based on an assessment of the future growth of the enterprise's computing resources, both in relation to networks and in host computers.

Destination Addresses and Routing

Direct and indirect destinations

IP uses the concepts of direct and indirect destinations in its routing logic (see Fig. 3.10). A *direct host* is a machine that is attached directly to the network and the network's gateway.

An *indirect host* is a destination host that is on a network other than that of the source host. Therefore, the datagram must be sent to an intermediate gateway before it is delivered to the destination host.

Due to the manner in which IP manages addresses and makes routing decisions, a machine only needs to examine the network address part of the IP address to determine if the destination host is directly or indirectly attached to the source host's network.

If it is indirectly attached, the IP module must then be able to select the next IP module to process the datagram. Therefore, the IP must keep a set of mappings between destination networks and the relevant gateway to reach the network and the physical port to that gateway.

The awkward nature of the IP address structure becomes readily evident from an examination of Fig. 3.10. Notice that gateway 9 has three IP addresses: 11.0.0.1, 13.0.0.4, and 10.0.0.1. While these addresses are certainly manageable, they do point out the need to carefully administer the IP addresses. Moreover, unless the vendor's routing algorithm is fairly sophisticated, the nature of the IP address structure could create a problem if a network could not be reached because it was not known in the routing table. For example, network 14.0.0.0 is reached from gateway 9 through a connection to network 13.0.0.0 out of the gateway's port 3 with an internet address of 13.0.0.2. However, if the communications link at 13.0.0.4 fails, IP does not know (unless the vendor is crafty enough to build this feature into its route discovery protocols) that alternate routes are available on other interfaces.

Of course, most vendors' products today have overcome some of the limitations of the IP address space by building secondary routes into the routing tables. In this example, the column labeled "Route the Datagram" would have a second dimension (or even third dimension) that describes alternate routes in case the first route fails. Again, this approach works well enough, but it does produce some fairly complex routing tables.

IP routing logic

The preceding discussion of direct and indirect routing implies that a gateway needs only the network part of an IP address to perform routing. Figure 3.11 shows a logic flow chart of the IP routing algorithm.

Each machine maintains a routing table containing (1) destination

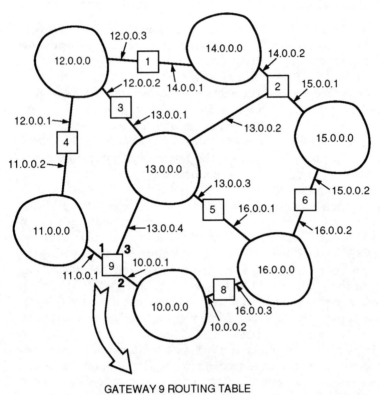

GATEWAY 9 ROUTING TABLE

To Hosts on Network	Route the Datagram	Across this Physical Port
10.0.0.0	Direct	**2**
11.0.0.0	Direct	**1**
12.0.0.0	11.0.0.2	**1**
13.0.0.0	Direct	**3**
14.0.0.0	13.0.0.2	**3**
15.0.0.0	10.0.0.2	**2**
16.0.0.0	10.0.0.2	**2**

Figure 3.10   Direct and Indirect Destinations.

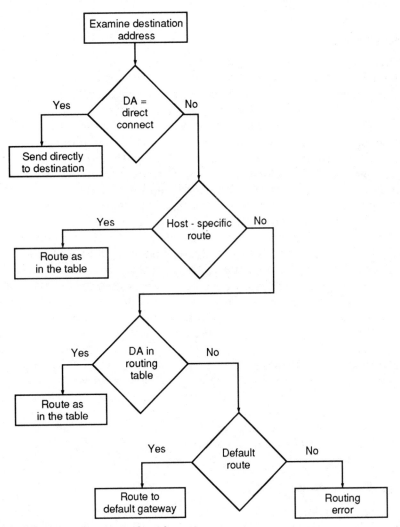

Figure 3.11   IP Routing Algorithm.

network addresses and (2) the specified "next hop" gateway. The table is used to perform three types of routing:

- Direct routing to locally attached machines
- Indirect routing for networks that must be reached via one or more gateways

- Default routing to the destination network in case the first two types of routing are unsuccessful

Multihomed hosts

As mentioned earlier, some gateways and hosts can have multiple connections to other networks throughout an internet. These machines have two or more physical connections and are called multihomed hosts. Multihomed hosts must have a unique IP address for each of their physical connections. The multihomed hosts, while providing flexible routing, can create some problems in managing traffic.

As a practical matter, it is a good idea to keep the host out of the gateway business. If the host routing table has no information for the destination IP address, it simply chooses a default gateway by selecting an entry in the routing table. The gateway should forward the datagram based on its routing table and return a message to the host stating that this has indeed occurred (as we shall see, this should entail a redirect message issued through the Internet Control Message Protocol [ICMP]). The host computer should then update its default entry to the appropriate designation returned by the gateway.

Multihomed hosts were originally intended to allow one physical interface to be identified by one IP address. However, in practice some vendors allow combinations of multiple internet addresses across one physical interface.

In addition, some interfaces are known as "logical hosts." This occurs when a host has more than one IP address, but these addresses have the same network number or the same subnetwork number, if any exist. Such a logical host interface could share one or several physical interfaces. The point of this discussion is that various combinations of multihoming can create confusion on how to handle routing.

Address Resolution Issues

As we learned earlier, each device attached to a single physical LAN is identified by a physical hardware address. We also learned that other addresses are assigned, such as network addresses. The vast majority of physical addresses are assigned by the manufacturer before the product is shipped to the customer or when the product is installed at the customer's site.

We find ourselves with an interesting problem, which we began to address in previous material: how to relate the physical address to a network address, and vice versa. As an example, if host A wishes to send a datagram to host D, it may not know the physical address of host D. To compound the problem, the higher-level network address may also be unknown to host A. Therefore, some means must be devised to relate different levels of addresses to each other.

The Address Resolution Protocol (ARP)

The IP stack provides a protocol for resolving addresses. The Address Resolution Protocol (ARP) is used to take care of the translation of IP addresses to physical addresses and hide these physical addresses from the upper layers.

Generally, ARP works with mapping tables (referred to as the ARP cache). The table provides the mapping between an IP address and a physical address. In a LAN (like Ethernet or an IEEE 802 network), ARP takes the target IP address and searches for a corresponding physical address in a mapping table. If it finds the address, it returns the 48-bit address back to the requester, such as a device driver or server on a LAN. However, if the needed address is not found in the ARP cache, the ARP module sends a broadcast onto the network.

The broadcast is called the *ARP request*. The ARP request contains an IP target address. Consequently, if one of the machines receiving the broadcast recognizes its IP address in the ARP request, it will return an ARP reply back to the inquiring host. This frame contains the physical hardware address of the queried host. Upon receiving this frame, the inquiring host places this address into the ARP cache. Thereafter, datagrams sent to this particular IP address can be translated into the physical address by accessing the cache.

The ARP system thus allows an inquiring host to find the physical address of another host by using the IP address.

The concepts of ARP requests and replies are shown in Fig. 3.12. Host A wishes to determine C's physical address. It broadcasts datagrams to B, C, and D. Only C responds because it recognizes its IP address in the incoming ARP request datagram. Host C places its ad-

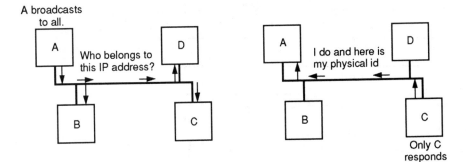

Figure 3.12 The ARP Request and Reply.

dress into an IP datagram in the form of the ARP reply. The other hosts, B and D, do not respond.

In addition to the mapping of IP addresses to physical addresses, ARP allows the designation of specific hardware types. Therefore, when an ARP datagram is received by the queried host, it can use a field in the datagram to determine if the machine is using a particular type of hardware such as an Ethernet interface or packet radio.

The ARP packet format is shown in Fig. 3.13. The ARP packet is encapsulated into the physical layer PDU. As an example, the physical layer PDU could be an Ethernet frame, described in Chap. 2. The EtherType field is set to 8035_{16} (32821_{10}) to identify an ARP frame (which is part of the field labeled "physical layer header" in Fig. 3.13). See Table 3.2 for the EtherType values.

A brief description of each field follows:

Physical Layer Header

Hardware: Specifies the type of hardware interface in which the inquiring host seeks a response. Examples are Ethernet and packet radio (see Table 3.3 for the assigned values).

Protocol: Identifies the type of protocol the sender is using; typically the EtherType (see Table 3.2).

Hardware Address Length: Specifies the length in bytes of each hardware address in the packet.

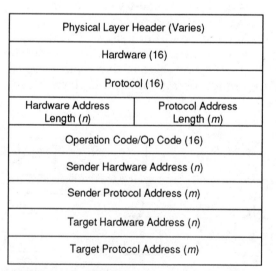

Figure 3.13 The ARP Request and Reply Packet.

TABLE 3.3   ARP Hardware Type

Type	Description
1	Ethernet (10 Mb)
2	Experimental Ethernet (3 Mb)
3	Amateur Radio X.25
4	Proteon ProNET Token Ring
5	Chaos
6	IEEE 802 Networks
7	ARCNET

Protocol Address Length: Specifies the length in bytes of the protocol addresses in the packet (for example, the IP addresses).

Opcode: Specifies whether this is an ARP request (1) or an ARP reply (2).

Sender Hardware Address: Contains the hardware address of the sender.

Sender Protocol Address: Contains the IP address of the sender.

Target Hardware Address: Contains the hardware address of the queried host.

Target Protocol Address: Contains the IP address of the queried host.

In the request packet, all fields are used except the target hardware address. In the reply packet, all fields are used.

The logic of ARP is depicted in Fig. 3.14. (Although extracted from RFC 826, the flow chart represents the writer's interpretation of the RFC.)

An ARP module also uses an incoming ARP packet to update (possibly) its cache. The module examines the sending IP address and hardware address to determine if its cache has these entries. In this manner it takes the opportunity to obtain as much information as possible from the traffic.

One might question why a network would go through all this activity to determine addresses. After all, why not perform the broadcasting operation each time and allow the networks to simply discard the traffic that is not destined for their hosts? This works well enough on a collision detection network, such as Ethernet and the IEEE 802.3 network. Indeed, these networks are designed as broadcast networks. However, the practice of broadcasting all datagrams could create a tremendous amount of traffic for any network, especially in packet-switched WANs. It is not hard to imagine the broadcast networks

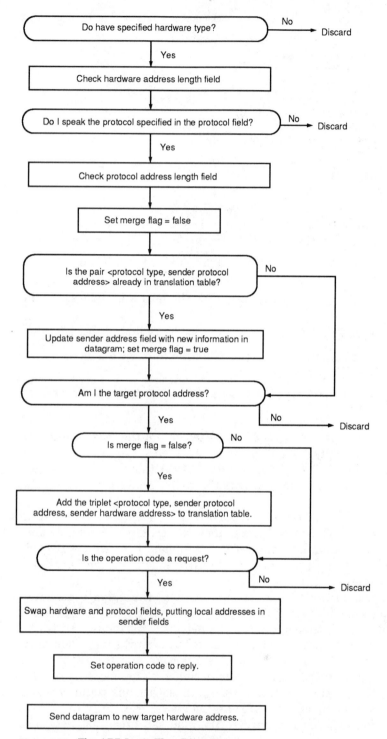

Figure 3.14 The ARP Logic Flow Diagram.

saturating packet-switched networks to the point of congestion. Consequently, the periodic query with a broadcast transmission makes very good sense and has proven to work well in operating networks, both LANs and WANs.

Experience has shown that when implementing ARP there should also be a mechanism for deleting old cache entries. This capability will prove useful to the user when addresses become invalid (to prevent the sending of invalid addresses in frames). One example that comes to mind is the changing of Ethernet addresses in a LAN. Furthermore, as discussed in the next section, the use of an additional protocol, called proxy ARP, tends to create even more invalid addresses.

The reader should check with vendors on the frequency with which ARP broadcasts are transmitted. There should be some method available for controlling the number of ARP requests for the same IP address. The simplest way to handle the broadcasting ARP problem is to establish a mechanism that prevents sending more than a given number within a given time.

It might also prove useful to save the first transmission of a PDU transmission. For example, imagine that a transmission was not delivered because of an invalid (unresolved) address. It is a good idea to save this first transmission and perhaps discard the remaining transmissions until the destination address has been resolved. In this manner, the system may not have to send out connection establishment messages that were created in a ULP (such as TCP or OSI's TP4) which might be using this initial PDU to determine round trip propagation time through the internet. This retransmission delay would bias the results.

ARP address translation table

The Internet defines a mapping table to be used with the address mapping protocols. This information is provided in RFC 1213. As depicted in Fig. 3.15, the mapping table consists of a row entry for each IP address on each host gateway (machine). Four columns are provided for each row entry. The contents of these columns are as follows:

The *ifIndex* contains the interface (physical port) for the specific interface for this address.

The *physical address* entry contains the media dependent address (for example, a MAC address).

The *IP address* entry contains the IP address, which corresponds to the physical address.

	IF Index	Physical Address	IP Address	Mapping Type
Address Entry 1				
Address Entry 2				
Address Entry *n*				

Figure 3.15   Address Translation Table.

The *mapping type* entry is set to one of four values: Other = 1 (none of the following), invalid = 2 (the mapping for this row entry is no longer valid), dynamic = 3 (the mapping does not change), static = 4 (entry may change).

Proxy ARP

Another protocol, called *proxy ARP* or *promiscuous ARP,* allows an organization to use only one IP address (network portion of address) for multiple networks. In essence, proxy ARP maps a single IP network address into multiple physical addresses. The concept is illustrated in Fig. 3.16. Gateway 1 (G1) hides the two networks from each other. For example, if host A wishes to send traffic to host D, host A might first

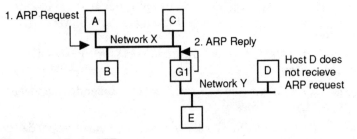

Figure 3.16   Proxy ARP.

form an ARP message in order to obtain the physical address of host D on network Y. However, the ARP message does not reach host D. The gateway intercepts the message, performs the address resolution, and sends an ARP reply back to host A with the gateway's physical address in the ARP target hardware address field. Host A then uses the ARP response to update its ARP table, and the ARP operation is complete. The example in this figure can be reversed. The hosts on network X can be serviced by the gateway in a similar manner just discussed for host A.

Proxy ARP is quite flexible, and nothing precludes mapping different IP address prefixes to the same physical address. However, some ARP implementations have diagnostic procedures that will display alarms to network control if multiple addresses are mapped to the same physical address. This problem is called *spoofing* and serves to alert network control of possible problems.

Proxy ARP works only if the organization has installed ARP. It is quite simple and does not work with complex topologies where more than one gateway services more than one network. It can be used without changing routing tables in other parts of an internet. As we mentioned at the start of this discussion, it hides physical networks through its mapping functions.

Reverse Address Resolution Protocol (RARP)

The ARP protocol is a useful technique for determining physical addresses from network addresses. However, some workstations do not know their own IP address. For example, diskless workstations do not have any IP address knowledge when they are booted to a system. The diskless workstations know only their hardware address.

The *reverse address resolution protocol (RARP)* works in a manner similar to ARP except, as the name suggests, it works in reverse order. The process is illustrated in Fig. 3.17. The inquiring machine (for

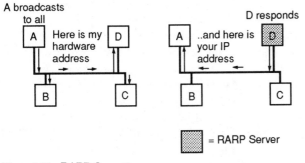

Figure 3.17   RARP Operations.

example, a diskless workstation) broadcasts an RARP request. This request specifies that machine A is the target machine in contrast to the ARP protocol, which would identify the receiving machine as the target machine. The RARP datagram contains the physical address of the sending machine. This transmission is sent out as a broadcast. Therefore, all machines on this physical network receive this request. However, only the RARP servers are allowed to reply.

The servers reply by filling in the target protocol address field, and they change the operation code in the RARP message from a request to a reply (3 = a request, 4 = a reply). The packet is sent back to the inquiring station, which then is able to use the information in the frame to derive its IP address. The EtherType field in the frame is coded as 8035_{16} (32821_{10}) to identify the I field as an RARP packet (see Table 3.2).

Primary and secondary RARPs

RARP is often used on LANs for booting the machines to the network. These types of networks experience low failure rates; the RARP messages are rarely lost, mishandled, or otherwise corrupted. However, in some networks more than one RARP server may be required due to the workload conditions. In order to ensure that the user stations obtain expeditious service from the RARP server, some LANs use transmit timers and time-outs. They evoke retransmissions of the RARP messages upon a time-out.

Other systems, in addition to using time-outs and retransmissions, will designate an RARP server as a primary or backup server. In the event that the primary RARP server is down or unable to fulfill a request, the request can be serviced by a designated backup server. Of course, on the down side, if the request is sent to multiple servers, these servers could create redundant traffic when they respond. Indeed, for an Ethernet type network, the replies from multiple servers will increase the chances of collisions, which results in reduced throughput.

The solution to this problem is simple. In many networks, a secondary server cannot respond until it ascertains that the primary server has not responded. The secondary station monitors the channel to check for the reply from the primary RARP. If the reply is not detected within the timer period, the secondary server times-out and assumes the role of the primary RARP. Another approach requires that the secondary server cannot use the time-out function. Rather, if the requesting machine does not receive the reply from the primary server, then it times-out and reissues the message. The secondary RARPs note that this is a rebroadcast of the same request. At this time, a secondary RARP (or RARPs) will service the message.

Be aware that not all vendors implement the RARP operations. The reader should check with the vendors to determine how or if RARP is used.

IP and X.121 Address Mapping

The CCITT X.121 specification is widely used throughout the world. The majority of public packet networks require X.121 as the network address. RFC 1236 provides guidance on the mapping of IP and X.121 addresses, as depicted through the DDN X.25/IP addressing conventions. Before discussing this standard, a brief tutorial on X.121 is provided.

International numbering plan for data networks (X.121)

X.121 uses a data network identification code (DNIC) based on the format DCCN, where DCC is a three-digit country code and N is the network digit to identify a specific network within a country. Figure 3.18 shows the structure for X.121.

XXXX XXXXXXXXXX
DNIC   NTN

Figure 3.18   X.121 Address Format.

Some countries have more than 10 networks. In this situation, multiple DCCs are assigned to the country. For example, the United States is assigned the DCC values of 310 through 316.

X.121 also defines a network terminal number (NTN). This value identifies the computer, terminal, etc. within the network and consists of a 10-digit identifier. Optionally, the NTN can be included as part of the terminal identifier. In this situation, the 11-digit field is called a *national number* (NN).

DDN IP addresses

The Internet DDN addresses consist of an ASCII text string of four decimal numbers separated by periods, which correspond to the four octet IP address. The four numbers are referred to as follows:

n = network

h = host

l = logical address

i = interface message processor or packet node

A class A address could be represented by n.h.l.i; a class B address could be represented by n.n.h.i; a class C address could be represented by n.n.n.h.i.

A user device can generate a 12- or 14-digit X.121 address. The last 2 digits of the 14-digit address are a subaddress and are not used on DDN.

An example of a class A IP address is 16.9.0.122, where n = 16, h = 9, l = 0, and i = 122.

Mapping X.121 and IP Addresses

The X.121 and IP address mapping is shown in Fig. 3.19. The DNIC is set to 0. The flag digit identifies physical or logical addresses in the address space. The host id is coded as values to represent i or h. The subaddress field is optional. The mapping rules depend on the class of address as well as the range of numbers used by the value h. The reader can study RFC 1236 if more information is needed.

Subnets, Subnet Addressing, and Address Masking

At first glance, it might appear that the IP addressing scheme is flexible enough to accommodate the identification of a sufficient number of networks and hosts to service almost any user or organization. But this is not the case. The Internet designers were not shortsighted; they simply failed to account for the explosive growth of the Internet as well as the rapid growth of the IPs in private networks.

The problem arises when a network administrator attempts to identify a large number of networks and/or computers (such as personal computers) attached to these networks. The problem becomes quite

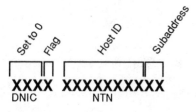

Host ID = Combinations of *h* and *i*

Figure 3.19 IP and X.121 Address Mappings.

onerous because of the need to store and maintain many network addresses and the associated requirement to access these addresses through large routing tables. As we shall see in later chapters, the use of the gateway protocols to exchange routing information requires immense resources if they must access and maintain big addressing tables.

The problem is compounded when networks are added to an internet. The addition requires the reorganization of routing tables and perhaps the assignment of additional addresses to identify the new networks.

To deal with this problem, the Internet establishes a scheme whereby multiple networks are identified by one internetwork address. Obviously, this approach reduces the number of network addresses needed in an internet. It also requires a slight modification to the routing algorithms, but the change is minor in comparison to the benefits derived.

Due to the practice of using one address to identify more than one network, the concept of a *subnet* was implemented in the Internet. A subnet is considered to be any network that operates transparently to a gateway that understands only the IP part of the internet address.

For example, the host part of the IP address is transparent to the gateway. As illustrated in Fig. 3.20, an internet address coming to gateway 1, an IP gateway, contains address 128.11.1.2. From the perspective of the networks attached to gateway 1, the internet only knows about the gateway address of 128.11.

It is the job of gateway G1 to resolve the local address values with either 1.0, 2.0, or 3.0, depending on which subnet is to receive the datagram.

Figure 3.20 also shows a subnet gateway labeled G2. This gateway

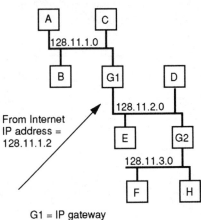

From Internet
IP address =
128.11.1.2

G1 = IP gateway
G2 = Subnet gateway

Figure 3.20 Subnet Addressing.

is concerned with mapping the address 3.0 to the host address attached to the subnetwork. In this example, it must establish the host addresses for hosts F and H. Ordinarily, this is done by accessing a look-up table in which the value of 3.0 is replaced with 3.n1, 3.n2, which identify hosts F and H, respectively.

Figure 3.21 shows the structure of the slightly modified internet address. All that has taken place is the division of the local address, heretofore called the host address, into the subnet address (in this example, 1.0, 2.0, 3.0) and the host address (in this example, the addresses for host F and host H).

It is evident that both the initial internet address and the subnet address take advantage of hierarchical addressing and hierarchical routing. This concept fits well with the basic gateway functions inherent in Internet. Referring once again to Fig. 3.20 and taking it from the top down, we find that the internet is only concerned with the first half of the internet address. G1 is only concerned with the subnet address, and G2 is only concerned with what is now called the host address. Taking it from the bottom up, the hosts F and H are not concerned with any of the higher-level addresses. They can communicate with each other and their gateway, G2, with physical addresses or, if necessary, a ULP address.

The choice of the assignments of the "local address" is left to the individual network implementors. However, a prudent designer is careful to keep the numbering and identification consistent through the whole local subnetwork. Notwithstanding, the values that are chosen can vary. For example, one byte can be used as a subnet address; the second byte can be used as a host address. Alternately, the first 12 bits can be used for the subnet address and a half byte can be used as a host address. There are many other choices in the definition of the local address. As we mentioned before, it is a local matter, but it does require considerable thought. It requires following the same theme of the overall internet ad-

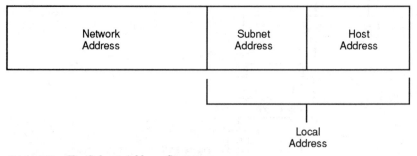

Figure 3.21   The Subnet Address Structure.

dress of how many subnets must be identified in relation to how many hosts must be identified that reside on each subnet.

Subnet masks

In order to support subnet addressing, the IP routing algorithm was modified to support a subnet mask. The purpose of the mask is to determine which part of the IP address pertains to the subnetwork and which part pertains to the host.

The convention used for subnet masking is to use a 32-bit field in addition to the IP address. The contents of the field (the mask) are set as follows:

Binary 1s: Identify the network address portion of the IP address.

Binary 0s: Identify the host address portion of the IP address.

The example in Fig. 3.20 would use the following mask for subnets 128.11.1, 128.11.2, and 128.11.3:

```
11111111    11111111    11111111    00000000
```

A *bitwise AND* function is used to extract the fields of the IP address as follows. A bitwise AND is performed on the IP address and the subnet mask. The results of this operation are matched against a destination address in a routing table. If the results are equal, the next hop IP address (relative to this destination address) is used to determine the next hop on the route. Therefore, the last octet (all 0s) identifies the host on the subnet.

The mask becomes part of the routing algorithm's conditional statement: If destination IP address and subnet mask equal my IP address and subnet mask, then send datagram to local network; otherwise, send datagram to gateway corresponding to destination address. Indeed, the use of masks handles routes to direct conventions, host-specified routes, and default routes.

An implementor should note the following guidelines for subnetting:

- The IP algorithm must be implemented on all machines in a subnet.
- Subnet masks should be the same for all machines.
- If one or more machines do not support masks, proxy ARP can be used to achieve subnetting.

Summary of broadcast rules.   Now that the subnet mask has been examined, the permissible formats for broadcast can be summarized.

Directed broadcast: This address allows broadcast to a specified network. It is used only in the destination address, and its format is [network number, 255].

Limited broadcast: The destination IP address is formatted so that every host on a physical network receives the datagram. This format will not allow the datagram to be routed outside the one physical network. Its format is [255,255].

Subnet directed broadcast: With the use of the subnet address mask value, an internet can also direct a broadcast to a specified subnetwork. Again, this format should only be used in the destination address field, and its format is [network number, subnetwork number, 255].

All subnetworks directed broadcast: This address format (again only in the destination field) allows a datagram to be broadcast to all subnetworks on a specified subnetted network. It is formatted: [network number, 255, 255].

Vendors vary on how they support broadcasting in their products. Some machines have not been programmed to understand subnetting, which can cause some problems if a subnet mask is used. Additionally, some machines do not understand the relationship of a link layer broadcast address and the IP broadcast address. The link layer and IP destination address should be complementary to each other. If one has a broadcast address, so should the other. At a minimum, if a link layer contains a broadcast address, the destination address field and the IP datagram should be an IP multicast address or an IP broadcast address.

It is also possible to build the address mask with noncontiguous ones. For example, this option is permissible: 0100110001100000. Since the operation simply does bitwise AND functions, any combination of the ones would identify the subnet. While this is possible, it is not a very good idea because it makes things unnecessarily complex.

Finally, before leaving the subject of subnet addresses, it should be emphasized that the selection of the address space is strictly up to the user. For example, using a class B address in which the host address space is 16 bits, the subnet address might be 8 bits, and the host address might be the other 8 bits, which allows the network administrator to configure 254 subnets with 254 hosts to each subnet (0 and 256 are not available). Or as another alternative, using 6 bits for the subnet address space gives the capability of identifying 64 networks $2^6 = 64$, which equals 10 bits for the host's identification attached to these networks, resulting in a maximum number of 10^{24} hosts for each network, $2^{10} = 1024$.

One scheme for the assignment of masks is to partition the subnet and host spaces (RFC 1219 provides further guidance). Assuming the use of a class C network with 8 bits available for the subnet and host addresses, the assignment of a number takes the following form: ssggghhh (where s = subnet, g = growth bits, and h = host bits).

The mask for this address space is 11110000. If it becomes necessary to add hosts to the subnet and enlarge the hosts' address space, the address space could be changed to ssgghhhh and the mask is still 11110000. Suppose the internet grows and needs more bits for subnet addresses. The address space could be changed to sssghhhh and the mask remains the same.

Of course, if the hosts on this internet grew to the extent that the final g bit had to be used (ssshhhhh), at this time the mask would be changed to 11100000.

Summary

Data networks need various types and levels of naming and addressing for the unambiguous identification of user and control traffic. The TCP/IP protocol suite provides a full array of these names and addresses as well as several protocols for mapping physical to network addresses and vice versa.

The IP address format has become a worldwide standard for network/host identification. The subnet address space and the subnet masking operations considerably reduce the overhead associated with IP address maintenance.

4

The Domain Name System (DNS)

Introduction

This chapter continues the discussion of naming and addressing and concentrates on naming and Internet name servers. The reader should be familiar with the material in Chaps. 2 and 3 before reading this chapter.

The Internet Protocol (IP) address structure (consisting of 32 bits) is somewhat awkward to use. Indeed, instead of using the IP address, many users have adapted the use of acronyms and meaningful terms to identify a numeric address. This practice presents an interesting problem if a network user is using acronyms as an address and must internetwork with a network that uses the numeric IP addresses. How is the non-IP identifier mapped to an IP address?

One could say that the user should conform and learn to use the IP addresses. Yet we cannot expect an end user to remember all the values on these addresses, much less to key in these addresses at the workstation. The solution is to devise a naming scheme wherein an end user can employ a friendly, easy-to-remember name to identify the sending and receiving entities.

In order for this worthy idea to be implemented, procedures must first be established to provide (a) a framework for establishing user friendly names and (b) conventions for mapping the names to IP addresses.

In the Internet, the organization and managing of these names was provided originally by the SRI Network Information Center. It maintained a file called HOST.TXT which listed the names of networks, gateways, and hosts and their corresponding addresses.

The original structure of *flat name* spaces worked well enough in the early days of internet. This term describes a form of a name consisting merely of characters identifying an object without any further meaning or structure. As stated earlier, the Internet Network Information Center was responsible for administering name spaces and assigning them to new objects that were identified in internet.

The Domain Name System (DNS)
Architecture

As the Internet grew, the administration of HOST.TXT became a very big job. In recognition of this problem, the Internet administrators decided in 1983 to develop a system called the DNS.

Like many addressing schemes (such as the ISO and CCITT standards), DNS uses a hierarchical scheme for establishing names. This concept should be familiar to the reader by thinking of an organization chart in a company. The Chief Executive Officer rests at the top of the tree hierarchy, with subordinates stacked in branches below. Another example of hierarchical naming is the telephone system, with country telephone codes at the top of the tree. Next in the tree are area telephone codes, then local exchange codes, and finally, at the bottom of the hierarchy, a local telephone subscriber number.

One attractive aspect of hierarchical naming is that it allows naming administrators to manage their own names at the lower levels of the hierarchy (e.g., the naming domain) and only use upper-level names if they have to operate outside their internal operations and networks.

This approach permits a high-level authority to assign to a lower level (an agent) in a *hierarchical name space* the responsibility for administering a subdomain name space. Even though authority for naming passes from a higher level, the designated agents are permitted to cross the hierarchy to send information to each other regarding names. Therefore, partitioning can be done in any manner deemed appropriate by an upper-level hierarchy, and the name space division can be made small enough to make the whole operation manageable.

The concept of the DNS is shown in Fig. 4.1. It is organized around a *root* and *tree* structure. A root has no higher entry and is also called a parent to the lower levels of the tree. The tree consists of *branches* which connect *nodes*. Each *label* of a node in the tree at the same node level must be completely unambiguous and distinct. That is, the label must be a relative distinguished name—distinguishable relative to this node level.

The hierarchical naming is established by tracing down through the tree, selecting the names attached to each label, and concatenating these labels together to form a distinguished name—distinguishable at all levels in the tree.

For example, the first node level under the root of the tree contains several names, and we will use COM as an example. Proceeding down the tree to the next level, several other names are listed (in this ex-

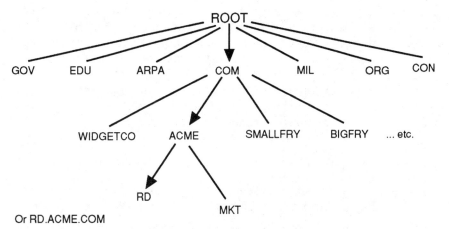

Or RD.ACME.COM

Figure 4.1   The Domain Name System (DNS).

ample, ACME). Finally, RD is the lowest level node in this tree. It is called a *leaf* node because it has no dependent nodes. The concatenated name is shown at the bottom of the figure as RD.ACME.COM.

The user may be wondering about the notation in this example. The tree shows the hierarchy pursuing the route down to the bottom of the leaf. However, the actual name is written with the local label first and the top-most domain label last. This approach is different from the practice of other standards, and it does take some adjustment if the reader has been using other naming conventions.

It should be emphasized that domain names are not intended to define addresses. Indeed, additional services are required to map names to addresses. As we will see shortly, these will be performed by name servers and name resolvers.

Internet names are no longer designated just for hosts. For example, an information class titled mail exchange (MX information) is available to allow an organization to transmit mail, not just to individual workstations or computers per se, but to any machine that is designed as a mail server. In addition, the use of a domain name allows an MX machine to have domain names without being attached to the Internet. They need only direct their mail to a mail server.

Domain Name Space

Each domain is identified by an unambiguous *domain name*. Because of the hierarchical nature of the DNS, a domain may be a subdomain of another domain. Subdomains are achieved by the naming structure, which allows encapsulation of naming relationships. In the example in Fig. 4.1, the domain RD.ACME. is a subdomain of RD.ACME.COM.

The DNS provides two ways of viewing a name. One is called an *absolute name,* which consists of the complete name in the DNS. In the example in Fig. 4.1, an absolute name is RD.ACME.COM. In contrast, a *relative name* consists of only a part of the name within a complete entry in the DNS. For example, in Fig. 4.1, RD would be used to define a relative name. These terms, absolute and relative names, are quite similar to the OSI Model's description of a relative distinguished name (RDN) and a relative name (RN), respectively.

Top-Level Domains

Presently, the DNS contains seven top-level domain names. They are shown in Fig. 4.1 and are as follows:

GOV   Any government body
EDU   An educational institution
ARPA   ARPANET-Internet host identification
COM   Any commercial enterprise
MIL   Military organizations
ORG   Any other organization not identified by previous descriptors
CON   Countries using the ISO standard for names of countries (ISO 3166)

Domain Name Resolution and Mapping
Names to Addresses

In order to map user friendly names to IP addresses, an internet user must work with the concepts of domain name resolution. RFC 1035 defines the procedures for these operations.

Fortunately, the user's task is quite simple for the resolving of these names. The user need only provide a set of arguments to a local agent called a *name resolver,* which is responsible for retrieving information based on a domain name or sending the request to a *name server.* The user has a few other minor tasks, such as forming the proper query to the name resolver and providing certain requirements for how the operation is performed. Figure 4.2 shows the structure for domain name resolution.

The user sees the domain tree as a single name (a single information space). Conversely, the resolver assumes the task of resolving the name or sending the name to independent cooperative systems (the name servers) for the name/address resolution. As the figure shows, the name server services a request from the name resolver. Thus, the resolver acts as a service provider to the user program. In turn, it acts as a user to the name server.

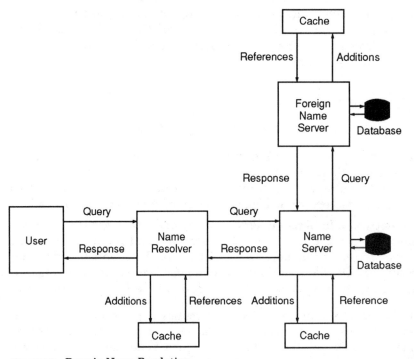

Figure 4.2 Domain Name Resolution.

The name servers may store some of the same information that is stored at the name resolvers for purposes of efficiency and backup. Regardless of how the information is stored at the name server, the name resolver must know the name of at least one name server in order to begin the query. The query is passed to the name server from the resolver. The server, in turn, must then provide a response or make a referral to yet another name server. With this approach, the resolver can learn more about the identities of other name servers and the information that they hold.

The determination of which name servers are to participate in the operation is based on the naming hierarchy tree shown in Fig. 4.1. Each leaf entry of this tree could correspond to a name server. A server at a subdomain (leaf entry) knows which servers are under its domain and can choose the appropriate server to answer a query.

Figure 4.2 shows another component attached to the resolver, called the *name cache*. Upon receiving a user query, it will check this local storage to see if the answer is available locally. If so, the answer is returned to the client in the form of a response. If it is not available in the name cache, the name resolver must then determine the best name servers to provide the response to the query.

The name cache is usually incomplete, but it provides the most frequently queried information in order to speed the process of name resolution. The information in the name cache is eventually erased through the use of timers.

Name Server Operations

The name server services the user's query with the following operations:

- The response of the name server to a query is one of the following: (a) the answer, (b) the identification of an error, or (c) referral to another server. It is now the responsibility of the resolver to reissue a query to specific name servers. This process is called a *nonrecursive* operation.

- In contrast, a local name server may contact other servers. In effect, this off-loads the task from the user host and requires the name server to return the queried IP address to the client. If it does not return the IP address, it must send a negative response. It is not allowed to return a referral. This operation is called a *recursive*.

The effect of the nonrecursive and recursive operations ensures that the user knows at least one server is at the address. It also ensures that a name server knows the IP address of at least one other name server.

The server is responsible for maintaining a portion of a subtree of a domain space, called a *zone*. It is a contiguous section of the domain space. Typically, a separate database exists for each zone. The name server is required to check periodically to make certain that its zone is correct and, if it is not correct, make certain that it is updated correctly. A zone can be updated only by the proper authority.

The name server uses a *zone transfer protocol* to allow more than one name server to store data about a zone. If a name server for a domain name fails for any reason, redundant copies of the naming and addressing information are available at other name servers.

A name server is classified as either a primary name server or a secondary name server. As suggested by these terms, the function of the primary name server can be duplicated in other machines, which, in turn, are called secondary name servers. This approach is implemented for purposes of reliability and efficiency in servicing the queries.

The query and reply messages transmitted between name servers can use either the Transmission Control Protocol (TCP) or the User Datagram Protocol (UDP). Typically, the connectionless UDP is used for ongoing queries because it gives better performance. However, for activities that require database updates, such as zone refresh operations, TCP is preferable in order to obtain reliable transfer. Whatever the case, name servers can use either protocol.

As stated earlier, internet domain servers are arranged (conceptually) in the same tree structure as the example in Fig. 4.1. Each leaf in this hierarchical tree represents a name server. This name server is responsible for a single domain (or subdomain). The entries in the conceptual tree in this figure do not represent any actual physical connections. They simply show the name servers about which other name servers know and with whom they are able to communicate. In order to participate in the DNS, an organization must agree to operate and support a domain name server.

Resource Records (RR)

We learned earlier that a domain name is used to identify a node. Each node contains information about its resources (if no resources are available, the node would have an empty resource). The resource information associated with a node and a name is called a *resource record (RR)*. A resource record is contained in a database and is used to define domain zones. The RRs are also used to map between domain names and network objects.

An RR is identified by its mnemonic type and numerical code. These types and their values are listed in Table 4.1, and are explained in more detail shortly.

TABLE 4.1   Type Values of the DNS

Type	Value and meaning
A	1 = Host address
NS	2 = Authoritative name server
MD	3 = Mail destination (now obsolete; use MX)
MF	4 = Mail forwarder (now obsolete; use MX)
CNAME	5 = Canonical name for an alias
SOA	6 = Start of zone authority
MB	7 = Mailbox domain name
MG	8 = Mailbox member
MR	9 = Mail rename domain
NULL	10 = Null RR
WKS	11 = Well-known service
PTR	12 = Domain name pointer
HINFO	13 = Host information (experimental)
MINFO	14 = Mailbox or mail list information
MX	15 = Mail exchange
TXT	16 = Text strings
RP	17 = Responsible person (experimental)
AFSDB	18 = AFS-type services (experimental)
X.25	19 = X.25 address, X.121 (experimental)
ISDN	20 = ISDN address, E.163/E.164 (experimental)
RT	21 = Route through (experimental)

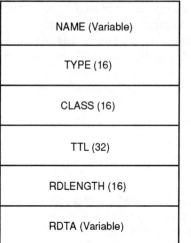

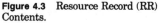

Figure 4.3 Resource Record (RR) Contents.

(*n*) = Number of bits in field

RRs are stored in a standard format. Figure 4.3 shows the format for the top-level part of an RR. The contents of an RR record have a standard format:

```
<name> <TTL> <class> <type> <data>
```

Some of these fields may be omitted in an RR. If the <TTL> field is blank, it defaults to a minimum time specified in another part of the database (explained later). If <class> is blank, it defaults to the last class specified in the database.

name: Contains the domain name of the node for this RR (it is an owner name). If blank, it defaults to the name of the previous RR.

TTL: The time to live parameter is optional and specifies the time (in seconds) that this RR definition is valid in the name server cache. If the value is 0, the RR should not be stored in cache (for example, if RR is volatile data). In practice, this value determines the time the resolver will use a server's data before it asks for an update.

class: Contains the values of the RR class code (where IN = the Internet; CH = Chaos system). If blank, it defaults to the last class specified.

type: Contains a value to represent the RR type codes (see Table 3.4).

RD length: Considered as part of the data field, it specifies the length in octets of the RDATA field.

data (RDATA):   A variable-length field describing the resource. The contents of RDATA vary depending on the type and class of RR. This field is examined in the next section of this chapter.

RDATA Field

Figure 4.4 shows one of the more common RDATA formats, the start of zone authority format (SOA). Only one SOA record per zone should exist.

As the figure reveals, the SOA RDATA contains seven subfields. Most of these fields are used for administration and maintenance of the name server. Their contents are as follows:

MNAME: Identifies the domain name that is the original or primary source of data for this zone.

RNAME: Identifies a domain name to be used for the mailbox of the person responsible for this zone.

SERIAL: This field contains the version number of the original copy of the zone. Any transfers of zones must preserve this value. It is incremented when a change is made in the zone.

REFRESH: A count (in seconds) to determine the interval for refreshing the zone.

RETRY: A count (in seconds) that describes the interval to elapse before an unsuccessful refresh should be reattempted.

EXPIRE: A value (in seconds) that specifies when this zone is no longer authoritative.

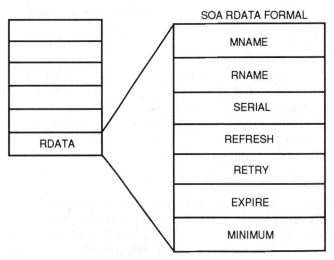

Figure 4.4   The Start of Zone Authority (SOA) Format.

MINIMUM: Contains the minimum value for the TTL field that should be exported from any RR from the subject zone. It is a lower bound on TTL for all RRs in a zone.

Explanation of DNS Types

Figure 4.5 shows the remainder of the fields for the RDATA formats. Each of these formats (actually, DNS types) is examined in the order they appear in this figure, from the top of the figure to the bottom. For purposes of simplicity, some of the optional entries in the formats are not shown. The reader may wish to refer to Table 4.1 during this discussion.

The *name server (NS)* RDATA format contains the domain name and the host name that provides the DNS service. One NS record should exist per server. Also, a name server does not have to be within the domain name. The following entry shows how NS appears in a resource record (as well as on a hard copy printout). Machines HOSTA.RD.ACME.COM. and HOSTC.MKT.COM. provide name service for the domain RD.ACME.COM.:

```
RD.ACME.COM.  NS  HOSTA.RD.ACME.COM.
                  HOSTC.MKT.COM
```

The *MG* RDATA format contains the name of a mailbox, which is a member of a mail group specified by the name. In the figure, this value appears as MGNAME.

The *CNAME* (canonical name) RDATA format contains a domain name which is an alias (nickname) for another name (the proper [canonical] name). CNAME allows a host to change its name (or use a shorter name, etc.) but keep its older name. For example, an alias for HOSTA.RD.ACME.COM. might be ACME.:

```
ACME.   CNAME   HOSTA.RD.ACME.COM.
```

The *HINFO* (host information) RDATA format contains two fields of string information. The first field identifies the CPU type and the second field identifies the operating system running on the CPU. This data format is quite useful in obtaining hardware and software information about a host machine. For example, the HINFO for HOSTA.RD.ACME.COM. might appear as

```
HOSTA.RD.ACME.COM.   HINFO   VAX-11 780 UNIX.
```

The MINFO (mail information) is in the experimental stages. It contains two fields. RMAILBX identifies a mailbox which is responsible for the mailing list. It may identify the owner of the RR, which means the owner is responsible for the mail. EMAILBX identifies the mailbox that is to receive error messages.

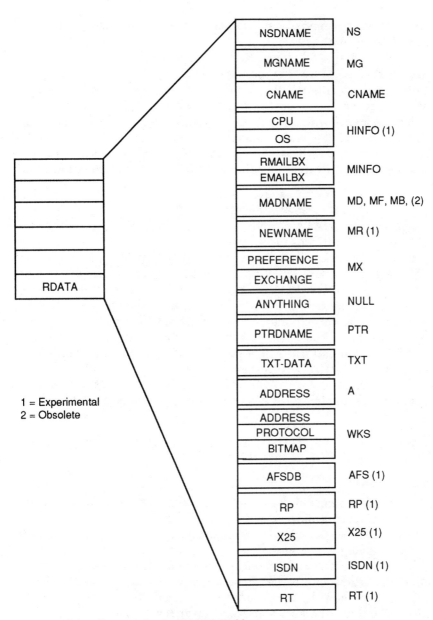

Figure 4.5 Other Contents for the RDATA Field.

Several type values are obsolete. These are listed in Fig. 4.5 as *MD*, *MF*, and *MB* RDATA formats. The reader should study RFC 1035 for guidance on these fields.

The *MR* RDATA is experimental. It contains a domain name which identifies a mailbox. It is a proper rename of a specified mailbox. This record is used principally as a forwarding entry if someone has moved to a different mailbox.

The *MX* (mail exchanger) RDATA format contains two fields. The first field is called a *preference field,* and its value specifies the precedence given to this RR for delivery to a host (low numbers are the highest priority). The second field is the *exchange field,* and it contains a domain name which identifies a host willing to act as a mail exchange for the owner name. The next example shows that HOSTA.RD.ACME.COM. wants its mail to be delivered to one of these machines, in the order indicated by the 10 and 20 values:

```
HOSTA.RD.ACME.COM.    MX  10  HOSTC.MKT.COM.
                      MX  20  HOSTD.HQ.COM.
```

The *NULL* RDATA format allows anything to be placed in this field, as long as it does not exceed 65,535 octets.

To continue the discussion of the RDATA fields, the *TXT* (text) RDATA field contains any kind of character string for descriptive text.

The *PTR* (pointer) RDATA format contains a domain name, which serves as a pointer to a location in the domain name space. This format is used for reverse mapping, in which internet addresses are converted to names. To understand this important feature of the DNS, we must first examine the A (address format) and digress briefly to examine the IN-ADDR-ARPA domain.

The *A* (address) RDATA format contains an internet address for a name. For example, HOSTA has an internet address of 128.11.1.1; its A record is

```
HOSTA.  IN    A     128.11.1.1
```

IN-ADDR-ARPA

The structure depicted in Fig. 4.1 facilitates name-to-address mapping by simply tracing down the domain tree and obtaining an address. However, since the index is organized around a name, an address-to-name mapping is not so easy.

To solve this problem, an address mapping domain name called *IN-ADDR-ARPA* was created. It provides a reverse mapping from address to host name by the use of the IN-ADDR-ARPA domain. The approach is to use the host address as an index to the host's RRs. Once the RRs are located, the name can be extracted. Within the IN-ADDR-ARPA domain are subdomains for each network with the proper network address.

As an example, consider that gateway 1 (GW1) needs to be located. (Gateways have the same PTR RRs as hosts and can be located by only the network number, if necessary.) Assuming that the gateway connects two networks, the A records could appear as

```
GW1.RD.ACME.COM.    IN  A  128.11.1.4.
                    IN  A  129.12.1.3.
```

In each of the networks' zones, one of these *number-to-name* entries is found (notice that the internet number octets are reversed for ease of use). With these entries stored in a database, the look-up for number-to-name resolution becomes a simple process using the PTR field.

```
4.1.11.128.IN-ADDR-ARPA.    PTR    GW1.RD.ACME.COM.
3.1.12.129.IN-ADDR-ARPA.    PTR    GW1.RD.ACME.COM.
```

Since gateways can be located by network number alone, each zone would have one of these number-to-name entries:

```
128.11.IN-ADDR-ARPA.  PTR    GW1.RD.ACME.COM.
129.12.IN-ADDR-ARPA.  PTR    GW1.RD.ACME.COM.
```

To continue with the other contents for the RDATA fields, the *WKS* (well-known services) RDATA format contains three fields. These fields are used to describe services supported at a particular internet address. The first field is a 32-bit internet address. The second field is called the protocol field and it identifies an IP number. The third field is a bit map. The bit map works as follows. Each bit contains the identification of a specified protocol. For example, the first bit in this field corresponds to port 0, the second to port 1, and so on. The appropriate values for these ports and protocols can be found in RFC 1010. If the bits are set to one, it means that the particular protocols are supported at that host. Typically, the bits are established to identify protocols such as TCP, FTP, SMTP, etc. As an example of the WKS entry, HOSTA supports TCP, FTP, SMTP, and TELNET:

```
HOSTA.RD.ACME.COM.    IN    WKS    128.11.1.1.
                                   TCP  FTP  SMTP    TELNET
```

Several other experimental resource records have been added to the DNS. The *AFS* (originally called the Andrew File System) RR type is used to map from a domain name in the DNS to the name of an AFS database server. The record contains a host name, which must be a domain name for a host that is providing a service for an AFS cell database server.

The *RP* (responsible person) record RR is another experimental record. The purpose of this record is to identify the responsible person for a particular system or host. Typically, this would be a contact in the event a problem occurs at a computer. This record uses a new RR type with the mnemonic RP. An example of an RP record is as follows:

```
GW1.RD.ACME.COM.  RP  UDB.IEI.ACME.COM.
```

Due to the importance and prevalence of X.25-based networks and the emerging ISDN technology, the Internet has added resource records for X.25 and ISDN addresses.

The X.25 resource record is defined with a mnemonic *X25*. It allows the coding of a CCITT X.121 address and the association of that address with a domain name. The value of this approach is that it only takes one more operation in a name server database to relate the IP address to the domain name which is associated with X.121 address in the record. An example of the X.25 RR is as follows:

```
ACME.COM.    X25    3110.123456789.
```

The ISDN RDATA format works in a similar manner (its mnemonic is *ISDN*). It allows a relationship to be established between an ISDN address coded typically with the E.164 format. As the reader might surmise, it is a simple step to do an additional look-up in the file to relate an ISDN address to the IP counterpart address through the use of the domain name (assuming these relationships have been created by the network administrator).

Additionally, the capability allows a mapping through the name server with the domain name as the pointer to all of the relationships of the addresses, that is, X.25, ISDN, and IP. While experimental, these services hold enormous potential.

The final experimental record that has been added to the DNS by the Internet is the route through (with a mnemonic of *RT*). The purpose of the route through record is to support a host that does not have its own WAN address. Its record provides the identification of an intermediate host that will serve as the domain name for the host that does not have a WAN address.

Example of a resource record

Figure 4.6 provides an illustration of a resource record and ties together several of the examples in the previous discussion. The top box shows the topology of two networks connected with a gateway (labeled G1). Host A is attached to network 128.11, as are workstations 1 and 2. Workstations 3 and 4 are attached to network 129.12. The internet addresses are shown as 128.11 and 129.12 for the two networks. The local addresses are shown in the boxes next to the workstations, gateways, or hosts.

The bottom part of the figure shows the RRs for this domain. The reader should be aware that this entry is written for pedagogical reasons and has been simplified. However, it contains the major parts of the records. The right part of the figure shows 11 notes. These notes are used to describe the entries in the database.

Note 1: This line describes the owner name as RD.ACME.COM. The IN identifies the class as the Internet. The SOA defines the type of RR record as the start of a zone authority. The right-most part of

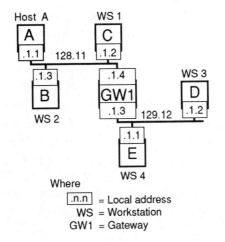

Figure 4.6 Example of an RR Record.

this line describes the first entry into the RDATA field for the SOA record. The HOSTA.RD.ACME.COM. describes the first field of the SOA RDATA segment called MNAME.

Note 2:   The value of 30 is in the SERIAL field.

Note 3:   The value of 3600 describes in seconds the time allotted to REFRESH the zone. This zone is to be refreshed every 60 minutes.

Note 4:   The value of 600 describes the interval before a failed REFRESH has to be reattempted. In this example, the value is 10 minutes.

Note 5:   The value of 604800 specifies an upper limit on the time that can elapse before the zone is no longer considered to be authoritative. This value translates into one week.

Note 6:   This field describes the minimum TTL value that should be exported from this zone. This value is 604800 (one week).

Note 7:   This note describes two entries in the RR file. The NS identifies the authoritative name server as HOSTA.RD.ACME.COM. The MX identifies the host for the mail exchange support operations. The precedence field of 20 is irrelevant since only one MX is identified.

Note 8:   This note shows the entry to identify HOSTA and its address of 128.11.1.1. The entry A is an example of a *glue* record. It specifies the address of the server and is used when the server for a domain is inside that same domain. The HINFO provides information about the host.

Note 9:   This line depicts an WKS RDATA entry. It establishes that host A, with an internet address of 128.11.1.1, uses TCP to support the well-known services of FTP, SMTP, TELNET, and NAMESRV.

Note 10:   Four entries exist to define the internet addresses for workstations 1, 2, 3, and 4.

Note 11:   This note shows the addresses for the gateway. The gateway is identified with two internet addresses: 128.11.1.4 and 129.12.1.3.

The structure of the DNS permits a relatively simple and easy addition of entries into the RR database. For example, assume that the networks depicted in Fig. 4.6 are connected to another network. This network has its own name server for its zone. All that is required to reflect this additional interconnection is to add the entry of the name server to the local domain's name server database and reference the other network by its specific name server. The entries would use NS and A type records to merely indicate that the server on the other network is the authority for the newly connected network. Consequently, queries for that network would be directed to the identified name server. The new configuration is shown in Fig. 4.7 with the resulting code in the local name server database. Workstations, etc. are not shown on the new network for purposes of simplicity.

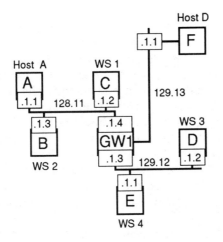

Where

.n.n = Local address
WS = Workstation
GW1 = Gateway

Code added to name server database
TRN.ACME.COM.   IN NS HOSTD.TRN.ACME.COM.
HOSTD.TRN.ACME.COM. IN A   129.13.1.1

Figure 4.7 Adding Another Network and Server to the Database.

DNS Messages

Figure 4.8 shows the format of the DNS message. These messages are transferred between name servers to update the RRs. Consequently, some of the fields in the message are similar to the format of the RR discussed in the previous section.

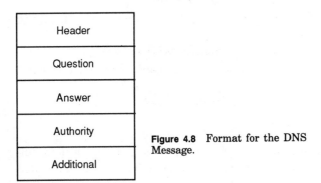

Figure 4.8 Format for the DNS Message.

As indicated in the figure, the message consists of five major sections. The *header* (which is always present) contains fields about the nature of the query and response. (We have more to say about all of these fields shortly.) The *question* section contains the data that is used to pose a query to the name server. The *answer* section contains the values of the RRs retrieved in response to the questions. The *authority* section contains RRs that point to the authoritative name server. The *additional record* section contains RRs to assist in the query; they are not specifically related to the answers to the question.

Figure 4.9 shows the format of the header section. The first field is the *ID* field, which consists of 16 bits. This identifier is used both with the query and reply in order to match the two together. The *QR* field is a 1-bit field, specifying that this message is a query (value of 0) or response (value of 1).

The *opcode* consists of 4 bits which contain the following information and values: 0 = standard query, 1 = inverse query, 2 = server status request, and 3–15 = reserved.

The *AA* (authoritative answer) bit is turned to a 1 for a response and identifies that the responding name server is the recognized authority for the domain name that is being queried. The *TC* (truncation) bit is turned on to notify that this message was truncated because it was too long. The truncation depends on the length of the data unit that is permitted on the transmission link. The *RD* (recursion desired) bit is set to 1 to direct the name server to do a recursive query. The *RA* (recursion available) bit is used in a response message to indicate if a recursive query capability is available in the name server. The three *Z* bits are reserved for future use.

The *RCODE* consists of 4 bits which are set to the following values:

0	No error occurred.
1	A format error has occurred and the name server is unable to interpret the query.
2	A problem has occurred at the name server.
3	A problem has occurred with the domain reference in the query; the server cannot find it.
4	The name server does not support this type of query.
5	The name server will not perform the operation for administrative or policy reasons.
6–15	Values are reserved for future use.

The *QDCOUNT* is a 16-bit value which specifies the number of entries in the question section. The *ANCOUNT* is a 16-bit value specifying the number of RRs in the answer section. The *NSCOUNT* is a

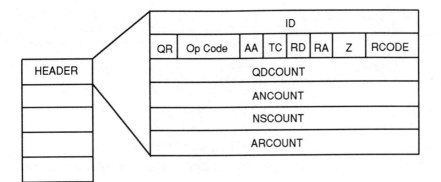

Figure 4.9 The DNS Message Header.

16-bit value which specifies the number of server resource records in the authority record section. The *ARCOUNT* is a 16-bit field which specifies the number of resource records in the additional record section. These last four fields are used by the receiver of the message to determine how to interpret the boundaries of the four fields.

Figure 4.10 shows the formats for these four sections. The *QUES-TION* section contains three entries. We learned earlier that it is used to carry the question of the query messages. The *QNAME* contains the domain name. The format of the field consists of a length octet followed by the appropriate number of octets. The *QTYPE* specifies the type of the query. The values in this field can contain the values of the type field discussed in the previous section (see Table 4.1). The

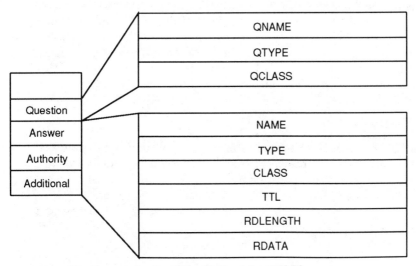

Figure 4.10 The Formats for the Other Fields of the DNS Message.

QCLASS is the last field in the question section. It specifies the class of the query. Typically, this value would be IN for the Internet.

As shown in Fig. 4.10, the *ANSWER, AUTHORITY,* and *ADDITIONAL* sections of the DNS message consist of the same format. The fields for this format are as follows:

NAME: This field identifies the domain name associated with the resource record.

TYPE: This field contains one of the RR type codes.

CLASS: This field specifies the data class that is contained in the RDATA field.

TTL: This is the time-to-live parameter discussed in the previous sections.

RDLENGTH: The field length is specified by this field.

RDATA: This field contains the information that is associated with the resource. Its contents depend on the type and class of the resource record. For example, it may be an internet address.

The *ANSWER, AUTHORITY,* and *ADDITIONAL* record sections contain a variable number of resource records (RRs). The contents and formats of these records were described earlier in conjunction with Fig. 4.3.

RR Compression

It is likely that the exchange of RR messages will entail duplicate domain names in succeeding occurrences of the traffic on the communications link. With this in mind, the DNS provides for message compression. The process is quite simple. Any duplicate domain name (or for that matter a list of labels) is replaced with a pointer which identifies the previous occurrence of the traffic.

Summary

The DNS provides the first international standard for name server protocols. It allows internet users to map names to addresses and addresses to names. It also supports mailbox operations and the storing of host profiles about operating systems, hardware, and applications architectures. Recent additions provide address and naming services for X.25 and ISDN systems.

5

The Internet Protocol (IP)

Introduction

As we learned in Chap. 1, the Internet Protocol (IP) is an internetworking protocol developed by the Department of Defense. The system was implemented as part of the DARPA internetwork protocol project and is widely used throughout the world. This chapter examines IP in more detail including its major features, its use of address and routing tables, and its relationships to other internet and IEEE protocols.

Major Features of IP

IP is quite similar to the ISO 8473 (the Connectionless Network Protocol or CLNP) specification explained in the last section of this chapter. Many of the ISO 8473 concepts were derived from IP.

IP is an example of a connectionless service. It permits the exchange of traffic between two host computers without any prior call setup. (However, these two computers usually share a common connection-oriented transport protocol.) Since IP is connectionless, it is possible that the datagrams could be lost between the two end users' stations. For example, the IP gateway enforces a maximum queue length size, and if this queue length is violated, the buffers will overflow. In this situation, the additional datagrams are discarded in the network. For this reason, a higher-level transport layer protocol (such as TCP) is essential to recover from these problems.

IP hides the underlying subnetwork from the end user. In this context, it creates a virtual network to that end user. This aspect of IP is attractive because it allows different types of networks to attach to an IP gateway. As a result, IP is reasonably simple to install, and because of its connectionless design, it is quite robust.

Since IP is an unreliable, best effort, datagram-type protocol, it has no reliability mechanisms. It provides no error recovery for the underlying subnetworks. It has no flow-control mechanisms. The user data (datagrams) may be lost, duplicated, or even arrive out of order. It is not the job of IP to deal with most of these problems. As we shall see later, most of the problems are passed to the next higher layer, TCP.

IP supports fragmentation operations. The term *fragmentation* refers to an operation wherein a protocol data unit (PDU) is divided or segmented into smaller units. This feature can be quite useful because all networks do not use the same size PDU. For example, X.25-based wide area networks (WANs) typically employ a PDU (called a packet in X.25) with a data field of 128 octets. Some networks allow negotiations to a smaller or larger PDU size. The Ethernet standard limits the size of a PDU to 1500 octets. Conversely, proNET-10 stipulates a PDU of 2000 octets.

Without the use of fragmentation, a gateway would be tasked with trying to resolve incompatible PDU sizes between networks. IP solves the problem by establishing the rules for fragmentation at the gateway(s) and reassembly at the receiving host.

IP and Subnetworks

As seen in Fig. 5.1, IP is designed to rest on top of the underlying subnetwork—insofar as possible in a transparent manner. This means that IP assumes little about the characteristics of the underlying network or networks. As stated earlier, from the design standpoint this is quite attractive to engineers because it keeps the subnetworks relatively independent of IP.

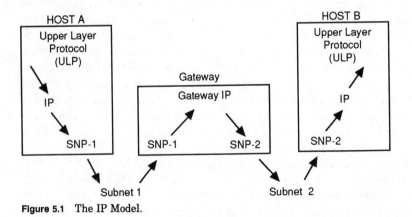

Figure 5.1 The IP Model.

As the reader might expect, the transparency is achieved by encapsulation. The data sent by the host computer are encapsulated into an IP datagram. The IP header identifies the address of the receiving host computer. The IP datagram and header are further encapsulated into the specific protocol of the transit network. For example, a transit network could be an X.25 network or an Ethernet LAN.

After the transit network has delivered the traffic to an IP gateway, its control information is stripped away. The gateway then uses the destination address in the datagram header to determine where to route the traffic. Typically, it then passes the datagram to a subnetwork by invoking a subnetwork access protocol (for example, Ethernet on a LAN, and X.25 on a WAN). This protocol is used to encapsulate the datagram header and user data into the headers and trailers that are used by the subnetwork. This process is repeated at each gateway, and eventually the datagram arrives at the final destination, where it is delivered to the receiving station.

It should be emphasized that an IP gateway is not completely unconcerned with the access protocol of an attached subnetwork. There is nothing magic about IP; the gateway interface must know how to access its connected networks. Consequently, some form of communications (however limited) must occur between the gateway and the attached subnetworks (see the section later in this chapter titled "IP Service Definitions and Primitives"). The important point is that an IP module does not care about the operations inside the networks.

The IP Datagram

A productive approach to the analysis of IP is first to examine the fields in the IP datagram (PDU) depicted in Fig. 5.2. An abbreviated description of the fields in the datagram is provided in Table 5.1.

The *version* field identifies the version of IP in use. Most protocols contain this field because some network nodes may not have the latest release available of the protocol. The current version of IP is 4.

The *header length* field contains 4 bits set to a value to indicate the length of the datagram header. The length is measured in 32-bit words. Typically, a header without QOS options contains 20 octets. Therefore, the value in the length field is usually 5.

The *type of service (TOS)* field can be used to identify several QOS functions provided for in Internet. It is quite similar to the service field that resides in the CLNP PDU. Transit delay, throughput, precedence, and reliability can be requested with this field.

The TOS field is illustrated in Fig. 5.3. It contains five entries consisting of 8 bits. Bits 0, 1, and 2 contain a precedence value used to

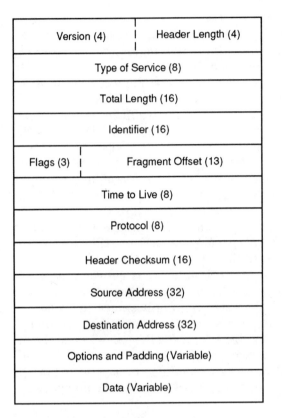

(*n*) = Number of Bits in Field

Figure 5.2   The IP Datagram.

indicate the relative importance of the datagram. Values range from 0 to 7, with 0 set to indicate a *routine precedence*. The precedence field is not used in all systems, although the value of 7 is used by some implementations to indicate a network control datagram. However, the precedence field could be used to implement some powerful flow control and congestion mechanisms in a network. This would allow gateways and host nodes to make decisions about the order of "throwing away" datagrams in case of congestion.

The next three bits are used for other services and are described as follows:

Bit 3 is the *delay bit (D bit)*. When set to 1 this TOS requests a short delay through an internet. The aspect of delay is not defined in the standard, and it is up to the vendor to implement the service.

TABLE 5.1   The IP Protocol Data Unit

Version field	Identifies the version of IP.
Internet header length	Specifies the length of the IP header.
Type of service	Stipulates quality of service functions.
Total length field	Specifies the total length of the IP datagram, including the header.
Identifier	Used with the address fields to identify the data unit uniquely (for fragmentation).
Flags	Used in the fragmentation operations.
Fragmentation offset	Describes where this datagram belongs within the original PDU.
Time to live	Used to determine how long the datagram is to remain in the internet.
Protocol	Used to identify a next-level protocol that is to receive the user data at the final destination.
Header checksum	Used to perform an error check on the header.
Source and destination addresses	Identifies the source and destination hosts and their directly attached networks.
Options	Used to request additional services for the IP user.
Padding	Used to give the datagram a 32-bit alignment.
User data	Contains user data.

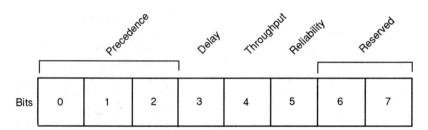

Bits | 0 | 1 | 2 | 3 | 4 | 5 | 6 | 7

Precedence
111 = Network Control
110 = Internetwork Control
101 = CEITIC/ECP
100 = Flash Override
011 = Flash
010 = Immediate
001 = Priority
000 = Routine

Delay
0 = Normal
1 = Low

Throughput
0 = Normal
1 = High

Reliability
0 = Normal
1 = High

Figure 5.3   The Type of Service (TOS) Field.

The next bit is the *throughput bit (T bit)*. It is set to 1 to request high throughput through an internet. Again, its specific implementation is not defined in the standard.

The last bit used is the *reliability bit (R bit)*, which allows a user to request high reliability for the datagram.

The next two bits, 6 and 7, are not used at this time.

The *TOS field* is not used in some vendors' implementations of IP. Nonetheless, it will be used increasingly in the future as the internet capabilities are increased. For example, it is used in the Open Shortest Path First (OSPF) protocol discussed in Chap. 8. Consequently, a user should examine this field for future work and ascertain a vendor's use or intended support of this field.

The *total length* field specifies the total length of the IP datagram. It is measured in octets and includes the length of the header and the data. IP subtracts the header length field from the total length field to compute the size of the data field. The maximum possible length of a datagram is 65,535 octets (2^{16}). Gateways that service IP datagrams are required to accept any datagram that supports the maximum size of a PDU of the attached networks. Additionally, all gateways must accommodate datagrams of 576 octets in total length.

The IP protocol uses three fields in the header to control datagram fragmentation and reassembly. These fields are the *identifier, flags,* and *fragmentation offset*. The identifier field is used to identify uniquely all fragments from an original datagram. It is used with the source address at the receiving host to identify the fragment. The flags field contains bits to determine if the datagram may be fragmented. If it can be fragmented, one of the bits can be set to determine if this fragment is the last fragment of the datagram. The fragmentation offset field contains a value which specifies the relative position of the fragment to the original datagram. The value is initialized as 0 and is subsequently set to the proper number if/when the gateway fragments the data. The value is measured in units of eight octets. We will devote a special section later in this chapter to fragmentation/reassembly and the use of these three fields.

The *time-to-live (TTL)* parameter is used to measure the time a datagram has been in the internet. It is quite similar to CLNP's lifetime field. Each gateway in the internet is required to check this field and discard it if the TTL value equals 0. A gateway is also required to decrement this field in each datagram it processes. In actual implementations, the TTL field is a number of hops value. Therefore, when a datagram proceeds through a gateway (hop), the value in the field is decremented by a value of one. Implementations of IP may use a time-counter in this field and decrement the value in one-second decrements.

The TTL field is used not only by the gateway to prevent endless loops, but it can also be used by the host to limit the lifetime that segments have in an internet. Be aware that if a host is acting as a gateway, it must treat the TTL field by the gateway rules. Check with the vendor to determine when a host throws away a datagram based on the TTL value. Ideally, the TTL value could be configured and its value assigned based on observing internet performance. Additionally, network management information protocols such as those residing in SNMP might wish to set the TTL value for diagnostic purposes. Finally, if your vendor uses a fixed value that cannot be reconfigured, make certain it is fixed initially to allow for your internet's growth.

The *protocol* field is used to identify the next-level protocol above the IP that is to receive the datagram at the final host destination. It is quite similar to the type field found in the Ethernet frame. The Internet standards groups have established a numbering system to identify the most widely used upper layer protocols. Table 5.2 lists and describes these protocols.

The *header checksum* is used to detect a distortion that may have occurred in the header. Checks are not performed on the user data stream. Some critics of IP have stated that the provision for error detection in the user data would allow the gateway at least to notify the sending host that problems have occurred. (This service is indeed provided by a companion standard to IP, called the ICMP, which is discussed in Chap. 6.) Whatever one's view on the issue, the current approach keeps the checksum algorithm in IP quite simple. It does not have to operate on many octets, but it does require that a higher-level protocol at the receiving host perform some type of error check on the user data if it cares about its integrity.

IP carries two addresses in the datagram. These are labeled *source* and *destination addresses* and remain the same value throughout the life of the datagram. These fields contain the internet addresses examined in Chap. 3.

The *options* field is used to identify several additional services. As we shall see later, it is similar to the option part field of CLNP. The options field is not used in every datagram. The majority of implementations use this field for network management and diagnostics.

Figure 5.4 illustrates the format of the option field. Table 5.3 contains the values that are currently defined in the standard.

The options field length is variable because some options are of variable length. Each option contains three fields. The first field is coded

TABLE 5.2   Internet Protocol Numbers

Decimal	Key word	Protocol
0		Reserved
1	ICMP	Internet Control Message Protocol
2	IGMP	Internet Group Management Protocol
3	GGP	Gateway-to-Gateway Protocol
4		Unassigned
5	ST	Stream
6	TCP	Transmission Control Protocol
7	UCL	UCL
8	EGP	Exterior Gateway Protocol
9	IGP	Interior Gateway Protocol
10	BBN-MON	BBN-RCC Monitoring
11	NVP-II	Network Voice Protocol
12	PUP	PUP
13	ARGUS	ARGUS
14	EMCON	EMCON
15	XNET	Cross Net Debugger
16	CHAOS	Chaos
17	UDP	User Datagram Protocol
18	MUX	Multiplexing
19	DCN-MEAS	DCN Measurement Subsystems
20	HMP	Host Monitoring Protocol
21	PRM	Packet Radio Monitoring
22	XNS-IDP	XEROX NS IDP
23	TRUNK-1	Trunk-1
24	TRUNK-2	Trunk-2
25	LEAF-1	Leaf-1
26	LEAF-2	Leaf-2
27	RDP	Reliable Data Protocol
28	IRTP	Internet Reliable TP
29	ISO-TP4	ISO Transport Class 4
30	NETBLT	Bulk Data Transfer
31	MFE-NSP	MFE Network Services
32	MERIT-INP	MERIT Internodal Protocol
33	SEP	Sequential Exchange
34–60		Unassigned
61		Any host internal protocol
62	CFTP	CFTP
63		Any local network
64	SAT-EXPAK	SATNET and Backroom EXPAK
65	MIT-SUBN	MIT Subnet Support
66	RVD	.MIT Remote Virtual Disk
67	IPPC	Internet Plur. Packet Core
68		Any distributed file system
69	SAT-MON	SATNET Monitoring
70		Unassigned

TABLE 5.2 Internet Protocol Numbers *(Continued)*

Decimal	Key word	Protocol
71	IPCV	Packet Core Utility
72–75		Unassigned
76	BRSAT-MON	Backroom SATNET Monitoring
77		Unassigned
78	WB-MON	Wideband Monitoring
79	WB-EXPAK	Wideband EXPAK
80–254		Unassigned
255		Reserved

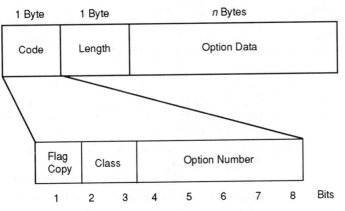

Figure 5.4   The IP Option Field.

TABLE 5.3 Option Codes

Class	Number	Length	Description
0	0	0	End of option list
0	1	0	No operation
0	2	11	Security
0	3	var	Loose source routing
0	7	var	Record route
0	8	4	Stream ID (obsolete)
0	9	var	Strict source routing
2	4	var	Internet timestamp

as a single octet containing the option code. The option code also contains three fields. Their functions are as follows:

Flag copy (1 bit)   0 = Copy option into only the first fragment of a fragmented datagram.

1 = Copy option into all fragments of a fragmented datagram.

Class (2 bits)   Identifies the option class (Table 5.3).

Option Number   Identifies the option number (Table 5.3).

The option class can be set to the following values:

0:   A user datagram or a network control datagram

1:   Reserved

2:   Diagnostics purposes (debugging and measuring)

3:   Reserved

The next octet contains the length of the option. The third field contains the data values for the option. The option field is described in more detail in the next section of this chapter.

The *padding* field may be used to make certain that the datagram header aligns on an exact 32-bit boundary.

Finally, the *data* field contains the user data. IP stipulates that the combination of the data field and the header cannot exceed 65,535 octets.

Major IP Services

This section provides an overview of the major services of IP. Be aware that vendors have different products for IP and some of them may not support all the features described in this section.

Internet header check routine

When a gateway receives the datagram, it checks the header to determine the type of traffic it is processing. If the traffic is an internet datagram, it passes the datagram to the internet header check routine. This module performs a number of editing and validity tests on the IP datagram header. The following checks are performed on the header:

Valid IP header length

Proper IP version number

Valid IP message length

Valid IP header checksum

Nonzero time to live field validity

If checks are performed and not passed, the datagram is discarded. If the checks are performed and passed, the internet destination address is examined to determine (a) if the datagram is addressed to this gateway, or (b) if the datagram is destined for another gateway. If it is not destined for this gateway, the datagram is passed to the IP forwarding routine for further routing.

IP source routing

IP can use a mechanism called *source routing* as part of its routing algorithm. Source routing allows an upper layer protocol (ULP) to determine how the IP gateways route the datagrams. The ULP has the option of passing a list of internet addresses to the IP module. The list contains the intermediate IP nodes that are to be transited during the routing of the datagrams to the final destination. The last address on the list is the final destination of an intermediate node.

When IP receives a datagram, it uses the addresses in the source routing field to determine the next intermediate hop. As illustrated in Fig. 5.5, IP uses a pointer field to learn about the next IP address. If a check of the pointer and length fields indicates that the list has been completed, the destination IP address field is used for routing. If the list is not exhausted, the IP module uses the IP address indicated by the pointer.

The IP module then replaces the value in the source routing list with its own address. Of course, it must then increment the pointer by one address (4 bytes) for the next hop to retrieve the next IP address in the route. With this approach, the datagram follows the source route dictated by the ULP and also records the route along the way.

Figure 5.5 provides an example of the use of route recording. In the first step, IP uses the pointer to locate the next address in the route data field. In this example, it locates address 128.2.3.4 and makes a routing decision based on this address. In the second step, it places its own address in the route data field in the same location of the current destination address. In the third step, it increments the pointer value to enable the next IP module to determine the next (or final) hop in the route.

Routing operations.   The IP gateway makes routing decisions based on the routing list. If the destination host resides in another network, the IP gateway must decide how to route to the other network. Indeed, if

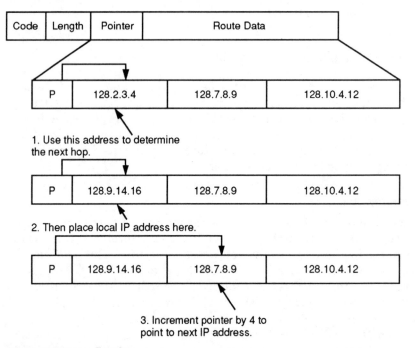

Code	Length	Pointer	Route Data

| P | 128.2.3.4 | 128.7.8.9 | 128.10.4.12 |

1. Use this address to determine the next hop.

| P | 128.9.14.16 | 128.7.8.9 | 128.10.4.12 |

2. Then place local IP address here.

| P | 128.9.14.16 | 128.7.8.9 | 128.10.4.12 |

3. Increment pointer by 4 to point to next IP address.

Figure 5.5 Source Routing.

multiple hops are involved in the communications process, then each gateway must be traversed and the gateway must make decisions about the routing.

Each gateway maintains a routing table that contains the next gateway on the way to the final destination network. In effect, the table contains an entry for each reachable network. These tables could be static or dynamic, although dynamic tables are more common. The IP module makes a routing decision on all datagrams it receives.

The routing table contains an IP address for each reachable network and the address of a neighbor gateway (that is, a gateway directly attached to this network). The neighbor gateway is the shortest route to the destination network. Otherwise, the IP gateway logic establishes that the gateway is directly connected to this network.

The IP routing is based on a concept called the *distance metric*. This value is usually nothing more than the fewest number of hops between the gateway and the final destination. The gateway consults its routing table and attempts to match the destination network address contained in the IP header with a network entry contained in the routing table. If no match is found, it discards the datagram and builds an ICMP message to send back to the IP source. This message would contain a "destination unreachable" code. If a match is found in the routing table, the gateway then uses it to determine the outgoing port.

Some implementations of TCP/IP have allowed a host to perform source route forwarding and to act as an intermediate hop through the full route. If the reader uses a system in which a host performs source routing, the host should adhere to all the rules of a conventional gateway in managing source routed datagrams. Again, this point is made to emphasize that the task of the host in any type of gateway function should be commensurate with the gateway, and the software should not be scaled down for purposes of efficiency. For example, the TTL field must be decremented by the host; and the host should be able to generate the ICMP destination unreachable messages in case the source route fails or in case fragmentation cannot be performed. It must also be able to perform the timestamp option (discussed shortly) in accordance with the proper rules of an IP gateway.

Loose and strict routing. IP provides two options in routing the datagram to the final destination. The first, called *loose source routing,* gives the IP modules the option of using intermediate hops to reach the addresses obtained in the source list as long as the datagram traverses the nodes listed. Conversely, *strict source routing* requires that the datagram travel only through the networks whose addresses are indicated in the source list. If the strict source route cannot be followed, the originating host IP is notified with an error message. Both loose and strict routing require that the route recording feature be implemented.

Route recording option

The route recording option operates in the same manner as source routing, with the recording feature which was just discussed. This means that any IP module that receives a datagram must add its address to a route recording list. The idea is illustrated in Fig. 5.6, except that this option is not using addresses in the recording field to determine the next hops. For the route recording operation to occur, the receiving IP module uses the pointer and length fields to determine if any room is available to record the route. If the route recording list is full, the IP module simply forwards the datagram without inserting its address. If it is not full, the pointer is used to locate the first empty full octet slot, the address is inserted, and the IP module then increments the pointer to the next IP slot.

The timestamp option

Another very useful option in IP is the provision for timestamping the datagram as it traverses each IP module through the internet. This idea allows a network manager not only to determine the route of the

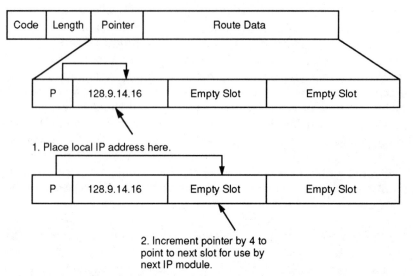

Figure 5.6   Route Recording.

datagram through the internet but also the time at which each IP module processed the datagram. This can be quite useful in determining the efficiency of gateways and routing algorithms.

The format for the options fields for timestamp operations is shown in Fig. 5.7. As with previous options, the length and pointer fields are used to identify the proper slot in which to place an IP address *and* the timestamp related to this address. Therefore, the pointer increments itself across an IP address and the timestamp for the address. The *oflw* field is only used when an IP module cannot register a timestamp due to (for example) lack of resources or an option field that is too small. This value is incremented by each module that encounters this problem.

A 4-bit flags field is used to provide guidance to each IP module about the timestamp operations. The values currently described are as follows:

0:   Timestamps are to be recorded only and are stored in consecutive 32-bit words.

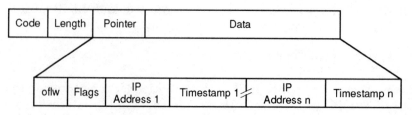

Figure 5.7   The Timestamp Option.

1:   Each timestamp is to be preceded by the IP address of the relevant module.

3:   IP addresses are already specified by the originator, and the gateway is tasked with recording the timestamp in its relevant IP address area.

The time used with the timestamp is based on milliseconds (ms) using universal time (the old Greenwich mean time). Obviously, the use of the universal time does not guarantee completely accurate timestamps between machines, because machines' clocks may vary slightly. Nonetheless, in most networks the universal time in milliseconds provides a reasonable degree of accuracy.

Fragmentation and reassembly

An IP datagram may traverse a number of different networks that use different PDU sizes, and all networks have a maximum PDU size, called the *maximum transmission unit (MTU)*. Therefore, IP contains procedures for dividing (fragmenting) a large datagram into smaller datagrams. It also allows the ULP to stipulate that fragmentation may or may not occur. Of course, it must also use a reassembly mechanism at the final destination which places the fragments back into the order originally transmitted.

When an IP gateway module receives a datagram which is too big to be transmitted by the transit subnetwork, it uses its fragmentation operations. It divides the datagram into two or more pieces (with alignment on 8-octet boundaries). Each of the fragmented pieces has a header attached containing identification, addressing, and, as another option, all options pertaining to the original datagram. The fragmented packets also have information attached to them defining the position of the fragment within the original datagram, as well as an indication if this fragment is the last fragment.

Referring to Fig. 5.3, the flags (the 3 bits) are used as follows:

Bit 0   = reserved

Bit 1:   0 = fragmentation and 1 = do not fragment

Bit 2 (M bit):   0 = last fragment and 1 = more fragments

Interestingly, IP handles each fragment operation independently. That is, the fragments may traverse different gateways to the intended destination, and they may be subject to further fragmentation if they pass through networks that use smaller data units. The next gateway uses the offset value in the incoming fragment to determine the offset values of fragmented datagrams. If further fragmentation is done at another gateway, the fragment offset value is set to the location that this fragment fits relative to the original datagram and not the preceding fragmented packet.

Figure 5.8 shows an example of multiple fragmentation operations across two gateways. Be aware that this example shows the *OL (overall length)* field. This field is not carried in the datagram but is used here to assist the reader in this analysis.

Subnet 128.3 uses a 1500-octet PDU size. It passes this data unit to gateway A. Gateway A decides to route the PDU to subnet 21.4, which supports a 512-octet PDU size. The gateway fragments the 1500 data

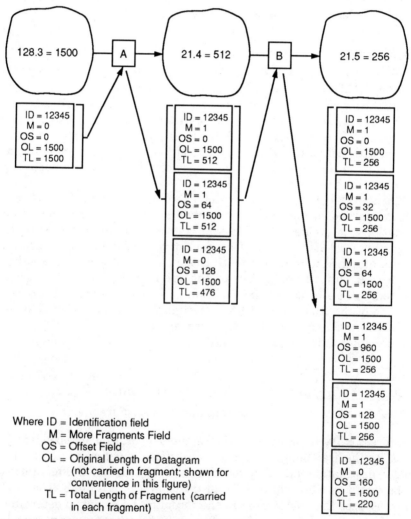

Where ID = Identification field
       M = More Fragments Field
      OS = Offset Field
      OL = Original Length of Datagram
           (not carried in fragment; shown for
           convenience in this figure)
      TL = Total Length of Fragment (carried
           in each fragment)

Figure 5.8 Fragmentation Operations at the Gateways.

unit into three smaller data units of 512, 512, and 476 octets. Thus, 1500 = 512 + 512 + 476. The last segment containing 476 octets is filled (padded) with zeros to equal a total of a multiple of 8. Therefore, this data field is 480 (480 = 476 + 4, which is an even multiple of 8).

Gateway A passes the data to subnetwork 21.4, which delivers it to gateway B. This gateway decides that datagram fragments are to be delivered to subnetwork 21.5. Since the gateway knows that this network uses a PDU size of 256 octets, it performs further fragmentation. It divides the 512 octet fragments into yet smaller data units and, using the offset values in the three incoming fragments, adjusts accordingly the offset values in the outgoing data units. Notice that the offset values are reset at gateway B, and their values are derived from the offset values contained in the preceding fragments.

As illustrated in Fig. 5.9, reassembly occurs at the receiving host. The IP module sets up buffer space when the first fragment is re-

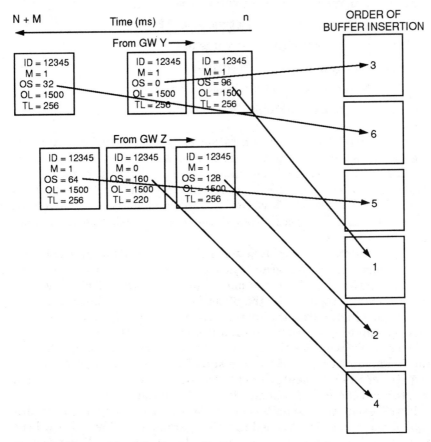

Figure 5.9 Reassembly of the Fragments.

ceived. A buffer is reserved for each fragment, and the fragment is placed in an area within the buffer relative to its position in the original datagram. As the fragments arrive, they are placed into the proper location in the buffer (pigeon holing). When all the fragments have been received, the IP module passes the data to the ULP in the same order that it was originally sent from the sending ULP.

For purposes of discussion, we assume that the datagram fragments depicted in Fig. 5.8 are routed to other gateways, say gateways Y and Z. To continue the analysis, Fig. 5.9 shows that the fragmented datagrams arrive from gateways Y and Z in the order depicted by the "time arrow," with earliest arrival at time n and the latest time of arrival at time $n + m$. Therefore, the fragments arrive in the following order (we are using the offset values in the figure to identify the fragment):

First: Fragment with offset value of 96

Second: Fragment with offset value of 128

Third: Fragment with offset value of 0

Fourth: Fragment with offset value of 160

Fifth: Fragment with offset value of 64

Sixth: Fragment with offset value of 32

The receiving machine has a rather easy job of figuring out where the fragments are to be placed. The IP module simply multiplies the offset value by 8 to determine which slot in the buffer is to receive the fragment. For example, the first arriving fragment's relative position in the buffer is computed as 96*8 = 768, or memory address 768. (If the reader wishes to test the calculations, we are using position 0, not 1, as the first position.)

In Fig. 5.9, the reassembling host initially does not know the length of the complete IP datagram until it receives the fourth fragment, which contains the M = 0 (no more fragments), the offset value, and the fragment length. Since the offset is 160 and the length is 220 octets, it now knows that the total datagram is (160 offset values *8 octets per value + 220 octets in final fragment = 1500 octets).

We now see why the M bit is so important. Since the length field in the fragment does not refer to the size of the original datagram but to the size of the fragment, the only method to determine the original length (and the final fragment) is the M = 0 indicator.

In the event that some fragments do not arrive or have been discarded because they exceeded the TTL parameter, IP will discard the fragments of the partially reassembled datagram. In addition, the receiving computer turns on a reassembly timer upon detection of the arrival of the first fragment. This timer, which is set by the network manager, can be used to ensure that all fragments arrive in a timely manner. If the timer times out before all fragments have arrived, the received fragments are discarded. If a user does not want fragmentation to occur, the fragment flag can be turned to 1, which indicates that fragmentation must not occur. This may be desirable if fragmentation creates excessive overhead because the reassembly timer continues to discard fragments which require retransmission from higher-layer protocols. However, this situation must be weighed against the fact that turning on the "don't fragment" flag means that datagrams will be discarded by gateways if the MTU exceeds the size of the subnetwork capability.

Reassembly at the gateways?   Connectionless gateways using dynamic routing (such as IP) do not reassemble datagrams. The task is impossible because all fragments belonging to the original datagram may not be processed by the same gateways. As a consequence, the gateway does not know how to compute the offset values for fragments it does not receive. In contrast, connection-oriented gateways can perform intermediate reassembly because, by the very nature of the system, all PDUs pass through the same gateway(s). For example, imagine in Fig. 5.8 that gateway A is a connection-oriented gateway. It could reassemble the fragments for transmission over a higher-capacity subnetwork by detecting the M = 0 in the fragment with an offset value of 128 and a length of 476 (128 offset values *8 octets per offset + 476 octets in final fragment = 1500 octets).

Retain fragments to await retransmission of other fragments?   Several of this writer's clients have expressed concern about IP discarding fragments based on the expiration of the fragmentation timer. In some instances, this can create a significant amount of replicated traffic on a network. This brief discussion should shed some light on the problem. First, we assume that discarded fragments are retransmitted by a higher-layer protocol (e.g., TCP). The traffic is fragmented (once again) by the originator and sent to the receiver.

The retransmitted fragments would contain the same values in the IP identification field as the original submission. Assuming that the receiver's software does not discard the fragments that were acceptable in the original transmission, one could argue that the identification field could be used to reconstruct a complete data unit by using the fragments of the retransmissions. Of course, this also means that if a pigeon hole is full, the received duplicate fragment would be discarded.

A brief analysis shows that it is not worth the effort. Filling vacant pigeon holes with retransmitted fragments is almost pure chance because some of the retransmitted fragments might undergo different fragmentation operations since the fragments were routed differently the second time. It is especially onerous if the transmitting end must determine which fragments should be transmitted and which should not. Indeed, making IP this smart moves it toward connection-oriented features—which should be avoided.

Also, be aware that the reassembly time-out is based on the remaining value of the TTL field in the IP header. This value does not work very well because the vast majority of TTL values are implemented with a hop-count metric and not a time metric. Therefore, an implementation of the reassembly time-out should be based on an actual clock.

Before leaving the subject of the options in IP, it should prove useful to reexamine the flag copy feature (see Fig. 5.4). A network administrator should determine if the flag copy should be used for certain options. For example, is it useful for all fragments to have the route recording option? After all, if these fragments move through different routes in an internet, the receiver might have difficulty in determining a single list of routes. On the other hand, such a feature still does not preclude examining the routes to determine the efficiency of the internet gateways and IP modules. However, for purposes of simplicity it may make sense (and the IP standard so requires) to stipulate that a route recording option is only used in one of the fragments of a fragmented datagram.

Next, consider when the option should be copied into all fragments. One that comes to mind is source routing. If the user wants source routing to be applied to a datagram, it is logical to assume the user wants it to be applied to all fragments of a fragmented datagram.

IP Address and Routing Tables

Address table

The Internet Activities Board (IAB) has published in RFC 1213 the definition for the IP address table. This table is depicted in Fig. 5.10. It consists of five columns and 1 to n rows. Each row pertains to an IP address at an entity (a host, gateway, etc.). There may be more than one row entry if the machine has more than one IP address. The contents of this table are as follows:

The *Entry Address* contains the IP address for this entry's interface.

The *Entry IfIndex* contains the interface number (port number) pertaining to this entity's connection to a subnetwork.

	Entry Address	Entry If Index	Entry Net Mask	Broadcast Address	Maximum Size of Datagram
Address Entry 1					
Address Entry 2					
Address Entry *n*					

Figure 5.10 The IP Address Table.

The *Entry Net Mask* column contains the subnet mask associated with the IP address in the entry address column.

The *Broadcast Address* contains a value for the least significant bit in the IP broadcast address. It is used for sending datagrams on the local interface and is associated with the IP address of this row.

The *Maximum Size of Datagram* represents the maximum size of a datagram that can be processed by this IP module.

Routing table

Until 1990, an IP routing table was designed based on an individual vendor's perception of the need for the entries in the table. With the publication of the Internet Management Information Base (MIB), a more formal definition of the IP routing table is now available. Figure 5.11 shows the IP routing table as defined in the MIB standard published as RFC 1213.

Each row of the IP routing table contains an entry for each route that is known to the IP module storing this table. The columns represent the information available on each route. A brief description of each column follows.

The *Destination* entry contains the IP address of the destination for this route. If this column is coded as 0.0.0.0, the route is considered a default route.

The *IfIndex* entry stands for the interface index. It identifies the local interface (more commonly known as a physical port) through which the next hop in the route can be reached.

	Destination	If Index	Metric 1	//	Metric 5	Next Hop	Route Type	Routing Protocol	Route Age	Routing Mask	Route Information
Route 1											
Route 2											
Route 3											
Route *n*											

Figure 5.11   The IP Routing Table.

The next five columns are labeled *Metric*. The metric entries contain information about the cost metric used for determining the route. With most systems, the cost metric is the number of hops to reach the destination. However, with the evolution of more sophisticated route discovery protocols (such as OSPF), it is possible that more than one cost metric may be used in calculating the route. As the table indicates, up to five cost metrics can be stored.

The *Next Hop* entry contains the IP address identifying the next hop for this route.

The next column in the table is the *Route Type*. It is set to one of four values to provide the following information: 1 = none of the following, 2 = an invalid route, 3 = a directly connected route (a directly connected subnet), and 4 = indirect (an indirect connection to reach this destination).

The next column is labeled *Routing Protocol*. This entry identifies the route discovery protocol by which this route was learned. If the route is discovered with RIP, the value in this column must be 8; if it is discovered with the Cisco internal group routing protocol, it must be set to 11; and so on.

The *Route Age* column is a value, in seconds, since the route was updated or verified.

The next field in the table contains the *Route Mask* for this route. Remember that this mask is logical ANDed with the destination address in the IP datagram before being compared to column 1 in this table (labeled *Destination*).

The last column, labeled *Route Information,* allows a reference to an MIB definition pertaining to a particular routing protocol. Its value depends on the type of routing protocol used in this row entry.

As an example of a row entry into the IP routing table, please refer back to Chap. 3, Fig. 3.10. This figure shows one of the destination networks as 14.0.0.0. Consequently, from the perspective of the routing table at gateway 9, the column entries for this network are as follows:

Destination = 14.0.0.0

Interface (port) Index = 3

Metric 1 = number of hops (the remaining metric columns are empty)

Next Hop = 13.0.0.2

Route Type = indirect (4)

Routing Protocol = egp (5)

Route Age = 5 seconds (for example)

Route Mask = several options

Route Information = value that depends on routing protocol entry

IP Service Definitions and Primitives

IP/ULP primitives

IP uses two primitives to define the services it provides to the adjacent ULP. The transmitting ULP utilizes the SEND primitive to request the services of IP. In turn, IP uses the DELIVER primitive to notify the destination ULP of the arrival of data. The interface of IP with the upper layer is quite simple, because IP is designed to operate with diverse ULPs.

These service definitions (implemented with primitives) are somewhat abstract to allow them to be tailored to the specific host operating system. For example, the SEND and RECV services on a UNIX-based system can be implemented with UNIX system library calls.

The relationship of IP and the ULP is shown in Fig. 5.12, which depicts host A sending data to host B. The arrows are reversed if host B sends data to host A.

The parameters associated with the primitives inform the ULP and IP about the operation requested from the ULP (SEND) and performed by IP (RECV).

The SEND parameters are also used to create the IP header. Con-

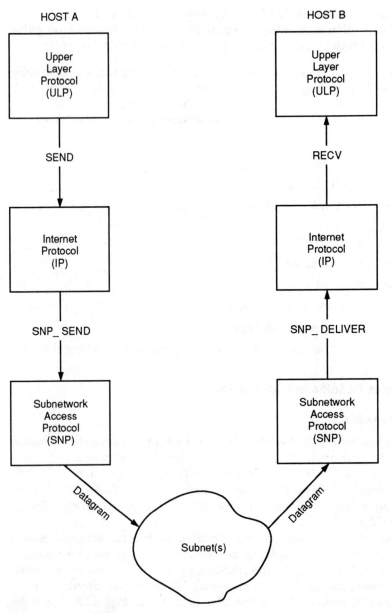

Figure 5.12 The IP Primitives.

sequently, they correlate closely to the IP header fields of a transmitted datagram, shown in Fig. 5.2. Likewise, the parameters in the RECV primitive correlate closely to the parameters of the received datagram. The SEND primitive contains the following information:

Source address: IP address of the host sending the data

Destination address: IP address of host to receive the data

Protocol: Name of the recipient ULP (e.g., TCP, UDP, etc.)

TOS indicators: precedence, reliability, delay, and throughput

Identifier: Optional, for fragmentation control

Don't fragment indicator: Yes or no

Time to live: In number of hops

Data length: Length of data being transmitted (0, if no data)

Buffer pointer: Pointer to the datagram

Option data: Options requested by a ULP (security, loose or strict source routing, record routing, stream identification, or timestamp)

Data: Present when data length is greater than 0

Result: Result of this SEND request:

  Datagram sent

  Error in arguments or network error

The RECV primitive contains the following information:

Source address: IP address of sending host

Destination address: IP address of recipient host

Protocol: Name of the recipient ULP as supplied by the sending ULP (e.g., TCP, UDP, etc.)

TOS indicators: Relative transmission quality associated with unit of data: precedence, reliability, delay, and throughput

Data length: Length of received data

Buffer pointer: Pointer to the datagram

Option data: Options requested by source ULP (security, loose or strict source routing, record routing, stream identification, or timestamp)

Data: Present when data length is greater than 0

Result: Result of this RECV request

IP/SNP primitives

The primitives between IP and the subnetwork access protocol (SNAP) are similar to the IP/ULP primitives. As shown in Fig. 5.12, two primitives are invoked for the IP/SNP operations. The SNP_SEND primitive is used by IP to invoke a service of the SNP; the SND_DELIVER is used by the SNP to deliver a datagram to the IP module. The SNP_SEND primitive contains the following information:

Local destination address: Subnetwork address of the destination

TOS indicators: precedence, reliability, delay, and throughput

Length of datagram

The datagram

The SNP_DELIVER primitive contains the datagram and error indicators (the latter is optional and not defined in the standard).

Other IP/SNP service definitions.   Many IP modules rest on top of IEEE LANs and interface with IEEE 802.2 (logical link control, LLC). Chapter 3 (Fig. 3.5) explains the method by which LLC and IP use the LSAP header extension to coordinate their operations. However, as of this writing, no RFC exists to explain the relationship of the IEEE 802.2 LLC primitives and IP. The next section provides this explanation.

Network layer/LLC primitives

The IP/SNP primitives explained in the previous section are not designed for the LLC interface. However, if an implementation only makes use of LLC connectionless data transfer service, the interface is simple. A brief explanation of this service follows (see Fig. 5.13).

Two primitives are used for connectionless data transfer. They are passed between LLC and its upper layer protocol (which could be IP or some other module).

DL-UNITDATA.request (source-address, destination-address, data, priority)

DL-UNITDATA.indication (source-address, destination-address, data, priority)

The request primitive is passed from the network layer to LLC to request that a link service data unit (LSDU) be sent to a remote link service access point. The address parameters are equivalent to a combination of the LLC SAP and MAC addresses. The priority field is passed to MAC and implemented (except for 802.3, which has no priority mecha-

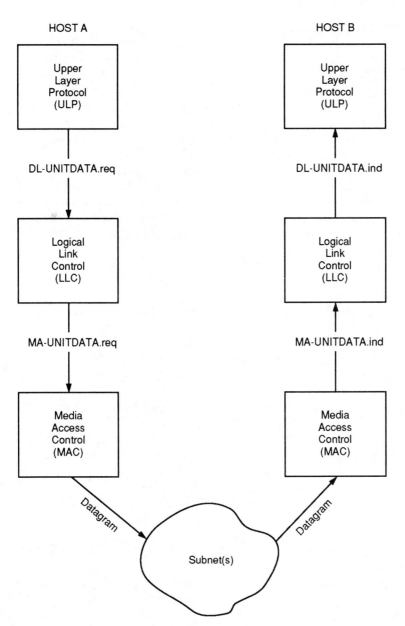

Figure 5.13 IP Over LLC in an IEEE LAN.

nism). The indication primitive is passed from LLC to the network layer to indicate the arrival of an LSDU from a remote entity.

A comparison of Figs. 5.12 and 5.13 reveals close similarities between IP/SNP and ULP/LLC operations, but differences exist in the parameters associated with the IP/SNP and ULP/LLC primitives.

If IP is placed on top of LLC, a convergence protocol must be implemented to map the SNP_SEND primitive and its parameters to the DL-UNITDATA.request and its parameters. The protocol must also map the SNP_DELIVER primitive and its parameters to the LLC DL-UNITDATA.indication and its parameters. The address fields present no major problem if RFC 1042 is followed (see Chap. 2, "Extension of LSAP Header"). A potential problem is deciding how to handle the TOS parameters. Perhaps the best approach is to ignore them at the LLC and MAC levels, since they are mostly irrelevant for use in a high-capacity LAN.

Multicasting

Like the physical layer, the internet network layer allows the use of multicasting PDUs. The concept is quite similar to LAN multicasting, in which a single PDU (in this case an IP datagram) is sent to more than one host. The set of hosts forms a *multicast group*.

IP multicasting allows hosts to operate on one or multiple physical networks. A host may belong to more than one multicast group, it may belong to a permanent multicast group (a *well-known* group), or it may dynamically enter and leave groups as the need dictates. Also, a host does not have to be a member of the multicast group to send data to the group.

Multicasting is accomplished through the use of the IP class D address discussed in Chap. 3. The first 4 bits of the 32-bit address field are set to 1110; the next 28 bits identify the specific multicast group. Due to the structure of the address space the classes of A, B, and C addresses are meaningless when using multicasting.

The permissible ranges for multicast addresses are from 224.0.0.0 through 239.255.255.255. The Internet does not allow the address space of 224.0.0.0 to be used, and the address space of 224.0.0.1 is reserved for an *all hosts* group. An all hosts group identifies all hosts and gateways that are participating in an internet IP multicast operation.

Figure 5.14 shows an example of how IP multicasting operates. Gateway 1 (G1) receives an IP datagram from another part of an internet. The destination IP address is a multicast address (a source address is not allowed to contain multicast values, for obvious reasons). The gateway is responsible for interpreting the multicast address and forwarding it to the proper hosts (for which it has authority)

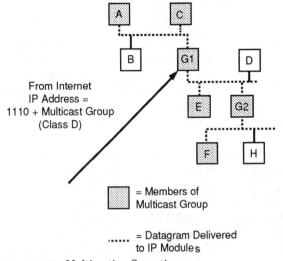

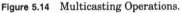

Figure 5.14   Multicasting Operations.

and to other participating multicast gateways (G2). In this example, hosts A, C, and E are members of the same multicast group. G2 and host F are also members.

One approach to sending this traffic to the proper host on a LAN is to map the IP multicast address to an Ethernet multicast address. The mapping is quite simple and proceeds as follows: The low-order 23 bits of the IP address are mapped into the low-order 23 bits of the Ethernet multicast address. This approach is not perfect because a one-to-one relationship does not exist between the 28 bits of the IP address and the 23 bits of the Ethernet address. However, it is a reasonable solution because the chances are quite small that any two groups will choose the same 23 bits for the multicast address value. In any event, it is prudent to make certain that the receiving software has the ability to discard datagrams that are not appropriate.

Hosts can be configured to either send or receive multicast datagrams. Alternately, hosts can be configured to send but not receive multicast datagrams or not to participate in any multicast operations.

The implementation of multicasting must ensure that the software is capable of allowing a host to join or leave a multicast group. A means must be devised to allow hosts to inform other hosts about the relationships and status of memberships. The IP software must keep bookkeeping operations about which host belongs to separate multicast groups and delete and add them accordingly. These administrative tasks are accomplished through the Internet Group Management Protocol (IGMP), which is discussed in the next section.

Internet Group Management Protocol (IGMP)

The IGMP allows gateways and hosts to inform each other about multicasting operations, such as joining and leaving multicast groups. Additionally, it allows the machines to communicate status messages about multicasting information. IGMP works in a manner quite similar to the Internet Control Message Protocol (ICMP). An IP datagram is used to transport the IGMP message between the machines. Be aware that IGMP is required for all machines that are going to implement IP multicasting.

IGMP also has some similarities to a LAN token bus protocol in how a machine is added as a member to a group. First, when a host wishes to join a multicast group, it must send out a message (just as, in a token bus, a LAN station sends out a set solicitor message). This message is an all-host multicast address in which the host establishes that it is a member of a multicast group. The IGMP message is received by the local multicast gateway that performs the necessary operations to route the traffic to other multicast gateways throughout an internet.

Once these operations have been performed, the multicast gateway must periodically query the host to determine if a host is still a member of a group. If the query does not get a response from the host, then the multicast gateway is required to stop advertising membership for that host to other multicast gateways.

The format for the IGMP message is quite simple and is illustrated in Fig. 5.15. The message consists of five fields.

The *version* field gives the current protocol version, which at this time is 1.

The *type* field identifies the field as a query with a value of 1 or a response with a value of 2.

Logically enough, the *unused* field is not used.

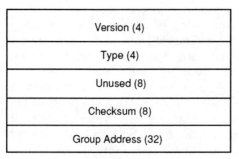

| Version (4) |
| Type (4) |
| Unused (8) |
| Checksum (8) |
| Group Address (32) |

(*n*) = number of bits in the field

Figure 5.15 The IGMP Message Format.

The *checksum* field is used to check for errors. The calculation uses the same algorithm as the IP and TCP protocols.

The *group address* field contains the group address for hosts to report their membership in the multicast group. This field has no meaning for a query message.

Other Thoughts on IP

The reader may be surprised at the brevity of the discussion of IP. We are not shirking our responsibility in the analysis; rather, we are merely reflecting the fact that IP does not contain a great number of functions. Indeed, one of the attractive aspects of IP is its simplicity and efficiency. However, as the reader may surmise, the supporting protocols to IP, such as TCP, and the addressing resolution and naming service protocols, discussed in earlier chapters, provide for a complex and rich internetworking environment.

It has been stated in earlier chapters that IP is one of the most widely used internetworking protocols in the world. Today, hundreds of products are available in the marketplace that use the IP architecture. Nonetheless, the use of IP will diminish gradually as users and vendors move to the ISO 8473 internetworking protocol.

The end user will most likely never know that the change has taken place if the implementation is well conceived. The network designer will see a similarity between the two protocols, but they are different enough that software must be written almost from scratch.

The next section introduces the ISO 8473 connectionless network protocol (CLNP).

Connectionless-Mode Network Service (ISO 8473)

ISO 8473 is a specification that describes the architecture for connectionless-mode network service. It is also called the connectionless network protocol (CLNP). It is quite similar to IP in the functions it performs, but it is not compatible with IP.

ISO 8473 has been designed to operate with the hosts attached to public and private networks and the gateways that service the hosts and networks. As will be seen, the protocol does not involve itself with the particular characteristics of the underlying subnetworks. Like IP, the basic idea is to demand little in the way of services from the subnetworks except to transport the PDU.

The protocol communicates by exchanging internetwork PDUs (IPDUs) in a connectionless (datagram) fashion. Each IPDU is treated independently and does not depend on the state of the network for any particular establishment connection time (since no connection exists in a connectionless network). Routing decisions are made independently by each forwarding internetworking node. It is also possible for the source user to determine the routing by placing the routing information in the IPDU source routing field.

The ISO 8473 connectionless-mode network service is provided by two primitives: N-UNITDATA.request and N-UNITDATA.indication. These two primitives are quite similar to the primitives used by the IP. The reader should note that the protocol uses no connection and clear primitives, which is a rather obvious indication of its connectionless attributes. The two primitives each contain four parameters: NS-Source-Address, NS-Destination-Address, NS-Quality-of-Service, and NS-Userdata. All parameters are explained shortly.

The ISO 8473 PDU

A brief description of the fields of the 8473 PDU is provided in Table 5.4. As the reader reviews this material, the similarity to the IP datagram will be evident. Figure 5.16 shows the format of the data unit. The next sections discuss how the fields are used in 8473 operations.

Quality of service (QOS) functions

An underlying subnetwork may provide several quality of service (QOS) functions. The services are negotiated when the primitives are exchanged between layers. Of course, the primitive parameters must be based on *a priori* knowledge of the availability of the services within the subnetwork. It does little good to ask for a QOS feature if it is known that the subnetwork does not provide it. Be aware that the values of QOS apply to both ends of the network connections (NC), even though the NC may span several subnetworks that offer different services.

Use of ISO 8348. For QOS choices, ISO 8473 uses the following QOS functions described in ISO 8348:

Transit delay: Establishment of the elapsed time between a data request and the corresponding data indication. This QOS feature applies only to successful PDU transfers. The delay is specified by a desired value up to the maximum acceptable value. All values assume a PDU of 128 octets. User-initiated flow control are not measured in these values.

Residual error rate (RER): The ratio of total incorrect, lost, or duplicated PDUs to total PDUs transferred:

TABLE 5.4   Functions of Fields in 8473 PDU

Protocol identifier	Identifies the protocol as ISO 8473.
Length indicator	Describes the length of the header.
Version/protocol	Identifies the version of ISO 8473.
Lifetime	Represents the lifetime of the PDU. It is coded in units of 500 ms.
Segmentation permitted	Indicates if segmentation is permitted. The originator of the PDU determines this value, and it cannot be changed by any other entity.
More segments	Indicates if more user data is forthcoming. It is used when segmentation takes place. When the bit equals 0, it indicates that the last octet of the data in this PDU is the last octet of the user data stream (the network service data unit, NSDU).
Error report	Indicates that an error report is to be generated back to the originator if a data PDU is discarded.
Type code	Describes the PDU as a data PDU or an error PDU.
PDU segment length	Specifies the entire length of the PDU (header and data). If no segmentation occurs, the value of this field is identical to the value of the total length field.
Checksum	Calculated on the entire PDU header. A value of 0 in this field indicates that the header is to be ignored. A PDU is discarded if the checksum fails.
Destination and source addresses and address lengths	Since the source and destination addresses are variable in length, the length fields are used to describe their length. The actual addresses are Network Service Access Points (NSAPs).
Data unit identifier	Identifies an initial PDU to reassemble a segmented data unit correctly.
Segmentation offset	If the original PDU is segmented, this field specifies the relative position of this segment in relation to the initial PDU.
Total PDU length	Contains the entire length of the original PDU, which includes both the header and data. It is not changed for the lifetime of the PDU.
Options	Optional parameters are placed in this part of the PDU such as route recording, quality of service parameters, priorities, buffer congestion indication, padding characters, and designation of security levels.
Data	Contains the user data.

Protocol Identifier
Length Indicator
Version/Protocol ID Extension
Lifetime
Segment/More/Error Report/Type Code
Segment Length
Checksum
Destination Address Length
Destination Address
Source Address Length
Source Address
Data Unit Identifier
Segmentation Offset
Total PDU Length
Options
Data

Figure 5.16   The ISO 8473 PDU.

$$RER = \frac{N(e) + N(1) - N(x)}{N}$$

where RER = residual error rate; N(e) = PDUs in error; N(1) = lost PDUs; N(x) = duplicate PDUs; N = number of PDUs.

Cost determinants: A parameter to define the maximum acceptable cost for a network service. It may be stated in relative or absolute terms. Final actions on this parameter are left to the specific network provider.

Priority: Used to determine preferential service in the subnetwork. Outgoing transmission queues and buffers are managed based on the priority values contained in the PDU header options field.

Protection against unauthorized access: Used to direct the subnetwork to prevent unauthorized access to user data.

Protocol functions

ISO 8473 includes several optional or required protocol functions. Each function provides a specialized service to the network user. In a sense, the ISO 8473 protocol functions are similar to the QOS features, except that they are performed as an integral part of the protocol.

Traffic management between subnetworks

This section provides an illustration of how a connectionless-mode internetwork protocol transfers data between subnetworks. While different vendors use various techniques for the provision of connectionless service, many use the concepts described herein.

When the protocol receives the NS-Source-Address and NS-Destination-Address parameters in the N-UNITDATA.request primitive from an upper layer, it uses them to build a source address and destination address in the header of the PDU. The source address and NS-Quality-of-Service parameters are used to determine which optional functions are to be selected for the network user. At this time, a data unit identifier is assigned to identify this request from other requests. This identifier must remain unique for the lifetime of the initial PDU and any segmented PDUs in the network(s). Subsequent and/or derived PDUs are considered to correspond to the initial PDU if they have the same source address, destination address, and data unit identifier. At first glance, this rule may appear to be connection oriented, but it applies only to PDUs created as a result of segmentation.

The PDU is then forwarded through the subnetwork(s). Each hop examines the destination address to determine if the PDU has reached its destination. If the destination address equals an NSAP (network service access point) served by the network entity, it has reached its destination. Otherwise, it must be forwarded to the next node.

When the PDU reaches its destination, the receiver removes the protocol control information (PCI) from the PDU. It also uses the addresses in the header to generate the NS-Source-Address and NS-Destination-Address parameters of the UNITDATA indication primitive. It preserves the data field of the PDU until all segments (if any) have been received. The options part of the PDU header is used to invoke any QOS parameters at the receiving end.

Unlike connection-oriented networks, an ISO 8473 connectionless-mode network has more flexibility in terminating service to a user. For example, if a new network connection request is received with a higher priority than an ongoing data transfer, the network may release the lower-priority transfer. Moreover, users may also have priorities established for the data transfers. The network connections (NC) with a higher priority will have their requests serviced first, and the remaining resources of the network are used to attempt to satisfy the lower-priority network connections.

User data is given a specific *lifetime* in the network(s). This mechanism is useful for several reasons. First, it prevents lost or misdirected data from accumulating and consuming network resources. Second, it gives the transmitting entity some control over the disposition of aged data units. Third, it greatly simplifies congestion control, flow control, and accountability logic in the network(s). (It should be emphasized that discarded data units can be recovered by the transport layer.)

The lifetime field in the PDU header is set by the originating network entity. The value also applies to any segmented PDUs and is copied into the header of these data units. The value contains, at any time, the remaining lifetime of the PDU. It is decremented by each network entity that processes it. The value is represented in units of 500 ms and is decremented by one unit by each entity. In the event that delays exceed 500 ms, the value is decremented by more than one unit.

If the lifetime value reaches zero before it reaches its destination, it is discarded. If the error report bit is on, an error report data unit is generated to inform the originator of the lost data. This feature may be considered by some to be a connection-oriented service. Whatever its name, it is obviously very useful if end-to-end accountability is required.

In addition to discarding aged data units, the network may also discard data for other reasons:

Checksum reveals an error (if checksum is used).

PDU is received which contains an unsupported function, such as a QOS function.

Local congestion occurs at the receiver.

Header cannot be interpreted accurately.

A PDU cannot be segmented, and it is too large for the underlying network to handle.

The destination address is not reachable or a path route is not acceptable to the network serving the PDU.

The PDU is transferred on a hop-to-hop (next node) basis. The selection of the next system in the route may be influenced by the QOS parameters and other optional parameters. For example, the next hop might be chosen because it supports the QOS requests.

Internetwork routing. The routing technique in ISO 8473 is called source routing and is quite similar to IP source routing. The route is determined by the originator of the PDU by placing a list of the intermediate routes in the options part of the PDU header. The route indicators are called *titles.* The relaying is accomplished by each network entity routing the PDU to the next title in the list. The indicator is updated by each relay point to identify the next stage of the route.

The protocol provides two types of routing: complete source routing and partial source routing. *Complete source routing* requires that the specified route be used in the exact order as in the route list. If this route cannot be taken, the PDU must be discarded with the option of returning an error report to the originator. *Partial source routing* allows a system to route to intermediate systems that are not specified in the list.

Another routing option, called the *record route function,* requires the intermediate systems to add their title to a record route list in the options field of the header. The list is built as the PDU is forwarded to its destination. This list can be used for troubleshooting internet or subnet problems. It can also be used as a tool for efficiency analysis, audit trails, or simply as a "directory" for a returning PDU.

If this option is invoked, either complete route recording or partial route recording is used. With the former, all intermediate systems are recorded and PDU reassembly is performed only if all derived PDUs took the same route. Otherwise, the PDU is discarded. The partial route recording also requires the full list but does not require that the derived PDUs visit the same intermediate systems.

CLNP and IP

The ISO 8473 standard was derived from the IP. From the standpoint of design, the routing should remain the same when an organization migrates to ISO 8473. The network topology should not be affected by the transition to ISO 8473. So the good news is that the two protocols are similar, and the bad news is that the conversion will still require rewriting a lot of software.

Summary

The IP is a widely used gateway protocol. It is implemented on both LANs and WANs and is designed to operate in a connectionless mode. Notwithstanding, it supports a number of quality service options called type of service (TOS). IP remains transparent to the underlying network. Consequently, it can be placed on a variety of networks. IP does not perform route discovery. It uses routing tables created by route discovery protocols.

Chapter 6

Internet Control Message Protocol (ICMP)

Introduction

The Internet Protocol is a connectionless-mode protocol, and as such, it has no error-reporting or error-correcting mechanisms. It relies on a module called the internet control message protocol (ICMP) to (a) report errors in the processing of a datagram, and (b) provide for some administrative and status messages. This chapter examines the major features of ICMP and provides guidance on its effective use.

ICMP resides in a host computer or a gateway as a companion to the IP (see Chap. 1, Fig. 1.7). As illustrated in Fig. 6.1, the ICMP is used between hosts or gateways for a number of reasons, such as (1) when datagrams cannot be delivered, (2) when a gateway directs traffic on shorter routes, or (3) when a gateway does not have sufficient buffering capacity to hold and forward protocol data units.

The ICMP will notify the host if a destination is unreachable. ICMP is also responsible for managing or creating a time-exceeded message in the event that the lifetime of the datagram expires. ICMP also performs certain editing functions to determine if the IP header is in error or otherwise unintelligible.

Certain implementations of TCP/IP have been rather "loose" in the returning of ICMP datagrams upon detection of an error. We will discuss several instances when ICMP error messages should be used prudently. There are some instances when they should not be used at all. The reader should check the product being used in the installation to make certain that ICMP datagrams are generated for errors and are generated logically. For example, there is a phenomenon in this protocol suite nicknamed the "black hole disease." Datagrams are sent out but nothing is returned, not even any ICMP

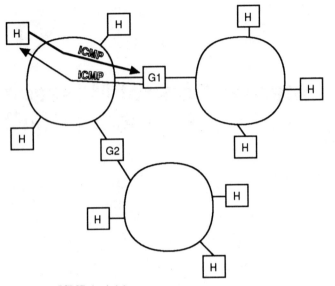

Figure 6.1 ICMP Activities.

errors. This happenstance implementation of ICMP makes trouble-shooting very difficult.

Some important aspects of ICMP should be emphasized:

- ICMP is a user of IP. IP encapsulates the ICMP data unit into IP datagrams for transport across an internet.

- IP must use ICMP.

- ICMP does not make IP reliable. Its function is to report errors. Therefore, even with the use of ICMP, datagrams may still be lost or delivered out of sequence. Reliability is the responsibility of a higher-layer protocol such as TCP or an application layer protocol.

- ICMP reports errors on IP datagrams, but it does not report errors on ICMP data units. To do so would create a Catch-22 situation wherein infinite repetitions could occur in error reporting.

- If IP is using fragmented datagrams, ICMP will report an error only on the first received fragment of the datagram.

- ICMP is not required to report errors on datagram problems. However, in actual situations, gateways generally create ICMP error messages. Reporting is less certain with regard to a host computer generating ICMP messages; the reader should check for individual variations in the vendor's product line.

ICMP Message Format

The ICMP message format is shown in Fig. 6.2. ICMP messages are carried in the user portion of the IP datagram. The protocol field in the IP header is set to 1 to signify the use of ICMP. All ICMP messages contain three fields: (a) the type field to define the type of message, (b) the code field to describe the type of error or status information, and (c) a checksum field for computing a 16-bit one's complement on the ICMP message. The ICMP error-reporting message also carries the internet header and the first 64 bits of the user data field. These bits are useful for troubleshooting and problem analysis.

ICMP Error- and Status-Reporting Procedures

The error-reporting and status-reporting services as reported by ICMP are listed below. They are explained further in the following material, and Fig. 6.3 provides an illustration of the major services.

Time exceeded on datagram lifetime

Parameter unintelligible

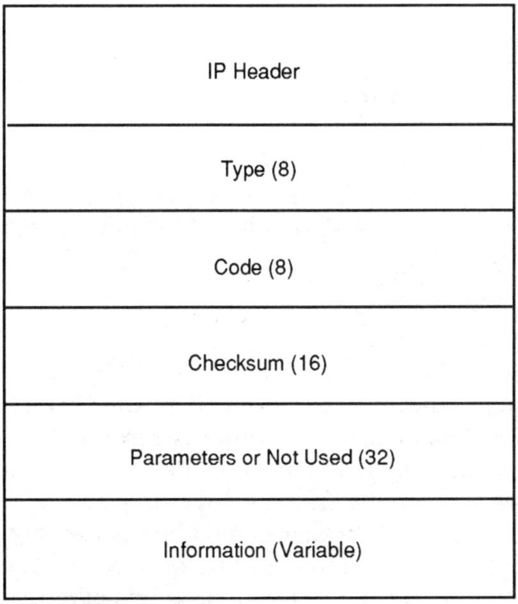

(*n*) = Number of bits in the field

Figure 6.2   The ICMP Message Format.

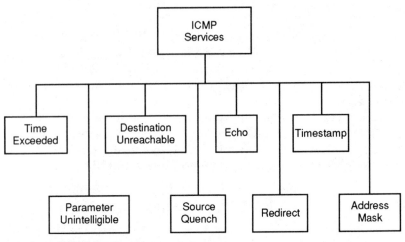

Figure 6.3 ICMP Services.

Destination unreachable (for a variety of reasons)

Source quench for flow control

Echo and echo reply

Redirect

Timestamp and timestamp reply

Information request or information reply

Address mask request and reply

As stated earlier, the type code is used to identify the type of message and the format of the ICMP protocol data unit. This field is coded as shown in Table 6.1.

Time exceeded

This service is executed by a gateway in the event that the time-to-live field in the IP datagram has expired (its value is zero) and the gateway has discarded the datagram. This service is also invoked if a timer expires during the reassembly of a fragmented datagram.

The ICMP message consists of the IP header and 64 bits of the original data in the first fragments (if fragmentation is used) of the datagram. The ICMP code field is set to (a) 0 = time to live exceeded in transit, and (b) 1 = fragment assembly time exceeded. Code 0 may be generated by the gateway; code 1 may be generated by the host.

TABLE 6.1   ICMP Type Codes

Type code value	Type of ICMP message
0	Echo reply
3	Destination unreachable
4	Source quench
5	Redirect
8	Echo request
11	Time exceeded
12	Parameter unintelligible
13	Timestamp request
14	Timestamp reply
15	Information request
16	Information reply
17	Address mask request
18	Address mask reply

Parameter unintelligible

The destination host or gateway can invoke this service if it encounters problems processing any part of an IP header. Typically, this occurs if a field is unintelligible and it cannot process the datagram.

The ICMP message contains a pointer field whose value points to the byte in the original datagram header that created the problem. In addition, the ICMP data unit carries the IP header and the first 64 bits of the problem datagram. The code field is set to 0 if the pointer is used. If the code field is set to 1, it indicates a problem with the IP service options.

Destination unreachable

This service is used by a gateway or the destination host. It is invoked if a gateway encounters problems reaching the destination network specified in the IP destination address. It can also be used by a destination host if an identified higher-level protocol is not available on the host or if a specified port is not available (inactive).

The ICMP message contains the IP header and the first 64 bits of the problem datagram. The code field of the ICMP header is coded as follows:

0 = Network unreachable

1 = Host unreachable

2 = Protocol unavailable

3 = Port unavailable

4 = Fragmentation needed

5 = Source route has failed

The gateway may send codes 0, 1, 4, and 5; codes 2 and 3 may be sent from the host.

Source quench

This service is a primitive form of flow and congestion control invoked by a gateway and is invoked if the machine has insufficient buffer space for queuing incoming datagrams. If the datagram is discarded, the gateway may send this message to the host that originated the datagram. It performs the same function as the receive not ready (RNR) format in many other protocols. The destination host can use the source quench message service if datagrams are arriving too fast for processing.

In actual operations, this service acts as a notification to the transmitting host to reduce the number of datagrams it is transmitting to the destination host. Therefore, this service acts as a flow control for the internet.

A gateway has the option of sending the source quench message for every datagram it discards. Upon receiving this message, the source host is required to reduce the datagram traffic. ICMP has no message to reinstate transmission. Flow control is reinitiated when the transmitting host no longer receives any source quench messages. Typically, this means the host can increase traffic (perhaps gradually) until it is running at a full transmit rate or until it receives another source quench message.

It is prudent to issue a flow-control signal before a machine's capacity is exceeded. Consequently, the source quench message may be issued when the machine's capacity is being approached. If this approach is used, the datagram that initiates the flow-control message may be delivered.

The ICMP data unit contains the relevant type value of 4. The code is set to 0 and, as with other ICMP error messages, the internet header and 64 bits of the problem datagram reside within the unit.

Echo request and reply

The echo request and reply is a valuable tool for determining the state of an internet. It can be sent to any IP address, such as a gateway. The gateway must return a reply to the originator. In this manner a network administrator can find out about the state of the network resources, because a reply is only sent in response to a request. If a problem exists, a reply is not returned.

This service can also be used to determine if another host is active and available in the network. To initiate the service, a sender host sends the ICMP data unit with the address of the destination host and the IP address field. If the queried host is indeed active, it returns an echo reply to the querying host.

This service is named PING in some systems. It uses the ICMP echo and echo reply but embellishes the basic operation with additional features, such as the interval between requests and the number of times to send the request. For example, the IBM version of PING can perform the following services:

PING LOOPBACK: Verifies the operation of TCP/IP software

PING my-IP-address: Verifies whether the network resource can be addressed

PING a-remote-IP-address: Verifies whether the network can be accessed

PING a-remote-host-name: Verifies the operation of the name server or name resolver

The ICMP message type field is used to identify the following: a = echo message and 0 = echo reply message.

Redirect

This service is invoked by a gateway; it sends the ICMP message to the source host. It is used to provide routing management information to the host. The redirect message indicates that a better route is available. Typically, this means the host should send its traffic to another gateway. Under most circumstances, the gateway generates a redirect message if its routing table indicates that the next hop, either the host or gateway, is on the same network as the network contained in the source address of the IP header.

The reader might wonder why a host would not know an optimum route to a destination. In many installations, the host IP tables are created initially with very little routing information. This simplifies the process of system generation at the host for the TCP/IP software and supporting tables. In the simplest form, a host routing table may begin with only an entry to one gateway. The table is then updated by gateways as gateways discover paths through the internet. Consequently, assuming that a host might not know a route, the redirect message can be sent from the gateway to the host informing it of a better choice.

Even though there is a better route to the final destination, the redirect message will not be sent if the IP datagram is using the source route option.

The code field is coded to convey the following information:

0 = Redirect datagrams for the network

1 = Redirect datagrams for the host

2 = Redirect datagrams for the type of service and network

3 = Redirect datagrams for the type of service and host

A host computer should not be allowed to send an ICMP redirect because the gateway should be tasked with this job; a host should only be tasked with updating its routing table according to receiving the redirect. Additionally, the rationale is to keep, insofar as possible, host machines out of the routing business.

Timestamp and timestamp reply

This service is used by gateways and hosts to determine the delay incurred in delivering traffic through a network or networks. The ICMP data unit contains three timestamp values:

Originate timestamp: Time the sender last processed the message before sending it (filled in immediately before sending).

Receive timestamp: Time the echoer first processed the message upon receiving it (filled in immediately upon receiving message).

Transmit timestamp: Time the echo last processed the message before sending it (filled in immediately before reply is sent).

RFC 792 requires that the timestamp values be in the number of milliseconds elapsed since midnight universal time (UT). If the time is not available in milliseconds or it cannot be provided with respect to midnight UT, then any time may be inserted in the timestamp values provided that the high-order bit of the timestamp is set to indicate that the timestamp values are nonstandard.

At first glance it might appear that the timestamp service provides a simple yet accurate method of synchronizing clocks between machines. On a general basis this is indeed the case, especially if the machines are on a point-to-point connection without any intervening network between them. Because point-to-point lines have nonvarying transit delays (with rare exceptions), the three timestamps can be used to coordinate the clocks between the two machines with acceptable accuracy. However, even in this simple situation, problems can arise. For example, the message must be timestamped immediately upon transmission for the originate timestamp, immediately upon reception for the receive timestamp, and immediately upon transmission for the transmit timestamp in order to achieve accurate clocking. If delays occur at the machines because of buffering or computation problems, then variation is built into the clocking coordination.

When intervening networks are involved, the timestamp and timestamp reply fields might be significantly inaccurate because of the variable delay experienced through the internet subnetworks. The best approach is to use some form of smoothing with statistical analysis to obtain some general idea of the clocks between the machines.

On a more realistic basis, the timestamp and timestamp reply are better utilized to ascertain delay through an internet. In this regard, the three timestamps can be used as a valuable tool to perform diagnostics of the performance of the internet resources.

Information request or information reply

This service enables a host to determine the identification of the network to which it is attached. A host sends the ICMP message with the IP header source and destination address fields coded as 0, which is used to convey "this network." A replying IP module (one designated as a server that is authorized to perform this task) will return the reply with the address fully specified in both the source and destination address fields of the IP header.

This service works like the reverse address resolution protocol (RARP), which enables a host to obtain its own IP address. It is not used much and has been replaced by RARP and BOOTP.

Address mask request and reply

This service is used by a host to obtain a subnet mask used on the host's network. (See Chap. 3 for a discussion on subnets and masks.) The requesting host can send the request directly to an IP gateway or may broadcast it.

While the address masked request and reply operations are quite useful, they must be approached with some forethought. At a minimum, an address mask reply should not be sent by any computer unless it is considered to be the authoritative originator for the address mask. The host should be designated as "an address mask agent." This approach will solve many problems in using this feature of ICMP, especially if the vendor has considered how to format and reply to the IP address mask field.

Other Thoughts on ICMP

Some implementations of ICMP have resulted in the proliferation of unnecessary status or error messages. The key in using protocols as flexible as the TCP/IP suite is to accept almost anything and send out almost nothing. Some ICMP messages that should not be sent are messages that pertain to broadcast and multicast addresses. Sending error messages on this type of traffic has a tendency to create broadcast storms on the network. As stated before, ICMP should not report on itself.

Additionally, ICMP messages should be cautiously sent on user datagram protocols (UDPs) traffic. Although we have not yet discussed UDPs, keep in mind that sending error messages relating to unidentified UDP ports could create some significant problems with the use of the ICMP destination unreachable report. This can occur in computers that have not established a client for the destination port identifier in the UDP segment.

Summary

ICMP is used by an internet to provide error, status, and administrative messages between gateways and hosts. The protocol relies on IP to deliver its messages, even though ICMP reports on some of the IP operations. ICMP is often used as a diagnostic tool because of its echo, timestamp, parameters unintelligible, and destination unreachable features. It must be implemented as part of the IP operations.

Transmission Control Protocol (TCP) and User Datagram Protocol (UDP)

Introduction

This chapter examines a widely used transport layer protocol known as the Transmission Control Protocol (TCP). As discussed earlier in this book, TCP was developed for use in ARPANET, but it is now used throughout the world and is found in many commercial networks as well as networks in research centers and universities. It has several similarities to the OSI transport protocol, and many of its features were incorporated into OSI's Transport Protocol Class 4 (TP4).

This chapter also examines the User Datagram Protocol (UDP), which is used in place of TCP in a number of applications.

Value of the Transport Layer

In previous chapters we emphasized that the Internet Protocol (IP) is not designed to recover from certain problems, nor does it guarantee the delivery of traffic. IP is designed to discard datagrams that are outdated or have exceeded the number of permissible transit hops in an internet.

Certain user applications require assurance that all datagrams have been delivered safely to the destination. Furthermore, the transmitting user may need to know that the traffic has been delivered at the receiving host. The mechanisms to achieve these important services reside in TCP (UDP is connectionless and does not provide these services).

The job of TCP may be quite complex. It must be able to satisfy a wide range of applications requirements and, equally important, it must be able to accommodate to a dynamic environment within an internet. It must establish and manage sessions (logical associations) between its local users and these users' remote communicating partners. This means that TCP must maintain an awareness of the user's activities to support the user's data transfer through the internet. These topics are covered in more detail in this chapter.

TCP Overview

As depicted in Fig. 1.7 (in Chap. 1) and Fig. 7.1, TCP resides in the transport layer of the conventional seven-layer model. It is situated above IP and below the upper layers. Figure 7.1 also illustrates that TCP is not loaded into the gateway. It is designed to reside in the host computer or in a machine that is tasked with end-to-end integrity of the transfer of user data. In practice, TCP is usually placed in the user host machine.

Figure 7.1 also shows that TCP is designed to run over the IP. Since IP is a connectionless network, the tasks of reliability, flow control, sequencing, opens, and closes are given to TCP. Although TCP and IP

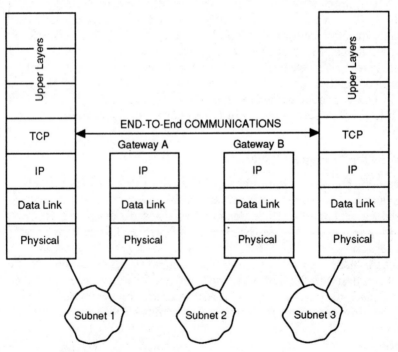

Figure 7.1 Relationship of Transport Layer to Other Layers.

are tied together so closely that they are used in the same context "TCP/IP," TCP can also support other protocols. For example, another connectionless protocol, such as the ISO 8473 (Connectionless Network Protocol, or CLNP), could operate with TCP (with adjustments to the interface between the modules). In addition, the application protocols, such as the File Transfer Protocol (FTP) and the Simple Mail Transfer Protocol (SMTP), rely on many of the services of TCP.

Many of the TCP functions (such as flow control, reliability, and sequencing) could be handled within an application program. But it makes little sense to code these functions into each application. Moreover, applications programmers are usually not versed in error-detection and flow-control operations. The preferred approach is to develop generalized software that provides community functions applicable to a wide range of applications, and then invoke these programs from the application software. This allows the application programmer to concentrate on solving the application problem and it isolates the programmer from the nuances and problems of networks.

Major Features of TCP

TCP provides the following services to the upper layers. This section introduces each of the services, and later sections in the book examine them in more detail.

Connection-oriented data management

Reliable data transfer

Stream-oriented data transfer

Push functions

Resequencing

Flow control (sliding windows)

Multiplexing

Full duplex transmission

Precedence and security

Graceful close

TCP is a *connection-oriented protocol*. This term refers to the fact that TCP maintains status and state information about each user data stream flowing into and out of the TCP module. The term used in this context also means that TCP is responsible for the end-to-end transfer of data across one network or multiple networks to a receiving user application (or the next upper layer protocol). Referring to Fig. 7.1,

TCP must ensure that the data are transmitted and received between the two hosts across three networks (Subnet 1, Subnet 2, and Subnet 3).

Since TCP is a connection-oriented protocol, it is responsible for the *reliable transfer* of each of the characters passed to it from an upper layer (characters are also called bytes or octets). Consequently, it uses sequence numbers and positive/negative acknowledgments. The term associated with these aspects of a connection-oriented protocol is a *virtual circuit*.

A sequence number is assigned to each octet transmitted. The receiving TCP module uses a checksum routine to check the data for damage that may have occurred during the transmission process. If the data are acceptable, TCP returns a positive acknowledgment (ACK) to the sending TCP module. If the data are damaged, the receiving TCP discards the data and uses a sequence number to inform the sending TCP about the problem. Like many other connection-oriented protocols, TCP uses timers to ensure that the lapse of time is not excessive before remedial measures are taken for either the transmission of acknowledgments from the receiving site and/or the retransmission of data at the transmitting site.

TCP receives the data from an upper layer protocol (ULP) in a *stream-oriented* fashion. This operation is in contrast to many protocols in the industry. Stream-oriented protocols are designed to send individual characters and *not* blocks, frames, datagrams, etc. The bytes are sent from an ULP on a stream basis, byte by byte. When they arrive at the TCP layer, the bytes are grouped into TCP *segments*. These segments are then passed to the IP (or another lower layer protocol) for transmission to the next destination. The length of the segments is determined by TCP, although a system implementor can also determine how TCP makes this decision.

Implementors of TCP who have worked with block-oriented systems, such as IBM operating systems, may have to make some adjustments in their thinking regarding TCP performance. TCP allows the use of variable-length segments because of its stream-oriented nature. Therefore, applications that normally work with fixed blocks of data (such as a personnel application that sends fixed employee blocks or a payroll application that transmits fixed payroll blocks) cannot rely on TCP to present this fixed block at the receiver. Actions must be taken at the application level to delineate the blocks within the TCP streams.

TCP also checks for duplicate data. In the event that the sending TCP retransmits the data, the receiving TCP discards the redundant data. Redundant data might be introduced into an internet when the receiving TCP entity does not acknowledge traffic in a timely manner, in which case the sending TCP entity retransmits the data.

In consonance with the stream transfer capability, TCP also supports the concept of a *push* function. This operation is used when an application wants to make certain that all the data that it has passed to the lower layer TCP has been transmitted. In so doing, it governs TCP's buffer management. To obtain this function, the ULP issues a send command to TCP with a push parameter flag set to 1. The operation requires TCP to forward all the buffered traffic in the form of a segment or segments to the destination. As we shall see later, the TCP user can use a close connection operation to provide the push function as well.

In addition to using the sequence numbers for acknowledgment, TCP uses them to *resequence* the segments if they arrive at the final destination out of order. Because TCP rests upon a connectionless system, it is quite possible that duplicate datagrams could be created in an internet. TCP also eliminates duplicate segments.

TCP uses an inclusive acknowledgment scheme. The acknowledgment number acknowledges all octets up to and including the acknowledgment number less one. This approach provides an easy and efficient method of acknowledging traffic, but it does have a disadvantage. For example, suppose that 10 segments have been transmitted, yet due to routing operations, these segments arrive out of order. TCP is obligated to acknowledge only the highest contiguous byte number that has been received without error. It is not allowed to acknowledge the highest arrived byte number until all intermediate bytes have arrived. Therefore, like any other connection-oriented protocol, the transmitting TCP entity could eventually time-out and retransmit the traffic not yet acknowledged. These retransmissions can introduce a considerable amount of overhead in a network.

The receiver's TCP module is also able to *flow control* the sender's data, which is a very useful tool to prevent buffer overrun and a possible saturation of the receiving machine. The concept used with TCP is somewhat unusual among communications protocols. It is based on issuing a "window" value to the transmitter. The transmitter is allowed to transmit a specified number of bytes within this window, after which the window is closed and the transmitter must stop sending data.

TCP also has a very useful facility for *multiplexing* multiple user sessions within a single host computer onto the ULPs. As we shall see, this is accomplished through some rather simple naming conventions for ports and sockets in the TCP and IP modules.

TCP provides *full-duplex transmission* between two TCP entities. This permits simultaneous two-way transmission without having to wait for a turnaround signal, which is required in a half-duplex situation.

TCP also provides the user with the capability to specify levels of *security* and *precedence* (priority level) for the connection. Even though these features are not implemented on all TCP products, they are defined in the TCP standard.

TCP provides a *graceful close* to a virtual circuit (the logical connection between the two users). A graceful close ensures that all traffic has been acknowledged before the virtual circuit is removed.

Another Look at Ports and Sockets

The reader may recall that a TCP upper layer user in a host machine is identified by a *port* address (see Chap. 3, Fig. 3.5). The port address is concatenated with the IP internet address to form a *socket*. This address must be unique throughout the internet, and a pair of sockets uniquely identifies each end point connection. For example,

Sending socket = source IP address + source port number

Receiving socket = destination IP address + destination port number

Although the mapping of ports to higher-layer processes can be handled as an internal matter in a host, the Internet publishes numbers for frequently used higher-level processes. Table 7.1 lists the commonly used port numbers along with their names and descriptions.

Even though TCP establishes numbers for frequently used ports, the numbers and values above 255 are available for private use. The remainder of the values for the assigned port numbers have the low-order 8-bits set to zero. The remainder of these bits are available to any organization to use as they choose. Be aware that the numbers 0 through 255 are reserved and should be avoided.

Examples of port assignments and port bindings

Figure 7.2 shows how port numbers are assigned and managed between two host computers. In event 1 (illustrated by the bold numeral 1), host A sends a TCP segment to host C. This segment is a request for a TCP connection to communicate with a higher-level process. In this instance, it is the well-known port = 25, which is the assigned number for the Simple Mail Transfer Protocol (SMTP). The destination port value is fixed at 25. However, the source port identifier is a local matter. A host computer chooses any number convenient to its internal operations. In this example, source = 400 is chosen for the first connection. The second connection, noted by the numeral 2, is also destined for host C to use SMTP. Consequently, the destination port = 25 remains the same. The source port identifier is changed; in this instance it is set to the value of 401. The use of two different num-

TABLE 7.1   Internet Port Numbers (Not Exhaustive)

Number	Name	Description
5	RJE	Remote Job Entry
7	ECHO	Echo
11	USERS	Active Users
13	DAYTIME	Daytime
20	FTP-DATA	File Transfer (Data)
21	FTP	File Transfer (Control)
23	TELNET	TELNET
25	SMTP	Simple Mail Transfer
37	TIME	Time
42	NAMESERV	Host Name Server
43	NICKNAME	Who Is
53	DOMAIN	Domain Name Server
67	BOOTPS	Bootstrap Protocol Server
68	BOOTPC	Bootstrap Protocol Client
69	TFTP	Trivial File Transfer
79	FINGER	Finger
101	HOSTNAME	NIC Host Name Server
102	ISO-TSAP	ISO TSAP
103	X400	X.400
104	X400SND	X.400 SND
105	CSNET-NS	CSNET Mailbox Name Server
109	POP2	Post Office Protocol 2
111	RPC	SUN RPC Portmap
137	NETBIOS-NS	NETBIOS Name Service
138	NETBIOS-DG	NETBIOS Datagram Service
139	NETBIOS-SS	NETBIOS Session Service

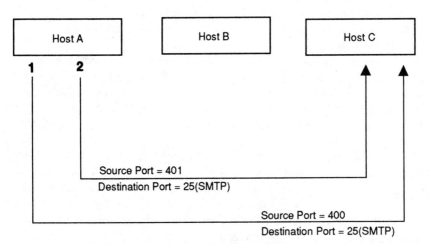

Figure 7.2   Establishing Sessions with a Destination Port.

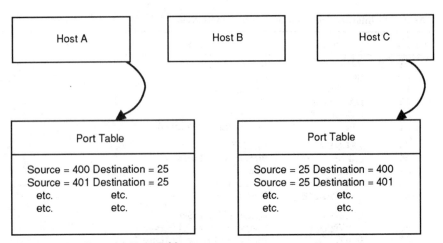

Figure 7.3 Binding with Port Tables.

bers for the FTP access prevents any mix-up between the two sessions in host A and host C.

Figure 7.3 shows the effect of the two segments that were used to establish the connections in Fig. 7.2. Host A and host C typically store the information about the TCP connections in tables. This example shows that the tables are called port tables. Notice the inverse relationship of these tables vis-à-vis the source destination. In the host A port table, the sources are 400 and 401, and the destination is 25 for both connections. Conversely, in the host C port table both sources are 25, and the destinations are 400 and 401. In other words, the source and destination port numbers are reversed by the TCP modules to communicate back and forth between each other.

Murphy's Law is alive and well, even with TCP. It is possible that another host might send a connection request to host C in which the source port and destination port are equal to the same values. It certainly would not be unusual for the destination port to be the same value since well-known ports are frequently accessed. In this case, destination port = 25 would identify the SMTP. Since source port identifiers are a local matter, Fig. 7.4 shows that host B has chosen source port = 400.

Without some type of additional identifier, the first connection between hosts A and C and the connection between hosts B and C are in conflict because they are using the same source and destination port numbers. In these cases, host C can easily discern the difference by the use of the IP addresses in the IP header of these datagrams. In this manner, the source port numbers may be duplicates and the internet address is used to distinguish between the sessions.

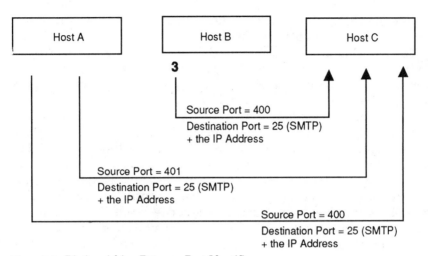

Figure 7.4 Distinguishing Between Port Identifiers.

In addition to IP addresses and port numbers, many systems further identify a socket with a "protocol family" value. For example, IP is a protocol family; DecNET is another protocol family. The manner in which protocol families are identified is dependent upon the vendor and the operating systems (discussed in Chap. 13).

Using sockets to support multiplexing.   Because the port numbers can be used by more than one end point connection, users can share a port resource simultaneously. That is, multiple users can simultaneously be multiplexed across one port. In Fig. 7.4, three users are sharing port 25 (UDP also supports port multiplexing, as explained later).

Passive and Active Opens

Two forms of connection establishment are permitted with TCP ports. The *passive open* mode allows the ULP (for example, a server) to tell the TCP and the host operating system it is to wait for the arrival of connection requests from the remote system (the foreign system) rather than issue an active open. Upon receiving this request, the host operating system assigns a port number to this end. This feature could be used to accommodate communications from remote users without going through the delay of an active open.

The applications process requesting the passive open may accept a connection request from any user (given some profile matching requirements, explained shortly). If any call can be accepted (without profile matching), the foreign socket number is set to all zeros. Unspecified foreign sockets are allowed only on passive opens.

The second form of connection establishment is the *active open* mode. In this situation, the ULP specifically designates another socket through which a connection is to be established. Typically, the active open is issued to a passive open port to establish a virtual circuit.

TCP supports a scenario in which two active opens are issued at the same time to each other. TCP will make the connection. This feature allows applications to issue an open at any time without concern that another application has issued an open.

TCP provides strict conventions on how the active and passive opens may be used together. First, an active open identifies a specific socket as well as its given precedence and security levels. TCP grants an open if the remote socket has a matching passive open or if it has issued a matching active open. Moreover, TCP defines two types of passive opens:

Fully specified passive open: The destination address in the active and passive open are the same. Therefore, the local passive open operation has fully specified the foreign socket. Also, the security parameter in the active open is within the range of the security parameter in the passive open.

Unspecified passive open: Addresses need not match, but the security parameters should be within an acceptable range.

The Transmission Control Block (TCB)

Because TCP must remember several things about each virtual connection, it stores information in a *Transmission Control Block (TCB)*. Among the entries stored in the TCB are the local and remote socket numbers, pointers to the send and receive buffers, pointers to the retransmit queue, the security and precedence values for the connection, and the current segment. The TCB also contains several variables associated with the send and receive sequence numbers. These variables are described in Table 7.2, and the next section examines how they are used.

TCP Window and Flow-Control Mechanisms

Using the entries in Table 7.2, we will examine in this section how TCP/IP provides flow-control mechanisms between two connection end points. To begin this analysis, please examine Fig. 7.5. The boxes labeled A and B depict two computers. Computer A is transmitting two units of data (two octets; although it is unusual to send just two octets,

TABLE 7.2   Send and Receive Variables

Send Sequence Variables	
Variable Name	Purpose
SND.UNA	Send Unacknowledged
SND.NXT	Send Next
SND.WND	Send Window
SND.UP	Sequence number of last octet of urgent data
SND.WL1	Sequence number used for last window update
SND.WL2	Ack number used for last window update
SND.PUSH	Sequence number of last octet of pushed data
ISS	Initial send sequence number
Receive Sequence Variables	
Variable Name	Purpose
RCV.NXT	Sequence number of next octet to be received
RCV.WND	Number of octets that can be received
RCV.UP	Sequence number of last octet of received urgent data
RCV.IRS	Initial receive sequence number

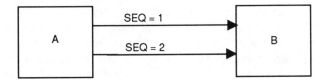

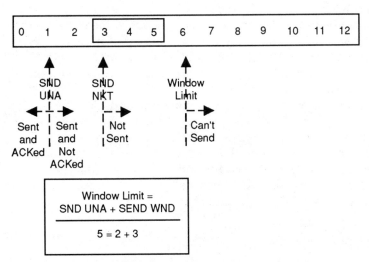

Figure 7.5   TCP Send Window Variables.

this example keeps matters simple) to computer B. These segments are labeled SEQ = 1 and SEQ = 2. The effect of this transfer can be seen by an examination of the send variables in the box at the bottom part of the picture. The SND UNA variable identifies the octets not yet acknowledged (2). Also, as indicated by the arrows below this variable name, the values less than this range have been sent and acknowledged (octet 0). Numbers greater (octets 1 and 2) have been sent but not acknowledged. The SND NXT identifies the sequence number of the next octet of data that is to be sent (octet 3). The window limit indicator provides the largest number that can be sent before the window is closed. The send window value is derived from the value in the TCP segment field called "window" (see Fig. 7.10). At the box at the bottom of Fig. 7.5, the window limit is computed as SND UNA + SND WND. This value is 5 because SND UNA = 2 and SND WND = 3.

Since host A has transmitted octets 1 and 2, its remaining send window is only 3. That is, it is allowed to transmit octets 3, 4, and 5. It is not allowed to send octet number 6. This window is indicated in the figure by the shaded area.

TCP is somewhat unique compared to other protocols in that it does not use just the acknowledgment number for window control. As just stated, it has a separate number carried in the TCP segment which increases or decreases the sending computer's send window. This concept is illustrated in Fig. 7.6. Computer B returns a segment to computer A. The segment contains among other fields, an acknowledgment field = 3 and a send window field = 6. The acknowledgment field simply acknowledges previous traffic. Used alone, it does not increase, decrease, open, or close computer A's window. Window management is the job of the send window field. Its value of 6 states that computer A is allowed to send octets based on this value of 6 plus the acknowledgment value. Hereafter, the window limit = ACK + SND WND. As depicted in the bottom part of this figure, the window is 9 as a result of 3 + 6. The window is thus expanded as indicated by the shaded area in this figure.

The credit for the window could have been reduced by computer B. Thus, the send window field permits the window to be expanded and contracted as necessary to manage buffer space and processing. This approach is a more flexible one than using the acknowledgment field for both the acknowledgment of traffic and window control operations. (Be aware that window shrinkage can have serious consequences on traffic flow. At best, it complicates matters.)

Retransmission Operations

TCP has a unique way of accounting for traffic on each virtual connection. Unlike many other protocols, it does not have an explicit *neg-*

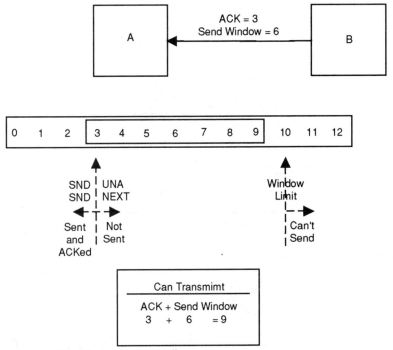

Figure 7.6   Result of a Window Update.

ative acknowledgment (NAK). Rather, it relies on the transmitting entity to issue a time-out and retransmit data for which it has not received a *positive acknowledgment (ACK)*. This concept is illustrated in Fig. 7.7. This figure shows eight operations labeled with shadowed numbers (1 through 8). Each of these operations will be described in order. The reader will notice that, for the purposes of simplicity, the window values and pointers described in Figs. 7.5 and 7.6 are not included in Fig. 7.7.

Event 1: TCP machine A sends a segment to TCP machine B. This example assumes a window of 900 octets (bytes) and a segment size of 300 octets. The sequence (SEQ) number contains the value of 3. As indicated in this event, 300 bytes are sent to TCP B.

Event 2: TCP B checks the traffic for errors and sends back an acknowledgment with the value of 303 (remember, this value is an inclusive acknowledgment which acknowledges all traffic up to and including 302: SEQ number 3 through 302; see Box 7.1). As depicted by the arrow in event 2, the traffic segment has not yet arrived at TCP A when event 3 occurs. (The tip of the arrow is not at A's location.)

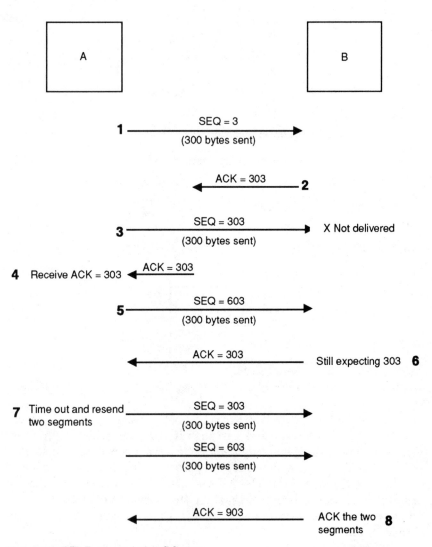

Figure 7.7 TCP Retransmission Schemes.

Event 3:   Because TCP A still has its window open, it sends another segment of data beginning with number 303. However, this traffic segment is not delivered to TCP B (for a number of reasons, discussed in previous chapters).

Event 4:   The acknowledgment segment transmitted in event 2 arrives at TCP A stipulating that TCP B is expecting a segment beginning with number 303. At this point, TCP A cannot know if the traffic transmitted in event 3 was not delivered or simply has not

BOX 7.1   Sequence Numbering and ACKs

I once sat in a meeting with two of my clients (who were writing some code for a proprietary transport layer). We were discussing sliding windows, rejects, selective rejects, and inclusive ACKs for a 512-byte PDU. These two individuals got into a rather heated debate on whether the inclusive ACK number should be 512 or 513. I told them the answer depended on whether the number zero is used as part of the *initial sequence (ISS)* number. Consider the following (for a 10-byte PDU, for simplicity). First, using an ISS of 0,

	ISS									
Sequence No.	0	1	2	3	4	5	6	7	8	9
	↓	↓	↓	↓	↓	↓	↓	↓	↓	↓
Bytes Sent	1	2	3	4	5	6	7	8	9	10

Therefore, an inclusive ACK = 10. A NAK = 0. (This protocol used NAKs.)
   Next, using an ISS number of 1,

	ISS									
Sequence No.	1	2	3	4	5	6	7	8	9	10
	↓	↓	↓	↓	↓	↓	↓	↓	↓	↓
Bytes Sent	1	2	3	4	5	6	7	8	9	10

Therefore, an inclusive ACK = 11. A NAK = 1.
   So, for Fig. 7.7, if TCP A were sending 10 bytes in a segment with an ISS number of 3,

	ISS									
Sequence No.	3	4	5	6	7	8	9	10	11	12
	↓	↓	↓	↓	↓	↓	↓	↓	↓	↓
Bytes Sent	1	2	3	4	5	6	7	8	9	10

The inclusive ACK = 13 and a NAK value would be 3 (although remember that TCP does not know how to NAK). Since this example sends 300 octets in a segment, the ACK value of 303 is the proper value.
   This discussion may seem somewhat trivial, but these types of simple misunderstandings can cause problems and result in bugs in the software of a communications system.

yet arrived due to variable delays in an internet. Consequently, it proceeds with event 5.

Event 5:   TCP A sends the next segment beginning with the number 603. It arrives error free at TCP B.

Event 6:   TCP B successfully receives the segment number 603, which was transmitted in event 5. However, TCP B sends back a segment with ACK 303 because it is still expecting segment number 303.

Event 7:   Eventually, TCP A must time-out and resend the segments for which it has not yet had an acknowledgment. In this example, it must resend to TCP B the segments beginning with numbers 303 and 603. Of course, the idea depicted in event 7 has its advantages and disadvantages. It makes the protocol quite simple, because TCP simply goes back to the last unacknowledged segment number and retransmits all succeeding segments. On the other hand, it likely retransmits segments which were not in error; for example, the segment beginning with number 603 which had arrived error free at TCP B. Nonetheless, TCP operates in this fashion at the risk of some degraded throughput for the sake of simplicity.

Event 8:   All traffic is accounted for after TCP B receives and error checks segments 303 and 603 and returns an ACK value equal to 903.

Estimating Timers for Time-Outs and Retransmissions

This section describes the approach taken by TCP to estimate a value for the time-out and retransmission. The discussion begins with some earlier approaches and concludes with recent changes to the TCP retransmission algorithm.

Choosing a value for the retransmission timer is deceptively complex. The reason for this complexity (see Fig. 7.8) stems from the fact that (a) the delay of receiving acknowledgments from the receiving host varies in an internet; (b) segments sent from the transmitter may be lost in the internet, which obviously invalidates any round trip delay estimate for a nonoccurring acknowledgment; and (c) in consonance with (b), acknowledgments from the receiver may be lost, which also invalidates the round trip delay estimate.

Because of these problems, TCP does not use a fixed retransmission timer. Rather, it utilizes an adaptive retransmission timer that is derived from an analysis of the delay encountered in receiving acknowledgments from remote hosts.

Returning to Fig. 7.8, the round trip time (RTT) is derived from adding the send delay (SD), the processing time (PT) at the remote host, and the receive delay (RD). If delay were not variable, this simple calculation would suffice for determining a retransmission timer. How-

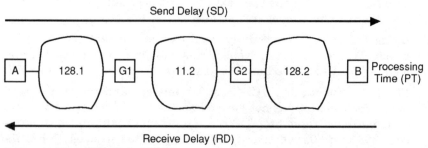

Figure 7.8 Round Trip Delay (RTT).

ever, as stated earlier, since delay in the internet is often highly variable, other factors must be considered.

The approach taken with earlier versions of TCP was to analyze each round trip sample and develop an average RTT for the delay. This simple formula for RTT is a weighted value based on the following:

$$SRTT = (\alpha*OSRTT) + ([1 - \alpha]*NRTT)$$

where SRTT = smoothed round trip time
α = smoothing factor (ranging close to 1 for accommodating the changes that last for a short period)
OSRTT = old smoothed RTT (close to 0 to respond to delays quickly)
NRTT = the new RTT sample

The next step in computing the timer is to apply a weighting factor to RTT as follows:

$$VT = \beta*SRTT$$

where VT = value for time-out; and β = a constant weighting factor which must be greater than RTT.

In addition, some implementations varied this formula, as follows:

$$VT = min (Ubound, max [Lbound, \{\beta*SRTT\}])$$

where Ubound = an upper bound on the time-out, and Lbound = the lower bound on the time-out.

This method of calculating the variable for the time-out did not work well due to the variable delay and the loss of acknowledgments in an internet. Ideally, one would wish the time-out timer to be quite close to RTT. However, due to the variable nature of RTT, it was discovered that the time-out timer expired too quickly in many instances and resulted in unnecessary segments being reintroduced into the internet. On the other hand, with a small value for the time-out, segment loss is handled more quickly.

One solution to the problem was provided by Phil Karn and is known as Karn's algorithm.* The approach is twofold: (a) TCP does not modify its estimate for any retransmitted segments, and (b) the time-out is increased each time the timer expires and initiates a retransmission. The reader might recognize that this approach is quite similar to the Ethernet back-off algorithm except that Ethernet

---

*D. E. Comer provides an excellent summary of early RFCs and other papers pertaining to this topic. This paragraph relies on the Comer discussion: see *Internetworking with TCP/IP*, D. E. Comer, Prentice Hall, 1991.

uses an exponential back-off in the face of increased traffic collisions on the network.

The Karn formula is

$$NVT = MF*VT$$

where NVT = new value for time-out, and MF = a multiplication factor (usually a value of 2 or a table of values).

The approach is to recalculate the RTT on a segment that was not retransmitted. It works well enough except in an internet with large variations in RTT.

RFC 1122 concedes that the original TCP approach to time-out and retransmission is inadequate. With new systems, the *Van Jacobsen's* slow start approach is used: Upon a time-out, TCP shuts its window to one. Upon receiving an ACK, it opens its window to half the size the window was before the time-out occurred.

Finally, the new TCP implementations take advantage of Poisson distribution and network utilization factors vis-à-vis RTT. This approach uses additional computations that take into account varying delay as a function of network utilization.

TCP and User Interfaces

TCP works with the service definition/primitive concept to interface with an upper layer user. The interface is achieved with the commands and messages summarized in Table 7.3. Be aware that primitives are abstract and their actual implementation is dependent on a host's operating system. Furthermore, RFC 793 defines those interfaces in a general way; vendor implementations vary. (Chapter 13 provides more information on this topic.) Figure 7.9 shows the relationship of the ULP, TCP, and IP.

The service definitions between TCP and its lower layer are not specified in the TCP standard. It is assumed in the TCP operations that TCP and the lower layer can pass information to each other asynchronously. TCP expects the lower layer to specify this interface. (The OSI Model follows the same practice.) This lower layer interface is defined in the IP specification (see Chap. 6) if IP rests below TCP.

The Segment (TCP PDU)

The PDUs exchanged between two TCP modules are called *segments*. Figure 7.10 illustrates the format for the segment. We examine each of the fields of the segment in this section.

The segment is divided into two parts, the header part and the data part. As depicted in Fig. 7.10, the data part follows the header part.

The first two fields of the segment are identified as *source port* and

TABLE 7.3 Typical TCP User Interfaces

Service Request Primitives (ULP to TCP)	
Command	Parameters
UNSPECIFIED-PASSIVE-OPEN	Local port, ULP time-out (1), time-out action (1), precedence (1) Security (1), options (1) → local connection name
FULL-PASSIVE-OPEN	Local port, destination socket, ULP time-out (1), time-out action (1), precedence (1), security (1), options (1)
ACTIVE-OPEN	Local port, foreign socket, ULP time-out (1), ULP time-out action (1), precedence (1), security (1), options (1)
ACTIVE-OPEN-WITH DATA	Source ports, destination address, ULP time-out (1), ULP time-out action (1), precedence (1), security (1), data, data length, push flag, urgent flag (1)
SEND	Local connection name, buffer address, byte count, push flag, urgent flag, ULP time-out (1), ULP time-out action (1)
RECEIVE	Local connection name, buffer address, byte count, urgent flag, push flag
ALLOCATE	Local connection name, data length
CLOSE	Local connection name
ABORT	Local connection name
STATUS	Local connection name

Service Response Primitives (TCP to ULP)	
Primitive	Parameters
OPEN-ID	Local connection name, foreign socket, destination address
OPEN-FAILURE	Local connection name
OPEN-SUCCESS	Local connection name
DELIVER	Local connection name, buffer address, byte count, urgent flag
CLOSING	Local connection name
TERMINATE	Local connection name, description
STATUS RESPONSE	Local connection name, source port and address, foreign port, connection state, receive and send window, amount-waiting-ack and -receipt, urgent mode, time-out, time-out action
ERROR	Local connection name, error description

Note: A notation of (1) means parameters are optional.

destination port. These 16-bit fields are used to identify the upper layer application programs that are using the TCP connection.

The next field is labeled *sequence number.* This field contains the sequence number of the first octet in the user data field. Its value specifies the position of the transmitting module's byte stream. Within the segment, it specifies the first user data octet in the segment.

The sequence number is also used during a connection management operation. If a connection request segment is used between two TCP en-

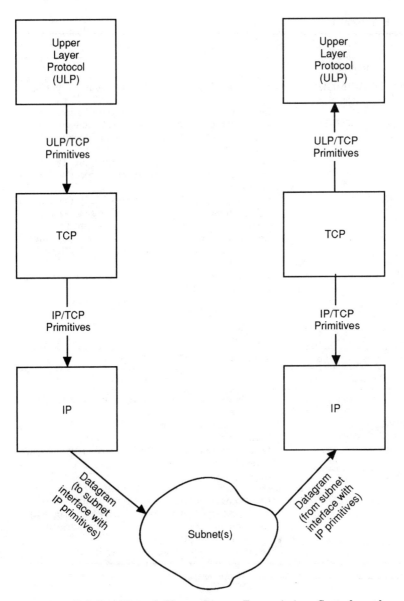

Figure 7.9 Relationships of Upper Layer, Transmission Control, and Internet Protocols (ULP, TCP, and IP, Respectively).

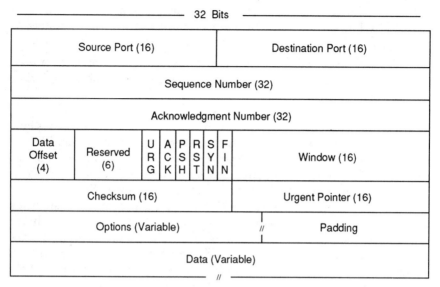

Figure 7.10   The TCP Segment (PDU).

tities, the sequence number specifies the *initial send sequence (ISS)* number that is to be used for the subsequent numbering of the user data.

The *acknowledgment number* is set to a value which acknowledges data previously received. The value in this field contains the value of the sequence number of the next expected octet from the transmitter. Since this number is set to the next expected octet, it provides an inclusive acknowledgment capability in that it acknowledges all octets up to and including this number, minus 1.

The *data offset* field specifies the number of 32-bit aligned words that comprise the TCP header. This field is used to determine where the data field begins.

As the reader might expect, the *reserved* field is reserved. It consists of 6 bits which must be set to zero. These bits are reserved for future use.

The next six fields are called *flags*. They are labeled as control bits by TCP, and they specify certain services and operations which are to be used during the session. Some of the bits determine how to interpret other fields in the header. The six bits are used to convey the following information:

URG: This flag signifies if the urgent pointer field is significant

ACK: This flag signifies if the acknowledgment field is significant.

PSH: This flag signifies that the module is to exercise the push function.

RST: This flag indicates that the connection is to be reset.

SYN: This flag indicates that the sequence numbers are to be synchronized; it is used with the connection-establishment segments as a flag to indicate that handshaking operations are to take place.

FIN: This flag indicates that the sender has no more data to send and is comparable to the end-of-transmission (EOT) signal in other protocols.

The next field is labeled *window*. It is set to a value indicating how many octets the receiver is willing to accept. The value is established based on the value in the acknowledgment field (acknowledgment number). The window is established by adding the value in the window field to the value of the acknowledgment number field.

The *checksum* field performs a 16-bit one's complement of the one's complement sum of all the 16-bit words in the segment. This includes the header and the text. The purpose of the checksum calculation is to determine if the segment has arrived error free from the transmitter.

The next field in the segment is labeled the *urgent pointer*. This field is only used if the URG flag is set. The purpose of the urgent pointer is to signify the data octet in which urgent data follows. Urgent data is also called *out-of-band* data. TCP does not dictate what happens for urgent data. It is implementation specific. It only signifies where the urgent data is located. It is an offset from the sequence number and points to the octet following the urgent data.

The *options* field was conceived to provide for future enhancements to TCP. It is constructed in a manner similar to that of the IP datagrams option field, in that each option specification consists of a single byte containing an option number, a field containing the length of the option, and last the option values themselves.

The option field is quite limited in its use. Currently, only three options are defined for the TCP standard:

0:   End-of-option list

1:   No operation

2:   Maximum segment size

Finally, the *padding* field is used to ensure that the TCP header is filled to an even multiple of 32 bits. After that, as the figure illustrates, user *data* follows.

Effect of segment size (length) on performance.   Since TCP is designed to support variable-length segments, the options field can be used by the receiver to inform the transmitter of the maximum buffer size that can be accommodated. In this manner, a limit is placed on the size (i.e., length) of the segment to be transmitted to the receiver. Notwithstanding, segments might vary in length up to the maximum length. If this is the case, the length of the segments could affect the length of the frames on the network because the segments are encapsulated into the frames.

Frame length is an important aspect of network performance, and it can affect the performance of bridges and gateways. To illustrate these points, imagine that two variable-length frames are sent across a network (our example is an Ethernet network). One set of frames each contains 1500 octets; another set of frames each contains 64 octets. Large frames provide better throughput on a local area network because the number of user bytes per overhead segment and Ethernet frame header is a greater ratio than the smaller 64-octet frame. Moreover, a point that is often overlooked is the *interframe gap* (the time between frames in which there is no transmission). TCP cannot directly affect the interframe gap; it is determined by lower layer protocols. However, the effect of using a larger frame gives a bridge or gateway more time to examine and make decisions on the frame than if a smaller frame is arriving with the same interframe gap as the large frame. Indeed, the manner in which TCP segments data and the speed at which these segments are sent to a lower layer should be examined carefully because the ability of a bridge to forward traffic and to filter irrelevant traffic is a function of both the frame length and the interframe gap.

This is not to say that TCP is solely responsible for these operations. As we mentioned before, some of these activities are determined by the lower LAN layers. Nonetheless, the situation warrants examination to tune the upper layers to the LAN protocol layers.

The TCP Connection Management Operations

TCP is a state-driven protocol. As such, its operations must conform to many rules on how and when specific segments are exchanged between the TCP entities. These rules are described in state transition diagrams. A general depiction of the TCP connection management operations is illustrated in Fig. 7.11. We use this figure to explain several features of TCP.

Examples of the TCP open, data transfer, and close operations

TCP open.   Figure 7.12 illustrates the major operations between two TCP entities to establish a connection. Before explaining the TCP operations, we need to pause briefly and define the terms *type* and *instance* in regard to a communications protocol.

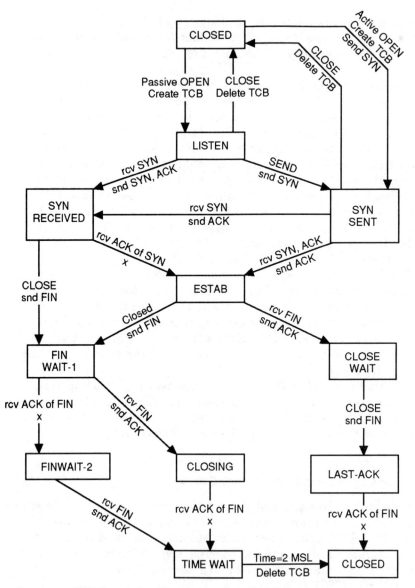

Figure 7.11   TCP Connection Management State Diagram.

First, a type describes an object. In this example, TCP is an object. Second, an instance describes the manifestation of an object. Therefore, in this example, each time TCP is invoked, it manifests itself. Since many user processes may use TCP simultaneously, each user session invokes the TCP logic and each invocation is an instance of

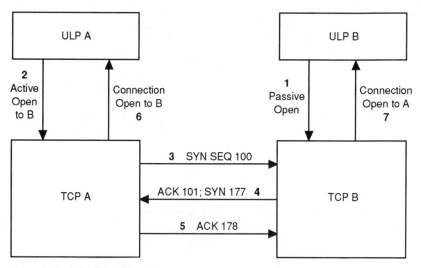

Figure 7.12   TCP Open Operations.

type TCP. In more pragmatic terms, each user invocation of TCP represents executing some of TCP's services to support a session.

Each instance of TCP requires that TCP maintain information about the event. These pieces of information are kept in the TCB about *each* user session. With this brief description behind us, we now can examine the operations of TCP in more detail.

As Fig. 7.12 depicts, TCP A's user has sent an active open primitive to TCP. The remote user has sent a passive open to its TCP provider. These operations are listed as events **2** and **1** respectively, although either event could have occurred in either order.

The invocation of the active open requires TCP A to prepare a segment with the SYN bit set to 1. The segment is sent to TCP B and is depicted in the figure as **3** and coded as SYN SEQ 100. In this example, sequence (SEQ) number 100 is used as the ISS number, although any number could be chosen within the rules discussed earlier. The SYN coding simply means the SYN bit is set to the value of 1.

Upon receiving the SYN segment, TCP B returns an acknowledgment with sequence number of 101. It also sends its ISS number of 177. This event is labeled as **4**.

Upon the receipt of this segment, TCP A acknowledges with a segment containing the acknowledgment number of 178. This is depicted as event **5** in the figure.

Once these handshaking operations have occurred with events 3, 4, and 5 (which is called a three-way handshake), the two TCP modules send opens to their respective users as in events **6** and **7**.

We can now use Fig. 7.13 to illustrate the relationship of the oper-

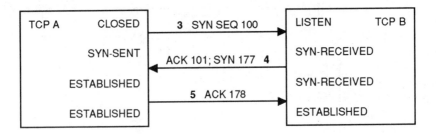

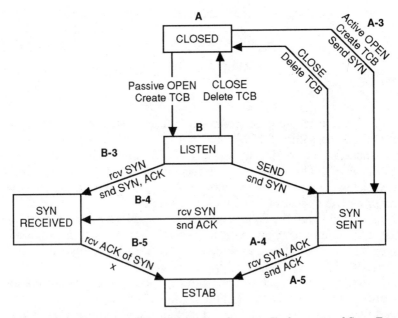

Figure 7.13 Relationship of Open Operations, Segment Exchanges, and State Transitions.

ations of Fig. 7.12 to the state diagram rules. Therefore, the information in Fig. 7.11 is condensed and redrawn as Fig. 7.13. This figure shows the relationship of the open operations with the segment exchanges and the state transactions. Notice that the top of the figure is derived from Fig. 7.12 but only contains the segment flow between the two TCP entities and not the operations between the upper layers and the TCP layers in each machine.

The bottom part of Fig. 7.13 shows the relevant portion of the state diagram for the open. The bottom of the diagram is labeled in outlined print as **A, B, A-3, A-4, B-3,** etc. These indicators can be matched to the outlined event numbers at the top of the figure to show how both TCP modules use the segments and the state diagrams.

For help in following the operations of Fig. 7.13, please look at the event labeled **3** at the top part of the figure. It shows TCP A issuing SYN SEQ 100. Prior to the transmission of this segment, TCP A is in state = CLOSED for this specific user session. Its state is changed to SYN-SENT after it sends the segment to TCP B.

Next, refer to the bottom diagram. The notation **A** indicates that TCP A is in the CLOSED state in regard to this user session. The state transition labeled **A-3** is matched to the segment issued by TCP A in the top part of the figure, labeled as **3**. Upon issuance of this segment, the state diagram shows that TCP A has entered the SYN-SENT state and has created a TCB entry for the connection.

Next we examine TCP B. As the top part of the figure shows, it is in the LISTEN state. The state diagram LISTEN state is labeled as **B** to show this relationship. The top part of the figure shows that upon receiving the SYN SEQ 100 segment, TCP B moves to the SYN-RECEIVED state. These events are shown in the state diagram with the label **B-3**, which also shows that TCP B sent back the SYN and ACK in event 4 at the top of the figure and **B-4** at the bottom of the figure. Figure 7.13 can be analyzed by continuing to match the numbers and events between the top and bottom part of the figure.

A newcomer to TCP often asks if TCP modules can initiate an open to a closed TCP socket. That is, must there be a passive open before a connection can occur. TCP does permit opens to closed sockets. Figure 7.14 shows this activity as well as how TCP handles opens that might be issued simultaneously from the two TCP modules. To answer the question about issuing an open to a closed TCP socket, the major requirement is that the open call must contain a local socket identifier as well as the foreign socket identifier. In addition, the open call may contain precedence, security, and user time-out information. If this information is available, the TCP module will issue the SYN segment. In Fig. 7.14, opens are sent from A and B at approximately the same time. The events in this figure occur as follows:

Event 1: After receiving these opens, the TCP modules create new transmission control blocks to hold the virtual connection information.

Event 2: This event shows that the SYN segments are sent from TCP A and B at approximately the same time. The position of the arrows are used in this figure to indicate the relative time sequence of the traffic. Consequently, the SYN segment from TCP A has not yet arrived at TCP B when TCP B's segment arrives at TCP A.

Event 3: In event 3, the SYN segment from TCP A finally arrives at TCP B. The results of the SYN segments in event 2 move the two TCP modules from CLOSED to SYN-SENT to SYN-RECEIVED.

Events 4 & 5: Both TCP modules issue an ACK segment, which, as

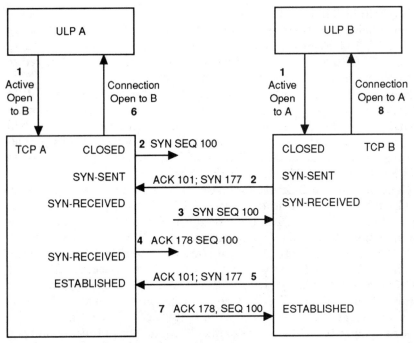

Figure 7.14   Simultaneous Opens from Closed States.

we learned earlier, is to acknowledge the SYN segments. TCP B's segment in event 5 arrives before TCP A's segment in event 4. This somewhat asynchronous aspect of TCP simply results from variable delay in an internet. The delay varies in both directions.

Event 6:   Upon receipt of the ACK at TCP A (in event 5), TCP A then sends a connection open signal to its ULP.

Event 7:   The ACK segment from TCP A finally arrives at TCP B.

Event 8:   To complete the connection, TCP B sends a connection open to its ULP.

Notice the effect of the arrival of the ACKs in events 5 and 7 with the issuance of the open primitives to the ULPs in events 6 and 8.

It should be noted that receiving a call at a receiving module in which a TCP does not exist will result in an error condition if the operating system has not generated some control information indicating that the user does have access to the connection identified in the open call.

TCP data transfer operations.   Figure 7.15 shows the TCP entities after they have successfully achieved a connection. In event 1, ULP A sends data down to TCP A for transmission with a SEND primitive. We as-

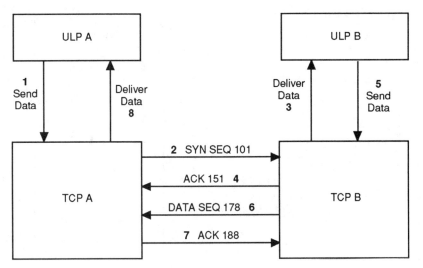

Figure 7.15   TCP Data Transfer Operations.

sume 50 octets are to be sent. TCP A encapsulates this data into a segment and sends the segment to TCP B with sequence number = 101, as depicted in event **2**. Remember that this sequence number is used to number the first octet of the user data stream.

At the remote TCP, data is delivered to the user (ULP B) in event **3**, and TCP B acknowledges the data with a segment acknowledgment number = 151. This is depicted in event **4**. The acknowledgment number of 151 acknowledges inclusively the 50 octets transmitted in the segment depicted in event **2**.

Next, the user connected to TCP B sends data in event **5**. This data is encapsulated into a segment and transmitted as event **6** in the diagram. The initial sequence number from TCP B was 177; therefore TCP begins its sequencing with 178. In this example, it transmits 10 octets.

TCP A acknowledges TCP B's 10 segments in event **7** by returning a segment with acknowledgment number = 188. In event **8**, this data is delivered to TCP A's user.

Remember that the data transfer operations pertaining to retransmission and time-outs were discussed in an earlier section (see Fig. 7.6).

TCP close operations.   Figure 7.16 shows a close operation. Event **1** illustrates that TCP A's user wishes to close its operations with its upper peer layer protocol at TCP B. The effect of this primitive (CLOSE) is shown in event **2**, where TCP A sends a segment with the FIN bit set to 1. The sequence number of 151 is a continuation of the operation

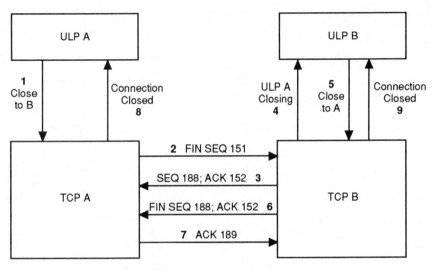

Figure 7.16   TCP Close Operations.

of Fig. 7.15. This is the next sequence number the TCP module is required to send.

The effect of this segment is shown as event **3** from TCP B. TCP B acknowledges TCP A's FIN SEQ 151. Its segment has SEQ = 188 and ACK = 152. Next, it issues a closing primitive to its user, which is depicted as event **4**.

In this example, the user application acknowledges and grants the close as event **5**. It may or may not choose to do this depending on the state of its operations. However, for simplicity, we assume the event depicted in **5** does occur. This primitive is mapped to event **6**, which is the final segment issued by TCP B. Notice that in event **6**, the FIN flag is set to 1, SEQ = 188, and ACK = 152. Finally, TCP A acknowledges this final segment with event **7** as ACK = 189.

The effect of all these operations is shown in events **8** and **9**, where connection closed signals are sent to the user applications.

To complete this analysis of TCP connection management, Fig. 7.17 shows the close operations in relation to the relevant part of the state diagram. Again, as we did in an earlier example of the open operations, the top part of the figure is a scaled-down version of Fig. 7.16 in which only the segment transmissions are shown. The effect of these operations is depicted with the state notations located inside each box and the outlined numbers and figures shown on the state diagram in the bottom part of the figure.

TCP connection table

The Internet MIB requires the use of a TCP connection table. The table contains information about each existing TCP connection. As de-

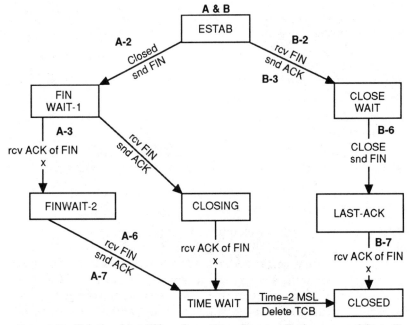

Figure 7.17 Relationship of Close Operations, Segment Exchanges, and State Transitions.

picted in Fig. 7.18, the table consists of five columns and a row for each connection.

The *Connection State* column describes the state of each TCP connection (for example, closed, listen, finWait 1, closing, etc.).

The *Local Address* column contains the local IP address for each TCP connection. In a listen state, this value must be 0.0.0.0.

	Connection State	Local Address	Local Port	Remote Address	Remote Port
Connection 1					
Connection 2					
Connection 3					
//					
Connection n					

Figure 7.18   The TCP Connection Table.

The *Local Port* column contains the local port number for each TCP connection.

The *Remote Address* column contains the remote IP address for each TCP connection.

The *Remote Port* number column contains the remote port number for each TCP connection.

Other Considerations in Using TCP

As explained earlier in this chapter, the TCP stream data are acknowledged by the receiver on a byte basis (not on a PDU). The acknowledgment number, returned by the receiver, refers to the highest byte in the data stream that has been received. The sending TCP software keeps a copy of the data until it has been acknowledged. Once acknowledged, it turns off a retransmission timer and deletes the segment copy from a retransmission queue.

If necessary, it will retransmit lost or errored data. From previous discussions in this book, the reader may know that the term associated with this technique is *inclusive acknowledgment*. It works well on systems that deliver data in sequential order, but the underlying IP may deliver data out of order or it may discard data. In such an event, TCP has no way to notify the sender that it has received certain segments of a transmission. It can only relay the value of the contiguous, accumulated bytes. Consequently, the sending TCP software may time-out and resend data segments that have already been successfully received.

A *push* function is available to force the TCP to send data immediately. This function is used to ensure that traffic is delivered to avoid deadlock at the other end. The stream concept does not deal with structured data streams, and it cannot delineate between records in a file transfer. Therefore, the applications must have some means of identifying the logical records before they begin their communications.

We also learned that TCP has a function similar to the OSI TP4 credit scheme. It is called the *window advertisement* field. A value is returned to the sending TCP in this field to inform it of the number of bytes of additional data the receiver is prepared to receive. If the sender receives a larger value in the window advertisement field, it can change the transmit window accordingly. It is not advisable to shrink the window advertisement past the previously acceptable positions in the data stream unless it is accompanied by a complementary acknowledgment. That is, the window size can change as it slides forward.

Finally, TCP has the potential for providing considerable information to the network manager (for example, if TCP is sending excessive retransmissions, it might provide a clue to problems in the network such as dead gateways or timers that are not functioning properly). The positive acknowledgments also could be used to determine how well certain of the components in an internet may be functioning.

User Datagram Protocol (UDP)

Previous chapters have discussed the concepts of a connectionless protocol. The reader may recall that the connectionless protocol provides no reliability or flow-control mechanisms. It also has no error recovery procedures. The UDP is classified as a connectionless protocol. It is sometimes used in place of TCP in situations where the full services of TCP are not needed. For example, the Trivial File Transfer Protocol (TFTP) and the Remote Procedure Call (RPC) use UDP.

UDP serves as a simple application interface to the IP. Since it has no reliability, flow-control, or error-recovery measures, it serves principally as a multiplexer/de-multiplexer for the receiving and sending of IP traffic. Figure 7.19 illustrates how UDP accepts datagrams from IP.

UDP makes use of the port concept to direct the datagrams to the proper upper layer applications. The UDP datagram contains a destination port number and a source port number. The destination number is used by the UDP module to deliver the traffic to the proper recipient.

Format of the UDP message

Perhaps the best way to explain this protocol is to examine the message and the fields that reside in the message. As Fig. 7.20 illustrates, the format is quite simple and contains the following fields:

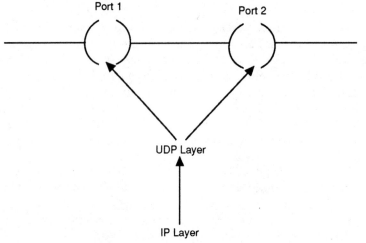

Figure 7.19   UDP Multiplexing.

32 Bits	
Source Port	Destination Port
Length	Checksum
Data	

Figure 7.20   Format for the UDP Datagram.

Source port: This value identifies the port of the sending application process. The field is optional. If it is not used, a value of 0 is inserted in this field.

Destination port: This value identifies the receiving process on the destination host machine.

Length: This value indicates the length of the user datagram including the header and the data. This value implies that the minimum length is 8 octets.

Checksum: This value is the 16-bit one's complement of the one's complement sum of the pseudo-IP header, the UDP header, and the data. It also performs a checksum on any padding (if it was necessary to make the message contain a multiple of two octets).

There is not a lot more to be said about UDP. It is a minimal level of service used in many transaction-based application systems. However, it is quite useful if the full services of TCP are not needed.

Summary

TCP provides a powerful yet simple set of services for the ULPs of internet. TCP has relatively few features, but the features are designed to provide end-to-end reliability, graceful closes, unambiguous connections, handshakes, and several quality of service operations. The internet transport layer also provides a connectionless operation called the UDP. This is a minimal level of service, principally to use the source and destination ports for multiplexing. With the use of UDP, the user application is typically tasked with performing some of the end-to-end reliability operations that would normally be done by TCP.

8

Route Discovery Protocols

Introduction

Since the TCP/IP protocol suite is based on the concept of internet-working, gateways and routers play a very important role in TCP/IP-based networks. Indeed, the IP protocol is designed around the concept of internetworking host computers with gateways and routers. This chapter is devoted to a discussion of the various types of route discovery protocols that are used in internet networks. It also examines the types of gateways and networks that are administered by public and private authorities. The last part of the chapter discusses several newer techniques used in internetworking and gateway operations. It is assumed that the reader has previously reviewed the material in Chap. 2, which deals with routers, bridges, and gateways.

This chapter uses the terms *gateway* and *router* interchangeably. More concise definitions are available in Chaps. 2 and 3.

As a reminder to the reader, IP is not a route discovery protocol. It makes use of the routing tables that are filled in by the protocols explained in this chapter.

Terms and Concepts

Individual networks may be joined together by a computer which acts as a switch between the networks. As discussed in Chap. 2, the switch operations are programmed to route the traffic to the proper network by examining a destination address in the protocol data unit (PDU) and matching the address with entries in a routing table. Those entries indicate (one hopes) the best route to the next network or next gateway.

Even though these individual networks may be administered by local authorities, it is common practice for a group of networks to be administered as a whole system. From the perspective of an internet, this group of networks is called an *autonomous system,* and it is administered by a single *authority.* Examples of autonomous systems are networks located on sites such as college campuses, hospital complexes, and military installations. The networks located at these sites are connected together by a gateway. Since these gateways operate within an autonomous system, they often choose their own mechanisms for routing data.

However, the routing of data between autonomous systems is usually controlled by a single ("global") administrative authority. This means that the local administrative authorities in the autonomous systems must agree on how they provide information (advertise) to each other on the "reachability" of the host computers inside the autonomous systems. The advertising responsibility can be given to one gateway, or a number of gateways may participate in the operation.

The autonomous systems are identified by autonomous system numbers. How this is accomplished is up to the administrators, but the idea is to use different numbers to distinguish different autonomous systems. Such a numbering scheme might prove helpful if a network manager does not wish to route traffic through an autonomous system which, even though it might be connected to the manager's network, may be administered by a competitor, does not have adequate or proper security services, etc. By the use of routing protocols and numbers identifying autonomous systems, the gateways can determine how they reach each other and how they exchange routing information.

Routing based on fewest hops

The vast majority of gateway products route traffic based on the idea that it makes the best sense to transmit the datagram through the fewest number of networks and gateways (hops). In the past, network designers held that this approach led to the most efficient route through an internet and, perhaps more to the point, it was easy to implement. The fewest-hops approach could be debated, but we will confine ourselves to how the approach works rather than its relative merits. Later in this chapter, the newer routing techniques are explored in considerable detail.

Figure 8.1 shows an example of how a "fewest-hops" routing directory may be employed. The routing directory contains values that represent the number of intermediate gateways (hops) between the originator of the traffic (for example, the source at node A) and the receiver (for example, the destination at node G). For simplicity, the intervening networks are not shown in this figure. With this approach, the datagrams are routed to the adjacent gateway that is closest to the final destination.

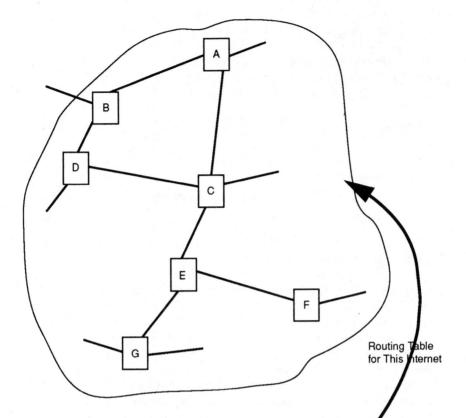

Destination

		A	B	C	D	E	F	G
	A	0	1	1	2	2	3	3
	B	1	0	2	1	3	4	4
Source	C	1	2	0	1	1	2	2
	D	2	1	1	0	2	3	3
	E	2	3	1	2	0	1	1
	F	3	4	2	3	1	0	2
	G	3	4	2	3	1	2	0

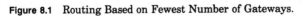

Figure 8.1   Routing Based on Fewest Number of Gateways.

A datagram at gateway A destined for a network connected to gateway G would be routed to gateway C, because C is closer to the destination than is the other alternative, gateway B.

Each gateway typically maintains its own routing directory. In this example, each gateway routes the traffic as follows:

1. Access the directory to determine the neighbor gateways (source to destination = 1).

2. Route the datagram to the gateway that is on the shortest path to the destination.

3. Repeat steps 1 and 2 until the datagram has reached its destination.

Routing based on type of service factors

Another type of internet routing that has seen rather limited use but is gaining acceptance is based on a number of criteria called *type of service factors (TOS)*. The OSI Model uses the term *quality of service factors (QOS)*. These factors are defined by the network administrators and users and may include criteria such as delay, throughput, security needs, etc. The path through an internet is chosen based on the ability of the gateways and networks to meet a required service.

Most implementations use adaptive and dynamic methods to update the directories to reflect traffic conditions, link conditions, and the gateway queue lengths. With such a method, the datagrams may take different paths through the internet and arrive out of order at the final destination. As we learned in Chap. 5, the receiving host machine then resequences the datagrams before passing them to the end user.

Figure 8.2a shows an example of adaptive routing, with estimated delay as the service criterion, as viewed by A. Datagrams are to be transported from A to J. The numbers on the links between the gateways reflect traffic conditions between the two gateways connected to the link. The larger numbers are weighted to indicate more delay. Each gateway communicates with its neighbor gateways (directly connected) by exchanging status messages. If the information in the message indicates that the status of the neighbor has changed, the routing table is changed. Periodically, this status information is broadcast to all other gateways and is used to update their routing tables.

In Fig. 8.2b, the dashed lines show that the datagrams are sent from $A \rightarrow C \rightarrow D \rightarrow E \rightarrow G \rightarrow I \rightarrow J$. The total time-weighted value for the end-to-end path is 15, which represents the path with the shortest overall delay between A and J.

It is possible that the datagrams from A may take different paths and traverse different gateways en route to J. If link, gateway, or net-

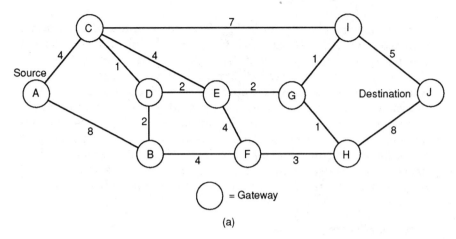

= Gateway

(a)

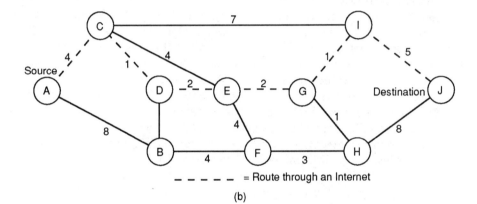

= Route through an Internet

(b)

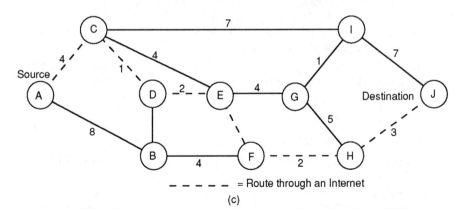

= Route through an Internet

(c)

Figure 8.2 Shortest Path Routing (with Adaptive Directories): (a) Adaptive Routing (with Shortest Path or Least Cost Algorithm); (b) Shortest Path from A to J; (c) Revised Route for A's Datagrams.

work conditions change, as in Fig. 8.2c, the end-to-end path may be changed (on the E–F, F–H, G–H, H–J, and I–J links). In this example, the datagrams are now sent from A → C → D → E → F → H → J. Care must be taken in the design and implementation of adaptive routing schemes to prevent the datagrams from "oscillating" in an internet. If the routing tables are updated too frequently because of unstable network performance, datagrams may take circuitous routes and perhaps never reach the final destination. It is easy to understand the value of the time-to-live parameter in the IP datagram in this situation. Eventually, oscillating datagrams are discarded and later retransmitted by the TCP module at the originating host computer.

Core and noncore gateways

Internet gateways are classified as *core* or *noncore* gateways. Core gateways are administered by a single authority. In the case of the Internet, it is the Internet Network Operation Center (INOC). Noncore gateways are outside the control of the single administrative authority. They are controlled by individual groups. From the perspective of the Internet, they are not controlled by the INOC.

When ARPANET was first implemented, it consisted of a single backbone network. With the implementation of Internet, ARPANET then provided attached gateways to local Internet networks. A protocol, called the *Gateway-to-Gateway Protocol (GGP),* was used for these core gateways to inform each other about their attached local networks. Traffic passing between two local networks passed through two gateways, and each core gateway had complete routing information on the other core gateway.

Since these gateways had complete routing information, they did not need the default route described in Chap. 3. However, things changed, and the Internet grew. Backbone networks were added to the original backbone network, and local networks were attached to other local area networks (LANs). The same types of growth also occured on many private internets. Therefore, the concept of a gateway holding complete routing information on an internet became too unwieldy.

Exterior and interior gateways

To approach this problem, gateways were given responsibilities for only a part of an internet. In this manner, a gateway did not have to know about all other gateways of an internet but relied on neighbor gateways and/or gateways in other autonomous systems to reveal their routing information. Indeed, if they had insufficient knowledge to make a routing decision, they simply chose a default route. This change gave rise to two other terms: *exterior gateways* and *interior gateways*. An exterior gateway is so named because it supports the exchange of routing information between different autonomous systems. Interior gateways are so named because they belong to the same autonomous system.

From these definitions we derive two other definitions. An *exterior neighbor* is a gateway that exchanges routing information between two autonomous systems. An *interior neighbor* exchanges information within the same autonomous system.

Figure 8.3 shows the relationship between external and internal gateway protocols. A set of packet-switched networks is labeled as autonomous system 1 and is connected to another set of packet-switched networks, labeled autonomous system 2. Gateway 1 (G1) and gateway 2 (G2) use an *external gateway protocol (EGP)* to exchange data and control information. The two internets use their own *internal gateway protocols (IGP)* for route management inside each autonomous system. Therefore, it is not unusual for a gateway to support two (or more) route discovery protocols, depending on where the traffic is destined. These gateways use an IGP within their autonomous systems and an EGP between each autonomous system.

Border routers and boundary routers

The terms described thus far would seem to cover all bases (or at least all nodes). Not quite. It is now accepted that an autonomous system may need to be divided further to achieve efficient and manageable routing tables and protocols. Therefore, an autonomous system can be divided into *areas*.

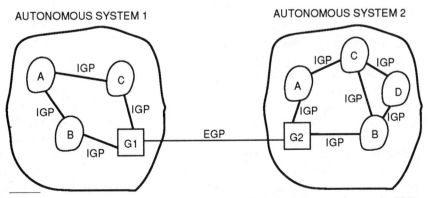

Figure 8.3 External Gateway Protocols (EGP) and Internal Gateway Protocols (IGP).

Areas may contain one to n subnets that exchange information through an IGP. In turn, areas have a designated *border* gateway that exchanges information with border gateways in other areas. Finally, designated *boundary* gateways exchange information between autonomous systems.

If some of these terms seem redundant to other terms described in the previous sections, you are following this narrative quite well because some of them *are* redundant. For example, an EGP gateway is the same as a border router. So why did the Internet authorities expand the vocabulary? The terms *border* and *boundary routers* were added to the internet vocabulary with the publication of OSPF (described in later in this chapter).

How autonomous systems or areas exchange information

Be aware that the example in this section is a generic example of route discovery. In later sections, we examine the specific rules for each internet gateway protocol.

Figure 8.4, as a slight alteration of Fig. 8.1, shows internetworking concepts in more detail. For simplicity, the networks between the gateways are not included in this figure. Gateways C and X are designated as core gateways for autonomous systems 1 and 2, respectively. The same concepts apply to areas, but this section will use the term *autonomous systems*. In Fig. 8.4a, gateway C's routing table (shown on the left side of the figure) is sent to gateway X, which uses it to update its routing table containing reachability information pertaining to gateways A, B, C, D, E, F, and G. Gateway X is not concerned with how this information was obtained by gateway C. It could have been obtained by an IGP method, but these internal operations remain transparent to gateway X.

To expand this discussion, let us assume that gateways F and K also exchange routing information. An autonomous system is not restricted to only one core gateway, but an area usually designates only one router for the area. Now assume (as in Fig. 8.4b) that the link or network connection is lost between E and F. Gateway C discovers this problem through its IGP and typically enters a value symbolizing infinity in its routing table entry to F (16, 256, or whatever the protocol stipulates). An "F = 16, through C" message is sent to gateway X, as shown by the arrow from C to X in Fig. 8.4b.

However, gateway X likely knows of a better route. Since F and K have exchanged routing information, the IGP exchange between X and K reveals that a better path than 16 exists to F. X stores in its routing table that this path is through K. It also sends an EGP mes-

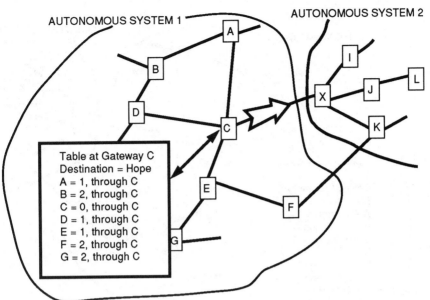

(a)

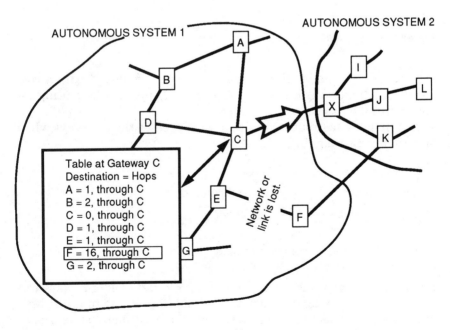

(b)

Figure 8.4 (a) Autonomous Systems (or Areas) Interactions; (b) Effect of Losing a Network Connection; (c) Receiving Routing Information from Gateway X.

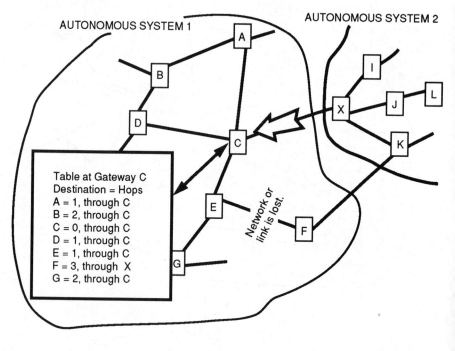

Table at Gateway C
Destination = Hops
A = 1, through C
B = 2, through C
C = 0, through C
D = 1, through C
E = 1, through C
F = 3, through X
G = 2, through C

(c)

Figure 8.4 (*Continued*)

sage to core gateway C that F can be reached through X with a cost metric of 3. Since 3 is less than 16, gateway C updates its routing table accordingly, as seen in Fig. 8.4c.

In summary, the routing tables are changed at the gateways when an arriving message indicates that

A new network has been found.

A better path to a network has been found.

A "better" path must be degraded.

Who participates in exchanging routing information and in executing routing logic?

We have said in previous chapters that both hosts and gateways can execute routing logic and that it is possible for a host to fulfill both functions. We have also said that the use of a host computer as a gateway must take into account the issues of delay, throughput, and efficiency. Typically, the host in an internet does not have as much knowledge about the network that the gateway has. The host usually routes traffic through the IP routing algorithm and default values in the routing tables; as a general practice, it routes traffic to gateways. These gateways have a more thorough knowledge of the network and perform more elaborate routing functions.

As stated earlier, the internet protocols are based on the use of partial routing tables at some gateways and full routing tables at others. This approach represents a compromise between, at one extreme, loading full routing tables in all machines and, at the other extreme, using directory-less schemes. The practice of using full routing tables could be unduly burdensome for a number of reasons. First, all machines do not need to know the locations of all other machines. Second, excessive memory could be consumed storing complete routing information in large tables. Third, searching the tables to extract the routing information could consume considerable CPU processing time. In any event, these factors should be considered very carefully before a decision is made to load these tasks onto an applications processor or a specialized switching processor.

The practical approach is to use a relatively small number of gateways that maintain complete routing tables for the networks. The outlying gateways keep only partial information (at the host level, the host may have even more limited routing tables). With this approach, the managers of "outlying" networks need not concern themselves with the onerous task of maintaining large tables of routing information. They need only be concerned with their specific networks.

In summary, the principal advantages to the use of partial routing tables are (a) storage saving, (b) CPU cycle saving, and (c) the ability of the outlying network managers to manage their routing operations in a relatively simple fashion without affecting other networks.

Clarifying terms

Before we move to an examination of specific gateway protocols, we should make certain that several terms that were introduced earlier in this chapter are understood. Note the following:

GGP: Used to provide routing information between core gateways

EGP: Used to provide routing information between autonomous systems

IGP: Used to provide routing information within an autonomous system and perhaps within an area

It is important to remember that some people use these three terms generically to describe a concept. This practice is acceptable as long as it is understood how the terms are used.

The terms *GGP* and *EGP* also identify two specific Internet gateway standards that are examined in this chapter. The term *IGP* does not identify a specific standard but rather (a) a concept, and/or (b) a family of interior gateway protocols.

Finally, as you read this chapter, keep in mind that the GGP is really a specialized autonomous system. Second, some autonomous systems use EGP internally; that is, the EGP is sometimes used as an IGP.

Now that we have analyzed the general concepts of gateways, we can turn our attention to the specific gateway protocols. First we introduce the Gateway-to-Gateway protocol (GGP). Next we examine the External Gateway Protocol (EGP). Then we examine three interior gateway protocols (IGPs). In the last section of the chapter, we examine the Open Shortest Path First (OSPF) standard.

The Gateway-to-Gateway Protocol (GGP)

Introduction

The GGP protocol was used in the Internet gateway system but has been replaced by SPREAD (not documented as of this writing). GGP is discussed here because it is a good example of a vector-distance protocol. We speak of it in the present tense because some networks still use variations of the protocol. The name is derived from the routing update message which contains pairs (V, D) of values in which V (the vector) identifies the destination and D (the distance) identifies the number of intermediate hops (networks/gateways) to the destination. It is similar to the earlier example in this chapter of fewest-hops networks.

Vector-distance protocols require that all gateways exchange information, because an option route is computed based on a sum of the distance between each gateway. Moreover, information is only exchanged between adjacent gateways that share a common network.

To begin our analysis of GGP, let us imagine that a GGP gateway is brought up (initialized) in a network. We assume that it has no knowledge of the network or its neighbors. Indeed, when a network gateway begins operations, it assumes that its neighbors are down and that it is not connected to them. Therefore, the distance to another node in a routing table would be an infinite number of hops (known as infinity).

The first order of business is to determine if a gateway can connect to its directly attached networks. Therefore, it must send messages to these networks to determine the state of the physical attachments. These operations are not defined in GGP and are network dependent. A gateway might actually send messages to itself to determine if it can communicate with a network. In other words, a gateway might periodically poll an attached network to determine if it can receive messages from the network. To accomplish this operation, it typically uses some of the GGP status messages discussed later in this chapter.

Neighbor connectivity analysis

Assuming that the gateway is operational, it ascertains its connectivity to its neighbors by using the Internet K-out-of-N algorithm. Every 15 seconds, the gateway sends a status message (called an echo message) to each of its neighbors. In turn, the neighbors send back an echo reply. If there is no reply to K-out-of-N echo messages, the neighbor is considered to be inoperable. The Internet standard states that the value of K is 3 and the value of N is 4.

On the other hand, if a neighbor is down and the gateway subsequently receives J-out-of-M echo replies, the neighbor is then declared to be up. The Internet standard states that the value of J is 2 and the value of M is 4. However, the values of J, K, M, and N can be set to any number deemed appropriate for autonomous systems.

Exchanging routing information

GGP gateways maintain several variables and numbers to manage the routing information exchanged within an internet. Figure 8.5 shows an example of the exchange of routing information between a gateway and its neighbor. We use this example to introduce the numbers and variables as well as the basic operations for the information exchange messages.

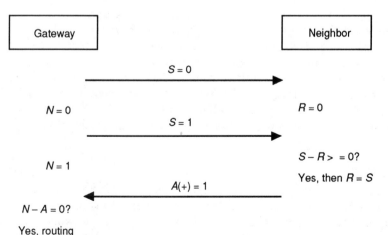

Figure 8.5   GGP: Exchanging Routing Information.

A sending gateway maintains a send sequence number N at its node. This number is used to sequence its updates to its neighbors. Upon the transmission of an update message, N is incremented by one. (It can be initialized to any value.) A neighbor also maintains a number; it is designated the receive sequence number R. Upon receiving an update from a gateway, the neighbor will compare its value R with the send sequence number contained in the message. The sequence number in Fig. 8.5 is labeled S.

The neighbor performs the comparison operation by subtracting R from S. If this value is greater than or equal to 0, it accepts the routing update message. As shown in the figure, the condition is true. Next, it sends back an acknowledgment (labeled A(+) = 1 in the figure). It then replaces the value R with the value S.

The acknowledgment is returned to the original sender (the gateway) in the acknowledgment message unit. In the example, the A value signifies an acknowledgment and the plus sign signifies a positive acknowledgment. The value 1 signifies the update value that is acknowledged.

Upon receiving this acknowledgment message, the transmitting gateway performs an N − A subtraction. If the result of this calculation is equal to 0, it knows that the routing update has been acknowledged by its neighbor. If it does not equal 0, then the gateway knows that an old routing update has been acknowledged and it will continue to transmit the S = 1 message until the neighbor sends the proper acknowledgment value back.

Figure 8.5 also indicates that the first message sent (S = 0) was not acknowledged by the neighbor. GGP states that if a second routing update is received before the first routing update is acknowledged, the neighbor need only acknowledge the second routing update.

In the event that negative acknowledgments are received, the gateway uses the A and N values in several checking routines to determine at which point it is to begin retransmitting.

The gateway must retransmit routing updates periodically until the messages are acknowledged and whenever its send sequence number changes. By use of the J, K, M, N algorithms, the gateway knows that it need not send updates to neighbors that are in the down state.

Computing routes

The internet procedure for exchanging routing information is described in RFC 823. We summarize the algorithms in this section.

An update to a routing table consists of (a) a list of networks that are reachable through the gateway, and (b) the number of hops required to reach each of these networks. For example, Fig. 8.6 shows

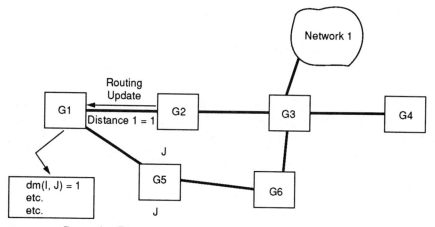

Figure 8.6 Computing Routes.

gateways 1 through 6 (labeled G1, G2, etc.) in which G2 is sending a routing update to G1. This routing update occurs because G2 thinks it is closer to G3 than is G1. Therefore, it must pass this information to G1 for G1 to be able to make an efficient routing decision.

Figure 8.6 shows that G2 is labeled with variable J and the network attached to G3 is labeled with variable I. The routing protocol works with the vector of dm (I, J), which contains the distance to I from J as reported by J. Since J is one hop away from I, dm (I, J) = 1.

Upon receiving the routing update message, G1 copies several of its fields into a routing table. In this example, it copies the information from G2 into the Jth entry of this table, which is the connectivity between G1 and its Jth neighbor. This entry is represented as d(J).

Next, G1 calculates a minimum distance vector which contains the minimum distance to each gateway from G1. In Fig. 8.6, G3 is represented as the Ith entry in this vector. The Ith entry is represented as MinD(I) and is calculated as

$$\text{MinD(I)} = \text{minimum over all neighbors of } d(J) + dm(I, J)$$

where d(J) is the distance between G1 and G2 (the Jth neighbor) and dm (I, J) is the distance from G2 (the Jth neighbor) to G3 (the Ith network attached to G3).

G1 would not store neighbor G5's distance to network I in MinD(I) because G5's dm(I, J) value to network I is greater than that of G3.

After the routes have been recomputed, G1 determines if it should notify its neighbors with routing update messages. It only sends updates if all three of the following conditions occur:

- A routing update from a neighbor is different from a previously received update
- A gateway's interface has changed its state
- A gateway's neighbor gateway has changed its state

Adding new networks. The addition of a new network to the routing tables is a fairly simple process. Upon receiving a routing update message, the gateway compares the address list to its list of neighbor addresses. If the address is not in the table, it adds the address to the table of neighbor addresses. It can use a polling message later to determine if the neighbor is up. It also adds the new network to its hop count matrix with the procedures discussed earlier.

Nonrouting gateways. The Internet standards allow the gateway to participate in forwarding datagrams without using the GGP routing operations. If such a topology is implemented, the gateways that are situated behind the nonrouting gateway must be known by the routing gateways.

GGP message formats

The GGP message format is depicted in Fig. 8.7. This message is encapsulated into an internet datagram. Therefore, although not shown in this figure, the internet header precedes the message fields. We now examine each of the fields in the GGP message.

The first field is the *type* field. This 8-bit field specifies that the message is a routing update message, for example. This field contains the value of 12 to distinguish it from other GGP messages. The next field is an *unused* field and is not defined at this time.

The *sequence number* field consists of 16 bits. It is used to sequence the routing updates between the sender and the receiver. The initialization of the sequence number must be agreed upon between both parties.

The next field is the *need update* field. This field is set to the value of one if the source gateway needs a routing update for the destination gateway. Otherwise, it is set to zero.

The next field, labeled *number distance groups,* is an 8-bit field. (This field is also labeled n-distance.) It contains the number of groups reported in this update message. Each distance group must contain a distance value and the number of networks followed by the actual network identification numbers that are reachable at that distance. GGP does not require that all the distances be reported.

Since the gateway protocols need not deal with the host address of the internet address structure, the GGP does not require that the host

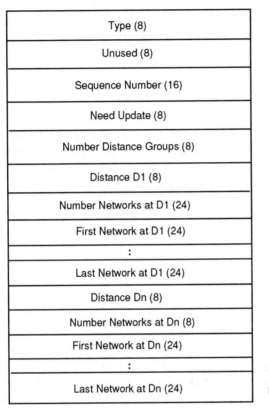

Type (8)
Unused (8)
Sequence Number (16)
Need Update (8)
Number Distance Groups (8)
Distance D1 (8)
Number Networks at D1 (24)
First Network at D1 (24)
:
Last Network at D1 (24)
Distance Dn (8)
Number Networks at Dn (8)
First Network at Dn (24)
:
Last Network at Dn (24)

Figure 8.7 GGP Message Format.

(*n*) = Number of bits in the field

portion of the address be included in the address fields. Therefore, the network address fields may be variable in length (1, 2, or 3 octets). GGP does not need a length field for the address fields; it need only examine the first bits of the network identifier to determine the number of octets in each address field.

The *distance D1* field is a value containing the hop count or some other distance indicator which is applicable to the distance group 1. The field labeled *number networks at D1* (often labeled *n1-dist*) contains the value representing the number of networks which are reported within distance group 1. The fields labeled *first network at D1* and *last network at D1* contain the identification of the networks in the group. As mentioned earlier, these are the actual IP addresses of the networks concerned.

The GGP message format then repeats itself until the last distance group has been described. This is labeled *Dn* in Fig. 8.7.

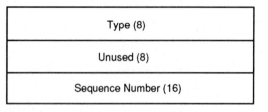

Figure 8.8   GGP Acknowledgment Message.

Figure 8.8 depicts the GGP acknowledgment message. The type acknowledgment, labeled *type* in this figure, simply identifies whether the acknowledgment is positive (type value = 2) or negative (type value = 10). The *sequence number* is used to acknowledge (either negatively or positively) previous traffic.

Figure 8.9 shows the format for the echo request and echo reply

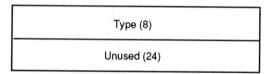

Figure 8.9   GGP Echo Request/Reply Message.

messages. These messages are used by the gateways to notify each other about their status and to test if the other gateway is responding properly. The message is a very simple structure consisting of the *type* of message (8 = echo, 0 = echo reply). The *source address* in the internet IP header is used in these messages to identify the two neighbors that are participating in the echo exchange.

Figure 8.10 shows the format for the network interface status mes-

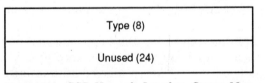

Figure 8.10   GGP Network Interface Status Message.

sage. It is used by a gateway to determine if it is able to send and receive traffic. Since the gateway may send these messages to itself, the *IP destination address* contains the address of the network interface of the gateway. The *type* field is set to 9.

Example of a GGP update message

Figure 8.11 shows an example of a GGP update message in relation to the internet topology examples discussed in previous sections. In this figure, the networks between the gateways have been labeled with the network portion of an internet address. The update message in this figure would be issued by gateway C to gateway X.

Three distance groups are reported: 0 = networks directly attached to C; 1 = networks one hop away from C; and 2 = networks two hops away from C.

External Gateway Protocol (EGP)

Introduction

The external gateway protocol (EGP) is used to provide network reachability information between neighboring gateways. Although the name of the protocol includes the term "exterior," these gateways may exist in the same or different autonomous systems. However, the more common approach is to use EGP between gateways not belonging to the same autonomous system.

The reader might wonder why yet another gateway protocol is needed. After all, why not use GGP to handle the exchange of routing information between autonomous systems? To understand the need for EGP, consider the following situation, shown in Fig. 8.12.

Gateways A, B, C, and D are core gateways and are used to manage the routing of traffic between networks 1, 2, 3, 4, and 6. Therefore, they can use the GGP operations for exchanging routing information.

These gateways use internet addresses to support routing between these networks. However, a problem is encountered when an attempt is made to route datagrams to networks 5 and 7. From the perspective of the core gateways, networks 5 and 7 do not exist. They are hidden from the view of the core behind network 6.

Therefore, we face the problem of how to provide information about networks between core gateways and noncore gateways. The situation is somewhat complex in that we must decide who is responsible for exchanging information with whom. The answer to the problem is to develop concise rules concerning which gateway is responsible for providing information to the core network about the existence and reachability of the *hidden* networks.

The internet solution is a scheme which allows an autonomous system to send *reachability* information to any other autonomous system. Furthermore, these messages must go to at least one core gateway. In practice, one gateway in an autonomous system usually assumes the responsibility for these tasks. From the perspective of Fig. 8.12, gate-

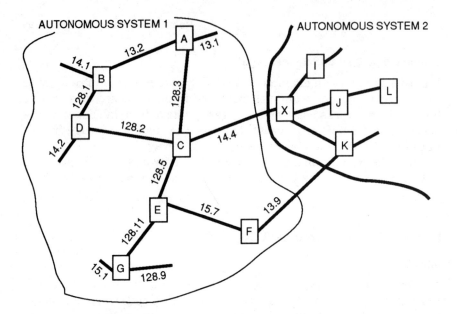

AUTONOMOUS SYSTEM 1

AUTONOMOUS SYSTEM 2

Type = 12
Unused
Sequence Number = 24 (for example)
Need Update = No (for example)
Number Distance Groups = 3
Distance D1 = 0
Number Networks at D1 = 4
14.4, 128.5, 128.3, 128.2
Distance D2 = 1
Number Networks at D2 = 6
15.7, 128.11, 14.2, 128.1, 13.1, 13.2
Distance D3 = 2
Number Networks at D3 = 4
15.1, 128.9, 13.9, 14.1

(n) = Number of bits in the field

Figure 8.11   A GGP Update Message Example.

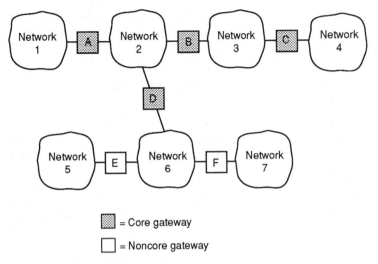

= Core gateway

= Noncore gateway

Figure 8.12 Core and Noncore Gateways.

way D assumes this responsibility. This means that gateway D belongs to an autonomous system consisting of networks 5, 6, and 7, as
well as gateways E and F.

Thus, the EGP serves to partition the responsibility for maintaining
and updating routing tables to specific gateways in an internet.

Major operations of EGP

EGP contains procedures to (a) acquire neighbors, (b) exchange information messages between neighbors, and (c) monitor the reachability
of neighbors. EGP uses polling procedures which allow the gateways
to monitor each other and to exchange routing update messages.

The EGP states

EGP is a state-driven protocol, which means that its operations are
described with state tables and state transition procedures. EGP contains five states numbered 0 through 4. If a machine has a number of
neighbors, it will maintain a state table for each neighbor. Shortly, we
will use the following states to clarify further how the protocol operates within a gateway:

Idle state (state 0): Defines a gateway which has no resources and
is not involved in any protocol activity. It can respond to initiation
messages, but it must ignore all other types of messages. Upon the

receipt of a message denoting some type of request, it can transition to a down state or, if it chooses to begin activities, it can transition to an acquisition state.

Acquisition state (state 1):   Allows the gateway to transmit request messages periodically. It may, however, receive messages and move to the down state, or it may return to the idle state.

Down state (state 2):   This state means that the gateway is down. It is not allowed to process polling messages and it is not allowed to send them. It is allowed to receive certain kinds of traffic, discussed in more detail shortly.

Up state (state 3):   Used to declare the neighbor gateway to be up. With this state, the gateway can process and respond to all the EGP messages. This state is used for the transmission of polling commands.

Cease state (state 4):   As the name implies, this is the state in which the gateway ceases updating operations, although it does continue to send a cease command and receive a cease-ack response.

Types of messages

The EGP messages are classified as (a) commands, which require some type of action to be performed; (b) responses, which are sent to give an indication of the status of an action; and (c) indications, which can be sent at any time. Table 8.1 lists the commands along with the permissible responses as defined in the state transition tables.

Like many protocols, EGP uses state transition tables in conjunction with timers, sequence numbers, parameters, and state variables to control the sending and receiving of these messages. Table 8.2 lists and describes briefly the sequence numbers, timers, and variables. Later discussions will show some examples of their use. The parameters P1–P5 are fixed, although their values (in parentheses) are suggested by RFC 904. All other values are set during an initial handshake (Request/Confirm exchange) between neighbors. The one exception to the last statement is the send sequence number S.

TABLE 8.1   EGP Commands, Responses, and Indications

Command	Responses/Indications
Request	Confirm, Refuse, Error
Cease	Cease-ack, Error
Hello	I-H-U (I heard you), Error
Poll	Update, Error

TABLE 8.2   **EGP Timers and Other Parameters**

Name	Description
R	Receive sequence number
S	Send sequence number
T1	Interval between Hello command retransmissions
T2	Interval between Poll command retransmissions
T3	Interval during which neighbor-reachability indications are counted
M	Hello polling mode
t1	timer 1—retransmission timer (for Request, Hello, and Cease)
t2	timer 2—poll retransmission timer (for Poll command)
t3	timer 3—abort timer
P1	Minimum interval acceptable between successive Hello commands received (30 seconds)
P2	Minimum interval acceptable between successive Poll commands received (2 minutes)
P3	Interval between Request or Cease command retransmissions (30 seconds)
P4	Interval during which state variables are maintained in the absence of command/responses (in Up/Down states) (1 hour)
P5	Interval during which state variables are maintained in the absence of responses in the Acquisition and Cease states (2 minutes)

EGP message types

EGP operates with 10 message types. These message types are listed and briefly explained in Table 8.3.

Figure 8.13 shows the format for the header that is included on all EGP messages. It consists of seven fields and may be followed by other fields. The EGP *version* number identifies the current version of the protocol. Its current value is 2. The value is used by communicating EGP modules to ensure that they are using compatible software.

TABLE 8.3   **EGP Messages**

EGP Message	Function of Message
Request acquisition	Request the acquisition of neighbor and/or initialize polling variables
Confirm acquisition	Confirm acquisition of neighbor and/or initialize polling variables
Refuse acquisition	Negative response to acquisition of neighbor
Cease request	Request deacquisition of neighbor
Cease-ack response	Confirm deacquisition of neighbor
Hello	Request neighbor reachability
I-H-U (I heard you)	Confirm neighbor reachability
Poll	Request network reachability update
Update	Network reachability update information
Error	Error response to a message

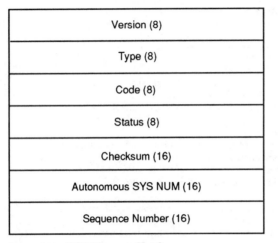

| Version (8) |
| Type (8) |
| Code (8) |
| Status (8) |
| Checksum (16) |
| Autonomous SYS NUM (16) |
| Sequence Number (16) |

Figure 8.13 EGP Message Header.

The *type* field identifies the type of message, such as a neighbor acquisition request. The *code* field contains a value to identify the code or subtype of message, such as a cease command. The value of the *status* field depends on the message type.

The *checksum* field is used to perform an error detection on the message. The algorithm used is the same one used by IP. The *autonomous system number* identifies the specific autonomous system of the sending gateway. The *sequence number* is used to sequence the messages properly between the gateways.

Figure 8.14 shows the format for the neighbor acquisition message. The fields in the message are coded to convey the following information (when the field information is the same as in Fig. 8.13, it is not repeated here):

Type: This field is always set to 3 to identify a neighbor acquisition message.

Code: This field is set to one of five values:

0 = Request command
1 = Confirm response
2 = Refuse response
3 = Cease command
4 = Cease-ack response

Status: This field is set to one of eight values (discussed in more detail shortly):

0 = Unspecified
1 = Active mode

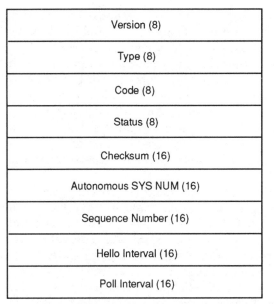

| Version (8) |
| Type (8) |
| Code (8) |
| Status (8) |
| Checksum (16) |
| Autonomous SYS NUM (16) |
| Sequence Number (16) |
| Hello Interval (16) |
| Poll Interval (16) |

Figure 8.14   EGP Neighbor Acquisition Message.

2 = Passive mode
3 = Insufficient resources
4 = Administratively prohibited
5 = Going down
6 = Parameter problem
7 = Protocol violation

Hello interval: Specifies the minimum Hello command polling interval in seconds.

Poll interval: Specifies the minimum Poll command polling interval in seconds.

The hello interval and poll interval are used only with request and confirm messages.

The status field is used by EPG to provide further information between the communicating modules. Briefly, a code of 0 is used when the protocol can find nothing else that is appropriate to place in the status field. A value of 1 is used when the message indicates an active status mode. The value 2 indicates a passive status mode.

In the event that the gateway does not have sufficient resources to process a request, it sets the status code to 3. RFC 904 suggests that this code be used if the machine is out of memory for the table management operations or otherwise out of system resources. A status code of 4 is used to indicate that the proposed action is not allowed. For example, the value in the autonomous system field cannot be identified or the gateway suggests the use of another gateway.

A status code of 5 indicates that the gateway is going down through an operator-initiated stop or through the expiration of the t3 abort timer. A status code of 6 indicates a parameter problem with the incoming message; possible scenarios include unintelligible parameters or the inability to assume a compatible mode. Finally, a status code of 7 signifies that a protocol violation has occurred because an incoming command or response message is incompatible with the state at the machine.

Figure 8.15 shows the format for the neighbor reachability messages. The *type* field is equal to 3. The *code* field is equal to 0 for a Hello command and 1 for an I-H-U response. The *status* field is equal to 0, which the standard identifies as indeterminate. The value of 1 signifies an up state and the value of 2 signifies a down state. Information for the other fields remains the same as described for Fig. 8.13.

Figure 8.16 shows the format for the Poll command. The *type* field is set to a value of 2. The *code* field is set to a value of 0. The *status* field is set to 0, which the standard states is indeterminate. The value of 1 signifies an up state and the value of 2 signifies a down state. The *IP source network* field contains the IP address of the network about which reachability information is required. It identifies a network that is common to the autonomous system of the neighbor receiving this message. As before, the information for the other fields remains the same as described previously.

Figure 8.17 shows the format for the update response/indication

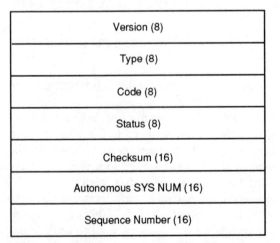

Figure 8.15   EGP Neighbor Reachability Message.

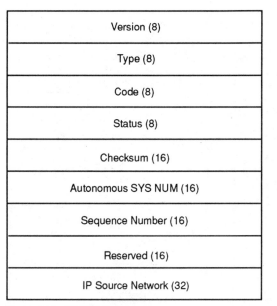

| Version (8) |
| Type (8) |
| Code (8) |
| Status (8) |
| Checksum (16) |
| Autonomous SYS NUM (16) |
| Sequence Number (16) |
| Reserved (16) |
| IP Source Network (32) |

Figure 8.16   EGP Poll Message.

message. To understand the protocol, this message must be studied in more detail. As the figure shows, the message contains a header (on the left side of the figure) and a repeating occurrence of fields for each gateway being reported (called a *gateway block*).

The *type* field for this message is set to 1. The *code* field is set to 0. The *status* field is set to one of the following values: 0, which is identified as indeterminate; 1 to signify up state; 2 to signify down state; and 128 to signify an unsolicited message state. The version, checksum, autonomous system numbers, and sequence number have been described previously.

The three remaining fields in the header provide the following information:

Number of int. GWs: Specifies the number of interior gateways reported in the message.

Number of ext. GWs: Specifies the number of exterior gateways reported in the message.

IP source network: Contains the IP address of the network about which reachability information is being reported.

Thereafter, the remainder of the message consists of the gateway block(s). The first field in a gateway block is the *gateway IP address*. It identifies the IP address of the gateway block. The *# distances* field

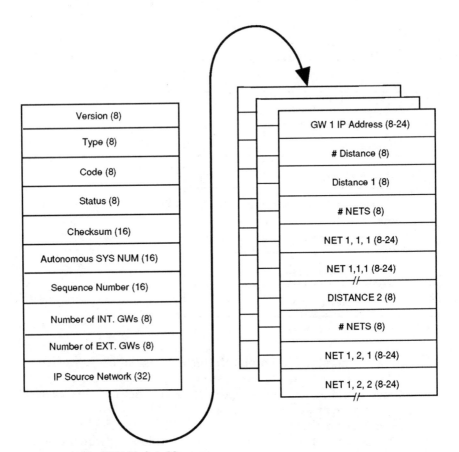

Figure 8.17   The EGP Update Message.

contains the number of distances reported in the gateway block. The distance field's contents differ depending on the architecture of the system. The *# nets* specifies the number of networks reported at each distance. Finally, the *net 1,1,1, 1,1, 2,* etc. contain the IP address of the networks reachable through the gateway.

Example of an EGP update message

Figure 8.18 provides an example of an EGP update message vis-à-vis a network topology. Autonomous system 1 contains networks 128.1, 128.2, 128.3, 128.4, and 128.5. Gateway 2 is designated as the EGP "server" for autonomous system 1. Gateways 1 and 3 are designated as EGP servers for autonomous systems 2 and 3, respectively.

A poll command from gateway 1 (event 1 in the figure) elicits a re-

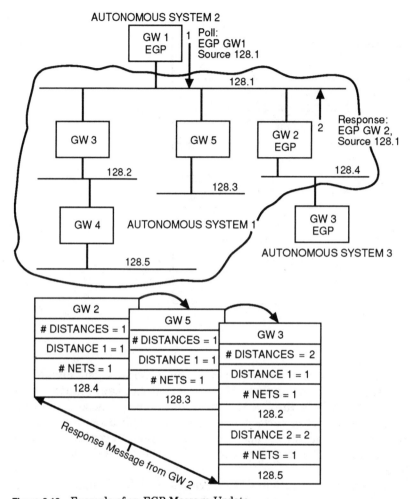

Figure 8.18   Example of an EGP Message Update.

sponse from gateway 2 (event 2 in the figure). The message sent from gateway 2 to gateway 1 is shown (excluding header) at the bottom part of the figure.

Figure 8.19 shows the format for the error response/indication message. This message is used to report on problems encountered by the gateway, usually based on the inability to process an incoming message. The *reason* field is coded with specific values to identify the nature of the error, and the *error message header* field contains the first 96 bits of the EGP header causing the problem. As before, the other fields were described previously.

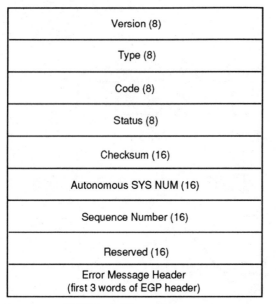

| Version (8) |
| Type (8) |
| Code (8) |
| Status (8) |
| Checksum (16) |
| Autonomous SYS NUM (16) |
| Sequence Number (16) |
| Reserved (16) |
| Error Message Header (first 3 words of EGP header) |

Figure 8.19 EGP Error Message.

EGP events

EGP is not only based on state transition diagrams, but also on an event list. The protocol defines 15 events that can cause state transitions. Table 8.4 lists the events and their names. These events are based on the receipt of certain messages, the expiration of timers, or operating system or human operator intervention. In conjunction with the state diagram logic, these events define the specific actions of the protocol.

To explain these events and state transition tables would entail explaining the entire protocol, which is beyond the scope of this book and best left to RFC 904. However, several examples of EGP operations during the up state are provided in the next section to clarify the protocol.

EGP operations during the up state

Table 8.5 lists the activities and state transitions vis-à-vis the events. We will use the row entries as beginning discussion points for an explanation of how the protocol operates in the up state. Please be aware that this example is a general overview of the activities of the gateway during the up state. Our goal is to give the reader a general understanding of the protocol without trivializing its operations. Some

TABLE 8.4   EGP Events

Name	Event
Up	At least j neighbor-reachability indications have been received within the last T3 seconds.
Down	At most k neighbor-reachability indications have been received within the last T3 seconds.
Request	Request command has been received.
Confirm	Confirm command has been received.
Refuse	Refuse response has been received.
Cease	Cease command has been received.
Cease-ack	Cease-ack response has been received.
Hello	Hello command has been received.
I-H-U	I-H-U response has been received.
Poll	Poll command has been received.
Update	Update response has been received.
Start	Start event has been recognized due to system or operator intervention.
Stop/t3	Stop event has been recognized due to (a) system or operator intervention, or (b) expiration of the abort timer t3.
t1	Timer t1 has counted down to zero.
t2	Timer t2 has counted down to zero.

TABLE 8.5   Events, Actions, and States in the EGP

	0 Idle	1 Acquisition	2 Down	3 Up	4 Cease
Up	0	1	3/Poll	3	4
Down	0	1	2	2	4
Request	2/Confirm	2/Confirm	2/Confirm	2/Confirm	4/Cease
Confirm	0/Cease	2	2	3	4
Refuse	0/Cease	0	2	3	4
Cease	0/Cease-ack	0/Cease-ack	0/Cease-ack	0/Cease-ack	0/Cease-ack
Cease-ack	0	1	2	3	0
Hello	0/Cease	1	2/I-H-U	3/I-H-U	4
I-H-U	0/Cease	1	2/Process	3/Process	4
Poll	0/Cease	1	2	3/Update	4
Update	0/Cease	1	2	3/Process	4
Start	1/Request	1/Request	1/Request	1/Request	4
Stop/t3	0	0	4/Cease	4/Cease	0
t1	0	1/Request	2/Hello	3/Hello	4/Cease
t2	0	1	2	3/Poll	4

entries in the table have two parts. They are read as n/a, where n = next state and a = action taken. This example will use the column labeled *3UP* and all the rows pertaining to the *3UP* column.

The row entry in the table labeled *Up* means that the proper *j* neighbor reachability indications have been received within the proper t3 time; therefore, the machine remains in the up state. The next row entry means the *Down* event takes the machine to state 2 (the down state). (Consult Table 8.4 for definitions of each event.) The machine stops timer t2, since polling transmissions are unnecessary.

The row entry labeled *Request* describes the actions taken when a request command message arrives at the gateway. This message is formatted as a neighbor acquisition message (see Fig. 8.14). It is used to request the acquisition of a neighbor and to set up the hello and polling intervals (whose values are transmitted in the message). The gateway must respond with a *Confirm* message. It also reinitializes all state variables and resets timer t1 to T1 seconds and timer t3 to P5 seconds.

The row entry labeled *Refuse* means the gateway has received a refuse message. It generally stays in the same state upon securing this message.

The row entry labeled *Cease* means the gateway has received a neighbor acquisition message with a code of cease command (3). The gateway must respond with a *cease-ack* response. It stops all timers and enters the idle state.

The row entry labeled *Hello* means that the gateway has received a hello command message. Since this message is used to determine neighbor reachability, the gateway responds with an I-H-U response and remains in the up state (state 3).

The row entry labeled *I-H-U* means that the gateway has received an I-H-U response. It processes the information and remains in the up state.

The row entry labeled *Poll* means that the gateway has received a poll command. Remember that this message (see Fig. 8.16) is used to request a network-reachability update and contains the internet address of the network about which the sending gateway wishes reachability information. Therefore, the responding gateway sends an update message (see Fig. 8.17), which contains the information to satisfy the polling query. As noted in the table, the gateway remains in the up state.

The receipt of an *Update* message (as seen in the table's row entry labeled *Update*) requires the gateway to process reachability information and remain in the up state. This message has been sent to the gateway because of a prior polling command. Therefore, it can act as an ACK to the poll.

The *Start* event is a result of an operator or operating system action. It results in a transition to the acquisition state and a request message.

The *Stop* event occurs due to a problem or the expiration of the abort timer (t3). The protocol requires that a *Cease* message be sent to request the deactivation of neighbors (placing them in an idle state). Timer t1 is set to P3 seconds, and timer t3 is set to P5 seconds.

The expiration of timer t1 requires that a Hello message be transmitted. The expiration of timer t2 requires that a Poll message be retransmitted. In both instances, the protocol entity remains in the up state.

Figure 8.20 shows several of the more important activities and the relationships of the messages at the gateway during the up state. Since EGP contains many more rules than we have covered here, the reader is encouraged to study RFC 904 for more information.

Other features of EGP

The reader should be aware that EGP is restricted to advertise reachability to those networks completely within the gateway's autonomous system. Therefore, an EGP gateway has a restricted authority. One of its values is to prevent a plethora of information from being transmitted around a network.

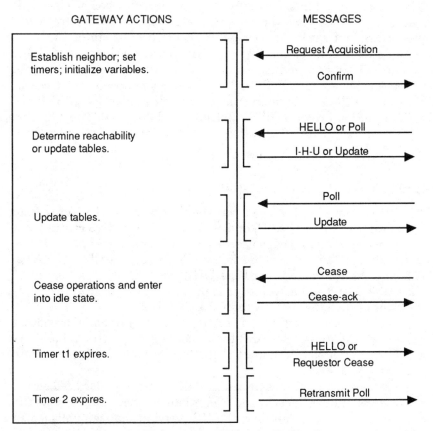

Figure 8.20 Summary of EGP Operations During the Up State.

EGP is similar to GGP except that the EGP messages advertise multiple gateways. As we learned in this section, the EGP gateway is able to send a sequence of reachability information blocks relative to a specified network.

However, it must be understood that EGP does not compute against the values contained in the routing update message. The software is designed only to establish that EGP can state that there is a path available. The name "Distances field" in the update message is really a misnomer. Therefore, EGP is used to advertise reachability information and cannot function with elaborate topologies which include looping gateways.

Interior Gateway Protocols (IGPs)

We stated earlier in this chapter that the term *interior gateway protocol (IGP)* is a generic term that refers to a concept as well as a variety of specific systems. Unfortunately, the internet has no clear IGP "leader" due to the somewhat unsystematic way the IGPs were developed and promulgated. In fairness, it should also be stated that network administrators prefer different IGP approaches because of different internal network management requirements. Nonetheless, since this book's subject is TCP/IP and the internet protocols, our focus in this section will be to highlight three internet-related IGPs: (1) Routing Information Protocol (RIP), (2) Hello, and (3) gated. The next section examines a better IGP called the Open Shortest Path First Protocol (OSPF).

Routing Information Protocol (RIP)

The RIP system was developed based on research at the Xerox Palo Alto Research Center (PARC) and Xerox's PUP and XNS routing protocols. Interestingly, its wide use was due to its implementation at the University of California at Berkeley (UCB) in a number of LANs. UCB also distributed RIP with its UNIX system. It is rather ironic that RIP is designed for LANs yet is now used in some wide area networks—if for no other reason than that it's there.

Since RIP was designed for LANs, it is based on a broadcast technology: A gateway periodically broadcasts its routing table to its neighbors. The broadcast aspect of RIP has brought forth complaints about its inefficiency.

The reader should also be aware that RIP is not standardized across vendor product lines. Most vendors offer value-added extensions to the protocol. This section describes the RIP version that is published in RFC 1058.

RIP is classified as a vector-distance algorithm routing protocol. RIP routing decisions are based on the number of intermediate "hops" to the final destination. Early descriptions of this type of protocol were provided by L. R. Ford and D. R. Fulkerson (*Flows in Networks,* Princeton University Press, Princeton, NJ, 1962). Therefore, RIP is sometimes called a Ford-Fulkerson algorithm, or a Bellman-Ford algorithm, because R. E. Bellman devised the routing equation (*Dynamic Programming,* Princeton University Press, Princeton, NJ, 1957).

RIP advertises only network addresses and distances (usually a number of hops). It is similar to GGP in that it uses a hop count to compute the route cost, but it uses a maximum value of 16 to indicate that a network is unreachable. GGP uses a value of 255 to designate a network unreachable. Also, RIP needs information on all networks within the autonomous system and, like GGP, it exchanges information only with neighbors.

Machines that participate in the RIP operations are active or passive devices. Active machines (usually gateways) advertise routes to other machines. Passive machines (usually host computers) do not advertise routes but receive messages and update their routing tables.

The hop count is a metric for the "cost" of the route. Other metrics may be used, such as delay, security, bandwidth, etc., but most implementations use a simple hop count.

RIP uses the user datagram protocol (UDP). UDP port number 520 is used by the RIP machines for sending and receiving RIP messages.

Each machine that uses RIP must have a routing table. The table contains an entry for each destination that is serviced by the machine. Each entry in the table must contain at least the following information:

Destination IP address

A metric (between 1 and 15) of the "cost" (number of hops) to reach the destination

IP address of the next gateway in the path to the destination

Indicators for determining if the route has changed recently

Timers associated with the route

RIP timers

Two timers are associated with each route: a *time-out timer* and a *garbage-collection* timer. The time-out timer is set each time a route is initialized or updated. If 180 seconds elapse before an update is received, or if the update contains a distance metric of 16, the route is considered obsolete. However, it is not removed until the garbage-collection timer has also expired. This timer is set for another 120 seconds, and after it expires the route is removed from the routing table. Until the garbage-collection timer expires, the route is included in all update messages.

Another timer is used to send updates (called *responses in RIP*) to neighboring machines. Every 30 seconds, these messages are broadcast by active gateways. They contain pairs of values. One value of the pair is an IP address; the other value is the hop count to that address from the source of the message.

Example of RIP operations

Figure 8.21 shows an example of RIP operations. Gateways G5 and G6 are reporting a (D, V) of (1, 5) in regard to network 5: They can reach network 5 with a metric cost of 1. This message is relayed to G3, which updates its routing table entry to network 5 with a cost of 2. Next, G3 sends a message to G1 and G2, which stores a cost of 3 to network 5. In turn, G1 and G2 advertise a (D, V) of (3, 5) to other gateways, and so on.

RIP requires that a route, once learned, cannot change until a (D, V) is received that represents a better route to the vector. Also, if a gateway receives a message of the same distance metric to a network (as G3 did by receiving messages from G5 and G6), it uses the first arriving message.

RIP problems

In retrospect, the Internet authorities would most likely have opted for a gateway protocol other than RIP. Indeed, changes have been

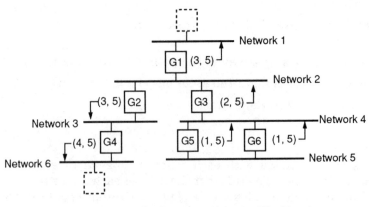

Where (D, V) = (D) distance to (V) vector (IP address)

Figure 8.21   Example of RIP Operations.

made to the original version to correct some rather serious deficiencies. One of these problems, called *counting to infinity,* is shown in Fig. 8.22. Gateway 5 has lost its connection to network 5. When this event occurs, it sends an RIP message through network 4 to gateway 3 with the (D, V) = (16, 5). This means that it has an infinity distance metric value to network 5 of 16. However, as noted in event 1, gateway 3 understands that it has a distance metric of 2 to gateway 5. Since this value is better than (16, 5), it maintains its routing table entry and advertises this value back to G5. G5, upon receiving the message that network 5 can be reached through G3 with a metric of 2, changes its update table as indicated in event 3 with (D, V) = (3, 5). That is, two hops through gateway 3 plus one more hop from gateway 5 equals 3. This message is related back to G3, and we see in event 4 that it changes its routing table to (D = V) = (4, 5) because it believes that to get to network 5 through G5 it must add one more hop to the value of 3 (which occurred in event 3). Thus, we find the two gateways incrementing their distance metric each time an RIP message is exchanged between them. Moreover, the two gateways will continue to send the datagram back and forth until the IP time-to-live value expires. Eventually the values will be incremented to the RIP infinity value of 16.

Recent RIP implementations handle this problem with a technique called the *split horizon* update. This approach requires a gateway to remember the neighbor from which the route was received. It is not allowed to send updates to a neighbor about a route that it learned

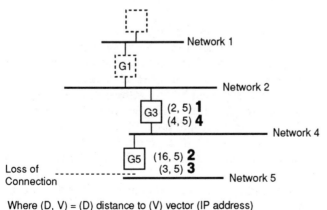

Where (D, V) = (D) distance to (V) vector (IP address)
  1 = Route to net 5 is through G5.
  2 = Connection gone, set to 16.
  3 = New route is through G3.
  4 = G3 adds one to its metric and sends to G5.

Figure 8.22 RIP Routing Problems.

from that neighbor. A variation to this idea is called the *split horizon with poisoned reverse*. This technique allows the routes to be included in the updates, but their metrics are set to infinity (16).

Another approach used in conjunction with the poison reverse technique is called a *triggered update*. This technique requires a gateway to send an immediate RIP message upon its receipt of messages indicating problems. It is not allowed to wait for the next ongoing broadcast. In other words, the approach requires that bad news about a connection or some other aspect of the network be propagated as quickly as possible.

These techniques ameliorate the routing exchange problems inherent in RIP. Even so, they are quite expensive for WANs in which bandwidth is precious and expensive. With smaller, more efficient, and higher-capacity LANs the enhanced approaches discussed in this section offer reasonable compromises. However, the preferable solution is to not use RIP but to migrate to a protocol like OSPF (discussed later in this chapter).

The RIP message format

The RIP message format is shown in Fig. 8.23. A header contains three fields:

Command: Set to 1 to specify the message as a request and 2 to specify a response

Version: Specifies the version number of the protocol

Reserved: Not used

Thereafter, a set of fields contains the values to identify a specific protocol family. Since RIP is intended to run over systems other than internet, the *family of net 1* field identifies the protocol family. For Internet applications, the value is 2. The next 12 octets contain the network ID (*net 1 address*) as reported by RIP. Obviously, an internet address needs only 4 of these 12 octets. RIP does not distinguish between the type of address in the message. It could be a subnet number, a network number, or a host number. If it contains a subnet number, the machine must know the mask structure; otherwise, the address will be ambiguous.

The *metric* field contains the metric value (usually the hop count) to the identified network.

The request and response

A request message can be sent to another gateway to ask for a routing update. The entries in the request are examined to determine how to respond. For each entry, the machine looks up the metric value in its

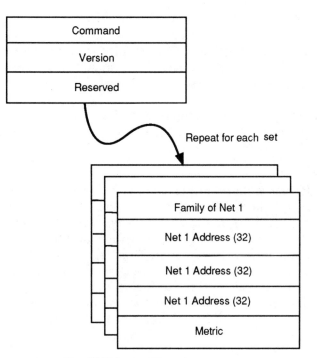

Figure 8.23 The RIP Message Format.

table and places the value into the metric field in a response message. An entire routing table can be obtained by coding the address family field as 0 and the metric field as 16.

RIP vs. OSPF

Due to the problems of RIP (technical deficiencies and lack of standardization), IAB's Internet Engineering Task Force has developed the Open Shortest Path First (OSPF) protocol. At this time, it is not widely implemented, but initial performances indicate that it eliminates the routing loops and dead ends described earlier in this chapter. The OSPF protocol does not broadcast its entire table to other routers. Rather, it sends each router information only about its own links. Each receiving router must acknowledge this traffic to the transmitting router. After receiving the information, each router builds appropriate entries in its routing table. OSPF is described later in this chapter.

The Hello Protocol

The Hello protocol is widely used throughout TCP/IP-based systems. Digital Equipment Corporation's LSI/11 minicomputer uses Hello in its "Fuzzball" software. It differs rather significantly from RIP, principally in that the Hello delay is based on time rather than hop counts. A gateway protocol advertising delay requires that the gateways have network clocks that are reasonably accurate in their alignment with each other. Therefore, Hello periodically provides messages for clock synchronization.

In addition to carrying routing information, a Hello message also contains a timestamp for use in checking time-related events.

The Hello message format

The Hello message format is shown in Fig. 8.24. The *checksum* field is used to check for errors in the message. The *date* field is the value of a local date of the message sender, and the *time* field contains the local time of the sender. The *timestamp* field is used by the machines to determine the round trip delay of the message. This field is important for a protocol, such as Hello, which uses delay as a metric for computing routes. The *offset* field is a pointer into the delay and offset entries. The *hosts* field specifies the number of entries that follow in the list of hosts. The *delay host* and *offset host* fields contain the delay to reach a host machine and an estimate between the difference (offset) between the sender's clock and the receiver's clock.

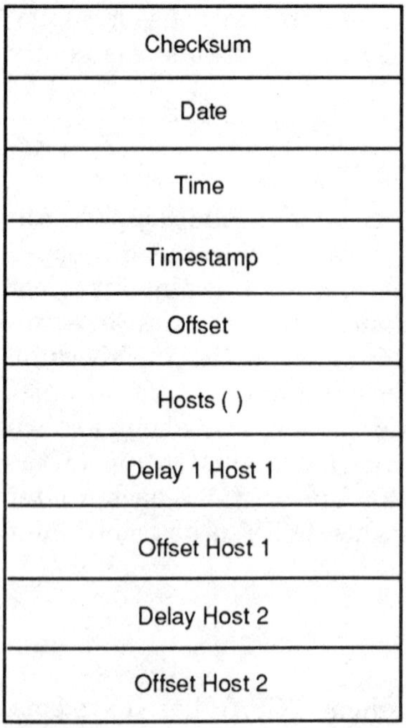

Checksum
Date
Time
Timestamp
Offset
Hosts ( )
Delay 1 Host 1
Offset Host 1
Delay Host 2
Offset Host 2

Figure 8.24 The Hello Message Format.

For those readers who wish more information on Hello, RFC 891 provides a description of the protocol.

Gated

This internal gateway protocol has also seen considerable use. For example, IBM uses it in its UNIX implementation on its newer personal computers. Gated combines many of the functions of RIP, Hello, and EGP. The program was developed at Cornell University and operates with UNIX. It allows the network manager to establish how gated may advertise routes to other exterior gateways. It is designed to accept either RIP or Hello messages and modify them for advertising within the gated framework.

Summary of Vector-Distance Protocols

We can summarize the major features of the vector-distance protocols as follows:

- Neighbor gateways exchange routing information.
- All gateways must participate in the operations, thus creating the potential for large message exchanges.
- Gateways may not know about other gateways beyond their neighbor. They only know that their attached networks are reachable through a neighbor gateway.
- Generally, messages are very large, containing all routing entries.
- Neighbors periodically test each other's status.
- They adjust slowly to topology changes.

Choosing the Optimum Path with a Shortest Path Algorithm

Recently, the Internet Engineering Task Force published RFC 1131, the OSPF (Open SPF) protocol. *SPF* means shortest path first. The term is inaccurate; the protocols described thus far in this chapter are designed to choose the shortest path. A better term is *optimum path,* but the former term is now accepted. The OSPF is based on well-tested techniques that have been used in the industry for a number of years. In this section, we describe these techniques. In the next section, we concentrate on the primary features of OSPF. In this discussion, the term *node* is synonymous with *gateway* and *router.*

Ideally, data communications networks are designed to route user traffic based on a variety of criteria, generally referred to as a least-cost routing or cost metrics. (Realistically, few are so designed, but the trend is toward these ideas.) The name does not mean that routing is based solely on obtaining the least-cost route in the literal sense. Other factors are often part of a network routing algorithm:

Capacity of the links

Delay and throughput requirements

Number of datagrams awaiting transmission onto a link

Load leveling through the network

Security requirements for the link

Type of traffic vis-à-vis the type of link

Number of intermediate links, networks, and gateways between the transmitting and receiving hosts

Ability to reach (connect to) intermediate nodes and, of course, the final receiving host

Even though networks vary in least-cost criteria, three constraints must be considered: (1) delay, (2) throughput, and (3) connectivity. If delay is excessive or if throughput is too little, the network does not meet the needs of the user community. The third constraint is quite obvious: The gateways and networks must be able to reach each other; otherwise, all other least-cost criteria are irrelevant.

As we have learned in this chapter, algorithms used to route data through an internet vary. Recently, the attention in the data communications industry has focused on two classes of routing algorithms. The first technique, called *bifurcated routing,* is designed to minimize the average network delay. The second technique, called *shortest path routing,* provides a least-cost path between the communicating pair of users and can be used to minimize the delay to the users. Since bifurcated routing is not used much, we only mention it in passing. For further information, the reader can examine *Computer-Communication Network Design and Analysis,* by M. Schwartz (Prentice Hall, 1977).

Several shortest path algorithms are used in the industry. Most of them are based on what is called *algorithm A.* It is used as the model for the newer internet SPF protocols and has been used for several years to establish optimum designs and network topologies. The concepts discussed here are from "A Note on Two Problems in Connection of Graphs," by E. Dijkstra, *Numerical Mathematics,* October, 1959; *The Design and Analysis of Computer Algorithms,* by A. V. Aho, J. E. Hopcroft, and J. D. Ullman (Addison-Wesley, 1974); and *Data Networks: Concepts, Theory and Practice,* by Uyless Black (Prentice Hall, 1989).

Figure 8.25 is based on an earlier example in this chapter (see Fig. 8.2) and shows an example of how algorithm A is applied, using node A as the source and node J as the destination (sink). (Please be aware that the topology represented in the figure was prepared for illustrative, not implementation, purposes.) Algorithm A is defined generally as follows:

- Least-cost criteria weights are assigned to the paths in the network (Fig. 8.25a).

- Each node is labeled (identified) with its least-cost criteria from the source along a known path. Initially, no paths are known, so each node is labeled with infinity. However, updates to the values (once the weights are established) are the same as an initialization.

- Each node is examined in relation to all nodes adjacent to it. (The source node is the first node considered and becomes the working node; see Fig. 8.25b). This step is actually a one-time occurrence wherein the source node is initialized with the costs of all its adjacent nodes.

- Least-cost criteria labels are assigned to each of the nodes adjacent to the working node. Labels change if a shorter path is found from this node to the source node. In OSPF, this would occur with the sending of link status messages on a broadcast basis to all other gateways.

- After the adjacent nodes are labeled (or relabeled), all other nodes in the network are examined. If one has a smaller value in its label, its label becomes permanent and it becomes the working node (see Fig. 8.25c).

- If the sum of the node's label is less than the label on an adjacent node, the adjacent node's label is changed because a shorter path has been found to the source node. In Fig. 8.25d, node E is relabeled because node D is a shorter route through node C.

- Another working node is selected and the process repeats itself until all possibilities have been searched. The final labels reveal the least-cost, end-to-end path between the source and the other nodes. These nodes are considered to be within a set N as it pertains to the source node.

The following general statements describe the preceding discussion:

1. Let $D(v)$ = sum of link weights on a given path.
2. Let $c(i, j)$ = the cost between node i and j.
3. Set $n = \{1\}$.

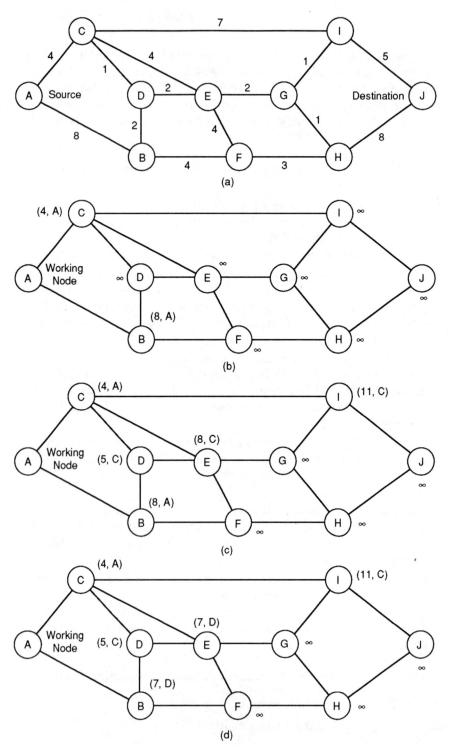

Figure 8.25 Application of Algorithm A.

4. For each node (v) not in N, set D(v) = C(1, v).

5. For each step, find a node w not in N for which D(w) is a minimum; add w to set N.

6. Update D(v) for all nodes still not in N by

$$D(v) = min [D(v), D(w) + c(w, v)]$$

7. Repeat steps 4 through 6 until all nodes are in set N.

The use of the algorithm is shown in Table 8.6. The steps are successively performed until all nodes are in N. The process is performed for each node, and a routing table is created for the node's use. Each node's table is constructed in the same manner just discussed.

The routing topology for node A is shown in Fig. 8.26. The numbers in parentheses represent the order of selection as reflected in Table 8.6.

It should prove useful to pause momentarily and examine the weighted paths in Fig. 8.25a. One might question why certain paths are weighted with large or small numbers. As an explanation, consider that node A could have two communication links available for transmission. The link from A to C could be a microwave land link, and the A to B link could be a satellite circuit. If an interactive user application were being routed through node A, the satellite link would be heavily weighted to discourage its use. As another example, the user data may need a secure link, and the A to B line may not use encryption/decryption devices. It should also be recognized that networks may not route traffic based on factors such as security or other QOS parameters, but they rely on performance criteria such as minimum delay.

If the least-cost criteria includes factors other than link and node capacity, then a separate capacity analysis is required to determine the ability of the network to handle the traffic. In this regard, the network capacity is like a chain, which is no stronger than its weakest

TABLE 8.6 Choosing the Nodes

Step	N	A(B)	A(C)	A(D)	A(E)	A(F)	A(G)	A(H)	A(I)	A(J)
Initial	{A}	8	4	·	·	·	·	·	·	·
1	{A,C}	8	(4)	5	8	·	·	·	11	·
2	{A,C,D}	7	4	(5)	7	·	·	·	11	·
3	{A,C,D,B}	7	4	5	(7)	11	·	·	11	·
4	{A,C,D,B,E}	(7)	4	5	7	11	9	·	11	·
5	{A,C,D,B,E,F}	7	4	5	7	11	(9)	14	11	·
6	{A,C,D,B,E,F,G}	7	4	5	7	11	9	(10)	10	·
7	{A,C,D,B,E,F,G,H}	7	4	5	7	11	9	10	(10)	18
8	{A,C,D,B,E,F,G,H,I}	7	4	5	7	(11)	9	10	10	15
9	{A,C,D,B,E,F,G,H,I,J}	7	4	5	7	11	9	10	10	(15)

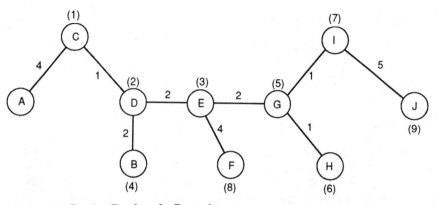

Figure 8.26   Routing Topology for Route A.

link. Likewise, a network has no more capacity than a specific combination of its lowest-capacity resources.

One might argue that network switching provides the means to route traffic around nodes and links that are either saturated or of insufficient capacity to handle the load. Nonetheless, at some point the traffic will reach an *area* within the network that is a bottleneck. This bottleneck limits the throughput of the entire network.

To determine why this limit exists, assume the least-cost weights in Fig. 8.25*a* represent the maximum link and node capacities for traffic flow in one direction. A set of nodes and links can be identified that act as the lowest common resource for network capacity.

One method to obtain this information is the *cut*. A cut is defined as the removal of connections (paths) between two nodes such that the two nodes are disconnected. In other words, they cannot reach each other.

Network designers look for the minimum cut through a network. This term describes an area with the minimum capacity and thus a potential bottleneck. Each cut is given a capacity which is the *sum* of the weights of the links through the cut. The cut with the lowest sum is the minimum cut.

Open Shortest Path First (OSPF) Routing Protocol

Introduction

This section provides an examination of OSPF. This protocol, designed by the OSPF working group of the Internet Engineering Task Force, is an IGP: Gateways/routers are all within one autonomous system. Also, as we stated earlier, OSPF is a link state or shortest path first protocol, in contrast to most of the internet protocols, which are based on some type of Bellman-Ford approach. The protocol, although it relies on techniques designed outside of the internet environment, is tailored specifically for an internet and includes such capabilities as subnet addressing and type of service (TOS) routing.

OSPF bases its routing decisions on two fields in the IP datagram: the destination IP address and the TOS. Once the decision is made on how to route the IP datagram, the datagram is routed without additional headers; that is, no additional encapsulation occurs. This approach is different from many networks in which PDUs are encapsulated with some type of internal network header to control the routing protocol within the subnetwork.

As we stated earlier in this chapter, OSPF is classified as a dynamic, adaptive protocol in that it adjusts to problems in the network and provides short convergence periods to stabilize the routing tables. It is also designed to prevent looping of traffic, which is quite important in mesh networks or in LANs where multiple bridges may be available to connect different LANs.

Also, it should be noted that the OSPF RFC 1131 uses the term *router* to describe the internetworking unit. We have learned in this book that many vendors use *router* and *gateway* synonymously. Furthermore, the OSPF PDUs exchanged between routers and networks are called *packets*.

OSPF operations

Each router contains a routing directory (called a *routing database* in OSPF). The database contains information about interfaces at the router that are operable as well as status information about each neighbor to a router. The database is the same for all participating routers.

The information focuses on the topology of the network(s) with a directed graph. Routers and networks form the vertices of the graph. Periodically, this information is broadcast (flooded) to all routers in the autonomous system. An OSPF router computes the shortest path to the other routers in the autonomous system with regard to itself as the working node (the working node is termed the *root* in this protocol). A very flexible and powerful approach to this protocol is that separate cost metrics can be computed for each TOS. If the calculations reveal that two paths are of equal value, OSPF will distribute the traffic equally on these paths.

OSPF can support one to many networks. The networks can be grouped into what is termed an *area,* and the design of the protocol allows an area to be hidden from other areas. Indeed, an area can be hidden from the full autonomous system.

Due to increasing concerns about security, OSPF includes authentication procedures. Routers must go through some simple procedures to authenticate the traffic between them. We have more to say about the authentication aspects of this protocol shortly.

OSPF works with directed graphs which are quite similar to the Dijkstra algorithm explained in Fig. 8.25. The graphs contain values between two points, either networks or gateways. The values represent the weighted shortest path value, with the router established as the root. Consequently, the shortest path tree from the router to any point in an internet is determined by the router performing the calculation. The calculation only reveals the next hop to the destination in the hop-to-hop forwarding process. The topological database used in the calculation is derived from the information obtained by advertisements of the routers to their neighbors, with periodic flooding throughout the autonomous system.

Thus far we have discussed in general terms how OSPF performs routing within the autonomous system. The method to determine routing information outside the autonomous system is referred to as *external routing*. Routing information pertaining to this capability is typically derived from OSPF as well as other protocols, such as the EGP. Alternately, routing information could be established through static routes between the autonomous systems. It could even be established by default routes. This information is also flooded through the autonomous system.

Two types of external routing capabilities exist with OSPF. In type 1 external routing, the external metrics are the same as the internal OSPF link state metric. Type 2 external metrics only use the cost of the router to the external autonomous system. The type 2 method is simple and based on the assumption that routing between autonomous systems is the major cost of routing the packet (which in some actual operations is not true). This approach eliminates conversion between internal link state metrics of OSPF and external costs (in which the autonomous system may have little influence).

The OSPF working group also adapted a very sound concept of autonomous system *areas* in which contiguous networks and hosts may be grouped together. In this situation, each area runs its own SPF algorithm. It also has its own topological database that differs from other areas. The purpose of the area is to isolate and partition portions of the autonomous system and to reduce the amount of information a router must maintain about the full autonomous system. Also, having such an area means that the overhead information transmitted between routers to maintain OSPF routing tables is substantially reduced.

OSPF uses the term *backbone* to define that part of an autonomous system that conveys packets between areas. For example, in Fig. 8.27

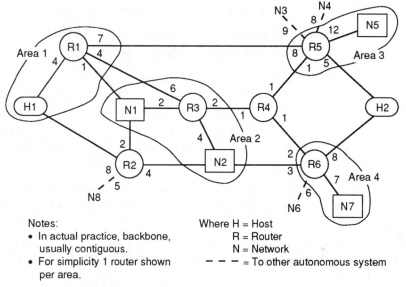

Figure 8.27   OSPF Concepts and Terms.

the routers R4 and R2 and their links serve as the backbone between the areas.

The full path of a packet proceeds as follows: (1) intra-area path to a router attached to the backbone; (b) the backbone path to the destination area router; and (c) the destination intra-area path to the destination network.

The resources (links, routers) of a backbone should be contiguous. For example, R2 in Fig. 8.27 has network N1 between it and backbone router R4. This configuration is permissible; the intervening networks simply become *virtual links* within the backbone for the purposes of constructing the topological database.

OSPF utilizes the Hello protocol for advertising state information between neighbors. Hello packets are used to confirm agreements among routers in a common network about a network mask and certain timers (dead interval, hello interval). In effect, the Hello protocol is used to make certain that neighbor relationships make sense.

Classification of routers

The OSPF routers are classified according to the functions they perform:

Internal router: All directly connected networks to this router belong to the same area. Also, all routers with only backbone interfaces are internal routers.

Border router: Any router that is not an internal router

Backbone router: Any router that has an interface to the backbone

Boundary router: A router that exchanges information with an-other autonomous system

Types of advertisements

The purpose of OSPF is for routers to inform each other about internet paths via advertisements. These advertisements are sent to routers by update packets. Four types of advertisements are used:

Router links advertisement: Contains information on a router's in-terfaces into an area. It is used by all routers and flooded through-out an area.

Networks links advertisement: Contains a list of routers connected to a network. It is used by a broadcast network and flooded through-out an area.

Summary links advertisement: Contains information on routes outside an area. It is used by border routers and flooded to the bor-der routers' areas (but inside the autonomous system).

Autonomous systems (AS) extended links advertisement: Contains information on routes in other autonomous systems. It is used by a boundary router and flooded through the autonomous system.

Example of the OSPF shortest path tree

This discussion expands earlier discussions of how OSPF uses least-cost-path logic to obtain a directed graph and the pruned tree. The ex-ample is a very simple topology for this general overview. RFC 1131 has an excellent and detailed example for the reader who needs more information. Figure 8.27 is based on the previous examination of al-gorithm A. In this example, the labels have been changed to identify hosts, networks, and routers (gateways). The autonomous system con-sists of areas 1, 3, 3, and 4. Routers 2, 5, and 6 provide connections to other autonomous systems with the EGP software.

The numbers have been rearranged from the previous examples us-ing this illustration. These numbers represent costs for each output port at each router. The cost is determined by the network adminis-trator. In this example, a lower-cost value determines a better route. Two numbers may be shown on a link in which two routers are di-rectly connected. The numbers reflect the cost at each router's output port. For example, a connection between routers R3 and R4 indicates that the cost of moving traffic from R3 to R4 is 2 and the cost from R4 to R3 is 1. The reason that this cost may vary could be the different traffic loads and queue sizes at the routers.

Also note that there are no costs associated with the ports emanating from the networks to the routers, nor are there costs associated with the hosts' interfaces to the routers. Since OSPF is a gateway protocol, it does not assume that a network or host computer is capable of participating in the shortest path operations. Notwithstanding, a network or host can participate in the operations by the same methods used by the gateways (if the network administration chooses to risk allowing a network or host to become involved in such a resource-intensive operation). In this context, a convenient way to view the directed graph is visually to remove the network from the picture and then view the arrows between the two routers.

Figure 8.28 depicts the directed graph of our hypothetical network. The direction of the arrows represents the cost of the path from a router to another router. The arcs with no value were explained in the previous paragraph.

The reader may notice that only one directional arrow is drawn from the routers to the hosts. In accordance with the rules of OSPF directed graphs, the figure shows what are known as *point-to-point networks,* in which a network is joined by a single router or a single pair of routers. This is depicted by the connection having one arrow in the direction toward the host.

Based on the values obtained with the directed graph, the OSPF is tasked with developing a pruned tree representing the shortest (best) path between a router and all the other nodes. Each router develops its

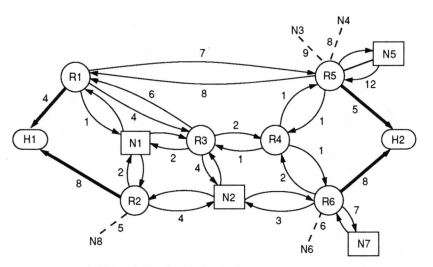

Figure 8.28 The Directed Graph with the Arcs.

own tree, and the router acts as the root in performing these calculations. Eventually, after messages have been exchanged between the routers and the topological database has been built, the tree will provide the destination to any network or host within the autonomous system.

In these examples, routers R2, R6, and R5 are responsible for providing connections to other autonomous systems. As explained earlier, these routers make their connections known to the other routers in the autonomous system through Type 1 or Type 2 metrics.

Finally, Fig. 8.29 shows the pruned tree as viewed by R1. It is quite similar to the tree developed in the discussion of algorithm A (see Fig. 8.25) except that the nodes have been relabeled as routers, networks, and hosts and no costs are associated with the output ports of the networks and hosts.

The tree and an accompanying topological database provide R1 with a route to all hosts and routers in the autonomous system. Once again, emphasis is on the arcs from N1 to R2 and N1 to R3. No values are associated with these arcs, since OSPF is designed as a gateway protocol. The direction of these arcs depicts that the network does not furnish information to the routers. In a sense, the routers establish virtual connections between the routers across transit networks. In this example, N1 is a transit network. Certainly these connections are significant as far as the least-cost-path value is concerned. In such a situation, the link state advertisement for a network (N1) must be generated by one of its attached routers, which is identified as the designated router for that network.

Based on what we have learned in this discussion, imagine the to-

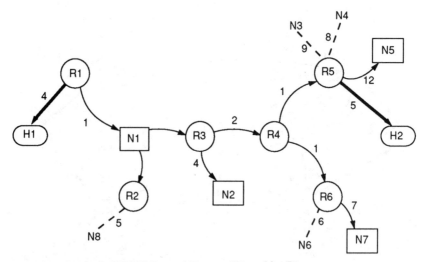

Figure 8.29 The Pruned OSPF Pruned Tree, as Viewed by R1.

pological database that is built by R4. Indeed, you may wish to experiment with Fig. 8.27 and draw the pruned tree as viewed by R4. To assist you in this exercise, the routing table for R4, based on Fig. 8.27, is shown in Table 8.7. (The host entries, H1 and H2, are usually not stored at a remote router.)

OSPF data structures

OSPF operates with five data structures. These data structures contain the information needed by OSPF to perform its operations. The data structures discussed in this section are

Protocol data structures

Area data structures (also backbone data structures)

Interface data structures

Neighbor data structures

Routing table structures

A useful way to view these data structures is depicted in Fig. 8.30. The *protocol data structure* consists of high-level data structures used in the autonomous system. Next are the *area data structures*, which contain information about the area. Next are the *interface* and *neighbor data structures*, which contain information on the router-to-network and router-to-router operations, respectively. Last is the *routing table structure* stored at the routers for routing an IP packet.

TABLE 8.7   Routing Table for R4

Destination	Next Hop	Distance Metric
H1	R3	7
H2	R5	6
N1	R3	3
N2	R6	4
N3	R5	10
N4	R5	9
N5	R5	13
N6	R6	7
N7	R6	8
N8	R3	8
R1	R3	3
R2	R3	3
R3	R3	1
R5	R5	1
R6	R5	1

Note: Use Fig. 8.27 with this table.

Protocol data structure

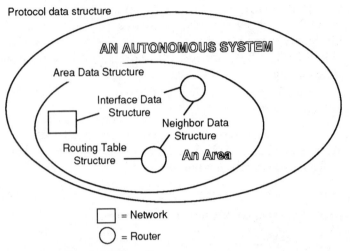

= Network
= Router

Figure 8.30 The OSPF Data Structures.

Protocol data structure. This high-level OSPF data structure provides the following information and services:

Router ID: The 32-bit identifier of the autonomous system router

Area structure pointers: ID to each area with which the router is concerned

Backbone structures pointer: ID to the backbone structure, which is the same as an area structure

Virtual links configured: ID of the router at the other end of virtual circuits

External routes list: List of routes that are external to this autonomous system

Routing table: Contains an entry for each destination to which the router can forward traffic

Area data structure. This data structure provides the following information and services:

Area ID: The identifier of the area

Address ranges: A list of IP addresses that define the area. A network is associated with an area depending on its IP address value

Router interfaces: The ID of those router interfaces that belong to the area

Advertisements lists: Description of the following information:

Network links: Advertisements of each router which is connected to a network

Summary links: Advertisements from border routers of routes with the autonomous system

Router links: Advertisements to routers in the area

Shortest path tree: The pruned tree, with this router as the root, based on the Dijkstra method described earlier in this chapter

Authentication type: The type of authentication (none, simple password) used in this area

Interface data structures.   This data structure describes the router and network connection. The interface belongs to the area in which the network resides. The following information and services are provided by the interface data structure:

Interface type: Type of attached network—broadcast, multiaccess (like a packet-switched network with two or more routers), point-to-point, or virtual

State: OSPF works with states and state transition diagrams. This value describes the current state of the interface (down, waiting, etc.).

IP address: The IP address for this interface

IP mask: The subnet mask for this interface

Area ID: The area associated with the network

HelloInterval: Time between a router issuing Hello packets on this interface (explained later)

DeadInterval: Time at which the machine considers a router down and will not accept Hello packets

InfTransDelay: Estimated time to send an update packet on this interface

Router priority: Priority of the router on this interface (highest priority becomes the designated router for this network)

Hello timer: Interval at which the Hello packet is launched (every HelloInterval seconds)

Wait timer: Interval at which this interface looks for a designated router (every DeadInterval seconds)

Neighboring routers: List of all routers attached to this network

Routers: IDs of designated router and backup router

Output cost(s):   The metric cost of sending traffic on this interface, based on (possibly) each IP TOS

RxmInterval: Timer of issuing link state advertisement retransmissions

Authentication key: Value to verify an authentication field in the OSPF header

Neighbor data structure.   This data structure is used between neighboring routers to control router roles and backup operations. The following information and services are provided by the neighbor data structure:

State: The neighbor routers operate with states and state transitions machines. This value identifies the states of the neighbor communications process (down, exchange, etc.).

Inactivity timer: Reveals that a Hello packet has not been received from this neighbor

Master/slave: Relationship of the neighbor routers (explained later)

Sequence number: Values used to coordinate exchange of packets between neighbors

Neighbor ID: Neighbor router ID

Neighbor priority (PRI):   Router priority used to select a designated router and its backup router

IP address: Neighbor router's IP address

Routers: IDs of neighbor's designated router and designated backup router

Lists: Three lists are used to manage link state advertisements:

   Link state retransmission: Advertisements not yet ACKed
   Database summary: List of advertisements that make up the area's database
   Link state requests: Advertisements still needed from a neighbor to synchronize the database

Routing table structure.   The OSPF routing table structure is used by IP packet forwarding. It contains the entries in our previous example (Table 8.7) plus other values. The entries in the table are as follows:

Destination: The destination's IP address (and mask)

Destination type: Identified as a network, border, or boundary router

Type of service: Possibly a separate set of routers for each TOS

Area: Identifies the area whose link information led to this entry in the table. Multiple entries are possible if two border routers share common areas.

Path type: Identified as intra-area, interarea, or external-to-autonomous systems

Cost: The full cost to the destination

Next hop: The next hop (router) for the datagram

Advertising router: Used for interarea and autonomous system links

The OSPF packets

This section describes the formats of all the OSPF packets. OSPF runs over the Internet Protocol (IP) and relies on IP for fragmentation services for large OSPF packets. In addition, some of the OSPF packets are multicast. OSPF requires the reservation of two multicast addresses:

ALLSPFrouters: This multicast address is reserved for all routers that support OSPF. Its value is 224.0.0.5.

ALLDrouters: This address is reserved for the designated router and a designated backup router. Address value is 224.0.0.6.

RFC1010 identifies the OSPF with IP protocol number 89. The OSPF routing protocol packets are always sent in an IP datagram with the IP TOS value equal to zero. It is recommended that OSPF packets be treated as high-priority traffic and be given precedence over regular IP traffic. The IP precedence field is useful in this regard.
   The discussion in this section begins with a description of two headers and then proceeds to an examination of the packets that are used with these headers.

The OSPF packet header. Figure 8.31 illustrates the 24-octet OSPF packet header. Each OSPF packet is appended with this header. The fields in the header mean the following. The *version* number describes which version of the protocol is currently used (currently, version 1). The *type* field identifies the type of packet. It may contain one of the following values:

1 = Hello

2 = Database description

3 = Link state request

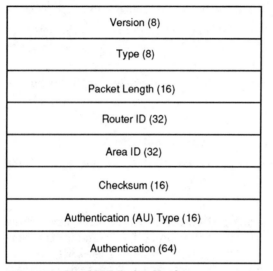

Version (8)
Type (8)
Packet Length (16)
Router ID (32)
Area ID (32)
Checksum (16)
Authentication (AU) Type (16)
Authentication (64)

Figure 8.31   The OSPF Packet Header.

4 = Link state update

5 = Link state ACK

The *packet length* field indicates the length of the field in octets, including the OSPF header. The *router ID* field contains the identification of the source of the packet. The *area ID* identifies the area from which the packet is transmitted. The *checksum* field is used to perform an IP-type checksum on the entire packet, including the authentication field.

The *authentication type (AUType)* identifies the type of authentication which will be used. Presently, two authentication types are used: 0 = none and 1 = a simple password. Finally, the *authentication* field contains the value used by the authentication scheme. The authentication field can be established on a per area basis. As just mentioned, two types of authentication are permitted.

The link state advertisement header.   OSPF uses one other header type: the link state advertisement header. This header comprises the topological database. The format for the header is shown in Fig. 8.32. All link state advertisements must use this header, which consists of 20 octets. Its purpose is to identify each advertisement between the routers.

The contents of the packet are as follows. The *LS age* field contains (in seconds) the time since the link state advertisement originated. The options field contains IP TOS values supported by the sender. The *LS type* describes the type of link advertisement, which further

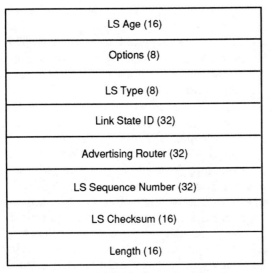

LS Age (16)
Options (8)
LS Type (8)
Link State ID (32)
Advertising Router (32)
LS Sequence Number (32)
LS Checksum (16)
Length (16)

Figure 8.32 The Link State (LS) Advertisement Header.

defines a format for the advertisement (discussed shortly). This field can be set to the following values:

1 = Router links (data on router-to-area interfaces)

2 = Network lengths (data on router-to-network interfaces)

3 = Summary link (data IP network)

4 = Summary link (data on autonomous system border router)

5 = AS external link (data on destinations external-to-autonomous system)

The *link state ID* field identifies that portion of the internet that is being described in the advertisement. Its contents can take values to depict router IDs and IP network numbers. Its value depends upon the LS type field.

The *advertising router* field is the identifier of the originating router for the link state advertisement. The *LS sequence number* is used to sequence the advertisements to detect duplicate or old packets. The *LS checksum* field is used to perform an error check on the contents of the packet. Finally, the *length* field contains (in octets) the size of the advertisement, including the 20-octet header.

The Hello packet. The Hello packet is used in OSPF to perform adjacent operations between neighbors. Parameters in the Hello packet allow the router neighbors to agree upon operating parameters such as a common network mask, the hello interval, and the dead interval.

The contents of the Hello packet are depicted in Fig. 8.33. The *OSPF header* is required for the packet. The next field is the *network mask* that is associated with the interface. The options field contains the IP TOS values supplied by the sender. The *dead interval (Deadint)* field contains a value to describe the number of seconds before a router is declared down. The *Hello interval (HelloInt)* field contains a value representing the number of seconds between the router sending another Hello packet. The *router priority (Rtr Pri)* field defines if a router will be designated as a backup. If this field is set to zero, the router is not allowed to become a designated backup router. The *designated router* field contains the identity of the router for the network in question. If this value is set to zero, there is no designated router. The *backup router* field contains the identity of the designated backup router for the network in regard to the advertising router. Finally, the repeating fields designated *neighbor router ID* contain the IDs of each router that have recently sent Hello packets on the network. *Recently* is defined by the value in the Deadint field.

Figure 8.34 illustrates the operations at a router that has received a Hello packet. Upon receiving this packet, the OSPF logic performs editing checks on the IP and OSPF headers. If any errors occur, the packet is discarded and processing stops. If no errors occur, OSPF checks the network mask, Hello interval, and DeadInterval fields for proper matches with the configuration at this interface. If the "no mis-

OSPF Header (192)
Network Mask (32)
Hello Int (16)
Options (8)
Router Priority (8)
Dead Int (32)
Designated/Backup Router (64)
Neighbor(s), 1 to n (32)

Figure 8.33 The Hello Packet for OSPF.

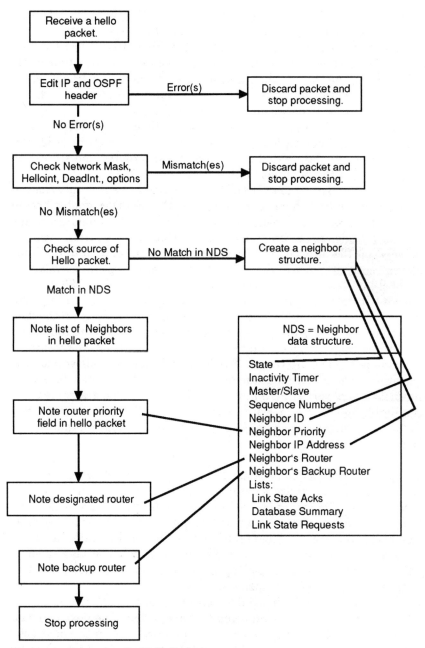

Figure 8.34 Processing the Hello Packet.

matches" occur, OSPF checks for the source of the Hello packet. If the source is not currently contained in its neighbor data structure, it creates a skeleton neighbor data structure for this source. The creation of the neighbor structure at this point consists of the insertion of the neighbor ID, the state of the interface, and the neighbor IP address. If there is a "match in NDS," OSPF examines and stores the list of neighbors that are contained in the Hello packet.

OSPF then examines the router priority field in the Hello packet and stores this information in the neighbor data structure. Additionally, it notes the designated router and backup router and stores this information in the neighbor data structure.

Once the Hello packet has been processed, OSPF then executes logic to establish or reestablish designated routers (DRs) and designated backup routers (DBURs). This process is shown in Fig. 8.35. First, OSPF discards any ineligible routers (those routers which have a priority value of 0). Next, all the attached routers are examined in relation to the information received in the Hello packets. Two major steps are involved in establishing routers and backup routers. In step 1 of Fig. 8.35, the designated backup router is chosen by an examination of the priority field relating to that router. In step 2, the designated router is established. Note that if no router has declared itself to be the designated router, the backup designated router is promoted. Then steps 1 and 2 are repeated to redesignate the backup router. The logic is designed to allow a smooth transition when either a backup or designated backup router fails in an internet. It is possible that a router could, for a time, be designated both as a router and a backup router. However, once this router detects that the primary router is inoperable, the logic requires that it remove itself as a designated router.

The database description packet. The purpose of the database description packet is to initialize a database at a router. The database packet may contain information on part of the pieces of the topological database, or it may contain the entire topology. These packets are managed through a master/slave relationship. One of the routers is designated as a master and the other becomes a slave. The master sends polls in the database description packets which must be acknowledged by database description responses.

The format of the database description packet is illustrated in Fig. 8.36. The *OSPF header* is required for this packet. The next three octets are reserved and set to zero. Three bits are used in the next octet and are labeled the *I bit,* the *M bit,* and the *MS bit.* The *I bit,* when set to zero, indicates that the packet is the first in a sequence of packets to follow. The *M bit* is the more data bit. When set to one it means that more database description packets follow. The *MS bit* designates the

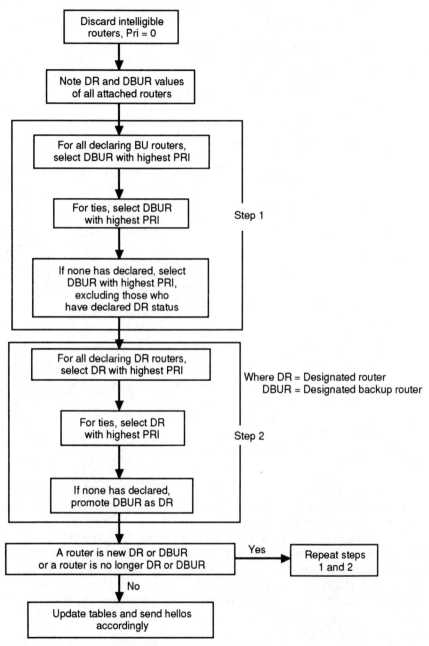

Figure 8.35 Establishing Routers and Backup Routers.

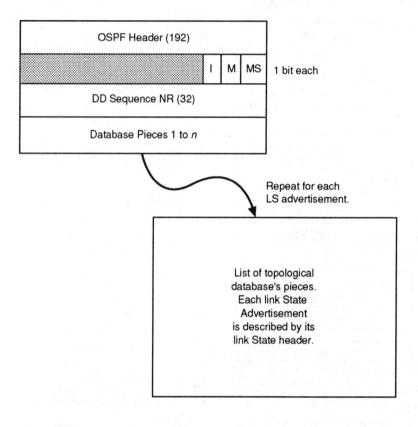

 = Reserved and set to 0

Figure 8.36   The Database Description Packet.

master/slave. When set to one it indicates that the router that originated the packet is the master. When set to zero it means that the
originating router is the slave.

   The *DD sequence number* is used to sequence the packets between
the master and the slave. The number is incremented by one with
each transmission of a packet. The remainder of the packet field repeats the number of advertisements for each piece of the topological
database. The *link state type, link state ID,* the *advertising router, LS
sequence number, LS checksum,* and *LS age* have been described previously in this chapter.

The link state request packet.   The purpose of the link state request
packet is to request additional information about a topological database from a neighbor (see Fig. 8.37). Typically, this packet is ex-

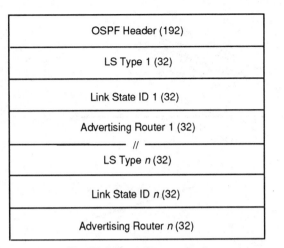

Figure 8.37   The Link State Request Packet.

changed when it is discovered that pieces of the database are missing or out of date. The contents contain the *OSPF header* and repeating fields for *LS type, link state ID,* and *advertising router.*

The link state update packets.   The link state update packets are used to provide four types of updates:

Router links

Network links

Summary links

AS external links

Each of these four types of update packets contains different formats. To provide an example of the use of these packets, Fig. 8.38 depicts a router which has three links in an internet labeled link 1, link 2, and link 3. Additionally, each link is labeled with the TOS required. Link 1's TOS requires low delay and high reliability. Link 2 requires high throughput. Link 3 has no additional TOS beyond the default value of zero.

Periodically the router advertises this information to its neighbors through the four types of packets described in this section. Figure 8.39 shows the principal advertisement packet of OSPF designated as the router links advertisement packet. It is drawn in this figure to illustrate how information is repeated for each link of the router and each TOS feature on each link.

The *OSPF header* is placed in front of the packet, as are the number

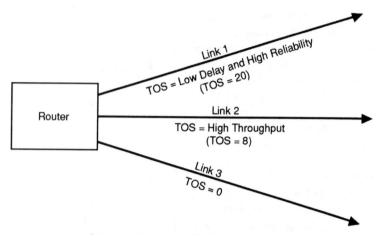

Figure 8.38 Example of a Link State Update.

of advertisements. The link state header precedes the advertisements. The *link state advertisement* part of the packet contains the *link state header,* followed by the *E* and *B bits*. If the E bit is set to one, it designates that the router is an AS boundary router. The designation E stands for external. When the B bit is set to one, it designates that the router is an area border router. The B designates border. The *number of links (NrLinks)* field designates how many advertisements are contained in the packet. OSPF requires that the router advertise all the links attached to it for the area. Next, repeating fields are placed in the packets to describe each link state advertisement.

The repeating fields contain information about each link attached to the router. In our example in Fig. 8.38, these fields would be repeated three times for each of the links at the router. The *link ID* identifies the type of router attached by the link. The actual value of this field depends on the type field. Likewise, the *link data* field value depends on the links type field. It may contain a network mask, or it may contain an IP interface address. The type field is set to one of three values:

1 = Connects to another router

2 = Connects to a transit network

3 = Connects to a stub network

The *number of TOS* field *(NR TOS)* describes how many TOS metrics are given for this link. At least one TOS metric must be given, which is designated TOS 0. If no additional TOS fields are contained

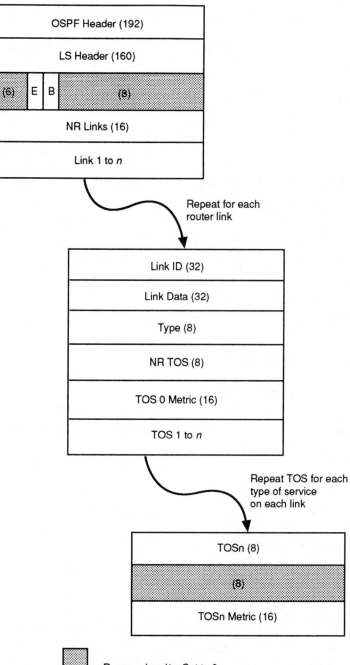

= Reserved and/or Set to 0

Figure 8.39 The Router Links Advertisement Packet.

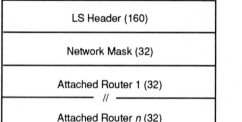

NETWORK LINKS
ADVERTISEMENT

SUMMARY LINKS
ADVERTISEMENT

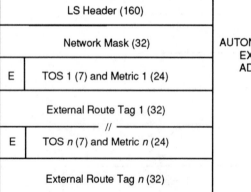

AUTONOMOUS SYSTEMS
EXTERNAL LINKS
ADVERTISEMENT

Figure 8.40 The Link State Update Packets.

in the packet, this field is set to zero. The *TOS 0 metric* field is a value containing the cost for this router for TOS = 0.

Finally, the figure shows that repeating sets of fields designated as *TOSn* and *TOSn metric* are contained in the packet for each TOSTOS value for each link. In our example there would be two sets of these

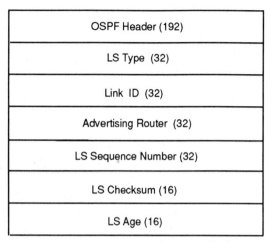

| OSPF Header (192) |
| LS Type (32) |
| Link ID (32) |
| Advertising Router (32) |
| LS Sequence Number (32) |
| LS Checksum (16) |
| LS Age (16) |

Figure 8.41   Link State Acknowledgment Packet.

fields for link 1, one set for link 2, and no occurrence of these fields for link 3.

Figure 8.40 depicts the remaining three formats for the link state update packets. These three formats (starting at the top of the figure) are used to advertise network links, summary links, and AS external links, respectively. The fields in these three formats have been discussed previously in this chapter.

The link state acknowledgment packet. The final OSPF packet is the link state acknowledgment packet, depicted in Fig. 8.41. OSPF requires that link state advertisements be acknowledged. They are acknowledged with the packet depicted in Fig. 8.41. The fields are largely self-descriptive and have been discussed previously.

Summary

The Internet system provides a number of protocols to provide routing and reachability information between gateways and autonomous systems and within autonomous systems. The EGP is widely used in many systems, and the GGP is an older example of a core gateway protocol. The internal gateway protocols are varied, and many systems use RIP, Hello, or gated. Without question, the OSPF protocol represents a giant leap forward in the Internet internetworking operations.

9

The Major Application Layer Protocols

Introduction

This chapter examines the application layer protocols that are used by most internet installations. Some of these protocols are very rich in function, and a full explanation of their operations would require an extensive discourse. Therefore, our goal is to provide a general overview of the major services they offer to an end user. The protocols that are covered in this chapter are

TELNET: For terminal services

Trivial File Transfer Protocol (TFTP):   For simple file transfer services

File Transfer Protocol (FTP):   For more elaborate file transfer services

Simple Mail Transfer Protocol (SMTP):   For message transfer services (electronic mail)

The TELNET Protocol

To begin this discussion, imagine that a manager is responsible for a computer operations center. A host computer in the operations center is tasked with supporting the communications operations among many terminals that have different characteristics. For example, a user at a DEC terminal needs to communicate with a user at a Hewlett-Packard terminal. It is not so easy. Both devices use different screen control and keyboard control characters, and both devices use different line protocols for the management of traffic on the communications link.

If the host computer must support a wide variety of terminals, precious resources are consumed in machine CPU cycles to resolve protocol differences, and the design and coding of supporting software to translate the protocols is a very expensive undertaking. The manager of the computer operations center must spend a great deal of time and expend considerable resources on developing or acquiring systems that provide translation facilities between the different machines.

TELNET provides some solutions to these problems. For example, it defines a procedure that permits host computers to learn about the characteristics of terminals attached to other hosts with which they communicate. Equally important, TELNET provides conventions for the negotiation of a number of functions and services for a terminal-based session between two machines. This approach ameliorates the protocol conversion problem because the negotiating machines have the option of not using a service that cannot be supported by either machine.

TELNET does not perform any protocol conversion between different machines. Rather, it provides a mechanism to determine the characteristics of the machines and a means to negotiate how the machines will interwork with each other to exchange data.

The TELNET protocol allows a program on a host machine (called the "TELNET client") to access the resources of another machine (called the "TELNET server") as if the client were attached locally to the server (see Fig. 9.1). Although TELNET provides a variety of features, some people call the standard a *remote login* protocol because it supports a remote device's login with a host machine.

Network virtual terminal

The TELNET standard is based on the idea of a network virtual terminal (NVT). The term "virtual" is used because an NVT does not ac-

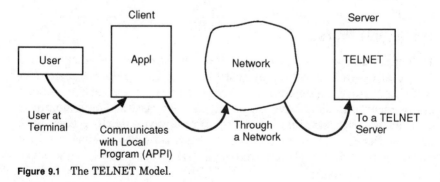

Figure 9.1 The TELNET Model.

tually exist; it is an imagined device that provides a standard means of representing a terminal's characteristics. The idea is to relieve the host computers from the tasks of maintaining characteristics about every terminal with which they are communicating.

With the TELNET standard, both the user and server devices are required to map their terminal characteristics into the virtual terminal description. The end result is that the devices appear to be communicating with the network virtual terminal because they are assuming that both parties are providing a complementary mapping.

Negotiations. The TELNET protocol, like other virtual terminal protocols, allows the communicating machines to *negotiate* a variety of options to be used during the session. The server and client are required to use a standard set of procedures to establish these options. We examine these options during the analysis of the TELNET protocol.

The use of negotiated options takes into consideration the possibility that host machines may provide services beyond those in a virtual terminal. Moreover, the TELNET model does not restrict the negotiated options to those stipulated solely in the protocols. Rather, TELNET allows the negotiation of different conventions beyond the TELNET specifications.

TELNET RFCs

The Internet standards include several RFCs that describe the TELNET options which can be negotiated. The user might find Table 9.1 useful in this regard. It lists the major TELNET options along with their number and the relevant RFCs, if available. Be careful that you do not assume that all these options are provided in each vendor product; many TELNET products do not support all of them.

Figure 9.2 shows how the options can be negotiated between two parties. One party can begin the negotiation by inquiring to another party about a particular option (function x in the figure). The response in this figure says that the responding party can support the option.

Next, the initiating party asks for the characteristics (regarding the option) from the responding party. The responding party then sends information about the option. This information describes certain characteristics of the responding party's terminal or other operating requirements.

The messages flowing between the two parties must adhere to a TELNET message format (which is called the *command structure*). For example, the initial signal of "do you support" or "will you support" is established by special TELNET codes *do* or *will*. In turn, the responder must return a TELNET code (in this example, the *will* code).

TABLE 9.1   TELNET Option Codes

Number	Name	RFC
0	Binary transmission	856
1	Echo	857
2	Reconnection	NIC 15391
3	Suppress Go ahead	858
4	Approximate message size negotiation	NIC 15393
5	Status	859
6	Timing mark	860
7	Remote controlled trans and echo	726
8	Output line width	NIC 20196
9	Output page size	NIC 20197
10	Output carriage-return disposition	652
11	Output horizontal tabstops	653
12	Output horizontal tab disposition	654
13	Output form feed disposition	655
14	Output vertical tabstops	656
15	Output vertical tab disposition	657
16	Output line feed disposition	658
17	Extended ASCII	698
18	Logout	727
19	Byte macro	735
20	Data entry terminal	732
21	SUPDUP	736
22	SUPDUP output	749
23	Send location	779
24	Terminal type	930
25	End of record	885
26	TACACS user identification	927
27	Output marking	933
28	Terminal location number	946
29	3270 regime	1041
30	X.3 PAD	1053
31	Window size	1073

Table 9.2 lists the names of the codes, their numeric values that are placed in the TELNET message, and brief description of their meaning. The table includes six line entries describing the six TELNET functions. These functions have been found to be common across almost all terminal-based applications; therefore, the TELNET standard defines a standard means of representing them.

The *interrupt process (IP)* function allows a system to suspend, interrupt, abort, or terminate a user process. For example, it allows a user to terminate an operation so it can get out of an endless loop.

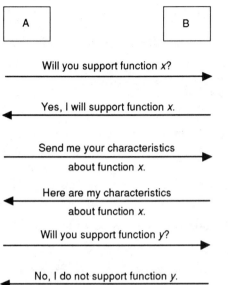

Figure 9.2   TELNET Negotiations.

TABLE 9.2   TELNET Command Codes

Code Name	Value	Meaning
SE	240	End of subnegotiation parameters
NOP	241	No operation
Data mark	242	The data stream portion of a Synch
Break	243	BRK Character
Interrupt process	244	The IP function
Abort output	245	The AO function
Are you there	246	The AYT function
Erase character	247	The EC function
Erase line	248	The EL function
Go ahead	249	The GA function
SB	250	Subnegotiation of the indicated option
Will (Option code)	251	Begin performing, or confirmation that device is now performing the indicated option
Won't (Option code)	252	Refusal to perform or continue to perform the indicated option
Do (Option code)	253	Indicates the request that the other party perform, or confirmation that you are expecting the other party to perform, the indicated option
Don't (Option code)	254	Demands that the other party stop performing, or confirm that party is no longer expecting the other party to perform, the indicated option
IAC	255	Interpret as command

The *abort output (AO)* function allows an application to run to completion but not send the output to the user's workstation. This function also clears output that is stored but is not yet displayed.

The *are you there (AYT)* function is a useful operation that is invoked when a user wishes to know that the application is executing. Typically, the AYT function is invoked if a user has not received messages for an extended time.

The *erase character (EC)* function enables the user to delete a character in a stream of data. In its simplest form, it is used to edit data on a screen if input mistakes are made.

The *erase line function (EL)* function allows a user to delete an entire line for editing purposes.

The *go ahead (GA)* function allows the session to follow a half-duplex transmission sequence.

In addition to the codes described in Table 9.2, TELNET has a number of codes for manipulating hard copy output on a printer. The codes are quite similar to their virtual terminal protocols, such as the CCITT X.3 PAD Recommendation. These codes perform operations such as horizontal tab (HT), vertical tab (VT), form feed (FF), back space (BS), Bell (BEL), line feed (LF), carriage return (CR), etc.

TELNET commands

The TELNET data unit is called a *command,* and the format is depicted in Fig. 9.3. If three bytes are used, the first byte is the *interpret as command (IAC)* byte. This is a reserved code in TELNET. It is also an escape character, because it is used by the receiver to detect if the incoming traffic is not data but a TELNET command.

The next byte is called the *command code.* This value is used in conjunction with the IAC byte to describe the type of command. The third byte is called the *option negotiation* code. It is used to define a number of options to be used during the session.

As discussed earlier, the TELNET command codes are listed and described in Table 9.2. The TELNET option codes are listed and explained in Table 9.1.

Byte 1   Byte 2   Byte 3 (Optional)

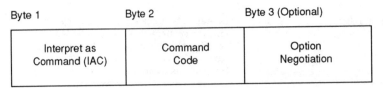

| Interpret as Command (IAC) | Command Code | Option Negotiation |

Figure 9.3 TELNET Command Format.

Example of TELNET commands

The RFCs listed in Table 9.1 should be studied if the reader wishes to gain an in-depth understanding of the many functions of TELNET terminals. This section provides an example of one of these functions: the echo service.

Echoes are used in practically all workstation environments to allow the data entered on the keyboard to be placed (echoed) onto the screen. In some situations, the echo occurs only locally; that is, the terminal keyboard entry is echoed to the screen. In other situations the echo is sent to the receiving machine and then echoed back to the transmitting machine. The particular implementation of this depends on the type of hardware and software that exists on the workstations.

The TELNET echo option allows two users to determine how echoing will occur during the session. The command format for the echo is as follows (the values in parentheses represent the IAC, command code, and option negotiation parameter that was explained in Fig. 9.3 and Table 9.1):

```
IAC WILL ECHO (255 251 1)
```

This command allows a user to begin echoing the characters it receives over the connection back to the sender of the data characters. Conversely, the following command

```
IAC WON'T ECHO (255 252 1)
```

specifies that the sender of this command will not echo, or wishes to stop echoing the data characters it receives back to the sender.

Another command is used for a request that the receiver of the command begin echoing. This takes the form of

```
IAC DO ECHO (255 253 1)
```

The last TELNET echo command is used by the sender to require the receiver of the command either to stop or not start echoing characters that it receives over the connection. This is formatted as

```
IAC DON'T ECHO (255 254 1)
```

The TELNET echo option defaults to *won't echo* and *don't echo*. That is, no echoing is done over the connection.

Another commonly used option is the transmit binary in which the data stream is interpreted as 8-bit binary images. To request permission to use this service, the sender issues

```
IAC WILL TRANSMIT-BINARY (255 251 0)
```

The sender of the next command, if it does not wish the connection to be operated with the transmit binary option, issues

```
IAC DON'T TRANSMIT-BINARY (255 254 0)
```

All the TELNET operations are conducted in a manner similar to these examples. Thus, the protocol is simple and easy to implement.

Trivial File Transfer Protocol (TFTP)

The trivial file transfer protocol (TFTP) is appropriately named because it is a simple file transfer protocol. It is not as complex as FTP (discussed next), nor does it have as many functions. It does not consist of a lot of code, nor does it consume much memory; consequently, it can be used on small machines.

TFTP has no security provisions or user authentication provisions. Indeed, it has very little end-to-end reliability because it rests on the User Datagram Protocol (UDP). It does not use TCP. Notwithstanding, TFTP has some integrity checks, supports timers, and has retransmission capabilities.

Typically, the transmitter sends a fixed block of data (512 bytes) and waits for an acknowledgment before sending the next block. This type of operation is known as a *flip-flop protocol,* because the transmitter must wait for an acknowledgment before it sends the next block of data, and the receiver must acknowledge each block before the transmitter can send the subsequent block.

Each block is numbered sequentially, and the acknowledgment field contains the number of the block that has been acknowledged. The end of a message is detected by sending a fragmented block that consists of a block of less than 512 bytes.

This protocol is not designed to be robust. Almost any type of problem will cause a termination of the connection. However, it does provide some error messages, and it also will support time-outs to detect when messages have been lost.

Generally, errors occur when (a) one party is unable to satisfy a request (for example, the format of the request is ill-formed, a file cannot be located, etc.); (b) a file can be found but the request cannot be fulfilled because the servicing party does not have sufficient resources; and (c) other errors have occurred (such as the duplication of the request).

TFTP is not used extensively today, although some vendors have brought it into their product line to ease compatibility problems. For example, IBM's TCP/IP product line for its personal computers implements the TFTP product to allow interaction between AIX and PC DOS machines.

TFTP and other protocols

As we discussed earlier, TFTP runs over UDP. Since a user datagram header is encapsulated into an IP protocol data unit (PDU), the TFTP can rely on these lower layer protocols to provide their services.

For example, TFTP uses the UDP source and destination ports to map the two TFTP users onto the file transfer session. This operation is accomplished by the use of TFTP transfer identifiers (TIDs). They are created by TFTP and passed to the UDP, which places them in the port identifier fields in the datagram.

TFTP uses the concept of port binding (discussed in Chaps. 1 and 7). To review the idea, the initiator of the file transfer (say, host A) selects a value for the source TID. The source TID is set to any value as determined by source A. The destination TID is the well-known port number 69 that is permanently assigned to TFTP. When host B returns an acknowledgment to the TFTP connection request, its source TID is the value 69, and its destination TID is the same identifier as host A's source TID.

TFTP packets

TFTP supports five types of PDUs, which are called *packets* in the standard:

Read Request (RRQ)

Write Request (WRQ)

Data (DATA)

Acknowledgment (ACK)

Error (ERROR)

The names of the packets describe their functions. The *read request (RRQ) packet* is transmitted to request a read operation on a foreign file. Conversely, the *write request (WRQ)* requests modification to a file. After receiving one of these requests, the foreign system may return an *acknowledgment data unit (ACK)*. This contains the block number of 0. After these handshaking operations have occurred, the data packets *(DATA)* are transmitted. They contain sequence numbers that identify each block of data. The block numbers are sequentially numbered from a value of one. The *error packet (ERROR)* contains information about problems that have occured during the operation.

The structure of these control packets is shown in Fig. 9.4. The *opcode (operation code)* contains the values used to identify the type of packet.

In the RRQ and WRQ packets, the opcode field is followed by the *filename* field. It identifies the file that is to be retrieved (typically performed at a terminal with GET <remote filename> {<local filename>}), or the name of the file that is to receive the data (PUT <remote filename> {<local filename>}).

2 Bytes	String	1 Byte	String	1 Byte
Opcode	Filename	0	Mode	0

RRQ = 1
WRQ = 2

2 Bytes	2 Bytes	*n* Bytes
Opcode	Block Number	0

DATA = 3

2 Bytes	2 Bytes
Opcode	Block Number

ACK = 4

2 Bytes	2 Bytes	String	1 Byte
Opcode	Block Number	ErrMsg	0

ERROR = 5

Figure 9.4 TFTP Packets.

The *mode* field is used to signify the mode of transfer that is to take place during the operation. As established in RFC 783, three modes are supported in TFTP:

NetASCII: USA Standard Code for Information Interchange

Byte: 8-bit bytes or binary data

Mail: Traffic goes to a user rather than to a file, but code is still NetASCII

The block number (*block #*) in the *data packet* begins with the value 1 and is incremented by 1 with each succeeding packet transmittal. The *data field* is a fixed-length block of 512 bytes. The last block in the file transfer contains between 0 and 511 bytes of data (and is labeled "0" in the figure).

The *acknowledgment (ACK) packet* also contains a block # field. This field acknowledges the transmitted data. It uses the same value that was received in the block # in the data packet.

The *error packet* contains an *ErrMsg* field to describe six types of errors:

0:   Not defined

1:   File not found

2:   Access violation

3:   Disk full or allocation exceeded

4:   Illegal TFTP operation

5:   Unknown transfer ID

Figure 9.5 shows the handshake and transfer operations between two machines using the TFTP standard. The initial handshaking activities are accomplished with the WRQ and ACK transactions. Thereafter, data are sent and acknowledged as depicted in the lower part of the figure.

File Transfer Protocol (FTP)

The Internet standards include a rather powerful file transfer protocol. It is called the *File Transfer Protocol (FTP)* and is a widely used upper layer standard. The purpose of FTP is to define procedures for the transfer of files between two machines.

FTP is rather unusual in that it maintains two logical connections between the machines. One connection is used for the login between machines and uses the TELNET protocol. The other connection is used for data transfer. The concept is shown in Fig. 9.6. The end *user* communicates with a *protocol interpreter (PI),* which governs the control connection. The PI must transfer information between the user and the PI's *file system.* Commands and replies are transmitted between the user-PI and the server-PI. As depicted in the figure, the other machine's (server's) PI responds to the TELNET protocol in managing connections.

During the file transfer, data management is performed by the other logical connection, which is called the *data transfer process (DTP).* Once the DTP has performed its functions and the user's request has been satisfied, the PI is used to close the connection.

FTP also permits the transfer between a device other than the original server and client. This operation is typically known as a *third*

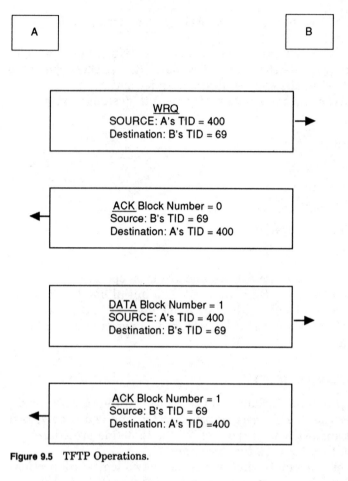

Figure 9.5   TFTP Operations.

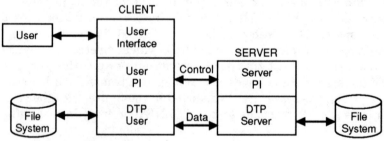

Figure 9.6   FTP Model.

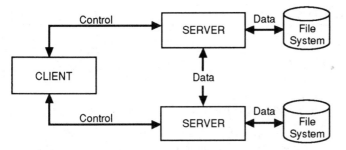

Figure 9.7 FTP Third Party Transfer.

party transfer. As shown in Fig. 9.7, a client opens a connection to two remote machines that both play the role as servers. The purpose of such a connection is to request that the client be given permission to transfer files between the two servers' file systems. If the requests are approved, one server forms a TCP connection with the other server and transfers data across the sending FTP module, the TCP modules, and into the receiving FTP module.

Data types

FTP is somewhat limited in its capability to support different *types* of data representation and the negotiation of the use of these types between machines. The FTP user is allowed to specify a type that will be used in the transfer (for example, ASCII, EBCDIC, etc.). ASCII is the default type, and FTP requires that all implementations support ASCII code. EBCDIC is also supported and is used rather extensively in data transfer between mainframe host computers.

Both ASCII and EBCDIC use a second parameter to indicate if the characters will be used for format control purposes. For example, the carriage control (CR), line feed (LF), vertical tab (VT), and form feed (FF) can be defined as control characters during the FTP session.

FTP also supports the transfer of bit streams, which it calls *image types*. With this operation, the data are sent in continuous bit streams. For the actual transfer, they are packed into 8-bit bytes. Most operations use this type for transmitting binary images, and therefore most FTP implementations support the image type.

A local type is also supported. This type is transferred in bytes whose size are determined by a parameter called *byte size*. FTP requires that the byte size value be a decimal integer.

FTP commands and replies

The FTP uses a number of *commands* for preliminary identification, password authentication, and the ongoing file transfer operations.

TABLE 9.3   FTP Commands

Commands	Function
USER	Identifies the user; required by the server
PASS	User password; preceded by USER
ACCT	User account id
CWD	Change working directory
CDUP	Change to parent directory
SMNT	Mount a different file system data structure
QUIT	Terminate connection
REIN	Terminate connection and start another
PORT	The port address
PASV	Request for passive open
TYPE	Specifies representation type (ASCII, EBCDIC, etc.)
STRU	File structure = file, record, or page
MODE	Transfer mode = stream, block, or compressed
RETR	Transfer copy of file to other party
STOR	Accept data and store it
STOU	Accept data and store it under different name
APPE	Accept data and append it to another file
ALLO	Allocate (reserve) storage for operation
REST	Restart marker (checkpoint) at which transfer restarts
RNFR	Old pathname of file to be renamed
RNTO	New pathname of file to be renamed
ABOR	Abort previous FTP command and associated data transfer
DELE	Delete specified file at the server site
RMD	Remove directory
MKD	Create (make) a directory
PWD	Return (print) name of current working directory
LIST	Transfer list of directories, files, etc. to DTP
NLST	Transfer a directory listing to user site
SITE	Provide services specific to user site
SYST	Query to determine type of operating system at the server
STAT	Return a status over the control connection
HELP	Retrieve helpful information from the server
NOOP	No operation

Table 9.3 lists the acronyms for these commands and a brief description of their function.

FTP also describes a number of *replies* that are used for the correct file transfer between the two processes. As the name suggests, these replies are invoked as a result of the FTP commands.

The replies consist of a three-digit number followed by some descriptive text. The first digit of the replies can take the values from 0 to 5. This digit is used to identify the five major types of replies. Table 9.4 lists the major types of replies and a brief description of their function.

The y value of the reply codes can be coded to contain additional information about the nature of the reply. The type of reply in this code is identified by five numerics, 0 through 5, to define replies relating to status commands, syntax errors, authentication commands, control,

TABLE 9.4   The FTP Reply Codes

Value Code	Function
1yz	A positive preliminary reply which means the command action is being initiated. The invoker of the command can expect another reply before proceeding to a new command.
2yz	A positive completion reply which informs the invoker that the command action has been completed successfully, and a new request may then be initiated.
3yz	A positive intermediate reply signifying that the command has been accepted, but the action is in a hold state because the performer needs additional information.
4yz	A transit negative completion reply signifying that the command is not accepted and an action did not take place. It also signifies a temporary error condition, and the action may be requested again.
5yz	A permanent negative completion reply stating that the action did not occur, the command is not accepted, and it is not expected that the reinitiation of the command will have any better success.

TABLE 9.5   The FTP Reply Codes

Value Code	Function
x0z	Identifies a syntax error; syntax is correct but the command makes no sense
x1z	Replies to requests for information, such as status
x2z	Replies that refer to connection management
x3z	Replies for authentication and accounting commands
x4z	Not specified
x5z	Replies on the status of file server system

data connection commands, etc. Table 9.5 lists and describes these codes.

The third digit defines an even finer level of detail about the meaning of the reply. These codes are numerous and beyond the scope of this book, but an example of their use is provided shortly. The reader is encouraged to refer to RFC 959 for more information on this level of detail about the FTP reply codes.

Sequence of operations in an FTP session

FTP follows several well-ordered steps to effect a data transfer between two users. They are discussed in this section in the order in which they occur.

Remote host login.   Before data transfer can occur between two users, the login operation must be completed. One of the functions of this login is to make certain that passwords, authorization codes, and other security features have been satisfied. At a minimum, a user must have an acceptable user name and password available for the other host machine.

During the login process, it is possible to change some tables that are used to control the data transfer. This is a very useful function if a user wants different types of support services for different types of connections.

Directory definition.   This feature may or may not be needed, but once the control connection is available, it may be necessary to change a directory to manage the space in which the data will reside.

File transfer definition.   Using the directory, this third operation is used to define the file to be transferred, through a list of subcommands. FTP supports a very wide repertoire of subcommands. The most common are GET and PUT subcommands, which allow a copying of the file from the remote host to a local file system, or from the local file system to the remote host.

Mode transfer definition.   The next step in the FTP file transfer process involves the definition of the type of mode to be used during the transfer. Basically, this entails defining how the data are to be represented and how the bits will be transferred. FTP supports several subcommands to support these operations:

Block: This parameter preserves the logical record within the file. It transfers the file in the same format as input to the transmitting module.

Stream: This mode is a default mode for the transfer. It is quite efficient, as it sends no block control information. Stream mode does not care what kind of data is transmitted, so it is code and block transparent.

TYPE: This mode is used with IMAGE, ASCII, or EBCDIC parameters.

ASCII: This is a default transfer mode for TYPE.

EBCDIC: EBCDIC is used frequently between hosts that use EBCDIC characters, such as IBM type machines.

IMAGE: This mode supports the transfer of contiguous binary bits packed in 8-bit bytes. It is the most widely used method for transferring straight binary data.

Starting the data transfer. This sequence of operations can begin with many of the FTP commands. For examples, the retrieve command can be used to begin operations, the append command can be used to "add" records to an existing file, etc.

Stopping the data transfer. This is a rather simple procedure involving the use of an FTP QUIT subcommand. This subcommand will disconnect the host running the FTP operations. It may be preferable to issue the CLOSE subcommand, which does not cause a disconnection. In this case, FTP stays active and another user can begin a new FTP session with the OPEN subcommand.

Examples of FTP operations

In this section, some examples of the FTP protocol are provided to summarize the operations and piece together bits of information we have been using to provide an overview of FTP.

FTP, like several other internet protocols, is a state-driven protocol. Consequently, we will find it useful to illustrate and explain several state diagrams with some examples. In all these examples, the letters mean the following:

B: The operations begin.

W: The protocol machine is waiting for a reply.

E: The operation was created in error.

S: The operation was a success.

F: The operation was a failure.

Each operation is depicted with the reply codes emanating from the function boxes. The reply codes are coded as 1yz, 2yz, 3yz, 4yz, and 5yz to denote the major reply codes discussed earlier. Remember that the yz values give more specific information about the replies.

The last general notation for these figures can be seen in Fig. 9.8. The figure shows a code labeled "CMD" that begins the operation. This command creates a wait state, after which reply codes signify the success or failure of the operation. With this in mind, we move to a discussion of several of the operations of FTP.

Refer again to Fig. 9.8. This figure illustrates a state diagram modeled for many of the FTP operations. The model in Fig. 9.8 supports the following commands: ABOR, DELE, CWD, CDUP, SMNT, HELP, MODE, NOOP, PASV, QUIT, SITE, PORT, SYST, STAT, RMD, MKD, PWD, STRU, and TYPE. (Refer to Table 9.3 for a brief description of these commands.)

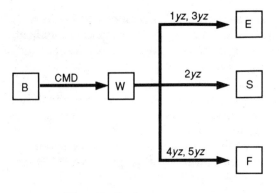

Where B = Begin
     W = Wait for reply
     E = Error
     S = Success
     F = Failure

Figure 9.8   FTP State Diagram for Elementary Operations.

The reader can simply insert one of these commands into the command notation (CMD) in the figure and follow the remainder of the flow chart to determine possible outcomes.

Figure 9.9 shows a similar state diagram, with the exception that reply code 1 entails the protocol machine returning back to a wait-to-reply state. This diagram supports the following commands: APPE, LIST, NLST, REIN, RETR, STOR, and STOU.

The last example shows a rather complex state diagram. Figure 9.10 depicts the operations in state transitions for the login procedure. As depicted in the figure, the operation begins with the issuance of a

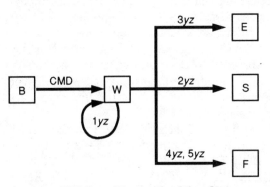

Figure 9.9   FTP State Diagram for Other Options.

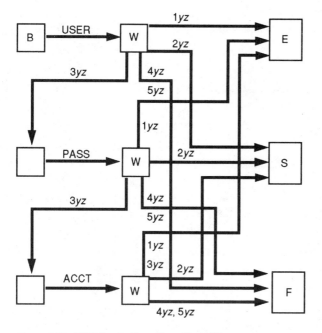

Figure 9.10 FTP Login Procedure State Diagram.

USER message. Subsequently, the password (PASS) and accounting (ACCT) messages are issued to determine if the login is a success, a failure, or an error.

Example of a file retrieval

Figure 9.11 shows an example of a file retrieval. The top part of the figure depicts the permissible replies that can be returned from a retrieve (RETR) command. The bottom part of the figure shows the sequence of the replies. RFC 959 uses the following convention for documenting reply sequences: Preliminary replies are listed first, followed by succeeding replies (which are indented under the preliminary replies). Next are the positive and negative completion replies.

To aid the reader in analyzing Fig. 9.11, the reply codes for RETR are listed in Table 9.6. Remember that many other reply codes are defined in the FTP standard.

Minimum implementation of FTP

All FTP implementations must support the services and commands as depicted in Box 9.1.

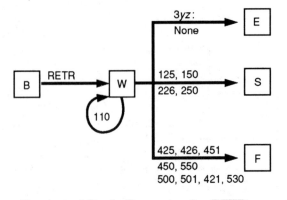

Command-Reply Sequence for RETR:

RETR
  125, 150

  (110)
  226, 250
    425, 426, 451
  450, 550
  500, 501, 421, 530

Figure 9.11   Example of a Retrieve Operation.

TABLE 9.6   Codes Relevant to Fig. 9.11

Code	Meaning
125	Data connection already open; beginning the transfer
150	File status correct; about to open data connection
110	Remark marker reply
226	Closing data connection; action was successful
250	Request action successfully completed
425	Cannot open data connection
426	Connection closed; action aborted
451	Local error; action aborted
450	Requested action not taken; file unavailable (e.g., busy)
550	Requested action not taken; file unavailable (e.g., not found)
500	Syntax error; command cannot be interpreted
501	Syntax error; parameters cannot be interpreted
421	Service not available; closing control connection
530	Not logged in

BOX 9.1   Minimum Implementation of FTP

Type:	ASCII Nonprint
Mode:	Stream
Structure:	File, Record
Commands:	USER, QUIT, PORT, TYPE, MODE, STRU, RETR, STRO, NOOP

Default values as follows:

TYPE:	ASCII, Nonprint
MODE:	Stream
STRU:	File

Simple Mail Transfer Protocol (SMTP)

The SMTP standard is one of the most widely used upper layer protocols in the Internet Protocol stack. As its name implies, it is a protocol that defines how to transmit messages (mail) between two users.

SMTP uses the concept of spooling. The idea of spooling is to allow mail to be sent from a local application to the SMTP application, which stores the mail in some device or memory. Typically, once the mail has arrived at the spool, it has been queued. A server checks to see if any messages are available and then attempts to deliver them. If the user is not available for delivery, the server may try later. Eventually, if the mail cannot be delivered, it will be discarded or perhaps returned to the sender. This is known as an *end-to-end delivery system,* because the server is attempting to contact the destination to deliver, and it will keep the mail in the spool for a period of time until it has been delivered.

SMTP is found in two RFCs. RFC 822 describes the structure for the message, which includes the envelope as well. RFC 821 specifies the protocol that controls the exchange of mail between two machines.

SMTP model

Figure 9.12 illustrates a general model of SMTP. The operations begin with the sender-SMTP establishing communications with the receiver-SMTP. Before the transmission of the mail, the two SMTP entities may exchange passwords or other authentication signals. Next, the sender transmits a special command called "MAIL," which gives the sender's identification and some other information for the mail exchange. The receiver must return an acknowledgment to the MAIL command. In SMTP, this acknowledgment is written as 250 or in some documents as "250 OK." Regardless of how it is written, it means that the requested mail action was completed.

The next step in the procedure is the transmission of an RCPT com-

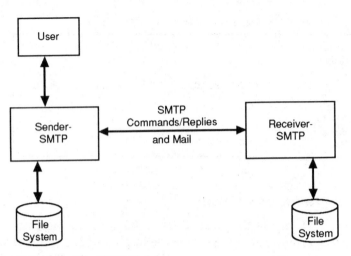

Figure 9.12   The SMTP Model.

mand. Its purpose is to identify the destination(s) of the message. Again, an acknowledgment is required from each potential receiver.

The third step in the process is the issuance of the DATA command. This message is sent by the sender-SMTP to alert the receiver(s) that a message is forthcoming. The data are then transmitted, line by line, until the sender sends a special sequence of control characters to signal the end of the message. At this time, the server may choose to terminate the process with a *QUIT* command.

Address field format

The sender-SMTP uses a standard format for its sending address and receiving address fields. They take the form

`local-part@domain-name`

Therefore, an SMTP name follows the Domain Name System concept, and some systems use the same server facility to derive an IP address from this name.

In practice, this format scheme could appear as

`Jones@beta.aus.edu`

where the local person's name is Jones and the beta.aus.edu is the domain identifier for the person.

The local-part@domain-name can take other forms to designate (1) a direct connection, user@host; (2) a mail receiver located at a non-

SMTP host via a mail gateway, user%remote-host@gateway-host; and (3) a relay between more than two hosts, @host-b@host-c@host-d.

Examples of SMTP operations

Figure 9.13 shows a simple operation of two SMTP users exchanging mail. The left side of the figure shows the sender establishing the connection. The receiver responds with 220 OK. The HELO command is used as an identifier exchange between the two machines. The MAIL FROM command tells Smith@Beta.com that a new mail transaction

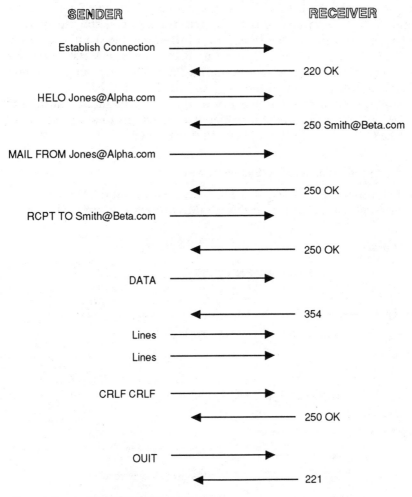

Figure 9.13   An SMTP Mail Transaction.

is beginning. The receiver uses this command to clear its buffers, reset state tables, and prepare for the message. Next, the RCPT command gives the forward path address of the receiver. In this example, it is Smith@Beta.com, which replies with 250 OK. The DATA command informs the receiver that message contents follow. The response is 354, which means start mail input and end it with CRLF CRLF.

The data are transmitted, and the end of transmission is signaled with CRLF CRLF. The receiver responds with 250 OK. Finally, the connection is taken down with QUIT and the responding 221, which means the server is closing the connection.

Figure 9.14 shows examples of other types of SMTP mail exchanges. The top part of the figure illustrates the use of the verification command (VRFY). Its purpose is to confirm the name of the receiver. In this example, JSmith should return a full name and a fully specified mailbox. The second operation in Fig. 9.14 depicts how SMTP can be used to confirm an identity in a mailing list. The respondents should return the full names and the fully specified mailboxes.

These figures provide only a few examples of the many features of SMTP. As stated before, the reader is encouraged to study the relevant RFC if more detailed information is needed.

SMTP and the Domain Name System (DNS)

If an installation runs the Domain Name System and SMTP, a name server must store the mail exchange (MX) reserve records (RRs). RFC

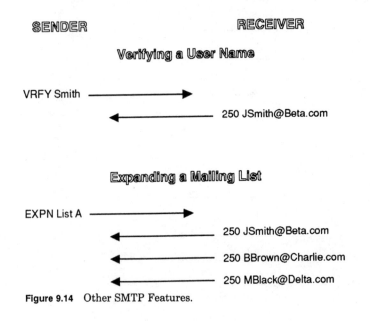

Figure 9.14   Other SMTP Features.

974 states that a sending SMTP should query the host to determine if a well-known (WKS) entry indicates that SMTP is supported.

An example of RRs to support an SMTP mailbox was provided in Chap. 3. Another example follows:

```
RD.ACME.COM.   IN   MX    1 0        RD.ACME.COM.
RD.ACME.COM    IN   MX    2 0        MKT.ACME.COM.
RD.ACME.COM    IN   WKS   12.14.1.1 TFCP (SMTP).
```

In this example, the mail for RD.ACME.COM. is delivered to the host. If RD.ACME.COM. is not available, mail is delivered to MKT.ACME.COM.

Summary

The Internet application layer protocols are the most widely used standards in the industry. They provide the user with relatively simple yet functionally rich services and can be run on large or small machines. Some of them are provided as part of a vendors network product. Their long-range future is questioned by some people who think the OSI application layer protocols will supplant them. For the near future, they remain the preferred approach for the majority of users in the industry.

Chapter 10

Other Protocols

Introduction

An internet uses scores of protocols. The focus in this book has been on TCP, IP, the gateway protocols, the naming/addressing protocols, and the operations of an internet. This chapter provides an overview of several other important protocols that are used in many internet systems.

X Windows

X Windows (also known simply as X) was developed at the Massachusetts Institute of Technology as a windowing system for bit map display computers. It has the term "windows" in its title because it allows a user to display several programs on the screen at one time. Thus, the workstation user need not have multiple screens to control multiple sessions. Notwithstanding, if necessary, X Windows and other software can support the running of multiple applications on separate terminals with the display of executions in the form of icons on the primary screen. The reader may recognize this feature in IBM's OS/2 Presentation Manager.

X Windows can be run on different types of CPUs or different types of networks (of course, the CPU operating system must support X). As we shall see shortly, an X message can be coded to stipulate the type of network communication that is needed (TCP, DECnet, etc.). Another attractive feature of the X Windows protocol is that it can be used with byte-oriented systems by using a block protocol on top of a stream protocol.

Both local and remote windows can be managed with X Windows. Remote windows are established by going through the TCP/IP protocols. Local windows are established with Berkeley UNIX sockets.

X Windows consists of two major modules: *xlib* and *X-server*. As in-

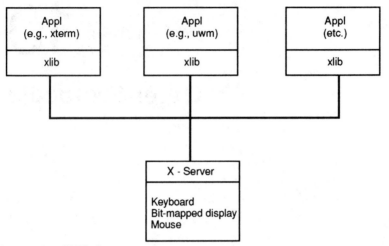

Figure 10.1   X Windows.

dicated in Fig. 10.1, xlib rests in front of the client application. Xlib is a C language module that accepts input from the user. The module is responsible for sending data back and forth to the user terminal. The user is also called the X-client. The X-server rests in the user's terminal. It is nothing more than the display software which receives data and sends data to and from the client application.

To further understand X Windows, it is useful to outline some of the principal rules and functions of the system:

- One X-server is installed per terminal, although more than one X-client may communicate with the X-server. As discussed earlier, the X-server will then display the application windows from the clients and, of course, send input to the appropriate X-client interface.

- The X-server does not maintain the windows. That is the responsibility of the X-client. The X-client is notified, via transactions called *events*, by the X-server when something has changed on the display.

- However, it is the responsibility of the X-server to keep track of the window visibility.

- Windows are managed through a concept called *stacks*, and parent and child windows. This approach is hierarchical in nature in that a child window rests beneath a parent window. In turn, a child window can be a parent window above other child windows. The rationale for this approach is to provide a means for subwindows to be visible on the screen when their parent is on top of its stack.

The xlib module is not the only available interface to X. A number of toolkits are available to mask the application from xlib, and they never use xlib directly.

The X Window System Protocol

Client applications and the server communicate with each other through the X Window System Protocol. Four types of messages are used:

Request: An instruction to the workstation server to perform an action, such as draw a line

Reply: Sent from the server in response to a request (or for some requests)

Event: Used by the server to inform the application of changes that affect the application (e.g., a user clicking a mouse, a foreign application changing a window)

Error: Sent to the client application by the server if something is wrong (e.g., the user selects an execution of a program which consumes more memory than is available)

The formats for these messages are shown in Fig. 10.2. The request format contains *major* and *minor opcodes* of one octet each. The *length* field is two octets, and the *data* field is variable. The reply, error, and event formats contain one octet for the *type* field and a 31-octet *data* field.

Many messages on X do not warrant a reply. For example a "move mouse" message is a one-way request. Additionally, these one-way messages are often buffered and sent in a *batch stream*. This approach

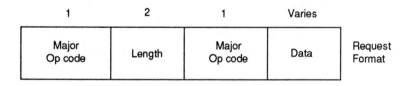

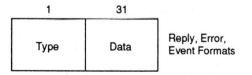

Figure 10.2   The X Window System Protocol Message Formats.

allows a user to issue an xlib request and go on to other operations. On the other hand, a round trip transaction with a returned request requires that the application wait for the reply.

An event message is sent only if an application has *solicited* the type of event that is being sent. This approach is quite important in that it allows an application to receive only relevant events.

A display connection

X Window applications must establish a display connection before they can communicate. The application uses an X request called *XOpenDisplay* from the xlib library to establish a connection with a workstation. The workstation and xlib exchange information with each other while establishing the connection; after which xlib creates a *display structure* that contains the necessary configuration data for proper communication between the application and the workstation. A reply to XOpenDisplay returns a pointer to the display structure.

After a *display connection* has been established, the application and workstation are ready to do work. Of course, the nature of the work depends on the application. For example, if the application wants to know what window the mouse pointer is in, it issues to xlib the *XQueryPointer* call. The position is returned in a reply.

As another example, suppose the application wishes to move the screen cursor (in contrast to it being moved by the mouse user). Issuing the *XWarpPointer* will move the cursor pointer in accordance with the arguments supplied to the call by the application.

While these are specific examples of X operations, on a more general level applications use standard X requests to operate on the following objects (resources):

Windows: The rectangular image on a screen that identifies the manipulated resource (user applications, database, file, etc.)

Graphic contexts: Control the "look" of objects (line size, boldness, etc.)

Color: Translates application commands to colors on the screen

Fonts: Support shape, size, style of text

Pixmaps: Hide displays for later use (a cut and a later paste, for example)

Cursors: Control the look of the cursor and its movement

It should be helpful to examine a few examples of X events that are generated to inform an application about something that happened.

These examples are far from being all inclusive and show only mouse-related events. A *ButtonPress* event is generated each time a mouse user presses a button (or buttons) on the mouse (when the pointer is within a specified window). The opposite holds true for the generation of a *ButtonRelease* event. The *MotionNotify* event is generated when the pointer moves within a specified window. It can be generated by manipulating the mouse or through program control.

We have only touched the surface of the capabilities of the X Window system. Many books and articles are available on the system, and RFC 1198 (FYI:6) provides more information and contact points within Internet.

Remote Procedure Call (RPC)

Remote Procedure Call is a widely used software module developed by Sun Microsystems, Inc. It is used on almost all UNIX-based systems. It greatly facilitates the distribution of applications to multiple machines. The RPC is published in RFC 1057.

RPC is a remote subroutine call program. It allows a caller program, named a client, to send a message to a server. The caller program then waits for a reply message. This call message includes parameters defining what is to be performed at the remote site. In turn, the reply message contains the result of the procedure call.

RPC can be implemented on either a TCP or a UDP transport layer. We know that UDP does not provide reliability. Therefore, it will be up to the end user application to provide for retransmissions, time-outs, and other transport layer mechanisms.

The RPC call message contains only three fields: (a) remote program number, (b) remote program version number, and (c) remote procedure number.

The purpose of the *remote program number* is to identify a group of procedures such as a database system, a file system, etc. Sun Microsystems administers numbers in the range of *0–1fffffff*. They are intended to be identical for all installations.

The procedures are really macros or catalogued procedures such as a read or write. The procedures are identified with *remote procedure numbers*.

Within the procedures, it may be necessary to change the system, in which case the *remote version number* is assigned as different releases are placed into production.

The RPC reply message is also quite simple. It provides the status of a procedure call with the replies shown in Fig. 10.3.

Possible RPC Replies

```
├─ MSG_ACCEPTED
│       ├─ Success (RPC execution was successful)
│       ├─ PROG_UNAVAIL (Program is not available)
│       ├─ PROG_MISMATCH (Version not supported)
│       ├─ PROC_UNAVAIL (Procedure is not supported)
│       └─ GARBAGE_ARGS (Parameters cannot be decoded)
└─ MSG_DENIED
        ├─ RPC_MISMATCH (RPC Version problem)
        └─ AUTH_ERROR (Authentication problem)
               ├─ AUT_BADCRED (Bad credentials)
               ├─ AUTH_REJECTEDCRED (Client must start again)
               ├─ AUTH_BADVERF (Bad verifier)
               ├─ AUTH_REJECTEDVERF (Verifier expired)
               └─ AUTH_TOOWEAK (Security problems)
```

Figure 10.3 Possible Replies to a Remote Procedure Call.

Network File System (NFS)

The Network File System (NFS) was also developed by Sun Micro-systems, Inc. to allow computers to share files across a network or networks. It is published in RFC 1094. NFS is computer independent and is independent of lower layers, such as the transport layer, because it rests above the RPC. NFS consists of two other protocols called the *mount protocol* and the *NFS protocol*. The purpose of the mount protocol is to identify a file system and its remote host that is to be accessed. The NFS protocol is responsible for performing the file transfer operations.

The NFS server procedures

An NFS server performs its operations through several procedures. These procedures are "stateless" in that no state tables are maintained to track the progress of the procedures' operations. This approach may seem a bit strange to the reader. After all, file reading, and especially writing, is inherently state oriented (sometimes called "stateful") because these operations must be tracked. NFS solves the problem by assuming that any required state-oriented services are implemented in other protocols. Therefore, a user application could contain the state-oriented logic (file locks, write positions, etc.) and call NFS for the use of its procedures.

The procedures of NFS are similar to other network transfer/management protocols. A user can invoke procedures to (a) create, rename, remove a file; (b) get attributes of files; (c) create, read, and remove a file directory; (d) read and write to a file; and (e) perform other procedures.

The user application is responsible for keeping track of the position in the file where reading and writing is to occur. For example, the NFS read file procedure, NFSPROC_READ, requires the application to furnish the position in the file where the reading is to begin as well as the number of bytes that are to be returned in the reply.

Remote Exec Daemon (REXECD)

The REXECD allows the execution of the REXECD command on a remote host through a TCP/IP-based network. The client is required to perform the REXECD processing. REXECD is designed to handle commands issued by host machines and to delegate these commands to slave machines for job execution. REXECD is responsible for authenticating the user (if a user ID/password is used). It also performs automatic login functions to the host. The protocol rests above TCP in the Internet Protocol (IP) suite.

IBM systems make extensive use of REXECD. IBM's VM, AIX, and DOS machines can run this protocol.

PING

PING is a very simple protocol that uses the user datagram protocol (UDP) segment. Its principal operation is to send a message and simply wait for it to come back.

PING is so named because it is an echo protocol and uses the ICMP echo and echo-reply messages. Therefore, each machine is operating with a PING server whenever IP is active on the machine. PING is used principally by systems programmers for diagnostic and debugging purposes. It is very useful because it provides the following functions:

- The *loopback ping* is used to verify the operation of the TCP/IP software.

- The *ping address* determines if a physical network device can be addressed.

- The *ping remote IP address* verifies whether the network can be addressed.

- The *ping remote host name* is used to verify the operation of a server on a host.

The reader can refer to Chap. 6 for more information on this protocol.

HOSTNAME

The HOSTNAME protocol (formerly titled the NIC Internet host name server) is a service provided by SRI for the Defense Communications Agency. The system is maintained by the DDN Network Information Center (NIC).

HOSTNAME is used to retrieve information about networks, hosts, gateways, and domains within an internet environment. A user that wishes to use HOSTNAME establishes a TCP connection to the NIC with established identifiers. TCP port 101 is used at the service host.

HOSTNAME is easy to use. The user simply keys in a single line with a key word and arguments. For example, a user keys in HNAME <HOSTNAME> followed by a carriage return. The response would then provide information on addresses and names stored in a host table. The specific retrieval would depend on the argument in the HNAME value. Notwithstanding, HOSTNAME's basic purpose is to provide information by matching host table entries.

HOSTNAME has other services. It allows a search across tables, a search within domains of tables, a search for known gateways, and a search for domain tables in conjunction with host tables. How these services are provided depends on the type of command that is entered from the user device.

Host Monitoring Protocol (HMP)

The Host Monitoring Protocol (HMP) is used to collect information from host computers in an internet. Typically, the information is used by a network control center (NCC) to determine the performance and the status of hosts. HMP uses the term *monitoring entity* to describe a monitored host and *monitoring host* to describe what would typically be the NCC doing the monitoring. This does not mean that one host could not monitor another.

Earlier implementations of HMP were used by NCCs to collect network information from gateways, cluster controllers, and other network entities. Some implementations have been used simply to exchange information between host machines.

HMP is a connectionless protocol. It operates at the transport layer over IP and ICMP. This approach does not preclude other layer suites; for example, HMP could rest over LLC Type 1, 2, or 3 in a LAN.

The idea of HMP is based on the realization that the following type of information needs to be exchanged between hosts, and between hosts and NCCs. First, it may be necessary for the monitored entity to send unsolicited traffic to a monitoring center. Once action that comes to mind is the sending of alarms from a monitored host. Second, the monitoring host (the control of the NCC) may need to gather information from the monitored entity for log control management. Finally, the NCC may need to set certain control parameters at the monitored host and ascertain if these control parameters have been set and carried out successfully.

To meet these needs, HMP is designed to collect three classes of data:

1. *Spontaneous events* are captured by the monitoring entity. These events are called *traps* in the internet. Typically, a trap would be on something that is deemed important enough to warrant the NCC's attention. The trap messages must contain identifiers to indicate the report, time, host, and, of course, any data relevant to the trapped message.

2. The second type of data collected by HMP deals with the current status of a host machine. The idea of *status information* is to collect information that is topical, not necessarily over a long period of time. HMP accomplishes this action by sending a typical poll message to a host. The poll requires the host to respond with its latest status information.

3. The third type of data collected by HMP is longer-range data, such as performance data over a period of time. Unlike status information, all this data is important because it is used for the analysis of the performance of the network and/or the host.

Discard Protocol

This protocol is also useful as a diagnostic tool. As its name implies, it discards any data it received. The usefulness of this protocol may initially escape the reader. Typically, it is used by the receiver to analyze the received data. The data likely is not actual end user data, but data introduced at the transmitting entity for network tuning considerations. Therefore, instead of passing this data up to an upper layer, the discard protocol discards it.

The discard protocol is used with TCP in which the discard server listens for the connections on TCP port 9. After the connection is established, any data coming in on this port is discarded.

The discard service is also provided for UDP service. The server listens for data on UDP port 9. Upon receiving the data, the datagram is discarded.

Finger

Finger is a very simple protocol that is used to obtain information about users logged on to a machine. The information given to an inquiring user depends entirely on the specific implementation of the finger. Typically, when the client sends a command, a list of users currently logged on to that host is provided in response. However, be aware that the implementation of Finger varies as does the information provided in the retrieval.

Typical information retrieved with the use of Finger is the name of the user, the job title of the job running on the machine, the interface to the user (that is, the terminal being used), the location of the workstation, etc.

Finger is now published as RFC 1196, which has clarified some ambiguities about the protocol.

The Bootstrap Protocol (BOOTP)

Earlier in this book we learned that the Reverse Address Resolution Protocol (RARP) is used to obtain an IP address from a physical address. Although widely used, RARP has some disadvantages. Since it is intended to operate at the hardware level, it is cumbersome to obtain and manage the routine from an applications program. It also contains limited information. Its purpose is to obtain an IP address, but not much other information is provided. It would be useful to have the reply of a message contain information about other protocols supported by the machine, such as the gateway address, server host names, etc. Due to these problems, the Internet now supports the Bootstrap Protocol, also known as BOOTP.

BOOTP uses an IP datagram to obtain an IP address. This approach seems somewhat circuitous at first glance, but the destination address in the IP datagram is a limited broadcast value (all ones yielding 255.255.255.255). A machine that chooses to use BOOTP sends out an IP limited broadcast. A designated server on the network receives the BOOTP message and sends a proper answer back to the inquirer in the form of yet another broadcast.

BOOTP utilizes UDP at the transport layer. Consequently, the operation is connectionless. The UDP uses a checksum to check for corruption of data. BOOTP performs some transport layer functions by sending a request to the server. Then a timer is started, and if no reply is received within a defined period, BOOTP attempts a retransmission.

The format for BOOTP is illustrated in Fig. 10.4. All fields are of fixed length, and the replies and requests have the same format. The field labeled *operation* is set to 1 to denote a request and 2 to denote a reply. The next two fields are identical to the ARP protocol, in that the *hardware type* and *hardware length* identify the type of hardware and the length of the hardware address. The *hops* field must be set to 0 in a request message. The server is allowed to pass a BOOTP message to another machine, perhaps in another network. If so, it must increment

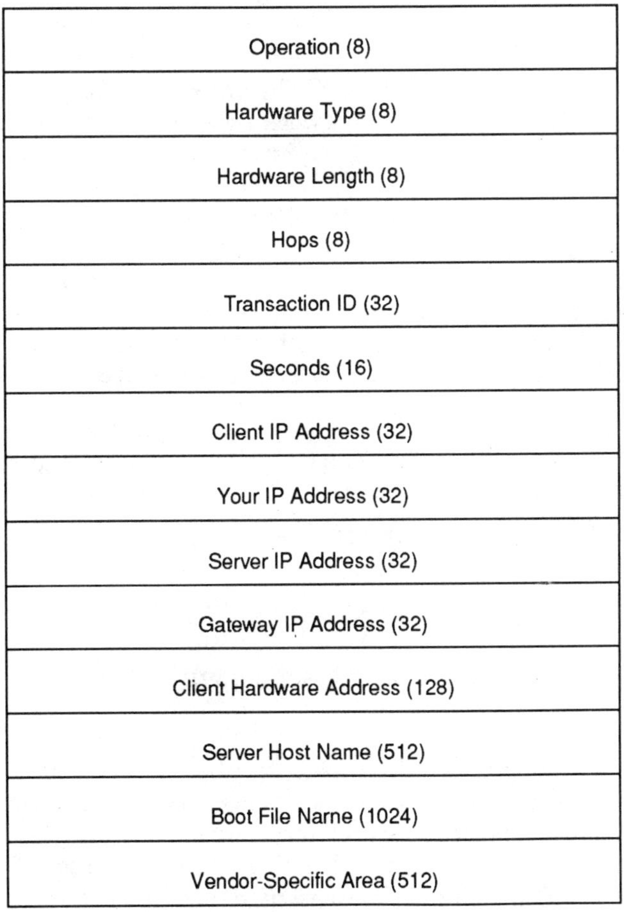

Operation (8)
Hardware Type (8)
Hardware Length (8)
Hops (8)
Transaction ID (32)
Seconds (16)
Client IP Address (32)
Your IP Address (32)
Server IP Address (32)
Gateway IP Address (32)
Client Hardware Address (128)
Server Host Name (512)
Boot File Narne (1024)
Vendor-Specific Area (512)

(*n*) = Number of bits in the field

Figure 10.4   BOOTP Message Format.

the hop count by one. The *transaction ID* field is used to coordinate requests and response messages. The *seconds* field is used to determine (in seconds) the time since the machine has started to establish the BOOTP procedure. The next four fields contain the IP addresses of the *client address,* as well as the *requestor's address, server address,* and *gateway address.* The *client hardware address* is also available. The message also contains the *client server* and the *boot file* names. The *vendor specific area* is not defined in the standard.

Network Time Protocol (NTP)

Chapter 6 discussed the use of an ICMP timestamp option in which communicating machines such as gateways and hosts coordinate their clocks. The question that remains is, how do these machines obtain their timing information? After all, who can say that one gateway has a more accurate clock than another gateway? The answer to this question is provided in this discussion on the network time protocol (NTP), published in RFC 1119. This standard is highly recommended for a reader who needs detailed information on clocking protocols, algorithms for smoothing the clock, developing clock offsets, as well as estimating round trip delays for synchronizing clocking values.

The NTP operation is depicted in Fig. 10.5. Clocking information for a network is provided through the primary time server designated as a root. The time server obtains its clocking information from master sources. In the United States, this is usually one of four sources:

1. *Fort Collins, Colorado:* Station WWV operated by the National Institutes of Standards and Technology (NIST) using high-frequency (HF) frequencies

2. *Kauai, Hawaii:* Station WWVH operated by NIST, also operating with HF frequencies

3. *Boulder, Colorado:* Station WWVB, operating with low-frequency transmissions

4. *Geosynchronous Orbiting Environmental Satellite (GOES):* Operated by NIST in the UHF range

These "master clocking sources" are used by the primary time server to derive accurate clocks. Other countries may have their own clocks that are used to provide clocking over large areas. Most of these clocks provide very accurate clocking synchronization on the order of less than 1 millisecond. Local clocks are even more accurate. Part of the problem with obtaining absolutely accurate clock information stems from the variable propagation delay due to different atmo-

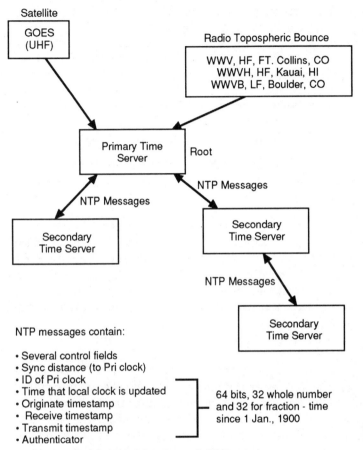

Figure 10.5 The Network Time Protocol (NTP).

spheric conditions, interrupt latencies at the machines, as well as small oscillator drifts in the clocks.

The primary time server, upon receiving clocking information from a master clocking source, then uses the NTP protocol to coordinate clocks at the secondary time servers. Secondary time servers may in turn provide clocking for other secondary time servers. The accuracy of the clocking decreases as NTP messages are propagated through the clocking hierarchy. Although Fig. 10.5 shows one primary time server servicing an internet, this need not be the case. Multiple primary time servers can service the clocking within the network.

The NTP messages contain, as one might expect, *timestamps* that are used by the primary and secondary time servers to calculate clock offsets and correct clocking inaccuracies. Several *control fields* are contained in the NTP message; they are beyond the scope of this discussion. The *sync distance* is an estimate of the round trip propagation delay to the primary clock, as seen by the originator of the NTP message. The *ID of the primary* clock contains the unique identifier of the primary time server. The next four fields contain timestamp information. They contain the following information:

Time local clock updated: The time that the originator of this message has had its local clock updated

Originate timestamp: The time that this message was originated

Receive timestamp: The time that this message was received

Transmit timestamp: The time that this message was transmitted after receiving it

All timestamps are 64 bits in length, with 32 bits reserved for a whole number and 32 bits for the fraction. Timestamps are benchmarked from January 1, 1900. Does the 32-bit field provide enough space for growth? The answer is, most definitely. The value 2^{32} provides magnitudes well beyond what we foresee as needed in the future.

The last field is *Authenticator*. It is an optional field used for authentication purposes.

In addition to RFC 1119, the interested reader might wish to refer to RFCs 956 and 957.

NTP uses port 37 and can operate above UDP or the TCP. Be aware that the information retrieved and displayed to the user on a terminal is not very readable. For example, the value gives the number of seconds since January 1, 1900, midnight (GMT). Consequently, the date of January 1, 1980 GMT at midnight would be retrieved and displayed as 2,524,521,600. Of course, a simple program can be written to translate this notation into a user friendly format.

Daytime

Daytime is similar to the Time protocol, except that it returns times which are easier to read. The returned string is an ASCII text. The information returned from the Daytime protocol is usually displayed as weekday, month day, year, time zone. This is used quite often in Internet standards when machine readable protocol is not required (as in the Time protocol discussed above).

Summary

The TCP/IP protocol suite contains a wealth of protocols beyond that of TCP and IP. The major applications protocols were examined in Chap. 9.

This chapter has summarized other popular protocols. The RPC and NFS systems are some of the most widely used upper layer protocols in use today. The internet has chosen to standardize these systems on Sun Microsystems products. X Windows is gaining in popularity for the use of bit-mapped, display-oriented protocol. Clocking protocols have been in existence for a number of years, and the Network Time Protocol represents the culmination of many of the earlier efforts.

Internet Network
Management Systems

Introduction

An internet is of limited long-term value if it cannot be managed properly. One can imagine the difficulty of trying to interconnect and communicate among different computers, gateways, etc. if the conventions differ for managing the use of alarms, performance indicators, traffic statistics, logs, accounting statistics, and other vital elements of a network.

In recognition of this fact, the Internet Activities Board (IAB) has assumed the lead in setting standards for TCP/IP-based internets and has sponsored two network management protocols. One protocol is intended to address short-term solutions and is called the *Simple Network Management Protocol (SNMP)*. The other protocol proposes to address long-range solutions and is called *Common Management Information Services and Protocol over TCP/IP (CMOT)*.

This chapter examines these Internet network management protocols. Emphasis is on the Internet Management Information Base (IMIB, or MIB) and the Structure for Management Information (SMI). The CMOT protocol is discussed in a more general way because it is not used much today. The Abstract Syntax Notation One (ASN.1) language is used in this chapter, but the examples are kept simple for the uninitiated reader.

A more thorough explanation is available from *Network Management Standards,* by Uyless Black (McGraw-Hill, 1991).

Summary of the Internet Network
Management Standards

Table 11.1 lists and describes the titles of the major Requests for Comments (RFCs) pertinent to the Internet network management standards.

RFC 1052 provides useful information on the background of the de-

TABLE 11.1   The Internet Standards for Network Management

RFC Number	Date	Title
1052	April, 1988	IAB Recommendations for the Development of Internet Network Management Standards
1155	May, 1990	Structure and Identification of Management Information for TCP/IP-based Internets
1213	March, 1991	Management Information Base for Network Management of TCP/IP-based Internets: MIB II
1157	May 1990	A Simple Network Management Protocol (SNMP)
1215		Using Traps with SNMP
1187		Bulk Data Retrieval with SNMP
1212		Concise MIB definitions
1095	April, 1989	The Common Management Information Services Protocol over TCP/IP (CMOT)
1085	December, 1988	ISO Presentation Services on top of TCP/IP-based Internets (LLP)

velopment of these standards. The standards themselves are contained in three documents. *RFC 1155* contains common definitions and identification of information used on TCP/IP-based networks. It is similar in intent to the OSI Network Management Standard IS 7498-4 and IS 10040.

RFC 1213 contains information dealing with an IMIB. This document is the second release of the MIB, which is known as MIB II.

The other important document is *RFC 1157,* which describes the Simple Network Management Protocol (SNMP). Although subsequent RFCs contain additional information for the use of SNMP, the reader may find *RFC 1215* (a convention for defining traps for use with the SNMP) and *RFC 1187* (bulk table retrieval with the SNMP) to be useful documents for ancillary information on SNMP. Additionally, *RFC 1212* (concise MIB definitions) is a very useful document that provides information on producing MIB modules.

Two other RFCs are listed in Table 11.1 as RFC 1095 and 1085. These RFCs deal with the Common Management Information Services and Protocol over TCP/IP (CMOT) and the Lightweight Presentation Protocol (LPP). As stated earlier, the CMOT approach has not proved to be successful. It is listed in this table in case the reader wants to analyze it for historical reasons.

Layer Architecture for Internet Network Management

Figure 11.1 depicts the internet layers for the network management standards. The SNMP forms the foundation for the management ar-

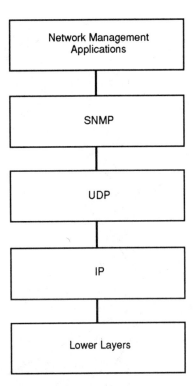

Figure 11.1 The Internet Network Management Layers.

chitecture. The network management applications are not defined in the internet specifications. These applications consist of vendor-specific network management modules such as fault management, log control, security and audit trails, etc. As illustrated in the figure, SNMP rests over the User Datagram Protocol (UDP). UDP in turn rests on top of IP, which then rests on the lower layers (the data link layer and the physical layer).

The Internet Naming Hierarchy

The objects within an internet have many common characteristics across the subnetworks, vendor products, and individual components. It would be quite wasteful for each organization to spend precious resources and time in using ASN.1 (and modified-ASN.1) to describe these resources. Therefore, the Internet MIB provides a registration scheme wherein resources (objects) can be categorized within a registration hierarchy. This concept is founded on the ISO/CCITT agreement convention, which identifies objects within a system.

Figure 11.2 shows the ISO and Internet registration tree for the Internet MIB. At the root level, three branches identify the registration

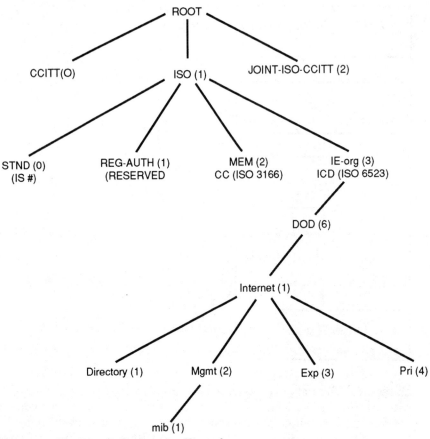

Figure 11.2 The Internet Registration Hierarchy.

hierarchy as either CCITT (0), ISO (1), or joint CCITT/ISO (2). Since we are concerned with the Internet activities, Fig. 11.2 shows the ISO branch. Notice branch 3, which is labeled IE-ORG. The next branch identifies the Department of Defense (DOD) with the value 6. Under this hierarchical tree, Internet is found with a value of 1. Next, within the Internet hierarchy are four nodes. One is labeled management (mgmt) with a value of 2. Finally, the leaf to this node is labeled mib (1).

The registration hierarchy permits the assignment of unique identifiers to managed objects. (*Managed object* is the term used to identify any internet managed resource, such as a router, a TCP connection, an IP address table, etc.) The identifier is derived by concatenating the numbers associated with each node in the tree. In Fig. 11.2, the Internet MIB is identified by 1.3.6.1.2.1.

Structure of Management Information (SMI)

SMI describes the identification scheme and structure for the managed objects in the internet. The SMI document deals principally with organizational and administrative matters. It leaves the task of object definitions to the other network management RFCs.

SMI describes the names used to identify the managed objects (that is, the network resources). These names are ASN.1 OBJECT IDENTIFIERS and use the naming convention depicted in Fig. 11.2. Referring to Fig. 11.2, the *Directory (1)* subtree is reserved at this time. It is anticipated that this subtree will be used to determine how the emerging OSI Directory services (X.500) will interface with an internet.

Mgmt (2) is used to identify the managed objects in the network. This subtree is managed by IAB, and the numbering is delegated by the IAB to other managed objects. Each definition in the tree is named as an OBJECT IDENTIFIER, which is a unique identifier of a managed object.

Exp (3) identifies objects that are used in experimental endeavors. Again, the authority for naming through this subtree rests with the IAB.

Finally, the *Pri (4)* tree permits private enterprises to register models of their own managed objects. The tree is still administered by IAB, but the private enterprise, upon receiving the node of the tree, may define new MIB objects within the hierarchy. Notwithstanding, the IAB recommends that all private names be registered under one authority.

Parts of the SMI standard are written in ASN.1-type coding. However, the syntax for SMI is simpler than the syntax for ASN.1. The objective of this approach is to provide a less rigorous convention for describing managed objects in the Internet. Shortly, we will examine the syntax rules for defining SMI objects. For the present, we need to concern ourselves with the types of managed objects that are defined in these standards.

SMI syntax and types

The Internet standards use ASN.1 constructs to describe the syntax of the object types. The full ASN.1 set is not allowed. The following primitive types are permitted: INTEGER, OCTET STRING, OBJECT IDENTIFIER, and NULL. In addition to the primitive types, these constructor types are allowed: SEQUENCE and SEQUENCE OF.

The SMI standard defines six major Internet managed objects (types):

Network Address: This type allows a choice of the Internet family of protocols. The type is defined in the modified ASN.1 notation as

CHOICE, which will allow choosing the protocol within the family. Presently, only the Internet family is identified.

IP Address: This address is used to define the Internet 32-bit address. The ASN.1 notation is an OCTET STRING.

Time Ticks: This type represents a non-negative integer, which is used to record events such as the last change to a managed object, the last update to a database, etc. The SMI standard requires that it represent a time increment in hundredths of a second.

Gauge: The SMI definition for this type is a non-negative integer which can range from 0 to 2^{31-1}. The gauge definition does not permit counterwraparound, although it may increase or decrease in value.

Counter: This defined type is described as a non-negative integer, again ranging from 0 to 2^{31-1}. However, this type differs from gauge in that the values can be wrapped around but can only increase in value.

Opaque: This defined type allows a managed object to pass anything as an OCTET STRING. It is so named because the encodings are passed transparently.

The Management Information Base (IMIB)

The Internet network management structure is organized around object groups. Presently, 10 object groups have been defined. Figure 11.3 depicts the composition of the object groups. The reader should be able to recognize the initials and acronyms in this figure. For example, several of the object groups were discussed in this book, notably, IP, ICMP, TCP, UDP, and EGP. Each of these object classes is defined further in the Internet MIB. RFC 1213 provides a detailed description in the modified ASN.1 notation for each of the object groups.

An organization is not required to implement all the MIB object

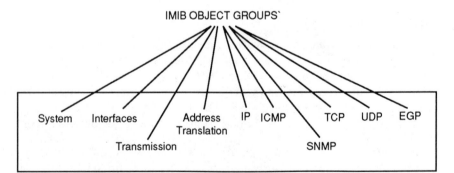

Figure 11.3   MIB Object Groups.

groups. Certainly, if one is using exterior gateways, the EGP group is mandatory. However, if an organization implements UDP at the transport layer, it need not implement the TCP group. These standards do require that if an object group is supported, all elements in that group also must be supported.

The object groups are made up of objects. An object is anything that is deemed to be important enough to manage in the network (a packet switch, PBX, modem, etc.). For the Internet MIB, each object must have a name, a syntax, and an encoding.

First, the name is an OBJECT IDENTIFIER, which must be identified through the internet registration hierarchy naming conventions, described earlier in this chapter. An object is also defined by a type and an instance. The object type and the object instance (in conformance with OSI conventions) serve to identify unambiguously an instantiation of the object.

Second, the syntax for each object uses ASN.1 for its description. As stated earlier, not all ASN.1 constructs are permitted. We will describe these later in this chapter.

The third aspect of an object is its encoding. This term describes how the object type is represented through the object type's syntax. In addition, encoding deals with how the object type is coded (represented) while being transmitted on the communications channel in the network. The encoding is done in conformance with the basic end-coding rules (BER) of ASN.1.

Overview of the object groups

Each object group (Fig. 11.3) is described briefly in this section. Be aware that this general explanation is to give the reader an idea of the major operations of the groups. RFC 1213 should be studied carefully to appreciate the full functions supported by the MIB definitions.

The *system* object group describes

The name and version of the hardware, operating system, and networking software of the entity

The hierarchical name of the group

When (in time) the management portion of the system was reinitialized

The *interfaces* object group describes the

Number of network interfaces supported

Type of interface operating below IP (e.g., LAPB, Ethernet, etc.)

Size of datagram acceptable to the interface

Speed (bit/s) of the interface

Address of the interface

Operational state of the interface (up, down, etc.)

Amount of traffic received, delivered (unicast or broadcast), or discarded, and the reasons

The *address translation* group describes the address translation tables for network-to-physical address translation. This group will eventually become obsolete, as its functions now reside in the IP group.

The *IP* group describes

If the machine forwards datagrams

The time-to-live value for datagrams originated at this site

The amount of traffic received, delivered, or discarded, and the reasons

Information on fragmentation operations

Address tables, including subnet masks

Routing tables, including destination address, distance metrics, age of route, next hop, and protocol from which route was learned (RIP, EGP, etc.)

The *ICMP* group describes

The number of the various ICMP messages received and transmitted

Statistics on problems encountered

The *TCP* group describes

Retransmission algorithm and maximum/minimum retransmission values

Number of TCP connections the entity can support

Information on state transition operations

Information on traffic received and sent

Port and IP numbers for each connection

The *UDP* group describes

Information on traffic received and sent

Information on problems encountered

The *EGP* group describes

Information on traffic sent and received and problems encountered

The EGP neighbor table

Addresses to neighbors

The EGP state with each neighbor

The *transmission* group was added to the second release of the MIB (MIB II). As of this writing, the group is empty, but it is intended to provide information on the types of transmission schemes and interfaces.

The *SNMP* group was also added to MIB II. It contains 30 objects that are used with SNMP. Most of the objects deal with error-reporting capabilities and will be explained later in this chapter.

Table 11.2 lists and briefly describes the objects for the System group. Similar tables could be created for each group, but this is beyond the scope of this book. This table is included to give the reader an idea of the MIB definitions. (All internet objects are described in my *Network Management Standards* book.)

All Internet objects are described further with certain *key words* (reserved words). Five notations are used to describe the format of a managed object:

Object descriptor: As the name implies, this describes the object in ASCII text.

TABLE 11.2   The System Group

Function: The System group provides general information about managed objects. This group must be implemented for all objects.

sysDescr	An octet string to describe the object, such as hardware, operating system, etc.
sysObjectID	An OBJECT IDENTIFIER to identify the object uniquely (with naming hierarchy values) within the naming subtree
sysUpTime	In TimeTicks, the time since the object was declared up and running (reinitialized)
sysContact	An octet string to identify the person/organization to contact for information about the object
sysLocation	An octet string containing the location of the object
sysServices	An integer value that describes the service(s) offered by the object, based on the location of the service within a layer

Syntax: The syntax describes the bit-stream representation of the object.

Definition: This notation allows the managed object to be described in text to aid the human reader in understanding the notation.

Access: This notation describes whether the managed object can be (a) read-only, (b) write-only, (c) read-write, or (d) not accessible.

Status: This notation is used to describe information such as (a) the version is mandatory, (b) the version is optional, (c) the object is obsolete.

Templates to describe objects

All object definitions are defined with templates and ASN.1 code. Templates are examined in this section. The next section examines the ASN.1 code. The template format is shown in Fig. 11.4. The fields were listed and described above.

Each of the 10 object groups in Fig. 11.3 is defined in RFC 1213 with the standard template format. It is of little value to the reader to repeat these templates—they consume almost 50 pages in the standard. Each group was described briefly in an earlier section to give the reader an idea of the principal functions of each group. The remainder of this section shows one example of the templates. The example is taken from the interfaces object group.

Figure 11.5 shows the template for a leaf entry of a registration tree for the TCP/IP interfaces. Be aware that several intermediate nodes are not included in this example. The notation of ifType { IfEntry 3 } means the IfType belongs to parent IfEntry 3 in the tree.

The syntax clause describes the abstract syntax (in ASN.1) of the object type. As the entry shows, the physical, data link, and subnetwork interfaces that exist below IP are described and assigned an integer value. Thus, two machines that exchange information about the inter-

OBJECT:
    A name for the object type, with its
    corresponding OBJECT IDENTIFIER

Syntax:
    The ASN.1 coding to describe the syntax
    of the object type

Definition:
    Textual description of the object type

Access:
    Access options

Status:
    Status of object type

Figure 11.4   Template for IMIB Object Type Definitions.

OBJECT:
    ifType {if Entry 3}
Syntax:
  INTEGER {
    other (1),   −none of the following
    regular1822 (2),
    hdh1822 (3),
    ddn-x25 (4)
    rfc877-x25 (5),
    ethernet-csmacd (6),
    iso88023-csmacd (7),
    iso88024-tokenBus (8),
    iso88025-tokenRing (9),
    iso88026-man (10),
    starLan (11),
    proteon-10Mbit (12),
    proteon-80Mbit (13),
    hyperchannel (14),
    fddi (15),
    lapb (16),
    sdlc (17),
    t1-carrier (18),
    cept (19),   −european equivalent of T-1
    basiclsdn (20),
    primarylsdn (21),
                            −proprietary serial
−... and others not shown,
        }

Definition:
  The type of interface...immediately "below"
  the IP in the protocol stack.
Access:
  read-only
Status:
  mandatory
Note: ... means sorne the material of RFC is omitted.

Figure 11.5   The Interface Type (ifType) Template.

face supported below the IP layer are required to use these values. For example, ifType = 6 must be used to identify an Ethernet interface.

Definition of high-level MIB

Figure 11.6 depicts the RFC 1213 ASN.1 notation for the MIB groups. The code can be understood in the context of the objects illustrated in Fig. 11.3 and the naming hierarchy tree in Fig. 11.2.

The IMPORTS statement designates that a number of definitions are imported from RFC 1155. All objects are tagged as OBJECT IDENTIFIERS and defined with yet another name within the naming tree ({mgmt1}, {mib 1}, etc).

RFC1213-MIB ::= BEGIN

IMPORTS
    mgmt, NetworkAddress, IpAddress, Counter, Gauge, TimeTicks
    FROM RFC1155-SMI;
    OBJECT-TYPE
      From RFC-1212;

mib-2   OBJECT IDENTIFIER ::= {mgmt 1}

    system   OBJECT IDENTIFIER ::= {mib-2 1}
    interfaces   OBJECT IDENTIFIER ::= {mib-2 2}
    at   OBJECT IDENTIFIER ::= {mib-2 3}
    Ip   OBJECT IDENTIFIER ::= {mib-2 4}
    icmp   OBJECT IDENTIFIER ::= {mib-2 5}
    tcp   OBJECT IDENTIFIER ::= {mib-2 6}
    udp   OBJECT IDENTIFIER ::= {mib-2 7}
    egp   OBJECT IDENTIFIER ::= {mib-2 8}
 -- cmot   OBJECT IDENTIFIER ::= {mib-2 9}
    transmission   OBJECT IDENTIFIER ::= {mib-2 10}
    snmp   OBJECT IDENTIFIER ::= {mib-2 11}
    END

Figure 11.6   The High-Level MIB Definition.

The SNMP

SNMP owes its origin to decisions made by the Internet Activities
Board (IAB) in early 1988. At that time, the IAB held meetings to discuss methods to develop network management protocols to operate on
TCP/IP-based networks. The result of that meeting was the decision to
develop two parallel management systems, SNMP and CMOT.

SNMP is designed to be a simple, short-range solution to network
management on internet. It is based on an earlier protocol called the
simple gateway monitoring protocol (SGMP). The reader can refer to
RFC 1028 for a description of this earlier protocol.

SNMP products began to appear on the marketplace in late 1988 and
early 1989. In 1988 the MIB to support SNMP was also published. In
September of 1988 at Interop '88, several announcements were made regarding implementations of SNMP. As the standard matured, other
RFCs were released to define its operation further. In early 1989, the
RFC 1098 titled *SNMP over Ethernet* was published. Today, SNMP is
widely implemented over many networks and vendor products.

SNMP administrative relationships

The SNMP architecture uses a variety of terms that were explained
earlier. Using Fig. 11.7 as a discussion point, entities residing at management network stations and network elements that communicate

SNMP COMMUNITY

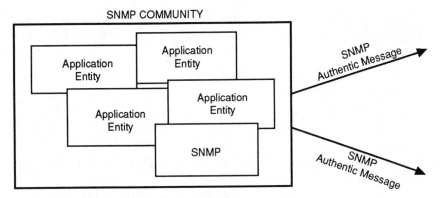

Figure 11.7 SNMP Community.

with each other using the SNMP standard are called SNMP *application entities*. The pairing of application entities with SNMP agents (agents are explained shortly) is called an *SNMP community*. Each community is identified by an Internet hierarchical name.

SNMP messages are originated by SNMP application entities. They are considered to belong to the SNMP community containing the application entity. These messages are termed *authentic SNMP messages*. Authentication schemes are used to identify the message and verify its authenticity. This process is called an *authentication service*.

Figure 11.8 provides a view of other administrative relationships for SNMP. An SNMP *network element* uses objects from the Internet MIB. The *subset of objects* pertaining to this element is called an SNMP MIB view. In turn, an SNMP access mode represents an element of the set (for example, read-only elements, write-only elements). A pairing of the SNMP access mode with the MIB view is termed the SNMP *community profile*. In essence, the profile is used to specify access privileges for an MIB view. These relationships are determined by the SNMP community pairing by the development of pro-

COMMUNITY PROFILE

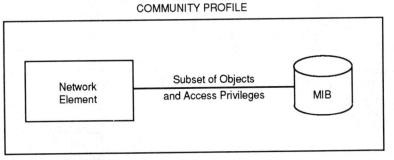

Figure 11.8 SNMP Community Profile.

files called SNMP *access privileges*. These access privileges then provide the directions on how SNMP agents and network elements can use the MIB.

Example of an SNMP operation

Figure 11.9 shows an example of how the operations of SNMP work. In this illustration, a network control center (which could be a host computer, gateway, or any other machine) communicates with an IP gateway which contains an IP *agent.* An agent performs the SNMP operations and accesses the MIB residing at the gateway. In turn, the IP agent can use SNMP messages to communicate with the network control. These messages support operations such as obtaining information regarding operations, changing information, issuing unsolicited messages in the event of alarms, etc. The SNMP messages are explained in the next section. The data that are operated on by these messages are defined by the IMIB, also illustrated in this figure. In a typical environment, network control will contain the MIB for all its managed resources (objects). However, it is not necessary for each agent to store the full MIB; rather, each agent stores that portion of the MIB relevant to its own operation. In this example, the IP gateway agent would have the MIB entries pertaining to IP routing tables, address translation, ICMP operations, and other tasks with which a gateway becomes involved. However, the gateway would not need to store the TCP MIB object group, because TCP does not reside in a gateway.

SNMP PDUs

SNMP uses simple operations and a limited number of protocol data units (PDUs) to perform its functions. Five PDUs have been defined in the standard:

Get request: This PDU is used to access the agent and obtain values from a list. It contains identifiers to distinguish from multiple

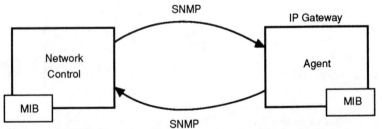

Figure 11.9 SNMP Operations Between an Agent and Network Control.

requests, as well as values to provide information about the status of the network element.

Get next request: This PDU is similar to the get request, except that it permits the retrieving of the next logical identifier in an MIB tree.

Get response: This PDU responds to the get request, get next request, and the set request data units. It contains an identifier that associates it with the previous PDU. It also contains identifiers to provide information about the status of the response (error codes, error status, and a list of additional information).

Set request: This is used to describe an action to be performed on a managed element. Typically, it is used to change the values in a variable list.

Trap: Trap allows the network object to report on an event at a network element or to change the status of a network element.

All the SNMP PDUs have a common coding format based on ASN.1. Figure 11.10 shows the encoding for the common format. The *Request*

```
Request ID ::=
    INTEGER
ErrorStatus ::=
    INTEGER{
        noError (0),
        tooBig (1),
        noSuchName (2),
        badValue (3),
        readOnly (4),
        genErr (5)
        }
Error Index ::=
    INTEGER
VarBind ::=
    SEQUENCE {
      name
        ObjectName,
      value
        ObjectSyntax
    }
VarBindList ::=
    SEQUENCE OF
      VarBind
```

Figure 11.10 The SNMP Common ASN.1 Code for PDUs.

ID field is used to distinguish between the different requests in the PDUs. The *ErrorStatus* coding provides a list to describe the type of error that is being recorded. This list is accessed through the *Error-Index* field, which is listed below the *ErrorStatus* field. The *ErrorStatus* field provides values for reporting problems. The *NoError* field simply reports that no error has occurred. The *tooBig* value is used to report that the results of an operation would not fit into an SNMP data unit. The *noSuchName* indicator is used to inform the controller that the variable name cannot be identified. The *badValue* is used if a variable cannot be identified or if its syntax makes no sense. The *readOnly* indicator is used to report that a variable has a profile of read only and cannot be written. The *genError* is used to report anything else.

The *VarBind* sequence is used to identify the name of the managed element and any associated value. The *VarBindList* is a set of values to set the variable bindings. Be aware that SNMP uses the term *variable* to describe an instance of a managed object, and the term *VarBind* simply describes the pairing of a variable to the variable's value. The VarBindList simply contains a list of the variable names and their corresponding values.

Figure 11.11 shows an actual example of ASN.1 coding of a Get Request. The parameters in this PDU were discussed previously in this chapter.

The SNMP MIB managed objects

MIB II contains managed objects pertaining to the SNMP group. Table 11.3 lists and summarizes these objects.

CMOT

CMOT was also designed by the Internet Engineering Task Force (IETF). It was based on the ISO network management standards and

```
Get Request - PDU ::=
    [0]
        IMPLICIT SEQUENCE {
            request-ID,
              Request ID,
            error-status                      -always 0
              ErrorStatus,
            error-index                       -always 0
              ErrorIndex,
            variable-bindings
              VarBindList
        }
```

Figure 11.11   The Get Request PDU.

TABLE 11.3   The SNMP Group

Function: The SNMP group provides information about SNMP objects, principally statistics relating to traffic and problems/error conditions. All these objects have a syntax of Counter, with the exception of the entry snmpEnableAuthTraps, which is integer.

snmpInPkts	An indication of the number of packets received from the layer below SNMP.
snmpOutPkts	Identifies the number of packets delivered from SNMP to the layer below.
snmpInBadVersions	Indicates the number of PDUs received with an erroneous version.
snmpInBadCommunityNames	Indicates the number of PDUs received with unidentifiable or unauthenticated community names.
snmpInASNParseErrs	Indicates the number of PDUs that could not be parsed to ASN.1 objects and vice versa.
snmpInBadTypes	Indicates the number of PDUs received which were indecipherable types.
snmpInTooBigs	Indicates the number of PDUs received with the tooBig error status field.
snmpInNoSuchNames	Indicates the number of PDUs received with an error status field NoSuchName field.
snmpInBadValues	Indicates the number of PDUs received with an error status in the badValue field.
snmpInReadOnlys	Indicates the number of PDUs received with an error status readOnly field.
snmpInGenErrs	Indicates the number of PDUs received with the genErr field.
snmpInTotalReqVars	Indicates the number of MIB objects that have been retrieved.
snmpInTotalSetVars	Indicates the number of MIB objects that have been changed/altered.
snmpInGetRequests *snmpInGetNexts* *snmpInSetRequests* *snmpInGetResponses* *snmpInTraps*	Indicate the number of the respective PDUs that were received.
snmpOutTooBigs	Indicates the number of PDUs sent with the tooBig field.
snmpOutNoSuchNames	Indicates the number of PDUs sent with the nosuchName field.
snmpOutBadValues	Indicates the number of PDUs sent with the badValue field.
snmpOutReadOnlys	Indicates the number of PDUs sent with the readOnly field.
snmpOutGenErrs	Indicates the number of PDUs sent with the genErr field.
snmpEnableAuthTraps	Describes if traps are enabled or disabled. This value can be read or written.
snmpOutGetRequests *snmpOutGetNexts* *snmpOutSetRequests* *snmpOutGetResponses* *snmpOutTraps*	Indicate the number of the respective PDUs that were sent.

can be used to run on a connection-oriented transport layer (such as TCP) or connectionless layer (such as UDP).

The CMOT layers

The CMOT architecture is depicted in Fig. 11.12. A reader familiar with OSI should be quite at ease with this illustration. Notice that the OSI association control service element (ACSE) is used in the application layer to provide services to the network management ASEs. The remote operations service element (ROSE) is also used.

The figure also shows an additional "layer" called the light-weight

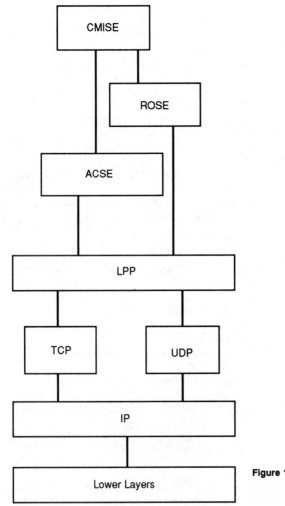

Figure 11.12 CMOT Layers.

presentation protocol (LPP). Since TCP and UDP have not been developed with OSI service definitions, the job of LPP is to interface the OSI application service elements to the TCP/UDP modules. In the spirit of OSI, the next lower level, which is the Internet Protocol (IP), is transparent to the CMOT applications in the upper layers.

The Lightweight Presentation Protocol (LPP)

RFC 1085 contains the specifications of the Lightweight Presentation Protocol (LPP). Its formal title is "ISO Presentation Services on top of TCP/IP-based Internets." LPP is needed in the CMOT protocol stack because of the presence of ACSE and ROSE. These protocols need certain services of the OSI presentation layer.

LPP provides these services by the following OSI presentation layer service definitions: (1) P-CONNECT, (2) P-RELEASE, (3) P-U-ABORT, (4) P-P-ABORT, and (5) P-DATA.

The following well-known port numbers are to be used between LPP, and TCP and UDP:

163/tcp: CMOT Manager

163/udp: CMOT Manager

164/tcp: CMOT Agent

164/udp: CMOT Agent

Summary

The Internet network management standards are widely used in both local and wide area networks. SNMP is the most prevalent network management standard in the industry. The Internet MIB defines the Internet managed objects and how they can be manipulated. CMOT has received very little support thus far in the industry, primarily because it is OSI based.

12

Operating TCP/IP with Other Protocols and Other Protocols without TCP/IP

Introduction

This chapter provides several examples of how TCP/IP can be stacked with other protocols. The initial focus of this discussion is on local area network (LAN) stacks. Subsequent discussions will examine wide area networks (WANs), ISDN, and the emerging Signaling Digital Hierarchy (SDH). In these later examples, the TCP/IP stacks are replaced by the OSI transport protocol class 4 (TP4) and connectionless network protocol (CLNP).

The first few examples show the encapsulation and decapsulation process of the protocol data units (PDUs) on the left and right sides of the figures. For simplicity of depiction, some later examples eliminate these notations. Each stack of protocols represents the protocols operating in each machine. For example, in Fig. 12.1, the left-side stack is in one machine and the right-side stack is in another machine.

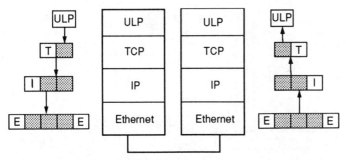

Figure 12.1 Minimum TCP/IP LAN Stack.

At first glance, it might seem that the placement of TCP/IP with other protocols is a relatively simple operation. The concept is made somewhat more complex by the requirement to discern (a) what services are needed in each layer, (b) if these services are available, and (c) equally important, if the layers perform redundant services. In many vendor products, stacking has been done in a rather lazy and haphazard manner, resulting in degraded throughput, degraded response time, and considerable redundancy of functions.

Several of the protocol stackings covered in this chapter are described in Internet RFCs. Others are not published in standards but are implemented through specific vendor products. Still others have been used by this writer with his clients.

A Minimum TCP/IP and LAN Stack

Figure 12.1 shows the familiar TCP/IP stack. It is considered a minimum implementation using only *Ethernet* at the lower layer to connect two stations on a LAN. This implementation is not used much today because of the somewhat awkward nature of interfacing *IP* directly with Ethernet (see Chaps. 2 and 3).

The *ULPs* consist of vendor software and the end user applications. It is a good idea to check the vendor's operations in considerable detail to determine their (1) functions, (2) ease of use, and (3) overhead in relation to the functions provided by the TCP and IP operations.

A Word About Operating System Dependency

Figure 12.2 adds the *operating system* notation to emphasize that the ability of these protocols to communicate with each other depends on how the operating system manages the interfaces between the layers in each machine. For example, a UNIX operating system provides dif-

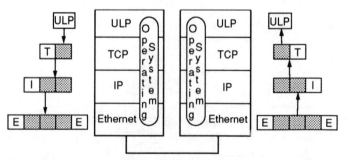

Figure 12.2   Operating System Dependency.

ferent interfaces of these layers than a DOS system. Notwithstanding, the two machines' communicating with each other (as shown in Fig. 12.2) does not require the operating systems in the two different machines to be compatible. The essential requirement is that the PDUs exchanged between the machines in the peer layers are understandable and invoke complementary functions in each machine.

TCP/IP over LLC

Figure 12.3 shows a more common LAN stack (also discussed in Chaps. 2 and 3) in which *logical link control (LLC)* and *media access control (MAC)* have been placed between *IP* and the *physical layer*. Typically, this approach uses *LLC type 1,* which is a connectionless data link protocol. The use of the LLC header is valuable because it provides destination and source service access points (SAPs) to identify the users of the layer above LLC. Of course, in this simple example, the user layer above LLC is IP.

A common approach for the IP/802 configuration is to use the address resolution protocol (ARP) to perform a mapping of the 32-bit Internet address to a 16- or 48-bit IEEE 802 address.

If LLC type 1 is used in this stack, most implementations support the full repertoire of the LLC standard. This means that unnumbered information (UI) commands, exchange identification (XID) commands and responses, and test (TEST) commands and responses must be supported. Additionally, when an XID or TEST command is received with a response flag, the destination/source SAP addresses must be swapped and the relationship of the P and F bits must be preserved. That is, a P bit solicits an F bit in all cases.

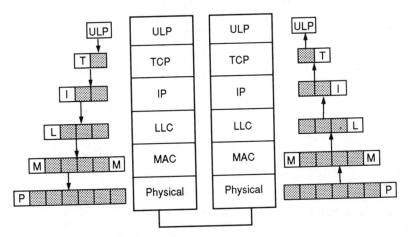

Figure 12.3   The 802 Stack.

IP need not run over LLC type 1 in a LAN. However, the LLC protocol does provide useful features with UI exchange, XID, and TEST
frames. Additionally, the use of the PSAPs and SSAPs provides a very
useful service for IP.

Regarding TCP for this stack, it might be considered "overkill" on a
LAN in which operations experience high throughput and high integrity. The user might consider a replacement for TCP, which is discussed in the next section.

Replacing TCP with UDP

Figure 12.4 shows a slightly different stack than the previous figure.
In this example the *User Datagram Protocol (UDP)* has replaced the
Transmission Control Protocol (TCP). This stack can be quite useful
because of its simplicity and because it still provides considerable integrity of traffic (which is typically offered by TCP) if the following
changes are made.

The biggest change is to implement the function with *LLC type 2*. In
effect, type 2 provides a connection-oriented link protocol, which ensures the delivery of traffic to the receiving LLC. Like TCP, LLC type
2 provides sequencing, flow control, and window control capabilities
with the establishment of a set asynchronous balanced mode (SABM)
link configuration. Therefore, some of the TCP functions are now
placed below IP. This approach also entails risks because LLC does
not have a graceful close. Therefore, some means must be taken at an
ULP to take care of connection management (closing).

One needs to weigh the trade-offs of achieving connection-oriented
services at LLC and/or the ULP. Again, check out the vendor's ULP
carefully, because some LLC type 2 and ULP connection-oriented services may be performing overlapping functions.

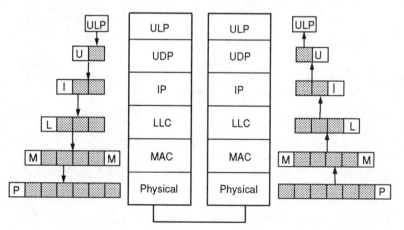

Figure 12.4 Using UDP in Place of TCP.

NetBIOS over TCP or UDP

Figure 12.5 shows a typical stack for personal computer-based networks that use IBM's NetBIOS. The illustration shows *NetBIOS* used above *TCP* or *UDP*. NetBIOS is designed principally to interconnect PC applications. It is used to locate application resources, establish connection between these applications, receive data between the applications, and then terminate the connections. NetBIOS provides both connection-oriented and connectionless modes. All the resources managed by NetBIOS are referenced by a 16-character name, and applications are registered through this name.

The NetBIOS is reached through internet well-known port numbers (described in Chap. 7) as follows:

Port 137 = NetBIOS name service

Port 138 = NetBIOS datagram service

Port 139 = NetBIOS session service

NetBIOS supports the NetBIOS name server (NBNS) node. In some installations the NBNS is mapped to the internet domain name system (DNS). NetBIOS contains a scope identifier which identifies the machines that operate under a specific NetBIOS area. The stacking of

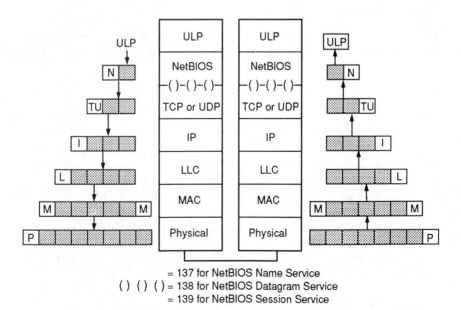

() () () = 137 for NetBIOS Name Service
= 138 for NetBIOS Datagram Service
= 139 for NetBIOS Session Service

Figure 12.5 Personal Computer Network Layers.

NetBIOS and TCP typically uses a NetBIOS name with its scope identifier to map to an internet DNS. One of the services provided in this
stack is the name discovery, in which an IP address can be used to
obtain an associated NetBIOS name.

After obtaining addresses through the naming services, a NetBIOS
session can be established. It consists of three phases:

1. Establishing a session in which IP addresses and TCP ports are
   mapped to the remote entity

2. Exchanging NetBIOS messages

3. Closing the session by the other entity

To establish a session, an entity must listen on a well-known service
port for incoming NetBIOS session requests. The NetBIOS session
server accepts requests for the end user application. It is important to
note that the TCP connection must be open before NetBIOS services
can occur. The NetBIOS session occurs with a request packet containing called and calling IP addresses as well as called and calling
NetBIOS names.

For a close operation, an end user requests to NetBIOS that the session be closed. Typically, the system obtains a TCP graceful close. If
this does not occur successfully and TCP connection remains open,
NetBIOS will take it upon itself to close the NetBIOS session.

IP over NetBIOS

Figure 12.6 shows yet another possibility with NetBIOS. In this scenario, *IP datagrams* are encapsulated in the *NetBIOS packets*. This

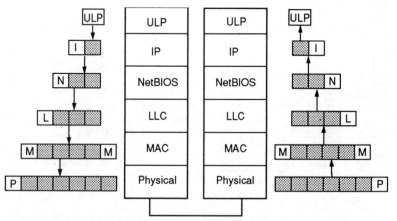

Figure 12.6 IP over NetBIOS.

implementation represents a minimum service stack wherein NetBIOS is run with connectionless services.

The principal consideration for this stack is the address mappings between IP and NetBIOS. The NetBIOS names must reflect the IP address; so part of the NetBIOS address space can be coded as IP.xx.xx.xx.xx. The IP value indicates an IP over NetBIOS operation, and the xx.xx.xx.xx represents the IP address. Broadcast addresses are of the form IP.FF.FF.FF.FF.

This stack provides connectionless services at IP, NetBIOS, and LLC. Consequently, any connection-oriented services for sequencing, flow control, data integrity, etc. must be addressed by the ULPs. As another option, LLC type 2 could be configured, which would provide a minimal level of data integrity, sequencing, and flow control. This writer recommends that the connectionless services be provided in an ULP and that LLC be kept simple and efficient.

XNS over IP

Figure 12.7 shows the widely used Xerox Network System (XNS) stack in a simplified version. XNS was developed in the 1970s and 1980s by the Xerox Corporation for use in some of its product lines. In most instances, the protocols were designed to work with Ethernet LANs. Xerox has made the XNS software available to the public, and the stacks have found their way into many other vendors' products. The lower layers come as no surprise. They have been discussed previously. XNS also uses the IP protocol. At the layer above, it uses the *Sequenced Packet Protocol,* which has some of the functions of TCP (although it is not as functionally rich).

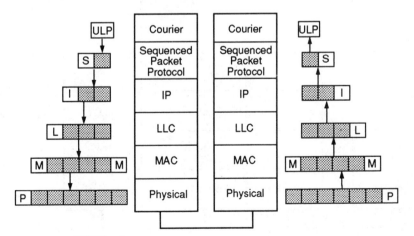

Figure 12.7   XNS Stack.

Figure 12.7 shows the *Courier* protocol resting in the ULP layer. The Courier entity provides general services associated with the OSI presentation and session layers. It also supports procedure calls in which a request for a service is made to another entity. The results are returned regarding the success or failure of the service request.

The figure also shows *IP* residing in the stack. The term used by XNS to define a set of complementary protocols is generally the *Internet Transport Protocols*. All of them may not be implemented in this module. They deal with functions such as error reporting (similar to ICMP) and the error protocol (similar to the echo function of ICMP). Additionally, the XNS IP layer typically uses the routing information protocol (RIP) for the exchange of routing information between routers, gateways, and host machines.

IP Router Stacks

Figure 12.8 shows the stacks of an *IP router*. In this example, the router is connecting two LANs: one an 802.3 CSMA/CD network and the other an 802.5 token ring network. The stacks at the router vary depending on which port is being managed. Notwithstanding, the only difference in the stacks exists at the physical and MAC layers; LLC and IP remain the same. The operations associated with this stack are covered in more detail in Chaps. 2, 3, and 5.

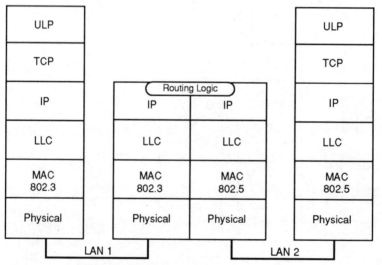

Figure 12.8 Typical LAN Router.

Relationship of IP and LAN Bridges

Figure 12.9 shows two LANs connected through a *bridge*. In this situation, IP does not exist at the bridge. The *MAC relay entity* is responsible for routing the traffic between the two ports (that is, the two networks). The reader might wonder why LLC is located at the bridge since its principal function is to provide an interface from the upper layers into MAC. The reason is that IEEE 802.1 MAC bridges allow the traffic to move from (1) the incoming MAC port across the relay entity to the outgoing MAC port; or (2) MAC into its LLC for bridge management functions. Once at the LLC at the gateway, traffic may be passed back down to MAC or to the relay entity for operations such as bridge learning and bridge forwarding. In any event, LLC is required for all 802 MAC bridges.

IP and X.25

IP, X.25, and LANs

Figure 12.10 shows the use of *X.25* on a LAN. In this example, *OSI TP4* is placed on top of IP, which is in turn stacked on X.25's network layer (called *packet layer procedures, (PLP)*. The LAN station does not invoke lower layer X.25 services, such as LAPB or the V Series support. Rather, it encapsulates the X.25 packet into the LLC and MAC PDUs for transport to the gateway. At the gateway, the traffic traverses the stacks in reverse order. At the X.25 PLP layer in the

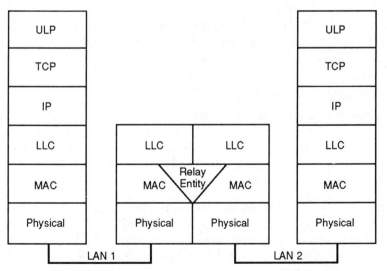

Figure 12.9   Typical LAN Bridge.

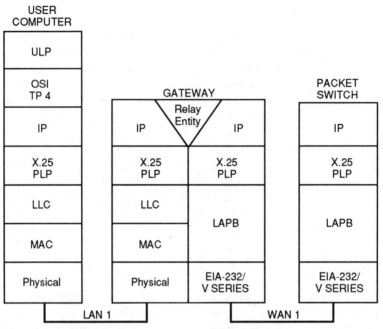

USER
COMPUTER

Figure 12.10   X.25 on a LAN.

gateway, the X.25 packet header is used to map a logical channel relationship between the user computer and the left side of the protocol stack in the gateway. IP is then invoked to perform its functions at the gateway, after which the gateway relays the traffic to the proper output port.

In this example, the LAPB data link control frame is used to encapsulate the X.25 packet, and the traffic is transmitted through EIA-232 or a V Series interface to the WAN packet switch.

IP, X.25, and public data networks (PDNs)

The placement of X.25 on a LAN is not very common. More typically, a user host computer connects with X.25 to the packet switch of a public data network (PDN). Figure 12.11 shows the layers for this configuration. RFC 877 establishes a few simple rules for the X.25-IP and X.25-packet switch interfaces:

- A virtual circuit is handled as usual—on demand. When the host computer receives a datagram by the X.25 module, it sends a Call Request packet to the switch. Upon receiving a Call Connected packet, the host transmits the IP datagram in the X.25 user data field of the X.25 packet.

USER
COMPUTER

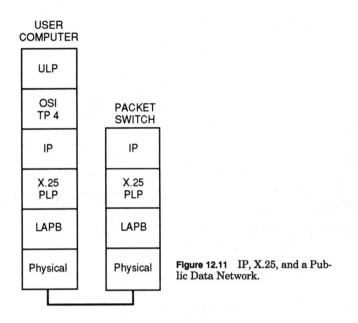

Figure 12.11   IP, X.25, and a Public Data Network.

- The first octet of the call user data field of the Call Request packet must contain hex CC to signify IP is running on X.25.

- M bit operations are allowed.

- Unless negotiated to other values, the maximum size of the IP datagram is 576 octets.

IP, X.25, and Amateur Packet Radio

Another possibility for an IP-X.25 combination is to encapsulate X.25 packets into IP datagrams. This technique is used to support the AX.25 protocol which runs on the Amateur Packet Radio system.

The procedure is very simple. One AX.25 packet is encapsulated into one IP datagram. LAPB flags are not used, nor is zero bit stuffing and unstuffing. LAPB CRC checks are included as well as LAPB address and control fields. Otherwise, AX.25 maintains all other LAPB and X.25 fields.

Using IPX with UDP/IP Networks

The Internet Packet Exchange Protocol (IPX) is Novell's Netware IP-type product. It is derived from the Xerox Network Systems (XNS) protocols. Since Netware is so widely implemented, a short discussion is appropriate to show how IPX traffic can be carried through internet networks (see Fig. 12.12). The stacking arrangement is from the top

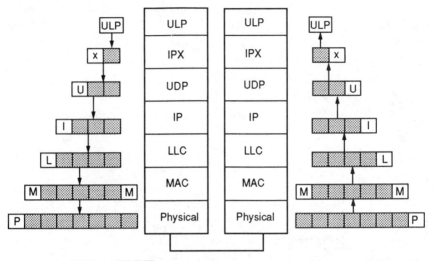

Figure 12.12   IPX over UDP/IP.

layer to the bottom layer as follows: ULP, IPX, UDP, IP, lower layer protocols (typically, LANs such as IEEE or Ethernets).

The IP and UDP headers are not affected by this stacking arrangement. The principal consideration for this stack concerns address mappings. An IPX address space consists of a network number and a host number. The network number is four octets, the host number is six octets. This combined number is used by IPX to route each IPX packet to the destination. Like the IP scheme, once the network number has fulfilled its function of reaching the destination network, the host number is used to route the traffic to the host attached to the destination network. For the IPX UDP/IP interface, RFC 1234 requires that the first two octets of the host number be set to 0 and the last four octets represent the node's IP address. This approach provides an easy method to handle unicast transmissions by simply discarding the first two octets of the host number.

The maximum transmission unit (MTU) for IPX is 576 octets. For this stack, the resulting PDU will be 604 octets (IPX of 576 + IP header of 20 + UDP of 8 = 604). All implementations supporting this stacking arrangement must be able to receive an IP packet of 604 octets.

Transmitting 802 LLC Traffic over IPX Networks

A different approach, depicted in Fig. 12.13, is the transmitting of IEEE 802 type 1 LLC traffic over IPX networks. This is a fairly common implementation for organizations that have configured their

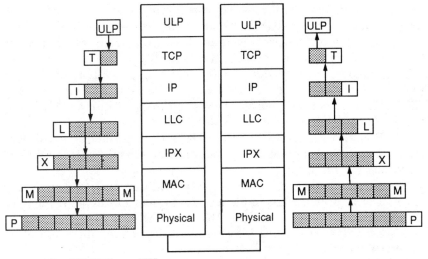

Figure 12.13   802 LLC over IPX.

LANs with IPX. It provides a convenient method of continuing to use IPX over an 802 LAN card.

The protocol stacking arrangement is as follows from higher layer to lower layer: ULP, TCP, IP, 802.2 LLC, IPX, and the physical layer.

RFC 1132 establishes these rules for this protocol stacking arrangement:

- Address mapping between IP addresses and IPX addresses is performed using ARP; however, the IPX physical address is 10 octets (4 bytes for IPX network address and 6 bytes for the IPX host address).

- This protocol stacking arrangement does not use the IPX checksum.

Transmitting IP Datagrams over ARCNET Networks

ARCNET is a widely used protocol for LANs. RFC 1201 establishes a procedure for the transmission of IP datagrams over ARCNET networks. As the reader might expect, IP datagrams are encapsulated into ARCNET PDUs in what is known as the *client data area* (see Fig. 12.13).

Several vendors have agreed on an ARCNET standard as published in "ARCNET Packet Header Definitions Standard," Novell Inc., November, 1989. This standard permits two types of frames to carry IP traffic. The short frame is 256 octets long and the long frame is 512 octets long. The IP datagram is placed in the client data area behind the ARCNET header. The largest amount of user data that can be sent across ARCNET is 504 octets. The remaining octets of the 512-octet frame consist of the ARCNET header. The header contains destination and source addresses as well as offset values and fragmentation flags to perform fragmentation and reassembly on the network.

This standard also provides for the mapping of a 32-bit IP address into the corresponding 8-bit ARCNET address. Mapping occurs using ARP. All IP broadcast addresses must be mapped into an ARCNET broadcast address with the value of 0.

RARP is also supported in RFC 1201, although some minor differences exist in the mapping. The reader should consult with the RFC if more detail is required.

The reader should be aware that Datapoint Corporation uses different ARCNET protocol IDs to identify protocols running on ARCNET. IP is designated as 212, ARP as 213, and RARP as 214. These numbers are not the same as the internet identification numbers described in Chaps. 2 and 3.

Transmitting IP Datagrams over FDDI Networks

The layer arrangement for this service is identical to the services described earlier in Fig. 12.3. The only difference is that FDDI contains two sublayers at the physical layer, which is completely transparent to IP and 802.2 LLC. The mapping arrangement for the physical and network addresses is in conformance with the Internet specifications described in Chaps. 2 and 3.

The FDDI standard permits a maximum frame size of 4500 octets. After preambles and the LLC/SNAP header, 4470 octets are available for user data. However, RFC 1188 makes an exception in this case in that it defines 4096 octets for data and 256 octets to be used for headers at the layers above MAC. Gateways supporting FDDI must be able to accept packets this large and, if necessary, perform fragmentation operations. Additionally, even though hosts can be expected to accept large packets, it is recommended that hosts not send datagrams greater than 576 octets unless they know the receiving host can support a larger size.

Addressing schemes on FDDI networks are quite similar to those discussed earlier for the other IEEE 802 networks. The only restriction is that interworking IP and ARP over FDDI requires only the use of a 48-bit physical level address.

As the reader might expect, IP over FDDI requires the use of 802 LLC type 1 using the conventional LLC frames: UI, XID, TEST. Be aware that IEEE specifies its control values with the least significant bit first (the "little-endian"). The internet protocols are just the opposite and document their control fields in big-endian order. This presents no problem as long as users working with IEEE and internet networks understand the documentation.

IP over Switched Multi-Megabit Data Service (SMDS)

SMDS is a public network offering packet-switched connectionless service. Its purpose is to support high throughput, with low delay, as well as large PDUs (up to 9188 user octets). It provides no explicit flow-control mechanisms; rather, it has a subscriber-to-network and a network-to-subscriber access class enforcement mechanism which provides for congestion control in the network.

IP can rest on top of an SMDS network by interfacing into the IEEE 802 LLC sublayer. In turn, LLC rests on top of the SMDS layers. This arrangement is straightforward because the interface protocol into SMDS is based on the IEEE 802.6 metropolitan area network (MAN) distributed-queue-dual-bus (DQDB) MAC protocol. This protocol has a rich MAC convergence function which allows connectionless services such as LLC, type 1, IP, etc. to be encapsulated into the DQDB PDU.

The concept of IP over SMDS is based on using an SMDS to support multiple logical IP subnetworks (known as LIS). Each LIS is managed by separate administrative authorities but uses the common SMDS for communications.

For LIS configuration, all stations within the LIS are accessed directly from one SMDS. This method requires that all LIS members have the same IP network and subnetwork numbers. Communications of stations outside LIS are performed through an IP router. An SMDS group address is used to identify all members within the LIS. This address permits SMDS to deliver traffic to the LIS members.

The layering arrangements for this stack are shown in Fig. 12.14. The IP interface occurs through the media convergence function (MCF), which interfaces directly into LLC. The queued-arbitrated functions (QA) define the procedures for sharing the DQDB. Resting beneath the QA are common functions, common to both queued, arbitrated, and prearbitrated (PA) functions. The PA functions are not relevant to this discussion but are used for isochronous services, such as voice and video. The physical layer provides the ongoing cabling and physical transmission for the dual cable bus. As the reader might expect, the services with this stack are quite common to other services which use LLC. The use of LLC type 1 frames is the same as for protocol stacks discussed earlier in this chapter.

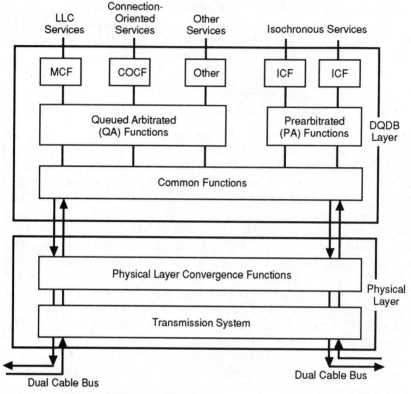

Figure 12.14 IP over SMDS with 802.6 DQDB.

OSI's Transport Protocol Class 0 over TCP

Figure 12.15 shows the stacking arrangement to run OSI's TP Class 4 (TP0) over TCP. One might wonder why such a stacking arrangement would be desirable. The principal advantage is that it provides a convenient and easy access to the upper layers of the OSI Model and allows an organization to continue using the widely used TCP/IP suite. Additionally, TP0 is a minimal level of service for the transport layer, so we are not risking redundancy of function by implementing both OSI's transport layer with TP0 and the Internet's TCP.

In the OSI Model, a connection between a transport layer user and the transport layer is achieved through service definitions, also known as *primitives*. These are defined in CCITT's X.214 and ISO's 8072 standards. For using the stack in this scenario, RFC 1006 defines the mapping of these OSI primitives to receive TCP service. It should be understood that the OSI transport layer does not work with a client-server approach. Therefore, an OSI indication primitive is used instead of a server listening on a well-known port.

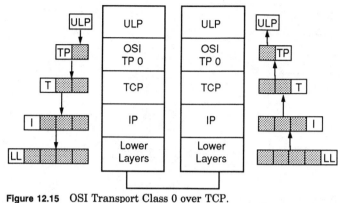

Figure 12.15 OSI Transport Class 0 over TCP.

TABLE 12.1 Mapping TP0 and TCP

TP0 ↔ NW Layer Definitions	TCP Service
N-CONNECT.request	Open completes
N-CONNECT.indication	Passive Open (Listen) finishes
N-CONNECT.response	Listen finishes
N-CONNECT.confirmation	Open (Active) finishes
N-DATA.request	Send data
N-DATA.indication	Data ready
TP0 ↔ Network Parameter	**TCP Parameter**
Called address	Server's IP addresses
Calling address	Client's IP address
Data (NDSU)	Data
Others	Ignored

The mapping between TCP and TP0 occurs through the use of the OSI service definitions. Table 12.1 lists these mappings as well as mappings of the parameters between the network service and TCP.

OSI Connectionless Transport Layer over UDP

This section describes a similar approach to Fig. 12.15, except that connectionless services are used, both at the OSI layer and the internet layer. The scheme is almost identical to that described in the previous section except that no connection-oriented services are in-

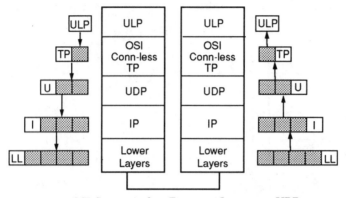

Figure 12.16   OSI Connectionless Transport Layer over UDP.

voked. Rather, the OSI network services of N-UNITDATA.request and N-UNITDATA.indication are the only services permitted between connectionless OSI and UDP. The parameter mapping is also quite simple. The source and destination addresses in the OSI layer map to the called and calling IP addresses for UDP services. User data maps directly to the UDP user data. Any other fields that exist in the OSI Model are ignored. The stacking arrangement is quite simple, as depicted in Fig. 12.16.

TCP/IP over ISDN

Figure 12.17 shows a typical protocol stack for interfacing a user workstation to a packet switch through an ISDN node. The reader will notice that IP is no longer included in this stack because most vendors are implementing these options with IP's OSI counterpart CLNP. Notwithstanding, nothing precludes using TCP or IP in the user computer in place of OSI TP4 and CLNP.

The traffic is transmitted from the user computer across the ISDN *R reference point* and the *terminal adapter* stack which maps the X.25 layers according to the X.25 specifications. Next, operations take place on the right side of the terminal adapter (TA). The TA operates the ISDN layers to establish proper D and B channel operations to the *ISDN node* across the *S/T reference point*. Although not depicted in this figure, after the three layers of ISDN are operational, the terminal adapter will dequeue the X.25 traffic and transport it transparently through the ISDN layers to the ISDN node. At the ISDN node, the traffic is passed up through the ISDN layers and then passed off to an ISDN *packet handler* (which, in the real world, is nothing more than a packet switch). The packet switch assumes the functions of

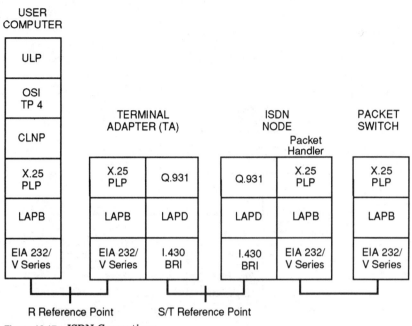

Figure 12.17   ISDN Connections.

X.25 and sends the packet down through the X.25 stack to communicate with the network *packet switch.*

Stacks for the 1990s

Figure 12.18 shows a set of protocol stacks for emerging technologies (one of several possibilities). The user machine could consist of the layers discussed in all these previous examples as well as voice images, such as telephone calls, and video images, such as high-definition television. The lower layers are labeled *user network communication layers.* These layers could be ISDN, LAN, TCP/IP layers, or whatever layers are needed to transmit the traffic from the user device and onto a network or communications channel. The *terminal adapter* is a much more sophisticated device than the present ISDN terminal adapters. On the left side, it has the layers used to accommodate the user layers. Also, it has a set of protocols (or a layer) called the *control plane* and the *user plane.* This software is used to accommodate the traffic coming out of and into the user layers. The plane acts as an intermediary between the user layers and the *adaptation layer.* The adaptation layer is application specific, so it is highly variable.

The adaptation layer passes the traffic to the *asynchronous transfer mode (ATM).* The ATM is the key component in the emerging commu-

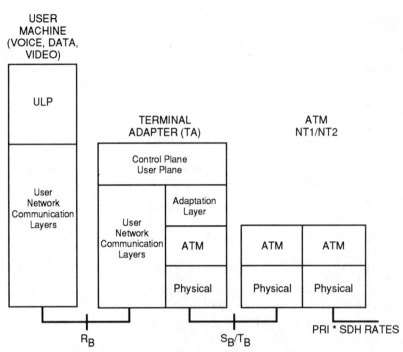

Figure 12.18   The Emerging Signalling Digital Hierarchy, BISDN, and ATM.

nications network technology for the 1990s. It forms the foundation for broadband ISDN (BISDN). Its job is to perform switching and multiplexing functions for traffic that it has received. Its physical connection might be to another ATM machine, labeled in this figure as *ATM NT1/ NT2*. This configuration is not required, and all the multiplexing and switching functions could be performed within the terminal adapter (although that probably will not be the case due to the expense involved). Therefore, in this example, the ATM NT1/NT2 is responsible for receiving traffic from other devices and terminal adapters and multiplexing the traffic into multiples of primary rates, which are labeled in this figure as *PRI*SDH* (signalling digital hierarchy) *rates*. SDH is the cornerstone of the merging of BISDN, metropolitan area networks (MANs), and integrated voice/data (IVD) applications.

Summary

TCP/IP exists in a wide variety of standards and vendor products. Most implementations are based on the layered protocol approach, in which TCP/IP is encapsulated into other PDUs or other protocols are encapsulated into TCP segments and IP datagrams.

Chapter

13

TCP/IP and Operating Systems

Introduction

This chapter provides an overview and examples of the relationship of
computer operating systems and the TCP/IP suite of protocols. The focus in this chapter is on the UNIX and IBM PC operating systems,
due to their prevalence in the industry. The reader should keep in
mind that many other interfaces are available. For example, C function calls, Fortran subroutine calls, etc. could be used (see Fig. 13.1).
The UNIX examples (included in this chapter) illustrate the implementation in the System UNIX V release from AT&T. The PC explanation focuses on higher-level calls to obtain services for an application layer or a PC keyboard user.

UNIX and TCP/IP

This section provides several examples of the UNIX operating system
and its interface with TCP. We cite the 4.3 BSD UNIX interfaces be-

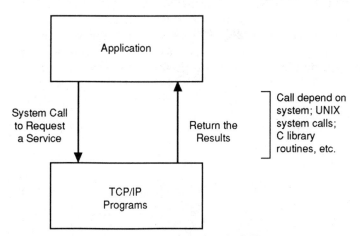

Figure 13.1 Accessing TCP/IP Through UNIX Calls.

cause of their prevalence in the industry. UNIX was developed at Bell Labs in the late 1960s. It was designed originally for single processor computers and includes many features that make it quite popular among software developers. Principal among those features are its time-sharing capabilities and its easy operations for the programmer through system calls.

Connection-oriented services

The concept of a *socket,* which is discussed several times in this book, is very much a part of the BSD UNIX I/O concept. A socket is really nothing more than an end point in the communications process. Unlike some socket concepts with I/O files, the TCP/IP BSD UNIX concept allows a socket to be created without providing a destination address. A destination address in a later system call will be used to create a final binding between the sending and receiving addresses.

Figure 13.2 shows the system call that creates a socket. It is identified as *socket* and consists of three arguments. The *domain* field describes the protocol family (a domain) associated with the socket. It could include the Internet family, PUP family, DEC family, Appletalk family, etc. The *type* argument stipulates the type of communications desired with this connection. The programmer can establish values to specify a datagram service, reliable delivery service, or a raw socket. The third argument allows the programmer to code the type of service that each of the *protocols* within the protocol family provides. This argument is required because protocol families usually consist of more than one protocol. It is the task of the programmer to supply the specific protocol in this argument. If it is left at 0, the system will select the appropriate protocol within the domain.

The domain values are available in the <sys/socket.h> file. The UNIX domain is AF_UNIX; the Internet domain is AF_INET. The socket types are also found in the file <sys/socket.h> file and are coded in the systems call as SOCK_STREAM = a reliable, stream service; SOCK_DGRAM = a datagram service; SOCK_RAW = a raw socket (to provide access to underlying protocols for communications programmers).

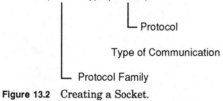

```
s= socket(domain,type,protocol)
                     └ Protocol

               Type of Communication

       └ Protocol Family
```

Figure 13.2   Creating a Socket.

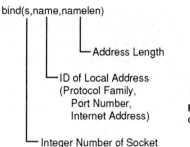

bind(s,name,namelen)

— Address Length

— ID of Local Address
(Protocol Family,
Port Number,
Internet Address)

— Integer Number of Socket

Figure 13.3 Establishing the Local Address.

We learned earlier that UNIX allows a socket to be created without furnishing addresses (in UNIX V, called a *name*) for the socket. Communications cannot occur until local and foreign internet addresses are declared for the association between the communicating entities. In the UNIX domain, local and foreign path names are used. Figure 13.3 shows the system call to establish the local address with the socket. The *bind* call sets up one half of an association. The first argument in the list is called *s* and contains the integer number value of the socket. The local *name* argument can vary but usually consists of three values: the protocol family, the port number, and an internet address. The *namelen* argument contains the length of the second argument.

Figure 13.4 shows the next step in mapping the TCP/IP connection between two machines. The *connect* system call allows the programmer to connect a socket to a destination address. As the figure illustrates, the *s* (socket number), the *name* (destination ID), and *namelen* (name length) are included as arguments. The name parameter identifies the remote socket for the binding.

The asymmetric nature of port bindings allows an easy implementation of a client-server relationship. The server issues a bind to establish a socket for a well-known service, such as FTP. It then listens passively for a client to send a connect request to the server's passive socket.

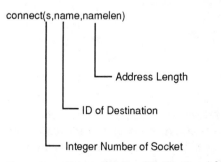

connect(s,name,namelen)

— Address Length

— ID of Destination

— Integer Number of Socket

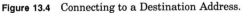

Figure 13.4 Connecting to a Destination Address.

If a connection is unsuccessful, an error is returned to the requestor. Over 20 error codes are available with the connect call, such as ECONNREFUSE = the host refusal of the connection because the server process cannot be found given the name furnished; and ETIME OUT = the connection attempt took too long.

After a server has set up a passive socket, it then listens for incoming connections that are requested (only supported on reliable stream delivery). This operation is performed with the *listen* system call. It takes the form shown in Fig. 13.5.

listen(s,backlog)

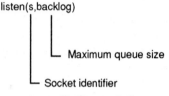

Maximum queue size

Socket identifier

Figure 13.5   The Listen Call.

The parameter *s* is the socket on which connections will occur; the *backlog* parameter establishes the maximum queue size for holding incoming connection requests. If the queue is full, an incoming connection request is refused with an indication of ECONNREFUSED. Other error codes associated with listen are EBADF = s is invalid; ENOISOCK = s is not a socket; EONOTSUPP = socket does not support a listen operation.

After the listen has been executed, the accepting entity (usually a server) must wait for connection requests. It uses the *accept* system call for this operation. The accept pulls the first entity in the queue to service. It takes the form shown in Fig. 13.6.

newsock = accept(s,addr,addrlen)

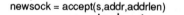

Address Length

Connecting Entity Address

Socket Identifier

Figure 13.6   The Accept Call.

The *s* parameter is the listening socket; the *addr* parameter contains the *sockaddr* of the connecting entity; and *addrlen* is the length of the address. If the operation succeeds, a new file descriptor *ns* is allocated for the socket and the new descriptor is returned to the requestor.

write(descriptor,buf,sizeobuf)

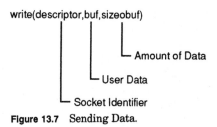

Amount of Data

User Data

Socket Identifier

Figure 13.7   Sending Data.

After all these system calls have executed successfully, the application entities can exchange data. Data exchange is accomplished through the *write* system call, which is depicted in Fig. 13.7. The call is quite simple. It contains three arguments.

The socket identifier (*descriptor*)

The buffer (*buf*), which is a pointer in memory containing the user data

The length field (*sizeofbuf*), which determines the length of the buffer search for the user data

To receive data, the *read* system call is invoked. Its format is illustrated in Fig. 13.8. The reader probably sees the repetitive aspects of the design of the system calls. This call contains the socket identifier (*descriptor*), the identification of the buffer (*buf*) in which the data will reside, and the length indicator (*sizeofbuf*) which describes the number of bytes that are to be read.

Other input/output calls

Input/output can also be achieved with the following calls:

```
send (S, buf, sizeofbuf, flags);
recv (S, buf, sizeofbuf, flags);
```

The only difference between these calls and the write and read calls is the extra *flags* parameter. It allows the programmer to use some other options in receiving/sending data to/from a connected socket.

read(descriptor,buf,sizeobuf)

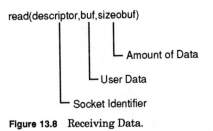

Amount of Data

User Data

Socket Identifier

Figure 13.8   Receiving Data.

The flags field (established in the <sys/socket.h> file) can be set to signify

MSG_PEEK: Examine the next message without reading it.

MSG_OOB: Receive out-of-band (urgent) data.

MSG_DONTROUTE: Send data but do not actually route it (for diagnostic/maintenance purposes).

Two other input calls are available. The *recvfrom* call is used to request input on a socket either in a connected or unconnected state. Its form is

```
recvfrom (s, buf, len, flags, from, fromlen)
```

Two other parameters are present with this call. The *from* parameter holds the message sender's address. The *fromlen* parameter returns the length of the sender's address.

The *recvmsg* call can also be used to receive input on an unconnected socket. It has fewer parameters than recvfrom and takes this form:

```
recvmsg (s, msg, flags)
```

The *msg* parameter defines a structure that includes the address and the size of the incoming message and some authentication entities.

Two other calls similar to *recvfrom* and *recvmsg* are *send to* and *sendmsg,* respectively, except that they send data.

Datagram services

The *send to* and *recvfrom* calls are used with UDP datagram services. In addition, a connect call is permitted with UDP operations to map a socket to a destination address. Accept and listen are not used with UDP.

Closing a connection

A socket can be closed if it is no longer needed with the following system call:

```
close (s)
```

Data may continue to be sent and or delivered even after the close is issued (check with your vendor for this feature). After some period of time, the data will be discarded. If the user does not wish to send and/or receive any more data, it can issue

```
shutdown (s, how)
```

where parameters for *how* are 0 = not interested in receiving data;

1 = no more data will be sent; 2 = no more data will be sent or received.

Other system calls

We have reviewed the most commonly used UNIX systems calls for invoking TCP/IP services. Several others are available and warrant an explanation (the parameters for these calls are not included in this general explanation):

select: Provides a capability to multiplex input/output operations on more than one socket

gethostbyname: Obtains host name (usually its domain name)

sethostbyname: Sets host name

getpeername: Obtains the name of a peer connected to a socket

gethostbyaddr: Obtains internet address of the host

getsockname: Obtains a socket and its associated local address

getnetbyname: Obtains network name

getnetbyaddr: Obtains network address

getprotobyname: Obtains protocol name

getprotobynumber: Obtains protocol number

All the UNIX calls are not included. Several others are available for domain sources, mapping and swapping network numbers, and obtaining information on servers and clients.

Example of programs to invoke UNIX-based TCP/IP services

Figure 13.9 shows an example of a program using UNIX calls to open a socket, read it, and close. Figures 13.10 and 13.11 show examples of reading and sending datagrams. These examples are from *UNIX SYSTEM V, Release 4, Programmers Guide: Network Interfaces* (Prentice Hall, 1990) and are reprinted with the permission of Prentice-Hall.

PC Interface Program

Vendors offer a number of interface programs to invoke TCP/IP services and internet applications services. This section highlights several user commands available in the IBM Interface Program. Further information is available in IBM manual number SC23-0812-0.

```
#include <sys/types.h>
#include <sys/socket.h>
#include <netinet/in.h>
#include <netdb.h>
#include <stdio.h>
#define TRUE 1
/*
   *This program creates a socket and then begins an infinite loop. Each time
   *through the loop it accepts a connection and prints out messages from it.
   *When the connection breaks, or a termination message comes through, the
   *program accepts a new connection.
   */
main()
{
     int sock, length;
     struct sockaddr_in server;
     int msgsock;
     char buf[1024];
     int rval;
     /*Create socket.*/
     sock = socket (AF_INET,SOCK_STREAM,0);
     if (sock < 0){
                         perror (''opening stream socket'');
                         exit (1);
     }
     /*Name socket using wildcards.*/
     server.sin_family = AF_INET;
     server.sin_addr.s_addr = INADDR_ANY;
     server.sin_port = 0;
     if(bind(sock,(struct sockaddr*)&server, sizeof server)<0){
                         perror(''binding stream socket'');
                         exit(1);
     }
     /*Find out assigned port number and print it out.*/
     length = sizeof server;
     if (getsockname (sock, (struct sockaddr*)&server,
       &length) < 0){
                         perror (''getting socket name:);
                         exit(1);
```

Figure 13.9   Accepting an Internet Domain Stream Connection.

```
        }
        printf(''Socket port#%d\n'', ntohs (server.sin_port));
        /*Start accepting connections. */
        listen(sock, 5);
do{
            msgsock = accept(sock, (struct sockaddr*)0,(int*)0);
            if (msgsock = -1)
                        perror (''accept'');
            else do {
                        memset(buf, 0, sizeof buf);
                        if ((rval = read(msgsock, buf, 1024)) < 0)
                                    perror(''reading stream message'');
                        if (rval = 0)
                                    printf(Ending connection\n'');
                        else
                                    printf(''-- > %s \n'', buf);
            } while (rval! = 0);
            close(msgsock);
} while (TRUE);
/*
    *Since this program has an infinite loop, the socket ''sock'' is
    *never explicitly closed. However, all sockets will be closed
    *automatically when a process is killed or terminates normally.
    */
    exit (0);
```

Figure 13.9   (*Continued*)

While studying this section, the reader should note the ease of use of the user commands to this interface program. Granted, the parameters associated with the commands require a user to have a firm grasp of how the TCP/IP protocols operate. Thus, in this context, a "user" of this interface would be a systems/communications programmer. An *end user* interface (with friendly screen menus and blinking color lights) is beyond this discussion.

IBM uses the syntax diagram shown in Fig. 13.12 to document many of its products, including the material in this section.

Sending mail through SMTP

The *netmail* command supports the transmitting of user mail through SMTP to another user or users. Figure 13.13 shows the syntax of the command. The *mail_file* parameter identifies the file to be sent. The *rcpt*

```
#include <sys/types.h>
#include <sys/socket.h>
#include <netinet/in.h>
#include <stdio.h>

/*
   *The include file <netinet/in.h> defines sockaddr_in as follows:
   *struct sockaddr_in(
   *      short sin_family;
   *      u_short sin_port;
   *      struct in_addr sin_addr;
   *      char sin_zero [8];
   *);
   *
   *This program creates a datagram socket, binds a name to it, then
     reads
   *from the socket.
   */
main()
{
          int sock, length;
          struct sockaddr_in name;
          char buf[1024];

          /*Create a socket from which to read.*/
          sock = socket (AF_INET, SOCK_DGRAM,0);
          if (sock < 0){
                    perror (''opening datagram socket'');
                    exit (1);

          }
          /*Create name with wildcards.*/
          name.sin_family = AF_INET;
          name.sin_addr.s_addr = INADDR_ANY;
          name.sin_port = 0;
          if (bind (sock,(struct sockaddr*)&name,
            sizeof name) < 0){
                    perror(''binding datagram socket'');
                    exit (1);
          }
          /*Find assigned port value and print it out. */
          length = sizeof (name);
          if (getsockname (sock, (struct sockaddr*)&name,
            &length) < 0)(
                    perror(''getting socket name'');
                    exit(1);
          )
          printf(''Socket port #%d\n'', ntohs(name, sin_port));
          /*Read from the socket. */
          if (read(sock, buf, 1024)<0)
                    perror(''receiving datagram packet'');
          printf(''-- > %s\n'', buf);
          close(sock);
          exit(0);
```

Figure 13.10   Reading Internet Domain Datagrams.

```
#include <sys/types.h>
#include <sys/socket.h>
#include <netinet/in.h>
#include <netdb.h>
#include <stdio.h>

#define DATA ''The sea is calm, the tide is full...''

/*
   *Here I send a datagram to a receiver whose name I get from the command
   *line arguments. The form of the command line is:
   *dgramsend hostname portnumber
   */
main(argc, argv)
          int argc;
          char*argv[];
{
          int sock;
          struct sockaddr_in name;
          struct hostend *hp, *gethostbyname();

          /*Create socket on which to send. */
          sock = socket(AF_INET, SOCK_DGRAM,0);
          if(sock<0){
                    perror(''opening datagram socket'');
                    exit(1);
          }
          /*
             *Construct name, with no wildcards, of the socket to send to.
             *gethostbyname returns a structure including the network
              address
             *of the specified host. The port number is taken from the
              command
             *line.
             */
          hp = gethostbyname (argv[1]);
          if (hp == 0){
                    fprintf(stdarr, ''%s: unknown host\n'', argv[1]);
                    exit(2);
          }
          memcpy( (char*)&name,sin_addr,(char*)hp- > h_addr,
            hp- > h_length);
          name.sin_family = AF_INET;
          name.sin_port = htons(atoi(argv[2]));
          /*Send message.*/
          if (sendto (sock, DATA, sizeof DATA, 0,
            (struct sockaddr*)&name, sizeof name)<0)
                    perror(''sending datagram message'');
          close(sock);
          exit(0);
```

Figure 13.11   Sending an Internet Domain Datagram.

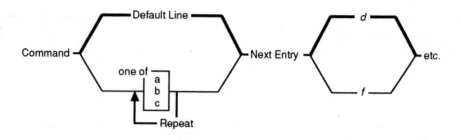

Where: Command = Enter command to invoke service
Default line = If no further user entry
One of = a, b, or c
Repeat = Choose at least one of a, b, c, but maybe more
Next entry = Further input
d = Default value, if nothing entered
f = Optional input
Bold line = Default
Non bold line = Nondefault

Figure 13.12   The Syntax Diagram.

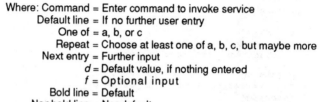

Figure 13.13   The *netmail* Command for SMTP Services.

parameter(s) use(s) the Internet naming convention for the user host. The *repeat arrow* signifies that more than one user can be identified.

An example of an entry on a PC in which the PC user wishes to send mail in the file called *sales memo* to *UBlack* at *ACME.COM.* would appear as

```
$ netmail sales memo UBlack@ACME.COM.
```

Sending a file through TFTP

Figure 13.14 shows the syntax for a user command to transfer files between hosts with the trivial file transfer protocol (TFTP). The *action* parameter is coded as

wrp: Writes the file designated as *localname* into the file system of the foreign host designated as *foreignname*

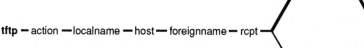

tftp — action —localname — host — foreignname — rcpt
                                                          — mode —

Figure 13.14   The *tftp* Command for Trivial File Transfer Protocol Operations.

rrg: Reads the file designated as *foreignname* from the foreign host into the local file designated as *localname*

o: Overrides or supersedes ongoing local files

The *mode* parameter is coded as follows: netascii = file transfer using standard ASCII characters; image = transfer files and binary images with no conversion performed; mail = appends the files stipulated to the end of a specified user mailbox, and afterward the user can retrieve this information with the PC/UNIX (AIX) mail command.

An example of an entry on a PC in which the PC user transfers the binary file /receipts from host4 to /tempreceipts at host10 is as follows:

```
$ tftp -w /receipts host4 /tempreceipts image
```

Sending a file through FTP

Figure 13.15 shows the syntax for invoking the FTP operations. This command supports the transfer of files to and from a foreign server. The *xftp* command assumes a packet size of 1576 bytes and a window size of 6K bytes. Files are transfered in the standard ASCII format, although other commands are available to request binary transfer. The *-n* parameter provides the user with automatic login, which precludes the user from having to enter an ID and password. The *host* parameter is the name of the client host. The *dbg* parameter is coded into one of four values to request the following services:

0: Obtain trace service messages.

1: Obtain error messages.

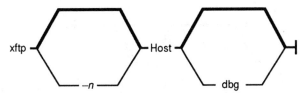

Figure 13.15   The *xftp* Command for File Transfer Protocol Operations.

2: Show all receipt packets.

4: Show all sent packets.

The xftp command, upon being executed, can be followed by several subcommands, which are provided to the user with the following prompt on the screen: xftp > . The user can then enter the subcommands. Here are several examples of subcommands:

acct: Provides accounting information.

append: Appends a file to another file.?

binary: Data transferred is binary.

dir: Display a listing of the directory.?

get: Retrieves a foreign file and stores it at the local host.

pass: Provides password information.

put: Sends a local file on a foreign host.

Here is an example of the xftp operation:

```
$ xftp host 4
...login operations (e.g., TELNET)
xftp > binary
xftp > put/receipts/tempreceipts
...status messages of file transfer
xftp > quit
...user is logged off
```

Using tn to invoke Telnet login services

Figure 13.16 shows the syntax for logging onto a foreign host through the Telnet interface. The tn command is used to access a Telnet protocol. It should be noted before discussing the remainder of the parameters that several subcommands can be used as part of tn by keying in control-T and single character subcommands. These subcommands allow the user to obtain many of the services of Telnet described in earlier chapters, such as are you there, break, keying in data, establishing echo modes, displaying status, etc.

The *host* parameter identifies the Telnet connection to the specific

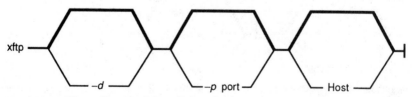

Figure 13.16 The *tn* Command for a Telnet Login.

host. If this parameter is not supplied, the user will be prompted to provide a host name. The *-d* indicates that the debugging option is on, and the *-p port* is used to identify the foreign port number for this connection. Otherwise, the system defaults to the Telnet port.

A typical example of a TELNET login is as follows:

```
$ tn host 4
... login occurs
... user can enter subcommands
```

Retrieving network statistics

The *netstat* command allows an end user to obtain various kinds of information about the state of the network and the state of connections. The netstat command is depicted in Fig. 13.17. Four options are available to obtain these services:

-a: Displays the state of all connections

-i: Displays the state of configurations that are automatically configured (connections that are loaded into the system)

-r: Displays the routing table

-v: Displays statistics about the LAN device driver on this internet interface

The following example is of a user keying in the netstat command to obtain the local IP routing table:

```
$ netstat -r
... routing table is displayed on the screen
```

Using PING to obtain echo services

Figure 13.18 shows the syntax for the PING service. After entering the command PING, the user chooses one of four parameters to obtain the PING service:

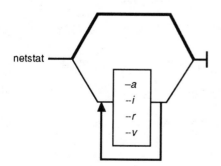

netstat

-a
-i
-r
-v

Figure 13.17 The *netstat* Command to Obtain Network Statistics.

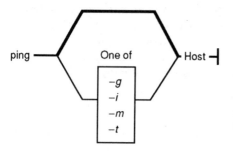

Figure 13.18 The PING Command to Obtain Echo Services.

-*g:*   A GGP echo request message is sent to a specified *host*

-*i:*   An ICMP echo request is sent to a specified host

-*m:*   A submask is returned for a specified host

-*t:*   An ICMP-type timestamp request is returned for a specified host

The following is an example of how a user executes PING to obtain the ICMP timestamp service:

```
$ ping -t host 4
... information on screen contains the three ICMP timestamp values:
(a/originated, (b) received, (c) transmitted
```

Using route to manipulate the IP routing table

Figure 13.19 depicts the syntax to add or remove routes from the IP routing table. The commands *add* and *delete* will add and remove a route, respectively. The -*f* command will clear the host gateway table. The *destination* parameter is an IP address identifying a host or network where the route is directed. The *gateway* parameter is an IP address which identifies the next gateway to process the datagram.

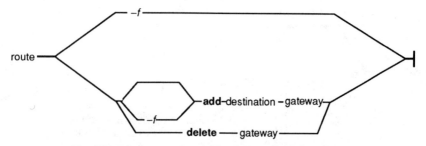

Figure 13.19   The ROUTE Command to Add and Remove IP Routes.

The following is an example of the route command in which gateway 14.3.2.1 is established as a default gateway:

```
$ route add 0 14.3.2.1.
```

Summary

Through the use of operating system calls, such as UNIX, a communications programmer can manipulate TCP/IP open and close sockets, transfer data, obtain name server support, as well as perform other services. On a higher level, programs such as the IBM interface program allow a user to obtain the upper internet application layer services such as file transfer, mail exchange, and remote terminal login without the need to understand the more complex operating system calls.

Chapter 14

Management Considerations

The Vendor Strategies with the Internet-Based Products

By 1990, many large enterprises (commercial banks, insurance companies, government departments) had either written a plan to migrate to the OSI standards or were planning to write such a plan. Indeed, the U.S. Government, which was the chief architect and sponsor of the Internet, has issued a directive for government agencies to migrate to GOSIP (The U.S. Government OSI Profile), which is an implementation of OSI.

Nonetheless, use of the Internet standards appears to be growing faster than the OSI standards. (I know of no accurate survey available—mostly nebulous opinion/questionnaires—but my day-to-day work leads me to this conclusion.)

Without question, every major communications vendor is planning to support one or more of the following scenarios:

- Migrate away from vendor-specific products toward the OSI and/or TCP/IP suites.

- Maintain the vendor-specific layers and provide interfaces between these layers and the OSI/TCP/IP suites.

The following scenario is *not* what the vendors and manufacturers are openly espousing:

- Vendor-specific protocols are the best approach, and their product lines will be built strictly on specific customer requirements (i.e., tailored to the individual customer).

The OSI concept is now accepted, and only the hopelessly inept manufacturer will state that OSI is not slated as part of its product line. It would be something like saying that motherhood is not sacrosanct.

It is equally evident that the TCP/IP protocols have a definite headstart on the OSI standards, in their use and acceptance by vendors, users, and just about everyone (except those folks that make a living selling or talking about OSI).

It should be emphasized that a company that is tasked with the design, manufacturing, and selling of computer and communications products must frequently produce a system that is tailored to the specific user environment. In a situation in which the environment does not fit the OSI or TCP/IP framework, what is to be done?

The answer is obvious: Build the product to meet the customer's needs, and try to design the product to have "hooks" into and out of the OSI and TCP/IP worlds.

A number of mainframe manufacturers are adapting to this approach with considerable success. Moreover, it is not contradictory to the spirit of OSI, and the TCP/IP standards do not address this issue. Remember, OSI does not care what the system does in its internal operations, nor does it care how the system does it. It only stipulates that a given and standardized input into *any* system must produce a predictable and standardized output from that system.

The vendors react to the marketplace

It might prove useful to move back in time and examine what was going on during the embryonic stages of the integration of computers and communications revolution. During the 1970s, several manufacturers realized that they could not afford to continue operating in an unorganized and ill-structured computer and communications environment, *even* within their own product lines. Consequently, they began to develop a more coherent approach to their own products and embarked on efforts to build a structured framework (architecture) for their communications protocols.

The implementation of vendor-specific architectures alleviated the incompatibility problem of the products within the vendor's product line; but it did nothing to address the serious problem of incompatibility between the different vendors' computers, terminals, and other equipment. If anything, the development of vendor-specific systems made matters worse, because each manufacturer embarked upon a separate course to invent a "better mouse trap."

At this time, several standards groups became active in these issues. The International Standards Organization (ISO) began work in 1979 on the Open Systems Architecture, now known as OSI. The OSI

Model was published in 1984 to serve as a standard model for computer communications.

Of course, we have learned that the Internet standards served as pioneers to some of the OSI protocols. Moreover, TCP and IP served as a valuable foundation for "launching" all the Internet standards. Without question, many dollars have been saved by the U.S. government and private industry because of the Internet standards.

So what about the future? Does it make sense to maintain both OSI and TCP/IP? Is one better than the other? Should a user care? With these questions in mind, let us examine some of the activities in the computer and communications standards arena and develop some answers.

A Comparison of the TCP/IP and OSI Stacks

Figure 14.1 shows the relationships of the OSI stack to the TCP/IP stack. A few points of emphasis are important in our discussion. Several organizations and many people have stated that some of these layers are functionally equivalent. Numerous reports and articles have been published stating that TCP and TP4, as well as IP and

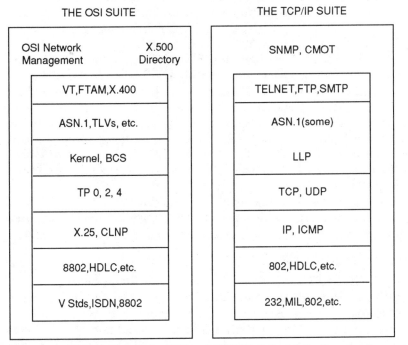

THE OSI SUITE

OSI Network Management	X.500 Directory
VT,FTAM,X.400	
ASN.1,TLVs, etc.	
Kernel, BCS	
TP 0, 2, 4	
X.25, CLNP	
8802,HDLC,etc.	
V Stds,ISDN,8802	

THE TCP/IP SUITE

SNMP, CMOT
TELNET,FTP,SMTP
ASN.1(some)
LLP
TCP, UDP
IP, ICMP
802,HDLC,etc.
232,MIL,802,etc.

Figure 14.1 Comparison of the OSI and TCP/IP Suites (not all protocols are shown).

CLMP, do the same things. It should be stated categorically: The OSI and Internet protocols perform similar functions, but there is definitely not a one-to-one mapping of their services.

The following discussion focuses on a comparison of the stacks and a general analysis of mapping the functions of one stack to the other.

The lower two layers of these two protocol stacks do not present any serious compatibility problems. Indeed, the top five layers can rest somewhat transparently over the bottom two layers. Both stacks plan to use existing international standards. For example, at the physical layer, the ubiquitous EIA 232-D standard is used in both stacks, although the OSI stack cites the use of the V Series Recommendations. EIA 232-D is compatible with its counterparts in the V Series (V.24 and V.28). EIA 232-D also aligns with ISO 2110 for the physical connection.

X.21 or X.21bis can also be applied to both stacks at the physical layer. The physical level LAN standards, as published by the IEEE 802 standards, apply to both stacks. No reason exists why the ISDN physical layer cannot be applied to both stacks, and the ISO publishes these standards under the 8802 numbers. Also, the emerging optical fiber standard, FDDI, can be used with both sets of standards.

The data link layer presents no major problems since most vendors have adapted a version of HDLC (e.g., LAPB in X.25-based networks, LAPD in ISDN networks for the control channel, and LAPM for error-correcting modems). Moreover, the LAN standards use compatible, physical data link protocols with the MAC sublayer of the 802 standards. Moreover, the IEEE 802.2 logical link control (LLC) standard works well with both stacks.

Mapping problems occur at the upper five layers and especially the upper three layers. As Fig. 14.1 illustrates, at layer three the OSI stack contains X.25 and CLNP. Admittedly, the functions of CLNP and IP closely parallel each other. However, CLMP is more functionally rich than IP.

There is no correlation between X.25 and the TCP/IP stack. X.25 is designed as a connection-oriented network interface. Some of the functions supported in X.25 are carried in TCP and to some extent in ICMP.

One could ask then, "Why can't we use X.25 as a functional equivalent to TCP and ICMP?" First, the mapping would be horrendous. Some of the functions do not map, and others are contradictory to the intent of the protocols. Second, TCP is designed to be a very reliable end-to-end protocol. X.25 is designed to be a reliable protocol, but it does not have the graceful close features of TCP since X.25 gives the network the option of discarding packets in certain situations (Reset,

Restart). Third, ICMP carries a number of diagnostic and status messages, but it does not support the number and type of diagnostic packets that X.25 supports.

So a question arises: What is to be done with X.25 vis-à-vis TCP/IP? The answer is that nothing prevents the network manager from mapping TCP/IP over an X.25 network, as we learned in Chap. 12. Moreover, it is technically feasible to use CLNP in place of IP and place it between TP and X.25.

The long-range goal of OSI is to migrate from TCP to TP4. However, TP4 is overkill for the X.25-based network. Therefore, TP2 is a more likely candidate at the transport layer for the X.25/CLNP stack.

TCP/IP does not have any comparable protocols to OSI in the session and presentation layers. ASN.1 is finding its way into the Internet network management standards, but it is not used to the extent it is used in OSI. TCP/IP does not have the OSI transfer syntax protocol (shown in Fig. 14.1 as TLV, for the type, length, value notation). However, nothing precludes a user from employing TLV with the internet protocols as long as each end of the communications channel knows how to use it. Some internet implementations use the External Data Representation (XDR) protocol, which is quite similar to but incompatible with TLV.

The session layer presents vexing problems. Its services are required by almost all the OSI application layer protocols. Therefore, it is not easy to bypass if a user is accessing an OSI application layer protocol. TCP/IP does not have a session layer, although several of the TCP/IP application layer protocols perform session services.

Other mapping problems occur in the applications layer, where the TCP/IP protocol stack is best known for FTP, SMTP, and TELNET. The OSI stack contains very elaborate protocols with FTAM, X.400 MHS, and the virtual terminal (VT). To say that these map to each other would be a disservice to the reader. Certain of the functions can be mapped on a limited scale, but the TCP/IP application layer protocols simply do not perform the many services of their counterparts in the OSI stack and vice versa.

For example, FTP permits third party transfers; FTAM does not. On the other hand, FTAM allows considerable manipulation of objects within a file. FTP does not have this level of granularity. FTP permits two logical connections between two FTP clients and control servers: a control connection and a data connection. This concept does not exist in FTAM.

The future OSI environment will rely heavily on the ISO OSI network management standards and the CCITT X.500 Directory services. TCP/IP is making great progress in this arena (with SNMP and

CMOT). Presently, the concept of X.500 does not exist in the TCP/IP suite.

IP and CLNP

We have made the point a number of times that CLNP and IP are quite similar. We have also made the point that they are not compatible. Figure 14.2 shows the protocol data units of CLNP and IP. Obviously, the formats are quite different.

TP4 and TCP

TCP is similar to many of the ISO/CCITT transport layer operations. Many of their support functions, such as multiplexing, end-to-end acknowledgment, and timer operations, are designed to achieve the same goals. However, the two protocols differ in many of their features, and in several instances the capabilities in one protocol do not exist in the other. Figure 14.3 compares the formats of the data units of TCP and TP4.

TP4 does not use port identifiers. Its identifiers are the destination

ISO CLNP PDU

IP DATAGRAM

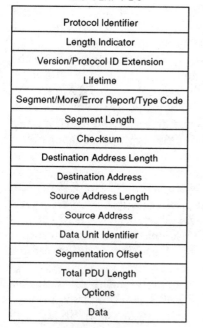
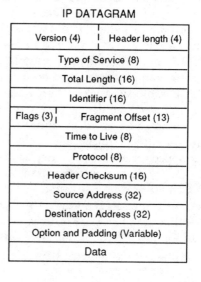

ISO CLNP PDU
Protocol Identifier
Length Indicator
Version/Protocol ID Extension
Lifetime
Segment/More/Error Report/Type Code
Segment Length
Checksum
Destination Address Length
Destination Address
Source Address Length
Source Address
Data Unit Identifier
Segmentation Offset
Total PDU Length
Options
Data

IP DATAGRAM	
Version (4)	Header length (4)
Type of Service (8)	
Total Length (16)	
Identifier (16)	
Flags (3)	Fragment Offset (13)
Time to Live (8)	
Protocol (8)	
Header Checksum (16)	
Source Address (32)	
Destination Address (32)	
Option and Padding (Variable)	
Data	

Figure 14.2 The ISO CLNP PDU and the IP Datagram.

OCTET

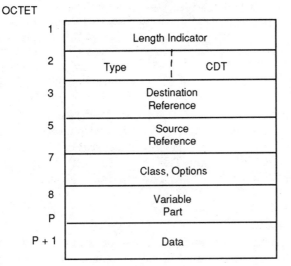

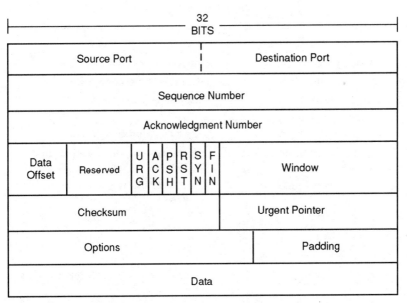

Figure 14.3 Comparison of the TP4 TPDU and the TCP TPDU.

and source reference fields and transport service access points (TSAPs, located in the variable part of the TPDU).

Both protocols support the sliding window concepts, TP4 with the CDT field and TCP with the window field. The variable part field of TP4 can be coded to negotiate many services, such as throughput, delay, etc. This capability does not exist in TCP. The OSI transport protocol is actually organized around five classes of protocols—each providing a specific set of services. One of these classes is TP4. TCP has no such capability.

A number of articles I have read state that TCP is more efficient than TP4. This finding is not surprising. TP4 provides more services—function rarely comes without cost. However, several options now exist that allow a user to run TP0 and TCP (see Chap. 12). The principal differences between TP4 and TCP are summarized in Table 14.1.

Migration Issues

Now that a general comparison has been made between IP and CLNP and TCP and TP4, it should prove fruitful to examine the migration issues. That is, how can an organization migrate from the internet stack to the OSI stack?

It is helpful to separate the migration issues into categories: (1)

TABLE 14.1   Comparison of TP4 and TCP

TP Class 4	TCP
Connection-oriented	Connection-oriented
Complex, with many functions	Simple, relatively few functions
Complex and varied TPDU	One format for segment
Data placed in specific SDUs from upper layer and sent as TPDUs	Data sent on a flow basis from upper layer and sent as segments
Expedited data may arrive out of sequence with earlier data	Urgent data stays in order within the stream and segment
Uses OSI service access point (SAP)	Uses the IP 32-bit address and the port number to achieve a socket
Push function nonexistent	Uses push function to force transfer
Supports multiple classes (0–4)	Does not use class concept
Uses OSI-based service definitions	Uses TCP-specific primitives
Uses TP-specific timers and state diagrams	Uses TCP-specific timers and state diagrams
No graceful close	Supports a graceful close

gateway, (2) network, and (3) host. The following discussions cover each issue.

Gateway migration issues

Consider Fig. 14.4a. Two hosts wish to exchange information using the FTP standard. They are transmitting the files through their respective networks and an intervening gateway.

Are there gateway migration issues with this scenario? The answer is no. The gateway should be transparent to the file transfer. Indeed, if the organization has implemented the protocol as it should, the upper layer migration should be completely transparent to the gateways. However, be aware that the network layer at the gateway must have the same software module as the network layer at the hosts because both IP and CLNP rely on the host to create the gateway header.

Figure 14.4b is an easy operation to implement at a gateway. Two hosts are to exchange file traffic through their own respective network directly connected to each other. Obviously, the gateway does not get involved. No gateway migration problems exist here.

Figure 14.4c is another matter. Examining the shaded areas, we see that the two networks are involved in transfer as are the two gateways. The gateway at the top part of the figure is connected to some other part of an internet, which is not shown. These gateways, as we have learned, must communicate with each other; therefore, they must have compatible gateway protocols. The transfer of an application layer protocol will not affect the operations at the gateways. However, extensive mapping must occur if one gateway uses IP and the other gateway uses CLNP.

What may not be so obvious is answering the question, "Does the vendor host care?" The answer is yes. Remember that IP and CLNP are source routing gateway protocols. Even though most of the work is done at the gateway, it starts at the host. Thus, we have to achieve compatibility with the software in the gateway and the software in the host machines.

Network migration issues

What are the migration issues with regard to the networks? From the standpoint of layer interactions, the migration is relatively straightforward. The CLNP or IP subnetwork access protocol (SNAP) is affected, but the upper layers should not be.

However, the effects on the networks of supporting TP4 instead of TCP can have major consequences in relation to throughput, delay,

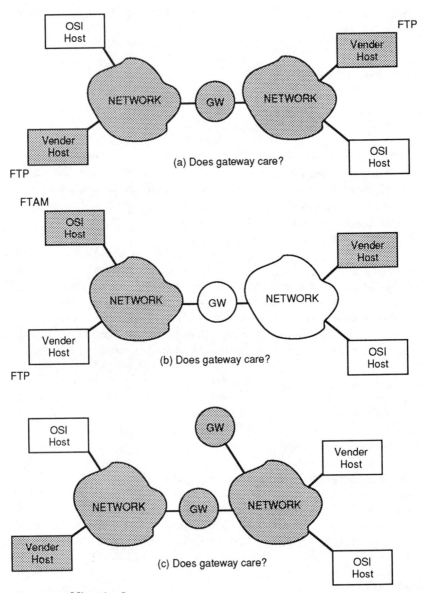

(a) Does gateway care?

(b) Does gateway care?

(c) Does gateway care?

Figure 14.4   Migration Issues.

congestion, flow control, time-outs, retransmissions, etc. The effects must be evaluated carefully.

Additionally, the replacements of, for example, FTP with FTAM, SMTP with X.400, and TELNET with VT will affect traffic conditions within the networks. These effects must also be evaluated carefully.

Host migration issues

Equally important is an assessment of migration issues in the host machines. Resolution between all layers is required because a host runs all internet layers. The only protocols which might not exist in a host are the route discovery protocols, such as EGP and OSPF.

Migration of Internet to OSI Network Architectures

Whatever one's thoughts are about defense expenditures, it remains a fact that in the computer and communications industry, many standards are established (developed, nurtured, and published) by the U.S. Department of Defense (DOD). Therefore, it is important to follow the activities of the DOD, because its decisions affect the marketplace.

Previous discussions in this book have examined how the DOD-developed TCP, ICMP, and IP are used throughout the world. We have also learned about the need to interconnect separate networks, some using DOD protocols and some using other schemes.

Internetworking DOD and non-DOD architectures

We have learned that when an OSI or internet network architecture is employed, a gateway is used to connect the separate networks. Obviously, an internetwork gateway must have the facilities to support each network that attaches to it.

An IP/CLNP gateway has been designed by the DOD to provide the transition between the DOD and the OSI protocol suites at the internetwork level. Basically, this gateway will discriminate between the different protocol suites employed during the transition period. When a packet arrives at a gateway interface, a module checks a network layer protocol identification field and then passes this data unit up to the appropriate internetwork module, either Internet's IP or OSI's CLNP. Thereafter, when the appropriate internetwork module has received the packet, the standard IP or OSI functions are performed.

The DOD has identified two ways of achieving DOD/OSI interoperability: dual DOD/OSI protocol hosts and DOD/OSI application layer gateways.

Dual DOD/OSI protocol hosts

This approach is simply a host machine that has complete protocol suites available as part of its capability. For example, the host machine can have a standard vendor-specific and/or DOD protocol stack, or it can have the pure OSI stack. Indeed, as the movement to OSI progresses, a host machine could have both stacks and select the protocols necessary for a particular configuration.

However, if a machine has only DOD protocols, a file transfer could be achieved by

- Using FTP on the originating DOD protocol host machine to transfer to a dual protocol host machine

- Using TELNET on the originating machine to remotely log into the dual host

- Using FTAM on the dual host machine to transfer the file to the destination OSI protocol host

With this scenario, we see a host providing gateway services between two other host machines.

Application layer gateways

The DOD also intends to develop application layer gateways which will allow the two protocol suites to communicate with each other. Basically, the application layer gateway acts as a protocol converter by performing a staging or conversion operation. It then invokes a corresponding application process using the other suite. The Defense Communications Agency will provide application layer gateways for file transfer (FTAM/FTP) and electronic mail (X.400/SMTP) gateways.

Activities of the Vendors

Almost all the vendors have announced or are planning to announce products based on the OSI network and transport layer protocols. However, most companies, organizations, and standards groups recognize that it is impossible to migrate immediately from a vendor-specific or mixed stack to a pure OSI stack. Invariably, the movement to OSI will require what are known in the industry as *transition aids*. Essentially, these transition aids act as convertors between the different layers in the stacks.

It is also recognized that a movement to OSI requires an extended period where different protocols exist and may even interoperate with each other. This coexistence is usually planned to be provided for an extended period of time because of cost considerations as a result of the migration.

Several standards groups, private companies, and government agencies are well into their planning and implementation stages for OSI. Due to the complexity and cost of this transition, some of the organizations have adapted several levels for achieving OSI functionality. For example, the DOD has specified three levels of OSI implementation and functionality: (1) limited, (2) OSI equivalent, and (3) advanced.

Limited OSI capability

With this approach, the users in an organization may specify and use OSI protocols in addition to or in place of the protocols that are attached to their networks. However, the full OSI model is not implemented. Rather, the most important protocols are acquired or developed.

In most organizations this immediate use of OSI entails the use of X.25. It also entails the use of standard NSAP address formats. Other products which allow the immediate use of OSI deal with the X.400 Message Handling System and the National Bureau of Standards phase one implementor agreements for FTAM.

Equivalent OSI capability

The second stage of implementation involves a more advanced implementation of OSI. For example, the DOD has established the next phase as bringing phase two of the National Bureau of Standards FTAM functions, as well as the virtual terminal protocols based on the ISO standards.

Advanced OSI capability

The last stage provides advanced OSI capabilities. This entails the implementation of many of the 1988 Blue Book specifications. The 1988 X.400 recommendation is substantially different from the 1984 recommendation. The final stage would bring the 1988 X.400 recommendation into the DOD protocol suite.

In addition, the ISO X.500 Directory services will be part of the advanced phase. The OSI management protocols will also be included here (although they are still in various stages of development). It is also anticipated that the international standards, for security services, will be brought into the last stage.

In some fashion, most forward-thinking companies are planning a migration strategy based on these ideas.

Summary

The TCP/IP and OSI standards are garnering the most support for use as international data communications network standards. They are rich in function, and they offer many options to the user. However, they are also incompatible. Fortunately, migration and transition strategies are in the works, and in the future we will see increased use of dual stacks and protocol converters.

Index

Absolute name, 80
Acquisition state (state 1), external gateway protocol (EGP), 202
Active open mode, Transmission Control Protocol (TCP), 153–154
Address field format, simple mail transfer protocol (SMTP), 272–273
Address mask request and reply, Internet control message protocol (ICMP), 143–144
Address Resolution Protocol (ARP), 61–69
  address translation table, 65–66
  ARP request, 61
  datagram format, 62–63
  logic flow diagram, 63–64
  proxy ARP, 66–67
  reverse address resolution protocol (RARP), 67–69
Address structure:
  Internet Protocol (IP), 54–56, 77
  TCP/IP, 54–56
Address table, Internet Protocol (IP), 116–117
Addresses:
  address resolution issues, 60–71
  Address Resolution Protocol (ARP), 61–75
  definition of, 39
  destination addresses and routing, 57–60
  IP address structure, 54–56
  link layer addresses (LSAPs), 45–47
  need for addressing levels, 49–50
  network addresses, 47–48
  physical addresses, 40–45
  upper layer (ULP) names/addresses, 50
Architectural model, TCP/IP, 12
Architecture:
  connectionless/connection-oriented protocols, 6–9
  Domain Name System (DNS), 78–79
  TCP/IP, 12
ARCNET networks, transmitting IP datagrams over, 325–326
Area data structure, OSPF (Open SPF) protocol, 234–335
ARP [see Address Resolution Protocol (ARP)]
ARPANET, 2, 9, 56, 145, 186
Autonomous systems:
  areas of, 187–188
  definition of, 181–182
  and information exchanges, 188–191

Bifurcated routing, 222
Bootstrap Protocol (BOOTP), 286–288

Bridges, 35
  spanning tree bridges, 36–38
Brouters, 35–36

Carrier sense, collision detection LANs, 28–29
Carrier sense multiple access with collision detection (see CSMA/CD LANs)
Cease state (state 4), external gateway protocol (EGP), 202
Checksum field, Hello protocol, 220
Circuit switching, WANs, 22
Class A addresses, 54–55
Class B addresses, 55
Class C addresses, 55
Class D addresses, 55
CMOT, 308–311
  layers, 310–311
  and Lightweight Presentation Protocol (LPP), 311
Command codes, TELNET protocol, 255
Computer-Communication Network Design and Analysis (Schwartz), 222
Connection management operations:
  Transmission Control Protocol (TCP), 167–176
    close operations, 173–174
    connection table, 174–176
    data transfer operations, 172–173
    open operations, 167–172
Connection-oriented operations, 7
Connection-oriented protocol, definition of, 147–148
Connection-oriented services, UNIX-based TCP/IP services, 334–337
Connectionless-mode network service (CLNP/ISO 8473), 97, 127–134
  definition of, 127–128
  field functions, 130
  and IP, 133–134
  ISO 8473:
    definition of, 127
    field functions, 130
    PDU, 128, 131
    use of ISO 8348, 128–129
  protocol functions, 129
  record route function, 133
  traffic management between subnetworks, 129–133
  Internetwork routing, 133
Connectionless-mode operations, 7–8
Core gateways, 186, 201
CSMA/CD LANs, 29–31
  data link layer, 30
  physical layer, 31

DARPA internet network, 2, 3, 56, 97

Data link layer, CSMA/CD LANs, 30
Data Networks: Concepts, Theory and Practice (Black), 222
Data structures, OSPF (Open SPF) protocol, 233–237
  area data structure, 234–235
  interface data structures, 235–236
  neighbor data structure, 236
  protocol data structure, 234
  routing table structure, 236–237
Data types, File Transfer Protocol (FTP), 263
Database description packet, OSPF (Open SPF) protocol, 242–244
Datagram services, UNIX-based TCP/IP services, 338
Date field, Hello protocol, 220
Daytime protocol, 290
Defense Advanced Project Research Agency (*see* DARPA internet network)
Delay host field, Hello protocol, 220
Department of Defense (DOD), 97
  application layer gateways, 362
  dual DOD/OSI protocol hosts, 362
  Internetworking, 361–362
  OSI implementation/functionality levels, 363–364
    advanced OSI capability, 363–364
    equivalent OSI capability, 363
    limited capability, 363
  standards, 361
  vendor activities, 362–364
Design and Analysis of Computer Algorithms (Aho/Hopcroft/Ullman), 222
Destination addresses and routing, 57–60
  direct host, 57–58
  indirect host, 57–58
  IP routing logic, 57–59
  multihomed hosts, 60
Discard protocol, 285–286
DOD [*see* Department of Defense (DOD)]
Domain Name System (DNS), 77–96
  architecture, 78–79
  domain name:
    definition of, 79
    resolution, 80–82
  illustration of, 79
  IN-ADDR-ARPA, 88–90
  messages, 93–96
    AA (authoritative answer) bit, 94, 96
    ADDITIONAL record section, 94, 96
    ANCOUNT, 94
    ANSWER section, 94, 96
    ARCOUNT, 95
    AUTHORITY section, 94, 96
    header, 94
    NSCOUNT, 94–95
    opcode, 94
    QCLASS, 96
    QDCOUNT, 94–95

Domain Name System (DNS), messages (*Cont.*):
    QNAME, 95
    QTYPE, 95
    QUESTION section, 94, 95–96
    RCODE, 94
  name server operations, 82–83
  resource records (RR), 83–85
    compression, 96
    example of, 88–93
    RDATA field, 85–86
  and simple mail transfer protocol (SMTP), 274–275
  structure of, 92
  top-level domains, 80
  types, 86–88
    HINFO (host information) RDATA format, 86
    MC RDATA format, 86
    MINFO (mail information) format, 86–87
    MR RDATA format, 87–88
    MX (mail exchanger) RDATA format, 88
    name server (NS) RDATA format, 86
    NULL RDATA format, 88
    PTR (pointer) RDATA format, 88
  type values of, 83
Down state (state 2), external gateway protocol (EGP), 202

Echo request and reply, Internet control message protocol (ICMP), 140–141
EGP [*see* External gateway protocol (EGP)]
Error- and status-reporting procedures, Internet control message protocol (ICMP), 137–138
External gateway protocol (EGP), 187, 192, 199–214
  acquisition state (state 1), 202
  cease state (state 4), 202
  definition of, 199–201
  down state (state 2), 202
  events, 210, 211
  idle state (state 0), 201–202
  major operations of, 201
  messages, 202–209
    error message, 210
    message header, 204
    message types, 203–208
    neighbor acquisition header, 205
    neighbor reachability message, 208
    poll message, 207
    update message, 208–209
  up state (state 3), 202
    operations during, 210–213

FDDI networks, transmitting IP datagrams over, 326–327
Federal Networking Council (FNC), 3–4

"Fewest-hops" routing directory, 182–184
File Transfer Protocol (FTP), 261–271
  commands/replies, 263–265
  data types, 263
  definition of, 261
  file retrieval, example of, 269
  FTP session, sequence of operations in,
    265–267
  minimum implementation of, 269–271
  model, 262
  operations, examples of, 267–269
  reply codes, 265
  sending files through, 345–346
Finger protocol, 286
Flags field, Internet Protocol (IP), 102
Flat name, 77
Fragmentation, 98, 111–116
Fragmentation offset field, Internet
  Protocol (IP), 102
Fully specified passive open, Transmission Control Protocol (TCP), 154

Garbage-collection timer, routing
  information protocol (RIP), 215–216
Gated protocol, 221
Gateways, 5, 35
Gateway-to-gateway protocol (GGP), 186,
  192–199
  acknowledgment message, 198
  computing routes, 194–196
  definition of, 192–93
  echo request/reply message, 198
  exchanging routing information,
    193–194
  message formats, 196–199
    distance D1 field, 197
    first network at D1/last network at
      D1, 197
    need update field, 196
    number distance groups field,
      196–197
    number networks at D1, 197
    sequence number field, 196
  neighbor connectivity analysis, 193
  network interface status message, 198
  update message, example of, 200

Header check, Internet, 106–107
Header checksum, Internet Protocol (IP),
  103
Header length field, IP datagram, 99
Hello packet, OSPF (Open SPF) protocol,
  239–242
Hello protocol, 219–221
  message format, 220–221
Hierarchical naming, DNS, 78
Host Monitoring Protocol (HMP),
  284–285
HOSTNAME protocol, 284
Hosts field, Hello protocol, 220
HOST.TXT, administration of, 78

IBM Interface Program, 339–349
  FTP, sending files through, 345–346
  manipulating IP routing table, using
    route, 348–349
  network statistics, retrieving, 347
  PING, using to obtain echo services,
    347–348
  SMTP, sending mail through,
    341–344
  Telnet login services, invoking with tn
    command, 346–347
  TFTP, sending files through, 344–345
ICMP [see Internet control message
    protocol (ICMP)]
Identifier field, Internet Protocol (IP),
  102
Idle state (state 0), external gateway
  protocol (EGP), 201–202
IEEE 802 LLC traffic, transmitting over
  IPX networks, 324–325
IEEE 802.3 standards, and CSMA/CD
  LANs, 29–31
IGPs [see Internal gateway protocols
    (IGPs)]
IN-ADDR-ARPA, 88–90
Indirect host, 57–58
Information/logic routing, participants
  in, 190–191
Information request/information reply,
  Internet control message protocol
  (ICMP), 143
Input/output calls, UNIX-based TCP/IP
  services, 337–338
Interface data structures, OSPF (Open
  SPF) protocol, 235–236
Interior gateway protocols (GPs), 214
Internal gateway protocols (IGPs), 187,
  214
Internet:
  layers of, 9–10
  migration to OSI network architec-
    tures, 361–364
  naming/addressing operation, 50–53
  network management standards,
    293–311
    CMOT, 308–311
    layer architecture, 294–295
    Management Information Base
      (MIB), 298–304
    naming hierarchy, 295–296
    SNMP, 304–308
    Structure of Management Informa-
      tion (SMI), 297–298
    summary of, 293–294
  organization of, 3–4
  typical topologies, 15–17
Internet Advisory Board (IAB), 3
Internet control message protocol
  (ICMP), 135–144
  address mask request and reply,
    143–144
  destination unreachable, 139–140
  echo request and reply, 140–141

Internet control message protocol (ICMP)
  (*Cont.*):
  error- and status-reporting procedures,
    137–138
  information request/information reply,
    143
  message format, 137
  parameter unintelligible, 139
  redirect, 141–142
  redirect service, 141–142
  source quench, 140
  time exceeded, 138–139
  timestamp/timestamp reply, 142–143
  unintelligible parameter, 139
  unreachable destination, 139–140
Internet Group Management Protocol
  (IGMP), 126–127
Internet Packet Exchange Protocol (IPX):
  transmitting IEEE 802 type 1 LCC
    traffic over, 324–325
  using with UDP/IP networks, 323–324
Internet Protocol (IP):
  address structure, 54–56, 77
  address table, 116–117
  and CLNP, 356
  connectionless-mode network service
    (CLNP/ISO 8473), 127–134
  flags field, 102
  fragmentation offset field, 102
  header checksum, 103
  header length filed, 99
  identifier field, 102
  Internet Group Management Protocol
    (IGMP), 126–127
  IP diagram, 99–106
  and LAN bridges, 321
  major features of, 97–98
  major services, 106–116
    fragmentation and reassembly,
      111–116
    header check routine, 106–107
    route recording option, 109
    source routing, 107–109
    timestamp option, 109–111
  multicasting, 124–125
  options field, 103–106
  over NetBIOS, 318–319
  padding filed, 106
  protocol field, 103
  router stacks, 320
  routing logic, 57–59
  routing table, 117–119
  service definitions/primitives,
    119–124
    IP/SNP primitives, 122
    IP/ULP primitives, 119–121
    network layer/LLC primitives,
      122–124
  and subnetworks, 98–99
  time–to-live (TTL) field, 102–103
  total length field, 101–102
  type of service (TOS) field, 99–101,
    102

Internet Protocol (IP) (*Cont.*):
  version field, 99
  and X.25, 321–323
  Xerox Network System (XNS) over,
    319–320
Internetworking, challenges of, 13–15
Internetworking architecture:
  connectionless/connection-oriented
    protocols, 6–9
  Internet layers, 9–10
  layer operations, example of, 10–12
  terms/concepts, 5–6
IPX [*see* Internet Packet Exchange
  Protocol (IPX)]
ISO 8473:
  definition of, 127
  field functions, 130
  PDU, 128, 131
  use of ISO 8348, 128–129

LAN bridges, and Internet Protocol (IP),
  321
LANs [*see* Local area networks (LANs)]
Layer operations, example of, 10–12
Lightweight Presentation Protocol (LPP),
  and CMOT, 311
Link layer addresses (LSAPs), 45–47
  SNAP convention, 46–47
Link state acknowledgment packet, 249
Link state advertisement header,
  238–239
Link state update packets, 245–249
LLC sublayer, 33–34
Local area networks (LANs), 27–34, 186
  classes of service, 34
  components of, 27–28
  definitions of, 27
  types of, 28–34
    carrier sense, collision detection
      LANs, 28–29
    CSMA/CD LANs, 29–31
    LLC sublayer, 33–34
    token bus LANs, 33
    token ring networks, 31–33
Logic flow diagram, address Resolution
  Protocol (ARP), 63–64
Logical link control (LLC), TCP/IP over,
  315–316
LSAPs [*see* Link layer addresses
  (LSAPs)]

MAC physical addresses, CSMA/CD
  frame and, 44–45
Major application layer protocols,
  251–275
  File Transfer Protocol (FTP), 261–271
  simple mail transfer protocol (SMTP),
    271–275
  TELNET protocol, 251–258
  trivial file transfer protocol (TFTP),
    258–261

Management Information Base (MIB), Internet, 298–304
  high-level MIB, definition of, 303–304
  object groups, 299–302
  template to describe objects, 302–303
MC RDATA format, 86
Message switching, WANs, 22–23
Messages:
  Domain Name System (DNS), 93–96
  external gateway protocol (EGP), 202–209
  gateway-to-gateway protocol (GGP), 196–199
  Hello protocol, 220–221
  Internet control message protocol (ICMP), 137
  routing information protocol (RIP), 218
MIB [see Management Information Base (MIB), Internet]
Migration issues, 358–361
  gateway, 359, 360
  network, 359–361
MR RDATA format, 87–88
Multicasting, Internet Protocol (IP), 124–125
Multihomed hosts, 55–56, 60

Name cache, 81
Name resolver, 80, 89
Name server, 80
Name server operations, Domain Name System (DNS), 82–83
Names, definition of, 39
Naming/addressing operation, Internet, 50–53
Neighbor data structure, OSPF (Open SPF) protocol, 236
NetBIOS:
  Internet Protocol (IP) over, 318–319
  over TCP/IP, 317–318
  over User Datagram Protocol (UDP), 317–318
Network addresses, 47–48
  physical and network address resolution, 48–49
Network clouds, definition of, 15
Network File System (NFS), 282–283
Network Information Center (NIC), 56
Network interface status message, gateway-to-gateway protocol (GGP), 198
Network links advertisement, OSPF (Open SPF) protocol, 230
Network management standards:
  Internet, 293–311
    CMOT, 308–311
    layer architecture, 294–395
    Management Information Base (MIB), 298–304
    naming hierarchy, 295–296
    SNMP, 304–308

Network management standards, Internet (Cont.):
    Structure of Management Information (SMI), 297–298
    summary of, 293–294
Network Time Protocol (NTP), 288–290
NFS [see Network File System (NFS)]
Noncore gateways, 186, 201
Nonrecursive operation, 82
Nonsource routing, 36
"Note on Two Problems in Connection with Graphs" (Dijkstra), 222

Offset host field, Hello protocol, 220
Open Shortest Path First Routing Protocol [see OSPF (Open SPF) protocol]
Open Systems Interconnection (see OSI)
Options field, IP diagram, 103–106
OSI, and TCP/IP, 4–5
OSI's Transport Protocol Class O, over TCP, 328–329
OSPF (Open SPF) protocol, 192, 214, 219, 221–226
  advertisements, types of, 230
  autonomous systems (AS) extended links advertisement, 230
  backbone router, 230
  border router, 230
  boundary router, 230
  data structures, 233–237
    area data structure, 234–235
    interface data structures, 235–236
    neighbor data structure, 236
    protocol data structure, 234
    routing table structure, 236–237
  external routing, 228
  internal router, 229
  network links advertisement, 230
  operations, 227–229
  packets, 237–249
    database description packet, 242–244
    Hello packet, 239–242
    link state acknowledgment packet, 249
    link state advertisement header, 238–239
    link state request packet, 244–245
    link state update packets, 245–249
    packet header, 237–238
  router classification, 229–230
  router links advertisement, 230
  routing database, 227
  shortest path tree, example of, 230–233
  summary links advertisement, 230

Packet switching, WANs, 23–27
Packets:
  ARP, 62–63
  OSPF (Open SPF) protocol, 227, 237–249
  trivial file transfer protocol (TFTP), 259–261
  X.25, 98–99

Padding field, IP diagram, 106
Passive open mode, Transmission Control
    Protocol (TCP), 153–154
PDUs [see Protocol data units (PDUs)]
Physical addresses, 40–45
    MAC physical addresses, CSMA/CD
        frame and, 44–45
    protocol identifiers, 41–44
    universal physical addresses, 41–44
Physical layer, CSMA/CD LANs, 31
PING protocol, 283–284
    services, 141
    using to obtain echo services, 347–348
Point-to-point networks, 231
Port numbers, 12–13
Ports/sockets:
    TCP, 150–153
    TCP/IP, 12–13
Protocol data structure, OSPF (Open
    SPF) protocol, 234
Protocol data units (PDUs), 181, 306–308
Protocol field, IP datagram, 103
Protocol stacks, for emerging technolo-
    gies, 331–332
Proxy ARP, 66–67
PTR (pointer) RDATA format, 88

Quality of service factors (QOS), 184

RARP [see Reverse address resolution
    protocol (RARP)]
RDATA field, 85–86
Record route function, CLNP, 133
Recursive operation, 82
Redirect service, Internet control
    message protocol (ICMP), 141–142
Relative distinguished name (RDN), 80
Relative name, 80
Remote Exec Daemon (REXECD), 283
Remote Procedure Call (RPC), 281–282
Repeaters, 35
Request for comments (RFCs), 2, 4
    TELNET protocol, 253–256
Resource records (RR), 83–85
    compression, 96
    example of, 88–93
    RDATA field, 85–86
Retransmission operations, Transmission
    Control Protocol (TCP), 156–160
Reverse address resolution protocol
    (RARP), 67–69
    primary and secondary RARPs, 68–69
RFCs [see Request for comments (RFCs)]
RIP [see Routing information protocol
    (RIP)]
Route discovery protocols:
    autonomous systems areas, and
        information exchange, 188–190
    border routers/boundary routers, 187–188
    core/noncore gateways, 186
    exterior/interior gateways, 186–187

Route discovery protocols (Cont.):
    external gateway protocol (EGP),
        199–214
    gated protocol, 221
    gateway-to-gateway protocol (GGP),
        192–199
    Hello protocol, 219–221
    information/logic routing, participants
        in, 190–191
    interior gateway protocols (GPs), 214
    OSPF (Open SPF) protocol, 221–226
    routing based on fewest hops, 182–184
    routing based on type of service
        factors, 184–186
    routing information protocol (RIP),
        214–219
    terms/concepts, 181–182, 191–192
Route recording option, Internet Protocol
    (IP), 109
Router classification, OSPF (Open SPF)
    protocol, 229–230
Router links advertisement, OSPF (Open
    SPF) protocol, 230
Routers, 35
Routes, definition of, 39
Routing information protocol (RIP),
    214–219
    definition of, 214–215
    family of net 1 field, 218
    message format, 218
    metric field, 218
    operations, example of, 216
    problems, 216–218
    request/response, 218–219
    split horizon update, 217–218
    split horizon with poisoned reverse,
        218
    timers, 215–216
    triggered update, 218
    versus OSPF, 219
Routing table, Internet Protocol (IP),
    117–119
Routing table structure, OSPF (Open
    SPF) protocol, 236–237
RR [see Resource records (RR)]

Services, Internet Protocol (IP), 106–116
    fragmentation and reassembly,
        111–116
    Internet header check routine, 106–107
    IP source routing, 107–109
    route recording option, 109
    timestamp option, 109–111
Shortest path routing, 222
Simple mail transfer protocol (SMTP),
    150, 271–275
    address field format, 272–273
    and Domain Name System (DNS),
        274–275
    model, 271–272
    operations, examples of, 273–274
    sending mail through, 341–344

SMI [see Structure of Management Information (SMI)]
SMTP [see Simple mail transfer protocol (SMTP)]
SNMP, 304–308
  administrative relationships, 304–306
  operation, example of, 306
  protocol data units (PDUs), 306–308
  SNMP MIB managed ojects, 308
Sockets, 12–13
Source quench, Internet control message protocol (ICMP), 140
Source routing, 36
  connectionless-mode network service (CLNP/ISO 8473), 133
  Internet Protocol (IP), 107–109
    loose and strict routing, 109
    routing operations, 107–109
Start of zone authority (SOA) format, 85
Structure of Management Information (SMI), 297–298
Subnetworks, 6
  examples of, 9
  and Internet Protocol (IP), 98–99
Summary links advertisement, OSPF (Open SPF) protocol, 230
Switched Multimegabit Data Service (SMDS), IP over, 327–328
System calls, UNIX-based TCP/IP services, 339

TCP/IP:
  architectural model, 12
  compared to OSI stacks, 353–356
  definition of, 2
  IP address structure, 54–56
  minimum TCP/IP and LAN stack, 314
  NetBIOS over, 317–318
  and operating systems, 333–349
  and OSI, 4–5
  over ISDN, 330–331
  over logical link control (LLC), 315–316
  ports/sockets, 12–13
  replacing TCP with User Datagram Protocol (UDP), 316–317
  [See also Wide area networks (WANs)]
TELNET login services, invoking with tn command, 346–347
TELNET protocol, 251–258
  command codes, 255
  commands, 256–258
    example of, 257–258
  network virtual terminal, 252–253
  negotiations, 253
  RFCs, 253–256
TFTP [see Trivial file transfer protocol (TFTP)]
Time-to-live (TTL) field, IP datagram, 102–103
Timers, routing information protocol (RIP), 215–216

Timestamp field, Hello protocol, 220
Timestamp option, Internet Protocol (IP), 109–111
Timestamp/timestamp reply, Internet control message protocol (ICMP), 142–143
Token bus LANs, 33
Token ring networks, 31–33
Top-level domains, 80
Topologies, Internet, 15–17
Total length field, IP datagram, 101–102
TP4, and TCP, 356–358
Transmission Control Protocol and the Internet Protocol (see TCP/IP)
Transmission Control Protocol (TCP), 82, 145–177
  active open mode, 153–154
  connection management operations, 167–176
    close operations, 173–174
    connection table, 174–176
    data transfer operations, 172–173
    open operations, 167–172
  fully specified passive open, 154
  major features of, 147–150
  overview, 146–147
  passive open mode, 153–154
  ports/sockets, 150–153
  retransmission operations, 156–160
  segments (TCP PDU), 162–167
    and performance, 166–167
  send and receive variables, 155
  sequence numbering and ACKs, 159
  time-outs/retransmissions, estimating timers for, 160–162
  Transmission Control Block (TCB), 154
  transport layer, value of, 145–146
  unspecified passive open, 154
  and user interfaces, 162–163
  window and flow-control mechanisms, 154–156
Triggered update, routing information protocol (RIP), 218
Trivial file transfer protocol (TFTP), 258–261
  operations, 261, 262
  and other protocols, 258–259
  packets, 259–261
    acknowledgment (ACK) packet, 259, 261
    error (ERROR) packet, 259, 261
    read request (RRQ) packet, 259
    write request (WRQ) packet, 259
  sending files through, 344–345
Type of service (TOS) factors, 184
Type of service (TOS) field, IP datagram, 99–101

UDP [see User Datagram Protocol (UDP)]
ULP [see Upper layer protocol (ULP)]

Unintelligible parameter, Internet
　　control message protocol (ICMP), 139
Universal physical addresses, 41–44
UNIX-based TCP/IP services, 333–339
　closing a connection, 338–339
　connection-oriented services, 334–337
　datagram services, 338
　input/output calls, 337–338
　programs to invoke, 339
　system calls, 339
Unreachable destination, Internet control
　　message protocol (ICMP), 139–140
Unspecified passive open, Transmission
　　Control Protocol (TCP), 154
Up state (state 3), external gateway
　　protocol (EGP), 202
　operations during, 210–213
Update message, gateway-to-gateway
　　protocol (GGP), 200
Upper layer protocol (ULP):
　names/addresses, 50
　and TCP, 148
User Datagram Protocol (UDP), 82, 144,
　145
　message format, 177–178
　NetBIOS over, 317–318
　OSI connectionless transport layer
　　over, 329–330
　replacing TCP with, 316–317

User network communication layers, 331

Vendor strategies, 351–353
Version field, IP datagram, 99

Wide area networks (WANs), 22–27
　circuit switching, 22
　message switching, 22–23
　packet switching, 23–27
Window and flow-control mechanisms,
　　Transmission Control Protocol
　　(TCP), 154–156

X.25:
　and Internet Protocol (IP), 321–323
　wide area networks (WANs), 98–99
X Windows, 277–281
　definition of, 277
　display connection, 280–281
　modules, 277–278
　principal rules/functions, 278
　system protocol, 279–280
Xerox Network System (XNS), over
　　Internet Protocol (IP), 319–320

Zone transfer protocol, 82

ABOUT THE AUTHOR

Uyless Black is president of Information Engineering
Incorporated, a Virginia-based telecommunications
consulting firm, He has designed and programmed many
data communications systems and voice and data networks.
As a former senior officer for the Federal Reserve, he
managed numerous large-scale data communications
systems. He has advised many companies, including Bell
Labs, AT&T, Bell Northern Research, and BellCore, on the
effective use of computer communications technology. He is
the author of ten books and numerous articles, including
The X Series Recommendations, *The V Series
Recommendations*, and *Network Management Standards*,
all published by McGraw-Hill. He is also a series advisor
for the *McGraw-Hill Series on Computer Communications*.